Accounting
for Non-Accounting Students

Fourth Edition

J R Dyson

Department of Accountancy and Finance,
Heriot-Watt University, Edinburgh

PITMAN
PUBLISHING

London · Hong Kong · Johannesburg · Melbourne · Singapore · Washington DC

PITMAN PUBLISHING
128 Long Acre, London WC2E 9AN
Tel: +44 (0) 171 447 2000
Fax: +44 (0) 171 240 5771

A Division of Pearson Professional Limited

Vist the Pitman PublishingWebsite at
http://www.pitman.co.uk

First published in Great Britain in 1987
Fourth edition 1997

© Pearson Professional Limited 1987, 1991, 1994, 1997

ISBN 0 273 62575 6

British Library Cataloguing in Publication Data
A CIP catalogue record for this book can be obtained from the British Library

10 9 8 7 6 5 4 3 2

Typeset by Pantek Arts, Maidstone, Kent.
Printed and bound in Great Britain

The Publishers' policy is to use paper manufactured from sustainable forests.

Contents

PART 6 PLANNING AND CONTROL

Preface

This is a book for non-accountants. It is intended primarily for students who are required to study accounting as part of a non-accounting degree or professional studies course. It should also be of value to those working in commerce, government or industry who find that their work involves them in dealing with accounting information. It is hoped that the book will help to explain why there is need for such information.

Non-accounting students (such as engineers, personnel managers, purchasing officers, and sales managers) are sometimes unable to understand why they are required to study accounting. This is often found to be the case when they have to take an examination in the subject, and they are then presented with a paper of some considerable technical rigour.

Accounting books written specifically for the non-accountant are also often extremely demanding. The subject needs to be covered in such a way that non-accounting students do not become confused by too much technical information. They do not require the same detailed analysis that is only of relevance to the professional accountant. Some accounting books specially written for the non-accountant go to the opposite extreme. They outline the subject so superficially that they are of no real practical help either to examination candidates or to those non-specialists requiring some guidance on practical accounting problems.

The aim of this book is to serve as a good introduction to the study of accounting. The subject is not covered superficially. In parts, the book goes into considerable detail, but only where it is necessary for a real understanding of the subject. It is appreciated that non-accountants are unlikely to be involved in the *detailed* preparation of accounting information such as, for example, in the compilation of a company's annual accounts. However, if such accounts are to provide the maximum possible benefit to their users, it is desirable that users should have a good knowledge of how they are prepared and how to extract the maximum possible information from them.

This concept is analogous to that of driving a car. It is perfectly possible to drive a car without knowing anything about how it works. However, to get the best possible performance from the car, it is useful to know something about the engine. It is not necessary to know as much about the car as a motor mechanic. All that is required is just sufficient knowledge to be able to drive the car so that is operates at its maximum efficiency. Similarly, it is not absolutely necessary to know how to prepare accounts to be able to use them, but they will mean a great deal more if the user knows something about their construction.

Accounting is now a compulsory subject for many non-accounting students on certificate, diploma and degree courses in colleges and universities. While the syllabuses for such courses have sometimes to be approved by external bodies, their detailed contents are often left to the individual lecturer to determine. This book was written with that type of course very much in mind.

The book is divided into six parts. Part 1 introduces the student to the subject of accounting and the profession of accountancy. Parts 2, 3 and 4 deal mainly with financial accounting, while Parts 5 and 6 are more concerned with management accounting.

Many further and higher education institutions have now adopted a modular structure for the delivery of their courses. The book will be useful, therefore, on those modules offered to non-accountants that include elements of both financial accounting and management accounting. However, it will also avoid students having to purchase two textbooks if financial accounting and management accounting are taken in separate modules. Equally, if some chapters in the various parts of the book are not relevant for some syllabuses, module leaders will find that it is quite easy to isolate those chapters that do relate to their particular module.

The Fourth Edition

In presenting the fourth edition, I am once again grateful to those lecturers and students who have been kind enough to suggest improvements that could be made in a new edition. I have tried to take all of their recommendations into account, but inevitably some material could not be accommodated because it was too specialist for a book aimed primarily at non-accountants taking a first- or second- year course.

The new edition has been revised and brought up to date, and number of changes have been made, the main ones being as follows:

1 The book has been divided into six parts (instead of four) in order to make it easier for lecturers to select those chapters that are most relevant for their respective modules.

2 Five of the six case studies contained in the third edition have been retained, but these now follow the main chapter to which they relate.

3 Students found the original Chapter 4 long and difficult. This chapter has now been split into two separate chapters. The new Chapter 4 deals with the preparation of basic financial accounts without any allowance being made for any final year end adjustments. The new Chapter 5 then deals with such adjustments (e.g. stocks, depreciation, accruals and prepayments, and bad and doubtful debts), and then incorporates them in a comprehensive example. Thus, when first dealing with Chapter 4, lecturers will have to take particular care to warn their students that the procedures covered up to that stage are only a preliminary step.

4 The old Chapters 17 to 20 (on annual reports) have been substantially rewritten, and they have now been included in the new edition as Chapters 10, 11, and 12.

5 All chapters now include some discussion questions at the end of each chapter. They should be especially useful to post-graduate students. These questions may be used literally as discussion questions in seminars or tutorials, or they may be set as essay questions. Some guidance notes relfecting the points that could be made in response to the questions are provided in the Instructor's Manual.

6 The new Chapter 7 on company accounts now excludes partnership accounts, as most lecturers felt that this was an irrelevant topic for non-accountants.

7 The chapter on cash flow statements (now Chapter 8) has been largely rewritten, as the overall feedback indicated that the original chapter was much too complex for non-accounting students.

8 The old Chapter 13 on product costing systems and recent developments has not been included as a separate chapter in the new edition. Instead, some brief reference to product costing systems is now included in Chapter 13 (Cost accounting procedures), as the general response indicated some topics covered in the old chapter (such as process costing) were much too detailed for non-accountants. Recent developments in management accounting are now included in a new and separate Chapter 20 (Contemporary issues in management accounting).

9 An opportunity has been taken to modernize and simplify a number of chapter and section headings.

While the book has not been written for a specific course or module, all of the above changes mean that it now has some identity with some national examination syllabuses. It will be found, for example, that the book covers BTEC's Higher National Programme Core Module Four: Managing Finance and Information, Section 1: Managing Finance, as well as most of the syllabus for Option Module One: Financial Accounting Framework, and part of the syllabus for Option Module Two: Business Information (particularly, Section One: Cost Measurement; and Section Three: Costing Systems and Techniques).

More specialist texts are, of course, available if a particular syllabus requires students to go into much more detail than is covered in this book, and some guidance on suitable reading is given in Appendix 1 (Further reading). Even so, unless particular modules are covered by national requirements, I would urge some caution. It is as well to consider whether most non-accountants really do need to know much more about accounting than is covered in this book.

How to use the book

Lecturers will have their own way of introducing the various subjects. It is to be hoped, however, that they will still use the various exhibits in the book to demonstrate particular accounting procedures. It is believed that lecturers spend far too much time (and money) photocopying questions for use in lectures. The students then spend *their* time in lectures trying to take down what the lecturer is writing on the blackboard without really listening to what is being said.

If this book is used as it is intended, it is not necessary for lecturers to photocopy additional exhibits and answers. The book contains sufficient exhibits for most modules or courses, and every exhibit is followed by a detailed solution. Thus there is no need for students to copy answers that have been written on the blackboard: they should be able to listen to the lecturer as each point is demonstrated step by step.

Most chapters are also followed by a number of tutorial exercises. Since detailed solutions for these questions are contained in Appendix 3, lecturers will also be spared having to provide solutions of their own.

There are, however, some additional questions (including some discussion questions) at the end of most chapters. The answers to these questions are included in a separate Instructor's Manual which is available at no cost to *bona fide* lecturers on application to the publishers.

A word to students

If you are using this book as part of a formal course, your lecturer will provide you with a work scheme which will outline just how much of the book you are expected to cover each week. In addition to the work done in your lecture, you will probably have to read each chapter two or three times. As you read a chapter, work through each exhibit, and then have a go at doing it without reference to the solution.

You are also recommended to attempt as many of the questions that follow each chapter as you can, but avoid looking at the solutions until you are absolutely certain that you do not know how to answer the question. The more questions that you attempt, the more confident you will be that you really do understand the subject matter. However, you must not spend all your time studying accounting, so make sure that you put enough time into your other modules.

Many students study accounting without having the benefit of attending lectures. If you fall into this category, it is suggested that you adopt the following study plan:

1 Organize your private study so that you have covered every topic in your syllabus by the time of your examination. You will probably need to allow for extra time to be spent on Chapters 3, 4, 5, 9, 16 and 18.

2 Read each chapter slowly, being careful to work through each exhibit. Do not worry if you do not immediately understand each point: read on to the end of the chapter.

3 Read the chapter again, this time making sure that you do understand each point. Try doing each exhibit without looking at the solution.

4 Attempt as many questions at the end of the chapter as you can, but do not look at the solutions until you have finished or you are certain that you cannot do the question.

5 If you have time, re-read the chapter.

One word of caution. Accounting is not simply a matter of elementary arithmetic. The solution to many accounting problems often calls for a considerable amount of personal judgement, and hence there is bound to be some degree of subjectivity attached to the solution.

The problems demonstrated in this book are not readily solved in the real world, and the suggested answers ought to be subject to a great deal of argument and discussion. It follows that non-accountants ought to be severely critical of any accounting information that is supplied to them, although it is difficult to be constructive in your criticism unless you have some knowledge of the subject matter. This book provides you with that knowledge.

Note: While this fourth edition was at proof stage, the ASB issued a revised version of FRS 1 on cash flow statements. Wherever possible this text has been corrected to incorporate the amended requirements of FRS 1 (Revised 1996).

Website resources for this book

A website has been constructed for this book which provides additional information and resources for lecturers and students. The site address is:

http://www.pitman.co.uk

The **open section** of the site, accessible to all, includes:

- information about the book
- information about the author
- ordering information
- a short quiz
- samples of the resource material which is included in the password-protected section of the site.

The **password-protected section** of the site, accessible only to adopting lecturers, includes:

- a section allowing lecturers' comments on the book to be recorded
- downloadable OHP Masters from the *Lecturer's Guide*
- a dialogue area for adopting lecturers
- further discussion and questions on the newspaper/journal article extracts that appear in the book
- an area where recent accounting developments that affect the book can be recorded
- extra questions and answers for lecturers' use.

In the future the website will be extended and will include a multiple-choice question bank, links to other websites, and a section on financial reporting on the web.

Acknowledgements

This book could not have been written without the help of a considerable number of people. Many of them have contributed directly to the ideas that have gone into the writing of it, while in other cases I am aware that I have absorbed their views without always being fully conscious of doing so.

I am indebted to far too many colleagues, friends and relatives to name them all individually, but I would like to place on record my thanks to all of my colleagues at Napier University. Without their ready assistance and tolerant benevolence, this book would be all the poorer. I would also like to thank all those lecturers and students elsewhere who have made various suggestions for improving the fourth edition.

My thanks are also due to the Chartered Institute of Management Accountants (CIMA), and to the Editors of *Accountancy Age, CA Magazine, The Financial Times,* and *The Scotsman* for permission to reproduce copyright material. This material may not be reproduced, copied or transmitted unless written permission is obtained from the original owner or publisher. I hope that the inclusion of some actual news stories does enliven the introduction to each chapter, and I also hope that it will encourage students to read regularly the financial pages of some high-quality newspapers and journals!

The CIMA definitions used in the text are from its own publication, *Management Accounting Official Terminology*, London: The Chartered Institute of Management Accountants, 1996.

An explanation
To avoid tedious repetition and tortuous circumlocution, the masculine pronoun has been adopted in this book. No offence is intended to anyone, most of all to my female readers, and I hope none will be taken.

PART 1

Introduction to accounting

CHAPTER 1

The accounting world

Directors condemned for lack of knowledge

Non-executive directors lack the knowledge to protect shareholders' interests, according to a KPMG survey.

A year after the collapse of Barings Bank, the survey found one in five UK company non-executive directors still in the dark about their firms' use of derivatives. And 18% said their companies had no formal control mechanisms governing their use.

Despite this, the survey found up to 19% of companies speculated with derivatives rather than just using them to hedge against risk.

KPMG reported that 20% of non-executives thought their companies' treasury function was run as a profit centre. This compared with just one in 20 that KPMG believed was the true figure.

'One explanation is that the 20% who saw their treasuries as profit centres were mistaken, suggesting a significant misunderstanding of corporate culture,' said Richard Raeburn, KPMG partner responsible for treasury and risk management.

Accounting Age, 29 February 1996

Exhibit 1.0 One day you too might be a director

This chapter is an introduction to the world of accounting. It begins with an explanation of the nature and purpose of accounting. This is followed by a section outlining the reasons why it is important for non-accountants to study the subject. The next section describes briefly the main branches of accounting. A further section summarizes the basic structure of the accountancy profession. The final section describes the major types of organizations or entities that may be found in the United Kingdom.

Learning objectives	**By the end of this chapter, you will be able to:**

- **define the nature and purpose of accounting;**
- **explain why non-accountants need to know something about accounting;**
- **identify eight main branches of accounting;**
- **list six United Kingdom professional accountancy bodies;**
- **describe three different types of business organizations.**

THE NATURE AND PURPOSE OF ACCOUNTING

The word *account* in everyday language is often used as a substitute for an *explanation* or a *report* of certain actions or events. If you are an employee, for example, you may have to explain to your employer just how you have been spending your time, or if you are a manager, you may have to report to the owner on how the business is doing. In order to explain or to report, you will, of course, have to remember what you were doing or what happened. As it is not always easy to remember, you may need to keep some written record. In effect, such records can be said to form the basis of a rudimentary accounting (or reporting) system.

In a primitive sense, man has always been involved in some form of accounting. It may have gone no further than a farmer (say) measuring his worth simply by *counting* the number of cows or sheep that he owned. However, the growth of a monetary system enabled a more sophisticated method to be developed. It then became possible to calculate the increase or decrease in individual wealth over a period of time, and to assess whether (say) a farmer with ten cows and fifty sheep was wealthier than one who had sixty pigs. Exhibit 1.1 illustrates just how difficult it would be to assess the wealth of a farmer in a non-monetary system.

Even with the growth of a monetary system, it took a very long time for formal documentary systems to become common, although it is possible to trace the origins of modern book-keeping at least as far back as the twelfth century. We know that from about that time, traders began to adopt a system of recording information that we now refer to as *double-entry book-keeping*. By the end of the fifteenth century, double-entry book-keeping was widely used in Venice and the surrounding areas. Indeed, the first-known book on the subject was published in 1494 by an Italian mathematician called Pacioli. Modern book-keeping systems are still based on principles established in the fifteenth century, although they have had to be adapted to suit modern conditions.

Exhibit 1.1 Accounting for a farmer's wealth

His possessions	A year ago	Now	Change
Cows	● ● ● ● ● ● ● ● ● ●	● ● ● ● ● ● ● ● ● ● ● ● ● ● ●	+5
Hens [● = 10]	● ● ● ● ● ● ● ● ● ●	● ● ● ● ● ● ●	−30
Pigs	● ● ● ● ● ●	● ● ● ●	−2
Sheep [● = 10]	● ● ● ● ●	● ● ● ● ● ● ●	+20
Land [● = 1 acre]	● ● ● ●	● ● ● ●	no change
Cottage	●	●	no change
Carts	● ● ●	●	−2
Ploughs	●	● ●	+1

Why has a recording system devised in medieval times lasted for so long? There are two main reasons:

1 it provides an accurate record of what has happened to a business over a specified period of time;
2 information extracted from the system can help the owner or the manager operate the business much more effectively.

In essence, the system provides the answers to three basic questions which owners want to know. These questions are depicted in Exhibit 1.2, and they can be summarized as follows:

1 What profit has the business made?
2 How much does the business owe?
3 How much is owed to it?

The medieval system dealt largely with simple agricultural and trading entities (an entity is simply the jargon accountants use to describe any type of organization). Modern systems have to cope with complex industrial operations and sophisticated financial arrangements. Furthermore, a business may be so big or so complex nowadays that the owners have to employ managers to run it for them. Indeed, the senior managers themselves may be largely dependent upon their junior colleagues telling them what is happening. A traditional book-keeping system was not designed to cope with situations where owners were separated from managers. It was designed largely to supply summarized information only to the owner-managers of a business who knew in detail from their own experience what was going on. The system was not intended to cope with frequent day-to-day reporting to managers remote from production or trading operations.

Exhibit 1.2 An owner's vital questions

Owed/ owned	A year ago	Now	Better or worse off now?
Animals owned	1 Cow	2 Cows	Better
Owed to Jim	50 Kilos of barley	100 Kilos of barley	Worse
Due from Hetty	4 Gross eggs	3 Gross eggs	Worse
Taking everything into account			?

As a result, Pacioli's system has had to be adapted so that it can satisfy the demand for information from two main sources:

1 from owners who want to know from time to time how the business is doing;
2 from the managers who need information in order to help plan and control it.

We shall be meeting the terms 'plan' and 'control' frequently in this book. Both terms can have several different meanings, but we shall adopt the following definitions:

> **To plan:** to determine what and how something should be done;
> **To control:** to ensure that the planned results are achieved.

Owners and managers do not necessarily require the same information, so this has meant that accounting has developed into two main specialisms:

1 financial accounting, which is concerned with the supply of information to the owners of an entity;
2 management accounting, which is concerned with the supply of information to the managers of an entity.

We shall be spending a great deal of time in subsequent chapters dealing with both financial and management accounting.

While it is useful to classify accounting into these two broad categories, Exhibit 1.3 shows that accountants are now involved in supplying information to a wide range of other interested parties, such as analysts, creditors, employees, the government, investors, lenders, and the public.

In this book, we are going to be mainly concerned with the supply of information to owners and managers, but first, we need to examine why non-accountants need to study accounting. We do this in the next section.

ACCOUNTING AND THE NON-ACCOUNTANT

Whatever your job, whether you repair machines in a factory, teach children in a school, or nurse sick patients in a hospital, you probably feel that you seem to spend all your time filling in forms and reading reports. Why? Why can you not just get on with repairing machines, teaching children, or nursing the sick?

It is true that in many organizations there is now an awful lot of paperwork. It can get out of hand, but usually there is a reason behind it all. A great

Exhibit 1.3 The main users of accounting information

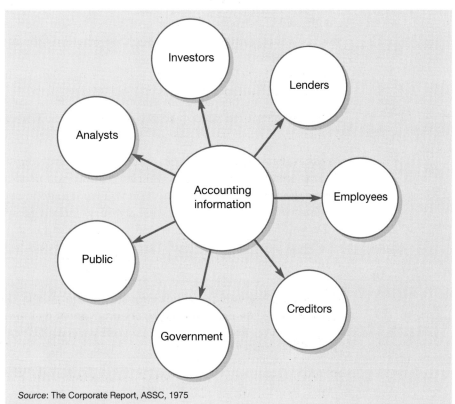

Source: The Corporate Report, ASSC, 1975

deal of information that is collected may, for example, be required by law. Some entities (such as public limited companies like ICI or Marks and Spencer) have a statutory obligation to publish (that is, to make available for public inspection) a certain amount of information about their affairs. This process requires a considerable amount of material to be collected about the company's activities before it can be summarized in a form suitable for publication. In the previous section, we referred to this process as *financial accounting*. As a manager it may be somewhat tiresome for you to become involved in financial accounting, but if the company is to comply with the law, you have no option.

However, unless you are at a very senior level in the entity, it is unlikely that as a non-accountant you will be directly involved in the detailed preparation of the financial accounts. You may have to supply *some* information, but you will probably not be involved to any great extent. Until you become a senior manager, the type of information that you have to provide is more likely to be needed for *management* accounting purposes.

As you have probably experienced, besides having to *supply* a great deal of information to senior management, you almost certainly *receive* an enormous amount as well. You know the feeling: your in-tray is constantly being topped up with scores of urgent memos and reports. Why?

The idea behind it all is very simple, although it may not appear so when you are constantly being harassed. The belief is that if you *know* what is going on, you will be much better placed to run your department much more efficiently and effectively. 'Efficient' and 'effective' are another two terms that we shall be using quite a lot in this book, so what do they mean? We will define them as follows:

> **Efficient:** the maximum output obtained from any given input;
> **Effective:** the success achieved in arriving at a desired outcome.

As your department gets bigger and more complex, you will not always know what is going on simply by casual observation. You need to be given information so that you can plan the direction you want to go in over (say) the next few weeks or months, and then ensure that you do indeed go in that direction.

Do you feel that all of this is unnecessary? It can be if the information you receive is irrelevant for your purposes. To be useful, it *has* to be what you want, and you have to be able to rely on it. This will not be the case if you have not been consulted about it, and the system has been imposed upon you by senior management. Furthermore, the information is likely to be inaccurate if it is prepared by employees who are unaware of its importance.

Perhaps you are thinking, 'This is all very well. It might possibly be of some benefit, but I still don't see why I have to study such a boring subject as accounting.' This is a fair point, so we will try to summarize the main reasons why you should study accounting:

1 **To make sure that you follow legal requirements**

As we have seen, some organizations are required by law to disclose publicly information about their activities. The required information is inevitably complex, it is normally written in a strange technical language, and it is often presented in a highly prescribed format. The responsibility for complying with the law rests ultimately with the senior management of the organization. While the accountants may help with the detailed preparation of the *accounts* (as they are called), the overall responsibility cannot be delegated to them. It follows that any non-accountant who aspires to being a senior manager cannot avoid having to know something about this process.

2 **To help you do a better job**

Larger organizations almost certainly have some form of detailed internal information supply. You may be involved in both supplying and receiving it. Its purpose is to help you and other managers do your respective jobs much more efficiently and effectively. It is supposed to help you plan your department's activities, to monitor and to control them, and to provide additional information about decisions you have to take about your department's affairs. This will often be translated and reported to you in financial terms (although you will also receive non-financial information). It will not mean anything and you will not be able to use it if you do not understand it. Furthermore, you certainly will not have been able to contribute to the development of the information system so that it is of particular benefit to you.

We believe that these arguments fully justify the time that you will be giving to the study of accounting. By the time that you have worked your way through this book, we hope you will find, despite your initial fears, that you agree accounting can be both interesting and useful!

Accounting has now developed into a considerable number of specialisms and, as you are likely to come across at least some of them in your career, it might be helpful if we provide a brief description of the main ones for you. We do so in the next section.

BRANCHES OF ACCOUNTING

The work that accountants now undertake ranges far beyond that of simply summarizing information in order to calculate how much profit a business has made, how much it owes, and much is owed to it. Although this work is still very important, accountants have gradually got involved in other types of work. Of course, other information specialists (such as market researchers and operational analysts) have also been drawn into the preparation of management information, and at one time, some observers expected accounting to be taken over by these newer and more scientifically-based disciplines. However, this has not happened. There are three main reasons: (a) financial information supply to external users still has a dominant influence on internal management information; (b) other information specialists have been reluctant to become involved in detailed accounting matters; and (c) accountants have been quick to absorb new methods and techniques into their work.

The main branches of accounting are shown in Exhibit 1.4, and a brief description of them is given below:

Accountancy and accounting

Accountancy is a profession whose members are engaged in the collection of financial data, the summary of that data, and then the presentation of the information in a form which helps recipients take effective decisions. Many writers use accountancy and accounting as synonymous terms, but in this book we shall use the term *accountancy* to describe the profession, and the term *accounting* to refer to the subject.

Auditing

Auditing forms a most important branch of accountancy. Once accounts have been prepared, they may have to be checked in order to ensure that they do not present a distorted picture. The checking of accounts and the reporting on them is known as *auditing*. Not all businesses have their accounts audited, but for some organizations (such as large limited liability companies) it is a legal requirement.

Auditors are usually trained accountants who specialize in checking accounts rather than preparing them. If they are appointed from outside the organization, they are usually referred to as *external* auditors. A limited company's auditors are appointed by the shareholders, and not by the management. The auditors' job is to protect the interests of the shareholders. They answer to them, and not to anyone in the company. By contrast, *internal* auditors are employees of the company. They are appointed by, and answer to, the company's management.

Exhibit 1.4 Branches of accounting

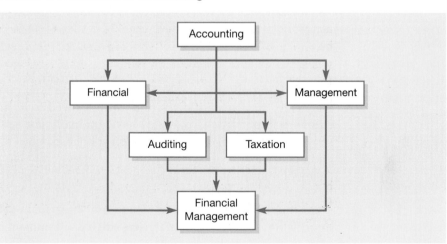

Internal auditors perform routine tasks and undertake detailed checking of the company's accounting procedures, whereas external auditors are likely to go in for much more selective testing. Nonetheless, they usually work very closely together, although the distinction made between them still remains important.

It might occur to you that as internal auditors are employees of the company, they must have much less independence than external auditors. In practice, however, even external auditors have limited independence. This is because the directors of a company usually recommend the appointment of a particular firm of auditors to the shareholders. It is rare for shareholders to object to the directors' recommendation so if the directors are in dispute with the auditors, they can always hint that they are thinking of appointing another firm. The auditors can always appeal directly to the shareholders, but they are not usually successful.

Book-keeping

Book-keeping is a mechanical task involving the collection of basic financial data. The data are first entered in special records known as *books of account*, and then extracted and summarized in the form of a *profit and loss account* and a *balance sheet*. This process normally takes place once a year, but it may occur more frequently. We shall be going into some detail in later chapters about profit and loss accounts and balance sheets. For the moment, all you need to remember is the following:

1 a profit and loss account shows whether the business has made a profit or loss during the year, i.e. it measures how well the business has done;
2 a balance sheet lists what the entity owns (its assets), and what it owes (its liabilities) as at the end of the year.

The book-keeping procedures usually end when the basic data have been entered in the books of account and the accuracy of each entry has been tested. At that stage, the *accounting* function takes over. Accounting tends to be used as a generic term covering almost anything to do with the collection and use of basic financial data. It should, however, be more properly applied to the use to which the data are put once they have been extracted from the books of account. Book-keeping is a routine operation, while accounting requires the ability to examine a problem using both financial *and* non-financial data.

Cost book-keeping, costing, and cost accounting

You may come across these terms used somewhat loosely. They form part of a branch of accounting that deals with the collection of detailed financial data for *internal* management purposes. The information is used in planning and controlling the entity.

Cost book-keeping is the process that involves the recording of cost data in books of account. It is, therefore, similar to book-keeping as described above, except that data are recorded in very much greater detail. Cost accounting makes use of those data once they have been extracted from the cost books in providing information for managerial planning and control. Accountants are now discouraged from using the term 'costing' unless it is qualified in some way, i.e. by referring to some branch of costing such as standard costing, but you will still find the term 'costing' in general use.

The difference between a book-keeping/accounting system and a cost book-keeping/cost accounting system is largely one of degree. A cost accounting system contains a great deal more data, and thus once the data are summarized, there is much more information available to the management of the company.

Financial accounting

Financial accounting is the more specific term applied to the preparation and subsequent publication of highly summarized financial information. The information is usually presented for the benefit of the owners of an entity, but it can also be used by management for planning and control purposes. The information will also be of interest to others, e.g. employees and creditors (as depicted in Exhibit 1.3).

Financial management

Financial management is a relatively new branch of accounting that has developed over the last 20 years. Financial managers are responsible for setting financial objectives, making plans based on those objectives, obtaining the finance needed to achieve the plans, and generally safe-guarding all the financial resources of the entity. Financial managers are much more heavily involved in the *management* of the entity than is generally the case with either financial or management accountants. It should also be noted that the financial manager draws on a much wider range of disciplines (such as economics and mathematics), and relies more extensively on non-financial data than does the more traditional accountant.

Management accounting

Management accounting is another all-embracing term. It was suggested earlier that cost book-keeping deals with the routine collection and summary of data for internal management purposes, whereas cost accounting is more involved in planning and control. Management accounting incorporates cost accounting data and adapts them for specific decisions which management may be called upon to make. It follows that a management accounting system incorporates *all* types of financial and non-financial information from a wide range of sources far beyond those used in traditional financial accounting.

Taxation

Taxation is a highly complex technical branch of accounting. Accountants involved in tax work are responsible for computing the amount of tax payable by both business entities and individuals. It is not necessary for either companies or individuals to pay more tax than is lawfully due, so it is quite in order for them to minimize the amount of tax payable. If tax experts attempt to reduce their clients' tax bills strictly in accordance with the law, this is known as tax avoidance. Tax *avoidance* is a perfectly legitimate exercise, but tax *evasion* (the non-declaration of sources of income on which tax might be due) is a very serious offence. In practice, the border line between tax avoidance and tax evasion is a fairly narrow one.

The main branches of accounting described above cannot always be put into such neat categories. Accountants in practice (that is, those who work from an office and offer their services to the public, like a solicitor) usually specialize in auditing, financial accounting or taxation. Most accountants working in industry or the public sector will be employed as management accountants, although some may deal specifically with auditing, financial accounting, or taxation matters.

One other highly specialist branch of accounting that you may sometimes read about is that connected with *insolvency*, i.e. with bankruptcy or liquidation. *Bankruptcy* is a formal legal procedure. The term is applied to individuals when their financial affairs are so serious that they have to be given some form of legal protection from their creditors. The term *liquidation* is usually applied to a company when it also gets into serious financial difficulties, and its affairs have to be wound up (that is, for it to go out of existence).

Companies do not necessarily go immediately into liquidation if they get into financial difficulties. An attempt will usually be made either to rescue them, or at least to protect certain types of creditors. In these situations, accountants sometimes act as *administrators*. Their appointment freezes creditors' rights and prevents the company from being put into liquidation during a period when the administrators are attempting to manage the company. By contrast, *receivers* may be appointed on behalf of loan creditors. The creditors' loans may be secured on certain property, and the receivers will try to obtain the income from that property, or they may even attempt to sell it.

We hope that you never come into contact with insolvency practitioners, so we will move on to have a look at another topic, the structure of the accountancy profession.

THE ACCOUNTANCY PROFESSION

Within the UK, there is nothing to stop anyone calling himself an accountant, and setting up in business offering accountancy services. However, some accounting work is restricted (such as the audit of large limited liability companies) unless the accountant holds a recognized qualification. Indeed, some accountants are sometimes described as being *qualified* accountants. This term is usually applied to someone who is a member of one of the major accountancy bodies (although many 'non-qualified' accountants would strongly dispute that they were not 'qualified' to offer a highly professional service). There are six major accountancy bodies operating in the British Isles, and they are as follows:

1 Institute of Chartered Accountants in England and Wales (ICAEW);
2 Institute of Chartered Accountants in Ireland (ICAI);
3 Institute of Chartered Accountants of Scotland (ICAS);
4 Association of Chartered Certified Accountants (ACCA);
5 Chartered Institute of Management Accountants (CIMA);
6 Chartered Institute of Public Finance and Accountancy (CIPFA).

The organization of the accountancy profession is also shown in Exhibit 1.5.

The Irish Institute (ICAI) is included in the above list because it has a strong influence in Northern Ireland.

As can be seen from the list, although all of the six major professional accountancy bodies now have a Royal Charter, it is still customary to refer only to members of ICAEW, ICAI, and ICAS as *chartered* accountants. Chartered accountants have usually had to undergo a period of training in a practising office, i.e. one that offers accounting services to the public, like a solicitor. Much practice work is involved in auditing and taxation but, after qualifying, many chartered accountants go to work in commerce or industry. ACCA members may also obtain their training in practice, but relevant experience elsewhere counts towards their qualification. CIMA members usually train and work in industry, while CIPFA members specialize almost exclusively in central and local government.

Apart from the six major bodies, there are a number of important (although far less well known) smaller accountancy associations and societies, e.g. the Association of International Accountants, the Society of Company and Commercial Accountants, the Association of Authorized Public Accountants, and the Association of Cost and Executive Accountants. All of these bodies offer some form of accountancy qualification, but they have not yet managed to achieve the status or prestige that is attached to being a member of one of the six major bodies. They are referred to as *secondary* bodies.

There is also another very important accountancy body known as the *Association of Accounting Technicians*. The Association was formed in 1980 as a professional organization especially for those accountants who *assist* qualified accountants in preparing accounting information. Although it is an independent body, it is sponsored by four of the six major professional bodies (the exceptions being ACCA and the Irish Institute). In order to become an accounting technician, it is necessary to take (or be exempt from) the Association's

Exhibit 1.5 Organization of the accountancy profession

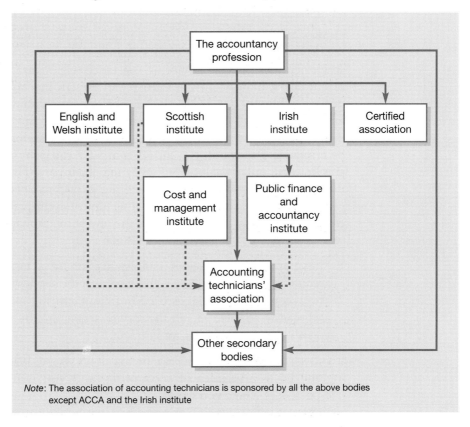

Note: The association of accounting technicians is sponsored by all the above bodies
except ACCA and the Irish institute

examinations. The examinations are not easy, although they tend to be less technically demanding and more practical than those of the six major bodies.

You can see that the accountancy profession is extremely diverse, and if you meet someone who calls himself an accountant, you may not be able to tell what that means. Nonetheless, whatever their qualifications, all accountants will have one thing in common: their job is to help *you* do your job more effectively. Accountants offer a service. They can do a lot to help you, but you do not necessarily have to do what they say. You should listen to their advice. However, as accountants are largely specialists in financial matters, you also should obtain advice from other sources, then make up your own mind what you should do. If things go wrong: never, never blame the accountant (or the computer!). As a manager, it is *your* decision, right or wrong.

You may be thinking 'This is all very well, but I am not really in a position to disregard the accountant's advice.' Exactly! That is what this book is about. By the end of it you will be in an excellent position to judge the quality of the advice given. We shall be examining the detailed material in later chapters, but before we end this chapter we need to look at the main types of entity which you may come across.

TYPES OF ENTITY

Entities can be categorized into two broad groups: manufacturing and servicing. Manufacturing entities *make* things (e.g. furniture, or chemicals), while service entities provide advice or assistance (e.g. a garage, or a hospital). In recent years, manufacturing industry in the UK has appeared to be on the decline, while the service sector has become much more important. For example, think of all the new supermarkets that have opened recently in your part of the country. Even within the manufacturing sector, however, there can be a servicing element, e.g. an oil company can provide a canteen for its employees. Similarly, a local authority may be involved in some form of manufacturing, such as designing and printing its own stationery.

In this book we shall be concentrating almost exclusively on manufacturing entities. This might appear a bit odd in view of the growing importance of the service sector, but there two good reasons:

1 The manufacturing sector enables us to use a much wider range of accounting techniques than is the case with the service sector.
2 The accounting techniques used in manufacturing industry can be easily and readily adapted to suit the service sector, and by the end of the book, you will be able to do this for yourself.

If you are involved in the service sector, don't worry! We shall only be covering the basic principles of accounting, and you will find them of use, irrespective of where you work!

In fact, it is not possible or necessary in a book of this nature to deal with every type of entity (Exhibit 1.6 depicts some of the main ones). We shall be concentrating on just two: sole traders, and limited liability companies.

Sole traders

Like much else in accounting, the term 'sole trader' is rather misleading. There are two main reasons why this is the case:

1 'sole' does not necessarily mean that only one person *works* for the entity;
2 it may not 'trade' in the sense of just selling a product, since it could be involved in manufacturing, or it may provide a service (like a plumber).

The term really refers to how the entity is owned and financed, the main requirement being that only one individual should own it.

Sole traders usually work on a very informal basis, and some private matters relating to the owner are often indistinguishable from those of the entity. Chapters 3, 4, and 5 of this book are concerned primarily with sole traders. In these chapters we shall be introducing you to how financial data are recorded and summarized. You will find that it is much easier to understand the procedures if we restrict ourselves to examples of sole trader entities.

You may also come across an entity known as a partnership. A partnership

Exhibit 1.6 Types of entity

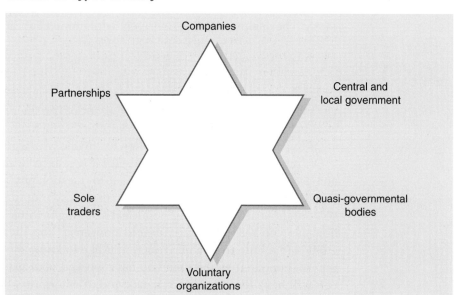

is very similar to a sole trader entity, except that two or more people are involved in the ownership of the business. Sometimes partnerships grow out of a sole trader entity, the sole trader perhaps realizing that he needs to put more money into the business, or that he wants someone to share the responsibility. In other cases, a new business may start out as a partnership, e.g. when two friends get together to start a home-decorating service.

The partners should arrange between themselves how much money they will each put into the business, what jobs they will do, how many hours they will work, and how the profits and losses will be shared. In the absence of any agreement (whether formal or informal), the provisions laid down in the Partnership Act 1890 are deemed to apply. Otherwise, partnerships are not covered by any specific legislation.

As the accounting procedures involved in dealing with partnerships are very similar to those that apply to sole traders, we shall not be dealing with them in this book.

Limited liability companies

A limited liability company is a formal type of business entity, so much so that, in law, it is regarded as having a quite separate existence from its owners. There are some extremely severe legal requirements, therefore, surrounding the creation and operation of such an entity, and its owners are restricted in what they can do with it (unlike sole traders or partnerships who have much more freedom). The restrictions are now contained within a consolidating Act of Parliament (the Companies Act 1985 as amended by the Companies Act 1989).

At this stage, we will not say any more about limited liability companies because we shall be examining them in some detail in Chapter 7. Thereafter we shall be dealing almost exclusively with limited liability companies.

CONCLUSION

The main aim of this chapter has been to introduce the non-accountant to the world of accounting. We have emphasized that the main purpose of accounting is to provide financial information to anyone who wants it.

Of course, information must be useful if it is to have any purpose but, as a non-accountant, you may feel reluctant to question any accounting information that lands on your desk. You may also not understand why the accountant is always asking you what you might think are irrelevant questions, so you respond with any old nonsense. You then perhaps feel a bit guilty and a little frustrated. You would like to know more, but you dare not ask. We hope that by the time you have worked your way through this book, you will have the confidence to ask and, furthermore, that you will understand the answer. Good luck!

Now that the world of accounting has been outlined, we can turn to more detailed subject matter. The first task is to learn the basic rules of accounting. These are covered in the next chapter, but it might be as well if you first read through this chapter again before you move on to the next one. It might also be a good idea to attempt some of the questions that end this chapter.

Key points	
	1 To account for something means to explain about it, or report on it.
	2 An entity is any type of organization, and it can be in either the profit-making sector or the not-for-profit sector (such as a local authority).
	3 Owners of an entity want to know (a) how well it is doing; (b) what it owes; and (c) how much is owed to it.
	4 Accounting is important for non-accountants because (a) they must make sure their own entity complies with any legal requirements; and (b) an accounting system can provide them with information that will help them do their jobs more effectively and efficiently.
	5 The main branches of accounting are: auditing, book-keeping, cost accounting, financial accounting, financial management, management accounting, and taxation.
	6 There are six main accountancy bodies: the Institute of Chartered Accountants in England and Wales, the Instiue of Chartered Accountants in Ireland, the Institute of Chartered Accountants of Scotland, the Chartered Association of Certified Accountants, the

> Chartered Institute of Management Accountants, and the Chartered Institute of Public Finance and Accountancy.
>
> 7 There are two main economic sectors within the British economy: manufacturing and servicing. There are different forms of ownership and control in both sectors. Profit-making entities fall into two main types: sole traders and limited liability companies.

CHECK YOUR LEARNING

1 Insert the missing words in each of the following sentences:
   (a) The word _____ in everyday language means an explanation or a report.
   (b) The owner of a business wants to know how much _____ it has made.

2 What are the two main branches of accounting?

3 State whether each of the following assertions is either true or false:
   (a) Auditors are responsible for preparing accounts   True/False
   (b) Management accounts are required by law   True/False

4 Which of the following activities is not an accounting function?
   (a) auditing (b) book-keeping (c) management consultancy (d) taxation

5 How many major professional accountancy bodies are there in the British Isles?
   (a) three (b) six (c) nine (d) ten or more

6 Fill in the blanks:
   (a) _____ trader (b) Partnership _____ 1890 (c) limited liability _____

Answers
1 (a) account (b) profit
2 (a) financial accounting (b) management accounting
3 (a) false (b) false
4 (c) management consultancy
5 (b) six
6 (a) sole (b) Act (c) company

QUESTIONS

1.1
State briefly the main reasons why a company may employ a team of accountants.

1.2
Why does a limited liability company have to engage a firm of external auditors, and for what purpose?

1.3
Why should a non-accountant study accounting?

1.4
What statutory obligations require the preparation of management accounts in any kind of entity?

1.5
What statutory obligations support the publication of financial accounts in respect of limited liability companies?

1.6
Describe briefly the nature and purpose of accounts.

ADDITIONAL QUESTIONS (WITHOUT ANSWERS)

1.7
Assume that you are a personnel officer in a manufacturing company, and that one of your employees is a young engineering manager called Joseph Sykes. Joseph has been chosen to attend the local University's Business School to study for a diploma in management. Joseph is reluctant to attend the course because it will include a subject called 'financial management'. As an engineer, he thinks that it will be a waste of time for him to study such a subject.

Required:
Draft an internal memorandum addressed to Joseph Sykes explaining why it would be of benefit to him to study financial management.

1.8
Clare Wong spends a lot of her time working for a large local charity. The charity has grown enormously in recent years, and the trustees have been advised to overhaul their accounting procedures. This would involve its workers (most of whom are voluntary) in more book-keeping, and there is a great deal of resistance to this move. The staff have said that they are there to help the needy, and not to get involved in book-keeping.

Required:
As the financial consultant to the charity, prepare some notes that you could use in speaking to the voluntary workers in order to try to persuade them to accept the new proposals.

DISCUSSION QUESTIONS

1.9
'Accountants stifle managerial initiative and enterprise.' Discuss.

1.10

It has been suggested that Germany is a far more successful country than the United Kingdom because it has far fewer accountants. How far do you agree?

1.11

Do you think that auditors should be responsible for detecting fraud?

1.12

Should companies be required to report not just to their shareholders, but to anyone else who has an interest in the company?

Financial accounting

CHAPTER 2

Accounting rules

F & C clarifies its accounting policy

By Jim Kelly

The directors of Foreign & Colonial Investment Trust have provided a fuller explanation in their annual accounts of their treatment of an associated undertaking, following the intervention of the Financial Reporting Review Panel, the accounts' watchdog.

In accounting for Hypo Foreign & Colonial Management (Holdings) Ltd in its 1994 accounts, the trust had shown it in the revenue accounts using the equity method – as recommended in the Statement of Standard Accounting Practice 1. The carrying value in the consolidated balance sheet was at directors' or market valuation. The panel said the trust had not explained this treatment adequately.

In its 1995 accounts, the trust explains that 'as the investment in HFCM forms part of the group's investment portfolio the directors believe adoption of the equity method in the balance sheet would not show a true and fair view.'

The difference between the two methods was shown in the later accounts – at £5.5m under the equity method compared to £49.7m at valuation. The panel welcomed the explanation and said its enquiry was concluded.

The Financial Times, 10 April 1996

Exhibit 2.0 Companies are expected to disclose their accounting policies

We suggested in Chapter 1 that accountancy is a profession engaged in the supply of financial information to a number of interested parties. In fact, the amount of information that is available is so enormous that it is necessary to place some limit on the type of data dealt with.

Modern accounting systems have evolved over a long period of time. They have not developed from any sort of theoretical model, but have grown out of practical necessity. As a result, a number of basic procedures have developed. These procedures may perhaps best be described as the *basic rules of accounting*. Some authors refer to them under a variety of other names, such as assumptions, axioms, concepts, conventions, postulates, principles, or procedures.

By the end of this chapter, you will be able to:

● **identify fourteen accounting rules;**

● **classify them into three broad groupings;**

● **describe each accounting rule;**

● **explain why each is important;**

● **outline the main features of a conceptual framework.**

In preparing and presenting information, accountants have considerable free-dom over which rules to adopt and how they should be interpreted. Since 1971, the accountancy profession has tried to restrict the room for manoeuvre by issuing a series of accounting guides. The guides issued prior to 1990 are known as Statements of Standard Accounting Practice (SSAPs). The ones issued since then are called Financial Reporting Standards (FRSs). When preparing accounting statements, qualified accountants are supposed to follow the letter and not just the spirit of the recommendations contained in SSAPs and FRSs. However, it is impracticable to lay down totally rigid rules for each and every situation, so accountants are still able to employ a great deal of individual discretion.

It would be possible, of course, to ignore all of the generally recognized accounting rules and to prepare accounts in an entirely novel way. This would be like trying to play football under different rules than the ones laid down by the Football Association. If the accepted rules were disregarded, any match played under entirely new rules would result in a game that would be almost incomprehensible to most of the spectators.

A similar situation would apply in accounting if the conventional rules were abandoned. Such rules include, for example, the amount and type of information to be collected, and the length of the accounting period. These are practical rules, like those in football covering the size of the pitch and the length of the match. Other accounting rules are more of an ethical nature, for example, all the rules should be applied consistently, and information should not be presented in a deliberately distorted fashion. These rules may again be compared with those in football that cover misconduct: for example, the ball must not be handled, or an opponent should not be kicked.

The basic accounting rules will be outlined in subsequent sections. For con-venience, they have been classified as follows:

1 boundary rules;
2 measurement rules;
3 ethical rules.

A diagrammatic summary of the main accounting rules that we are going to examine is shown in Exhibit 2.1.

Exhibit 2.1 The basic accounting rules

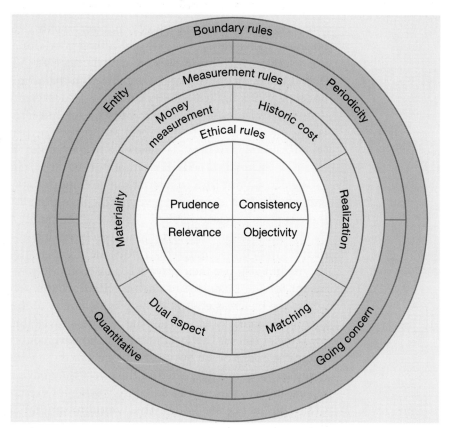

This classification is largely arbitrary. It has been chosen to help you examine more clearly some of the most important accounting rules. There are something like 150 identifiable accounting rules, but we are only going to look at the 14 that are of particular relevance to non-accountants.

BOUNDARY RULES

In small entities, the owners can probably obtain all the information that they want to know by finding out for themselves. In larger entities, this is often impracticable, so a more formal way of reporting back to the owners has to be devised. However, it would be difficult to inform the owners about literally *everything* that had happened to the entity. A start has to be made, therefore, by determining what should and should not be reported. Hence, accountants have devised a number of what we will call *boundary rules*. The boundary rules attempt to place a limit on the amount and type of data collected and stored within the entity.

There are four main boundary rules, and they will be examined in the following sub-sections.

Entity There is so much information available about any organization that accountants start by drawing a boundary around what we have referred to as an *entity*. As we explained in the last chapter, an entity could be a profit-making business, such as a shop buying and selling goods, or a firm of solicitors offering a service. Such businesses are usually referred to as *profit-making* entities. A profit-making entity may be organized in the form of a sole trader, a partnership, or of a limited liability company. However, an entity might well be a *non-profit making* (some accountants prefer the term *not-for-profit making*) entity, such as a charity or a local authority. The primary purpose of such organizations is to provide a service to the public, the profit motive being either irrelevant or of secondary importance.

The accountant tries to restrict the amount of data collected to that of the entity itself. This is sometimes very difficult, especially in small entities where there is often no clear distinction between the public affairs of the entity and the private affairs of the owner. In a profit-making business, for example, the owners sometimes charge their household expenditure to the business, and they might also use their private bank account to pay for goods and services meant for the business. In such a situation, the accountant has to decide where the business ends and the private affairs of the owners begin. He has then to establish exactly what the business owes the owner and the owner owes the business. The accountant will, however, only be interested in recording in the books of the business the effect of these various transactions on the *business*. He is not interested in the effect they have on the owner's private affairs. Indeed, it would be an entirely different exercise if the accountant did deal with his private affairs. This would mean that he was accounting for a different entity altogether, i.e. the private entity, instead of the public one, although there may be a great deal of overlap between the two entities.

Periodicity Most entities have an unlimited life. They are usually started in the expectation that they will operate for an indeterminate period of time, but it is clearly unhelpful for the owner to have to wait years before any report is prepared on how it is doing. The owner would almost certainly wish to receive regular reports at frequent short intervals.

If an entity has an unlimited life, any report must be prepared at the end of what must inevitably be an arbitrary period of time. In practice, *financial accounting* statements are usually prepared annually. Such a time period has developed largely as a matter of custom. It does, however, reflect the agricultural cycle in Western Europe, and there does seem to be a natural human tendency to compare what has happened this year with what happened last year. Nonetheless, where entities have an unlimited life (as is usually the case with manufacturing organizations), the preparation of annual accounts presents considerable problems in relating specific events to appropriate accounting periods. We shall be having a look at these problems in Chapter 5.

Apart from custom, there is no reason why an accounting period could not be shorter or longer than twelve months. Management accounts are usually prepared for very short periods, but sometimes this also applies to financial accounts. For example, in the fashion industry, where the product designs may change very quickly, managers may want (say) quarterly reports. By contrast, the construction industry faced with very long-term contract work may find it more appropriate to have (say) a five-year reporting period. In fact, irrespective of the length of the main accounting period (i.e. whether it is quarterly or five yearly), managers usually need regular reports covering a very short period. Cash reports, for example, could be prepared on a weekly, or even on a daily basis.

It must also not be forgotten that some entities (e.g. limited liability companies) are required by law to produce annual accounts, and as tax demands are also based on a calendar year, it would not be possible for most entities to ignore the conventional twelve-months period. In any case, given the unlimited life of most entities, you will appreciate that *any* period must be somewhat arbitrary, no matter how carefully a particular entity has tried to relate its accounting period to the nature of its business.

Going concern The periodicity rule requires a regular period of account to be established, regardless either of the life of the entity or of the arbitrary nature of such a period. The going concern rule arises out of the periodicity rule. This rule requires us to assume that an entity will continue in existence for the foreseeable future unless we have some strong evidence to suggest that this is not the case. It is important to make absolutely certain that this assumption is correct, because a different set of accounting rules would be adopted if its immediate future is altogether uncertain.

Quantitative Accountants usually restrict the data that are collected to those which are easily quantifiable. For example, it is possible to count the number of people that an entity employs, but it is difficult to calculate the *skill* of the employees. Such a concept is almost impossible to quantify, and it is, therefore, not included in a conventional accounting system.

MEASUREMENT RULES

The boundary rules determine *what* data should be included in an accounting system, whereas the measurement rules explain *how* that data should be recorded. There are six main measurement rules, and we outline them briefly in the following sub-sections.

Money measurement It would be very cumbersome to record information simply in terms of quantifiable amounts. It would also be impossible to make any fair comparisons between various types of assets (such as livestock and farm machinery), or different types of transactions (such as the sale of eggs and the purchase of corn). In order to make a meaningful comparison, we need to convert the data into a common and recognizable measure.

As we suggested in Chapter 1, the monetary unit serves such a purpose. It is a useful way of converting accounting data into a common unit, and since most quantifiable information is capable of being translated into monetary terms, there is usually no difficulty in adopting the monetary measurement rule.

Historic cost The historic cost rule is an extension of the money measurement rule. It requires transactions to be recorded at their *original* (i.e. their historic) cost. Subsequent changes in prices or values, therefore, are usually ignored. Increased costs may arise because of a combination of an improved product, or through changes in the purchasing power of the monetary unit, i.e. through inflation.

As we shall see in Chapter 12, inflation tends to overstate the level of accounting profit as it is traditionally calculated. Over the last 25 years, there have been several attempts in the UK to change the method of accounting in order to allow for the effects of inflation. There has been so much disagreement on what should replace what we now call *historic cost accounting* (HCA), that no other method has been acceptable. Throughout most of this book, we shall be adopting the historic cost rule.

Realization One of the problems of putting the periodicity rule into practice is that it is often difficult to relate a specific transaction to a particular period. For example, assume that a business arranges to sell some goods in 1997, it delivers them in 1998, and it is paid for them in 1999. In which year were the goods *sold*: 1997, 1998, or 1999? In conventional accounting, it would be most unusual to include them in the sales for 1997, because the business has still got a legal title to them. They could be included in the accounts for 1999 when the goods have been paid for. Indeed, this method of accounting is not uncommon. It is known as *cash flow accounting* (CFA). In CFA, transactions are only entered in the books of account when a cash exchange has taken place. By contrast, in HCA, it is customary to enter most transactions in the books of account when the legal title to the goods has been transferred from one party to another and when there is an obligation for the recipient to pay for them. This means that in the above example, the goods would normally be considered to have been sold in 1998.

The realization rule covers this point. It requires transactions relating to the sale of goods to be entered in the accounts for that period in which the legal title for them has been transferred from one party to another. In the jargon of accounting, they are then said to be realized. It is important to appreciate that for goods and services to be treated as realized, they do not need to have been paid for: the cash for them may be received during a later period (or for that matter, may have been received in an earlier period).

The realization rule is normally regarded as applying to sales, but *purchases* (meaning goods that are intended for resale) may be treated similarly. Thus, they would not be included in an entity's accounts until it had a legal title to them (i.e. in law, it would be regarded as owning them).

The realization rule can produce some rather misleading results. For example, the company may treat the goods as having been sold in 1998. In 1999, it finds that the purchaser cannot pay for them. What can it do? Its accounts for 1998 have already been approved. It is too late to change them, but obviously the sales for that year were overstated (and so too, almost certainly, was the profit). The customer defaults in 1999, so how can the *bad debt* (as it is known) be dealt with in *that* year? We shall be explaining how in Chapter 5.

Matching The realization rule relates mainly to the purchase and sale of goods, in other words, to what are known as *trading* items. However, a similar rule known as the *matching* rule applies to other incomes (such as dividends and rents received) and expenditure (such as electricity and wages).

A misleading impression would be given if the cash received during a particular period was simply compared with the cash paid out during the same period. The exact period in which the cash is either received or paid may bear no relationship to the period in which the business was transacted. Thus, accountants normally adjust cash received and cash paid on what is known as an *accruals and prepayments* basis. An accrual is an amount that is *owed* by the entity at the end of an accounting period in respect of services *received* during that period. A prepayment is an amount that is *owing* to the entity at the end of the accounting period as a result of it paying in advance for services to be rendered in respect of a future period.

The conversion of cash received and cash paid on to an accruals and prepayments basis at the end of an accounting period often involves a considerable amount of arithmetical adjustment. Account has to be taken for accruals and prepayments at the end of the previous period (i.e *opening* accruals and prepayments), as well as for accruals and prepayments at the end of the current period (i.e. *closing* accruals and prepayments). We shall be dealing with accruals and prepayments in more detail in Chapter 5.

An accruals and prepayments system of accounting enables the incomes of one period to be matched much more fairly against the costs of the same period. The comparison is not distorted by the accidental timing of cash receipts and cash payments. However, as the matching rule requires the accountant to estimate the level of both accruals and prepayments as at the end of each accounting period, a degree of subjectivity is automatically built into the estimate.

Dual aspect The dual aspect rule is a useful practical rule, although it really only reflects what is obvious. It is built round the fact that every time something is given, someone (or something) else receives it. In other words, every time a transaction take place, there is always a twofold effect. For example, if the amount of cash in a business goes up, someone must have given it, or if the business buys some goods, then someone else must be selling them.

We explained in Chapter 1 that this twofold effect was recognized many centuries ago. It gave rise to the system of recording information known as *double-entry book-keeping*. This system of book-keeping is still widely used. Although the concept is somewhat obvious, it has proved extremely useful, so much so that even modern computerized recording systems are based on it. From long experience, it has been found that the system is a most convenient way of recording all sorts of useful information about the entity, and of ensuring some form of control over its affairs.

There is no real need to adopt the dual aspect rule in recording information: it is entirely a practical rule that has proved itself over many centuries. Voluntary organizations (such as a drama club, or a stamp collecting society) may not think that it is worth while to adopt the dual aspect rule, but you are strongly recommended to incorporate it into your book-keeping system in any entity with which you are concerned. If you do, you will find that it gives you more control over the entity's affairs besides providing you with a great deal more information.

Double-entry book-keeping will be examined in more detail in the next chapter.

Materiality Strict application of the various accounting rules may not always be practical. It could involve a considerable amount of work that may be out of all proportion to the information that is eventually obtained. The materiality rule permits other rules to be ignored if the effects are not considered to be *material*, that is, if they are not significant.

Hence, the materiality rule avoids the necessity to follow other accounting rules to the point of absurdity. For example, it would normally be considered unnecessary to value the closing stock of small amounts of stationery, or to maintain detailed records of inexpensive items of office equipment. However, it should be borne in mind that what is immaterial for a large organization may not be so for a small one.

If you decide that a certain item is immaterial, then it does not matter how you deal with it in the accounts, because it cannot possibly have any significant effect on the results. When dealing with insignificant items, therefore, the materiality rule permits the other accounting rules to be ignored.

ETHICAL RULES

There is an old story in accounting about the company chairman who asked his chief accountant how much profit the company had made. The chief accountant replied by asking how much profit the chairman would like to make. Accountants recognize that there is some truth in this story, since it is quite possible for different accountants to use the same basic data in preparing accounting statements, and yet still arrive at a different level of profit!

You might think that by faithfully following all of the accounting rules, *all* accountants should be able to calculate exactly the same amount of profit. Unfortunately, this is not the case since, as we have seen, most of the main accounting rules are capable of wide interpretation. The matching rule, for example, requires an estimate to be made of amounts owing and owed at the end of an accounting period, while the materiality rule allows the accountant to decide just what is material. Both rules involve an element of subjective judgement, and so no two accountants are likely to agree precisely on how they should be applied.

In order to limit the room for individual manoeuvre, a number of other rules have evolved. These rules are somewhat ethical in nature, and indeed some authors refer to them as accounting *principles* (thereby suggesting that there is a moral dimension to them). Other authors, however, refer to *all* of the basic accounting rules as principles, but it really does not matter what you call them as long as you are aware of them. Basically, the ethical rules require accountants to follow not just the letter, but the spirit of the other rules.

There are four main ethical accounting rules, and we will review them individually in the following sub-sections.

Prudence
The prudence rule (which is sometimes known as *conservatism*) arises out of the need to make a number of estimates in preparing periodic accounts. Managers and owners are often naturally over-optimistic about future events. As a result, there is a tendency to be too confident about the future, and not to be altogether realistic about the entity's prospects. There may be, for example, undue optimism over the credit-worthiness of a particular customer. Insufficient allowance may, therefore, be made for the possibility of a bad debt. This might have the effect of overstating profit in one period, and understating it in a future period. We shall come across this problem again in Chapter 5.

The prudence rule is sometimes expressed in the form of a simple maxim:

If in doubt, overstate losses and understate profits.

Consistency
As we have seen, the preparation of traditional accounting statements requires a considerable amount of individual judgement to be made in the application of the basic accounting rules. To compensate for this flexibility, the *consistency* rule states that once specific accounting policies have been adopted, they should be followed in all subsequent accounting periods.

It would be considered quite unethical to change those rules just because they were unfashionable, or because alternative ones gave better results. Of course, if the circumstances of the entity change radically, it may be necessary to adopt different policies, but this should only be done in exceptional circumstances. If different policies are adopted, then the effect of any change should be clearly highlighted and any comparative figure adjusted accordingly.

The application of this rule gives confidence to the users of accounting statements, because if the accounts have been prepared on a consistent basis they can be assured that they are comparable with previous sets of accounts.

Objectivity Accounts should be prepared with the minimum amount of bias. This is not an easy task, since individual judgement is required in interpreting the rules and adapting them to suit particular circumstances. Owners may want, for example, to adopt policies which would result in higher profit figures, or in disguising poor results.

If optional policy decisions are possible within the existing rules, it is advisable to fall back on the prudence rule. Indeed, it tends to be an overriding one. If there is any doubt about which rule to adopt (or how it should be interpreted), the prudence rule tends to take precedence.

It must be recognized, however, that if the prudence rules is always adopted as the easy way out of a difficult problem, you could be accused of lacking objectivity. In other words, you must not use this rule to avoid making difficult decisions. Indeed, it is just as unfair to be as excessively cautious as it is to be widely optimistic. Extremism of any kind suggests a lack of objectivity, so you should avoid being either over-cautious or over-optimistic.

Relevance The amount of information that could be supplied to any interested party is practically unlimited. If too much information is disclosed, it becomes very difficult to absorb, so it should only be included if it is it going to help the user.

The selection of relevant information requires much experience and judgement, as well as calling for a great understanding of the user's requirements. The information needs to be designed in such a way that it meets the *objectives* of the specific user group. If too much information is given, the users might think that it is an attempt to mislead them, and as a result, all of the information may be totally rejected.

In this context, accountants try to present accounts in such a way that they represent 'a true and fair view'. The Companies Act 1985, for example, requires company accounts to reflect this particular criterion, and it is advisable to apply it to all entities. Unfortunately, the Act does not define what is meant by 'true and fair', but it is assumed that accounts will be true and fair if an entity has followed the rules laid down in appropriate accounting and financial reporting standards.

Financial reporting standards are formulated by an Accounting Standards Board (ASB), and professionally qualified accountants are required to follow its recommendations. As we mentioned earlier, these are contained in Financial Reporting Standards (FRSs) and in Statements of Accounting Standards (SSAPs) issued by the former Accounting Standards Committee (ASC) and not yet withdrawn by the ASB. FRSs are not statutory requirements, although as will be seen in Chapter 10, some recognition in law is given to them, and the ASB has much greater power to enforce its recommendations than had the old ASC.

By the time that the ASC had been disbanded in 1990, it had issued 25 SSAPs (three of which had been withdrawn). By late 1996, the ASB had issued eight FRSs and withdrawn four of the old SSAPs.

Such standards are considered to represent the most authoritative view of how certain matters should be dealt with in the 'financial statements of a reporting entity that are intended to give a true and fair view of its state of affairs at the balance sheet date and of its profit or loss (or income and expenditure) for the financial period ending on that date' (as the ASB's 'Foreword to accounting standards' puts it). This is perhaps rather a strange way of requiring compliance with the standards, because it suggests that some accounts are not meant to give a true and fair view!

The standards cover such diverse subjects as the accounting policies adopted by an entity, and the treatment of depreciation, taxation and stock valuations. Although professionally qualified accountants are supposed to follow the recommendations contained within the standards, they still leave room for considerable individual interpretation, and no real disciplinary action has yet been taken against any accountants for not following either the letter or the spirit of them.

SUMMARY OF THE BASIC ACCOUNTING RULES

It would be convenient at this stage if we summarized the basic accounting rules outlined in the previous section, so that it will be easy for you to refer back to when studying later chapters. In summary, therefore, they are as follows:

Boundary rules

1 **Entity**. Accounting data must be restricted to the entity itself. They should exclude the private affairs of those individuals who either own or manage the entity, except insofar as they impact directly on it.

2 **Periodicity**. Accounts should be prepared at the end of a defined period of time, and this period should be adopted as the regular period of account.

3 **Going concern**. The accounts should be prepared on the assumption that the entity will continue in existence for the foreseeable future.

4 **Quantitative**. Only data that are capable of being easily quantified should be included in an accounting system.

Measurement rules

1 **Money measurement**. Data must be translated into monetary terms before they are included in an accounting system.

2 **Historic cost**. Financial data should be recorded in the books of account at their historic cost, that is, at their original purchase cost, or at their original selling price.

3 **Realization**. Transactions that reflect financial data should be entered in the books of account when the legal title to them has been transferred from one party to another party, irrespective of when a cash settlement takes place.

4 **Matching**. Cash received and cash paid during a particular accounting period should be adjusted in order to reflect the economic activity that has actually taken place during that period.

5 **Dual aspect**. All transactions should be recorded in such a way that they capture the giving and the receiving effect of each transaction.

6 **Materiality**. The basic accounting rules must not be rigidly applied to insignificant items.

Ethical rules

1 **Prudence**. If there is some doubt over the treatment of a particular transaction, income should be under-estimated and expenditure over-estimated, so that profits are more likely to be understated and losses overstated.

2 **Consistency**. Accounting rules and policies should not be amended unless there is a fundamental change in circumstances that necessitates a reconsideration of the original rules and policies.

3 **Objectivity**. Personal prejudice must be avoided in the interpretation of the basic accounting rules.

4 **Relevance**. Accounting statements should not include information that prevents users from obtaining a true and fair view of the information being communicated to them.

Before we finish this chapter, we ought to have a brief look at some accounting theory. No! Don't close the book just yet. It won't be as bad as you think!

A CONCEPTUAL FRAMEWORK

As we explained at the beginning of this chapter, the basic accounting rules have evolved over a period of time: nobody worked them out on paper before they were applied in practice. This means that when some new accounting problem arises, we do not know how to deal with it. Some accountants (especially university lecturers), argue, therefore, that what is needed is a *conceptual framework*. In other words, we ought to devise a theoretical model of accounting, and then any new accounting problem could be solved merely by running it through the model.

It sounds very sensible, but it is not easy to devise such a model. Several attempts have been made, and none of them have been successful. Basically, there are two approaches that can be adopted:

1 We can list all the accounting rules that have ever been used, and then extract the ones that are the most widely used. There are two main problems in adopting this approach:

(a) To be meaningful, we would have to conduct an extremely wide survey of existing practice. As yet, the sheer scale required by this exercise has defeated most researchers.

(b) Such an exercise would simply freeze existing practice: it would not improve it.

2 Alternatively, we could determine

(a) who uses accounting statements;

(b) what they want them for (i.e. we would need to establish user *objectives*); and

(c) what rules we need to adopt to meet those objectives.

Again, the scale of the exercise has defeated most researchers. Furthermore, even if some agreement could be reached on the users of accounting statements and their objectives, it is not easy to select appropriate rule that would be generally acceptable.

It follows that the ASB (whose job would presumably be easier if it could solve new accounting problems by running them through some sort of model) may still have to deal with new issues on a fire-fighting basis. As new problems arise, it may have to put forward a solution which it hopes will be acceptable, but if not then it has to try again.

That is all the theory with which we shall be dealing (it wasn't too bad, was it?), although we shall be returning to some of these problems in later chapters.

CONCLUSION

In this chapter we have identified 14 basic accounting rules that accountants usually adopt in the preparation of accounting statements. We have described four of these rules as boundary rules, six as measurement rules and four as ethical rules. We have argued that the boundary rules limit the amount and type of information that is traditionally collected and stored in an accounting system. The measurement rules provide some guidance on how that information should be recorded, and the ethical rules lay down a code of conduct on how all the other rules should be interpreted.

The exact number, classification and description of these various accounting rules is subject to much debate amongst accountants. Most entities can, in fact, adopt what rules they like, although it would be most unusual if they did not accept the going concern, matching, prudence and consistency rules.

In the next chapter, we shall examine the dual aspect rule in a little more detail. This rule is at the heart of double-entry book-keeping and most modern accounting systems are based upon it.

Key points	
	1 In preparing accounting statements, accountants adopt a number of rules that have evolved over a number of centuries.
	2 There are four main boundary rules: entity, periodicity, going concern, and quantitative.
	3 The six main measurement rules are: money measurement, historic cost, realization, matching, dual aspect, and materiality.
	4 Ethical rules include: prudence, consistency, objectivity, and relevance.
	5 No satisfactory conceptual framework of accounting has yet been developed by the accountancy profession (although the ASB is attempting to do so). Thus, new accounting problems have to be dealt with on a fire-fighting basis.

CHECK YOUR LEARNING

1 State whether each of the following comments is true or false:

   (a) Accounting is based on a theoretical framework.   True/False
   (b) All of the basic accounting rules are codified in law.   True/False
   (c) Accountants can adapt accounting rules to suit particular circumstances.   True/False

2 Fill in the missing blanks in the following statement:
If in doubt, _____ losses, and _____ profits.

3 Indicate the category of the following six accounting rules:

	Boundary	Measurement	Ethical
(a) going concern	☐	☐	☐
(b) matching	☐	☐	☐
(c) money measurement	☐	☐	☐
(d) objectivity	☐	☐	☐
(e) periodicity	☐	☐	☐
(f) prudence	☐	☐	☐

Answers
1 (a) false   (b) false   (c) true
2 over-state; under-state
3 (a) boundary   (b) measurement   (c) measurement   (d) ethical
   (e) boundary   (f) ethical

QUESTIONS

In questions 2.1, 2.2 and 2.3 you are required to state which accounting rule the accountant would most probably adopt in dealing with the various problems.

2.1

1 Electricity consumed in period 1 and paid for in period 2.
2 Equipment originally purchased for £20 000 which would now cost £30 000.
3 The company's good industrial relations record.
4 A five-year construction contract.
5 A customer who might go bankrupt owing the company £5000.
6 The company's vehicles which would only have a small scrap value if the company goes into liquidation.

2.2

1 A demand by the company's chairman to include every detailed transaction in the presentation of the annual accounts.
2 A sole-trader business which has paid the proprietor's income tax based on the business profits for the year.
3 A proposed change in the methods of valuing stock.
4 The valuation of a gallon of petrol in one vehicle at the end of accounting period 1.
5 A vehicle which could be sold for more than its purchase price.
6 Goods which were sold to a customer in period 1, but for which the cash was only received in period 2.

2.3

1 The proprietor who has supplied the business capital out of his own private bank account.
2 The sales manager who is always very optimistic about the credit-worthiness of prospective customers.
3 The managing director who does not want annual accounts prepared as the company operates a continuous 24 hours a day, 365 days a year process.
4 At the end of period 1, it is difficult to be certain whether the company will have to pay legal fees of £1000 or £3000.
5 The proprietor who argues that the accountant has got a motor vehicle entered twice in the books of account.
6 Some goods were purchased and entered into stock at the end of period 1, but they were not paid for until period 2.

2.4

The following is a list of problems which an accountant may well meet in practice:

1 The transfer fee of a footballer.
2 Goods sold in one period, but the cash for them is received in a later period.
3 The proprietor's personal dwelling house has been used as security for a loan which the bank has granted to the company.
4 What profit to take in the third year of a five-year construction contract.
5 Small stocks of stationery held at the accounting year end.
6 Expenditure incurred in working on the improvement of a new drug.

Required:

State:

(a) which accounting rule the accountant would most probably adopt in dealing with each of the above problems; and

(b) the reasons for your choice.

ADDITIONAL QUESTIONS (WITHOUT ANSWERS)

2.5

The Companies Act 1985 lists five prescribed accounting principles, while SSAP 2 (Disclosure of accounting policies) refers to four fundamental accounting concepts.

Required:

Write a report for your managing dirctor comparing and contrasting the five accounting principles laid down in the Companies Act 1985 with the four fundamental accounting concepts outlined in SSAP 2. (*Note*: before preparing your report, you are advised to consult both the Act and the Standard.)

2.6

The adoption of the realization and matching rules in preparing financial accounts requires a great deal of subjective judgement.

Required:

Write an essay examining whether it would be fairer, easier, and more meaningful to prepare financial accounts on a cash flow basis.

DISCUSSION QUESTIONS

2.7

Do you think that when preparing a set of financial accounts the prudence rule should override the objectivity rule?

2.8

'The law should lay down precise formats, contents, and methods for the preparation of limited liability company accounts.' Discuss.

2.9

It has been suggested that before any more financial reporting standards are issued, the Accounting Standards Board should first devise a conceptual framework for financial reporting. How far do you agree with this suggestion?

CHAPTER 3

Recording data

Wickes shares frozen

SHARES in the DIY group Wickes were suspended yesterday pending an investigation into accounting irregularities stretching back over three years.

The shares were suspended at the company's own request after it said it had discovered serious accounting problems relating to the timing of recognition of profits from its supplier contributions. Wickes warned that it was probable that 1995 profits, and shareholders' funds, had been overstated.

Discounts from suppliers for bulk orders appear to have been credited to the profit and loss account even though some of them were not paid. 'If sales do not meet the expected volumes and discounts are later rescinded the profit margins can be overstated,' said Robert Snaith, a SG Strauss Turnbull analyst.

Shares opened the day at 109p before plunging 40p ahead of the suspension. Wickes said a statement will be forthcoming today. One analyst said he was not surprised by the turn of events and cited the lack of transparency surrounding management and 'the spread sheets not adding up' as reasons for his scepticism. Major investors said they may consider a range of options including calls for a board shake-up following the suspension of the shares.

The beleaguered group slumped into the red with losses of £258 million for the year to 31 December 1995 after swallowing huge write-offs following the disposal of its Hunter Timber business. In April the group warned that profits in the first half would fall 'significantly below those of last year'.

The Scotsman, 26 June 1996

Exhibit 3.0 When to record appears to have been part of the problem here

In the last chapter, a number of basic accounting rules were outlined, including the dual aspect rule. In this chapter, the dual aspect rule will be examined in much more detail.

Most modern book-keeping systems adopt the dual aspect rule, irrespective of whether they are hand written, mechanized or computer based. While it is unlikely that as a non-accountant you will be involved in the recording of accounting data, you may well be presented with information based on such data. In presenting it to you, it is sometimes assumed that you have some knowledge of double-entry book-keeping.

This chapter has been specially designed to introduce the *non-accountant* to the subject of double-entry book-keeping. The chapter contains a number of book-keeping examples, and while it might seem unnecessary for you to work through them, you are recommended to do so for two main reasons:

1 it will help you to become familiar with accounting terminology;
2 a knowledge of the methods used in preparing accounting information will help you to assess its *usefulness* in doing your job much more effectively and efficiently.

We had better warn you that this will not be an easy chapter for you to work through. And we mean *work*, rather than just read through. Most sections contain an exhibit which illustrates a particular book-keeping procedure. These exhibits must be studied most carefully.

To help you get the most out of this chapter, you are recommended to adopt the following procedure:

1 read the descriptive material in each section very carefully;
2 make sure that you understand the requirements of each exhibit;
3 examine the answer to each exhibit, paying particular attention to the following points:
    (a) the way in which it has been presented, i.e. its format;
    (b) how the data in the exhibit have been converted in response to the requirements of the question;
4 once you have worked through the answer, try to do the question on your own without reference to the solution;
5 if you go wrong, or you find that you do not know how to do the question, re-read the earlier parts of the chapter, and then have another go at it.

We begin our study of the dual aspect rule by examining its basic fundamental concept. We do so in the next section.

By the end of this chapter, you will be able to:

● **describe what is meant by the terms 'debit' and 'credit';**

● **write up some simple ledger accounts;**

● **extract a trial balance;**

● **identify six accounting errors not revealed in a trial balance.**

THE DUAL ASPECT RULE

The dual aspect rule arises from a recognition that every time a transaction takes place, there must always be a two-sided effect *within* the entity (a transaction is simply the doing or performing of any business). A few examples should help to make the point clear:

1 If an owner of an entity pays £10000 into his business bank account out of his private bank account, the business bank account will go *up* by £10000, but the amount owed by the business to the owner will also go *up* by £10000.
2 If the business owes Jones £3000 and it sends him a cheque for £2000, the amount that it owes Jones will go *down* by £2000, but its bank account will also go down by £2000.
3 If a business receives £1000 in cash from Smith in part-payment of an amount owed by him to the business, the business's cash will go *up* by £1000, but the amount owed by Smith will go *down* by £1000.
4 If a business pays £5000 in cash for a car, the total value of the cars it owns will go *up* by £5000, but its cash balance will go *down* by £5000.

These examples are illustrated in diagrammatic form in Exhibit 3.1

Transaction 1 results in an up/up effect; transaction 2 results in a down/down effect; and transactions 3 and 4 have an up/down effect. Thus, although some transactions move in the same direction, other transactions can move in opposite directions. Nonetheless, there is *always* a twofold effect: there are no exceptions. Note that this twofold effect takes place *within* the entity. We are not interested in the effect that it may have on outside parties: that is their own affair and not ours, except insofar as it has an impact on our business.

The recognition of the twofold effect of all transactions gave rise to the system of recording accounting data that we now refer to as *double-entry book-keeping*. Its main objective is very simple: it is to record the dual effect of all transactions. But why should we want to record everything twice over? There are two main reasons:

1 it provides valuable information about the effect of each transaction in respect of the business;
2 as every transaction is recorded twice, it provides a check on the accuracy of the recording system: in other words, it is a form of control.

The recording of accounting data is achieved by classifying all transactions into appropriate groupings. These are then stored separately in what are known as *accounts*. An account is simply a history or a record of a particular type of transaction. In a manual system all of the accounts are usually kept in bound books known as *ledgers*. Nowadays, however, many entities store information in computer-based systems, although hand-written recording systems may still be found in some small businesses.

Exhibit 3.1 Examples of the twofold effect when a transaction takes place

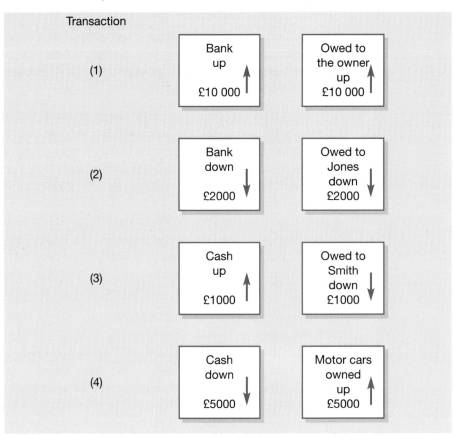

The effect of a particular transaction on an account is to cause the balance on the account either to go up or to go down, and so a particular transaction could either *increase* the total amount held within an account, or it could have the opposite effect and *decrease* it. We can put it another way, and suggest that the account either *receives* an additional amount, or it *gives* (or releases) it. It is this receiving and giving effect that has given rise to two Latin terms commonly used in accounting. These two terms are as follows:

> **Debit**: meaning to receive, or value received;
> **Credit**: meaning to give, or value given.

Accountants judge the twofold effect of all transactions on particular accounts from a receiving and giving point of view, and each transaction is recorded on that basis. Thus, when a transaction takes place, it is necessary to ask the following questions:

1 which account should *receive* this transaction (i.e. which account should be *debited*?);

2 which account has *given* this amount (i.e. which account should be *credited*?).

Accounts have been designed to keep the debit entries separate from the credit entries. This helps to emphasize the opposite, albeit *equal* effect that each transaction has within the recording system. The separation is achieved by recording the debit entries on the left-hand side of the page, and the credit entries on the right-hand side. In a hand-written system, each account is normally kept on a separate page (known as a folio) in a *book of account* (although if there are a lot of accounts, it may be necessary to keep several books of account). A book of account is also sometimes known as a *ledger*, and hence accounts are often referred to as *ledger* accounts. The format of a typical handwritten *ledger account* is illustrated in Exhibit 3.2.

There is no logical reason why debits should be entered on the left-hand side of an account, and credits on the right-hand side. It is purely a matter of custom, like driving on either the left-hand or the right-hand side of the road.

In the next section we will show you how particular transactions are recorded in appropriate ledger accounts.

Exhibit 3.2 Example of a ledger account

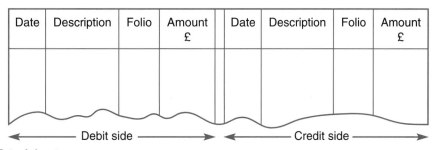

Date	Description	Folio	Amount £	Date	Description	Folio	Amount £

←———— Debit side ————→ ←———— Credit side ————→

Tutorial notes

1 The columnar headings would normally be omitted.

2 The description of each entry is usually limited to the *title* of the corresponding account in which the equal and opposite entry may be found.

3 The folio column is used to refer to the folio (or page) number of the corresponding account.

4 This example of a ledger account may nowadays only be found in a fairly basic handwritten book-keeping system. Computerized and mechanized systems of recording information usually necessitate an alternative format.

WORKING WITH ACCOUNTS

It would not be helpful to either the owners or the managers of a business if the information was not recorded systematically. What has evolved, therefore, is a practical method of capturing the twofold nature of all transactions in separate accounts. Normally, each transaction is recorded in two quite separate accounts, so the book-keeper has to decide in which two accounts to enter a particular transaction. The following sub-sections illustrate the procedure that the book-keeper will adopt.

Choice of accounts

Most transactions can be easily assigned to an appropriate account. The total number and type will depend partly upon the amount of information that the owner wants (for example, salaries and wages might be kept in separate accounts), and partly upon the nature of the business (a manufacturing entity will probably need more accounts than a service entity). In practice, there are a number of accounts that are common to most entities, but if you do not know which account to use, you should adopt the following rule:

If in doubt open another account.

If an account does eventually prove unnecessary, it can always be closed down. While some accounts are common to most entities, it will not always be clear what they should be used for. An idea of the overall system is shown in Exhibit 3.3, and we also list below a brief summary of the main types of accounts:

Capital The **Capital Account** records what the owner has contributed (or given) to the entity out of his private resources in order to start the business and keep it going. In other words, it shows what the business owes him.

Cash at bank The **Bank Account** records what money the entity keeps at the bank. It shows what has been put in (usually in the form of cash and cheques) and what has been taken out (usually by cheque payments).

Cash in hand The **Cash Account** works on similar lines to that of the Bank Account, except that it records the physical cash received (such as notes, coins and cheques) before they are paid into the bank. The cash received may be used to purchase goods and services, or it may be paid straight into the bank. From a control point of view, it is best not to pay for purchases directly out of cash receipts, but to draw an amount out of the bank specifically for sundry cash purchases. Any large amount should be paid by cheque.

Creditors **Creditor Accounts** record what the entity owes its suppliers for goods or services purchased or supplied on credit (see also trade creditors).

Exhibit 3.3 The inter-linking of different types of accounts

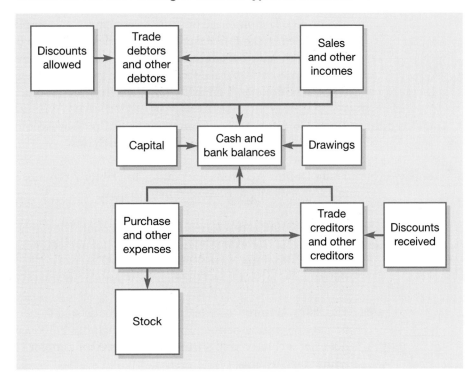

Debtors **Debtor Accounts** record what is owed to the entity by its customers for goods or services sold to them on credit (see also trade debtors).

Discounts allowed **Discounts allowed** are cash discounts granted to the entity's customers for the prompt settlement of any debts due to the entity. The amount of cash received from debtors who claim a cash discount will then be less than the total amount for which they have been invoiced.

Discounts received **Discounts received** relate to cash discounts given by the entity's suppliers for the prompt payment of any amounts due to them. Thus, the amount paid to the entity's creditors will be less than the invoiced amount.

Drawings The term *drawings* has a special meaning in accounting. The **Drawings Account** is used to record what cash (or goods) the owner has withdrawn from the business for his/her own personal use.

Petty cash The **Petty Cash Account** is similar to both the Bank Account and the Cash Account. It is usually limited to the recording of minor cash transactions, such as bus fares, or tea and coffee for the office. The cash used to finance this account will normally be transferred from the Bank Account.

Purchases The term *purchases* has a restricted meaning in accounting. It relates to those goods that are bought primarily with the intention of selling them (normally at a profit). The purchase of some motor cars, for example, would not usually be recorded in the **Purchases Account** unless they have been bought with the intention of selling them to customers. Goods not intended for resale are usually recorded in separate accounts. Some purchases may also require further work to be done on them before they are eventually sold.

Trade creditors **Trade Creditor Accounts** are similar to Creditor Accounts except that they relate specifically to trading items, i.e. purchases.

Trade debtors **Trade Debtor Accounts** are similar to Debtor Accounts except that they also relate specifically to trading items, i.e. sales.

Trade discounts **Trade discounts** are a form of special discount. They may be given for placing a large order, for example, or for being a loyal customer. Trade discounts are deducted from the normal purchase or selling price. They are not recorded in the books of account, and they will not appear on any invoice.

Sales The **Sales Account** records the value of goods sold to customers during a particular accounting period. The account includes both cash and credit sales. It does not include receipts from (say) the sale of a motor car purchased for use within the business.

Stock Stock includes the value of goods which have not been sold at the end of an accounting period. In accounting terminology, this would be referred to as **closing stock**. The closing stock at the end of one period becomes the **opening stock** at the beginning of the next period.

Once the book-keeper has chosen the accounts in which to record all the transactions for a particular accounting period, it is then necessary to decide which account should be debited and which account should be credited. We examine this problem in the next sub-section.

Entering transactions in accounts

There is one simple rule that should be followed when entering a transaction in an account.

> **Debit the account which receives**
> and
> **Credit the account which gives.**

This rule is illustrated in Exhibit 3.4 which contains some common ledger account entries.

Exhibit 3.4 Example of some common ledger account entries

Example 1
The proprietor contributes some cash to the business.

Debit: Cash Account   *Credit:* Capital Account

Reason: The Cash Account receives some cash given to the business by the owner. His Capital Account is the giving account and the Cash Account is the receiving account.

Example 2
Some cash in the till is paid into the business bank account.

Debit: Bank Account   *Credit:* Cash Account

Reason: The Cash Account is the giving account because it is releasing some cash to the Bank Account.

Example 3
A van is purchased for use in the business; it is paid for by cheque.

Debit: Van Account   *Credit:* Bank Account

Reason: The Bank Account is giving some money in order to pay for a van, so the Bank Account must be credited as it is the giving account.

Example 4
Some goods are purchased for cash.

Debit: Purchases Account   *Credit:* Cash Account

Reason: The Cash Account is giving up an amount of cash in order to pay for some purchases. The Cash Account is the giving account, and so it must be credited.

Example 5
Some goods are purchased on credit terms from Fred.

Debit: Purchases Account   *Credit:* Fred's Account.

Reason: Fred is supplying the goods on credit terms to the business. He is, therefore, the giver and his account must be credited.

Example 6
Some goods are sold for cash.

Debit: Cash Account   *Credit:* Sales Account

Reason: The Cash Account receives the cash from the sale of goods, the Sales Account being the giving account.

Example 7
Some goods are sold on credit terms to Sarah.

Debit: Sarah's Account   *Credit:* Sales Account

Reason: Sarah's Account is debited because she is receiving the goods, and the Sales Account is credited because it is supplying (or giving) them.

It is not easy for beginners to think of the receiving and of the giving effect of each transaction. You will find that it is very easy to get them mixed up and to then reverse the entries. If we look at Examples 6 and 7 in Exhibit 3.4, for example, it is difficult to understand why the Sales Account should be credited. Why is the Sales Account the giving account? Surely it is *receiving* an amount and not giving anything? In one sense, it is receiving something, but that applies to any entry in any account. So, in the case of the sales account, regard it as a *supplying* account, because it gives (or releases) something to another account.

If you find this concept difficult to understand, think of the effect on the *opposite* account. A cash sale, for example, results in cash being increased (not decreased). The cash account must, therefore, be the receiving account, and it must be debited. Somebody (say Jones) must have given the cash, but as it is a cash sale, we credit it straight to the sales account. If you find it easier, think of the Sales Department having supplied, given or *sold* the goods to Jones.

Most students find it easier, in fact, to work out the double-entry effect of respective transactions by relating them to the movement of cash. You might find it useful, therefore, to remember the following procedure:

> *Either* Debit: the Cash (or Bank) Account and
> Credit: the corresponding account, if the
> entity **receives** some cash.
>
> *Or* Debit: the corresponding account and
> Credit: the Cash (or Bank) Account, if
> the entity **gives** some cash.

If a movement of cash is not involved in a particular transaction, work out the effect on the corresponding account on the assumption that one account is affected by a cash transaction. In the case of a credit sale, for example, the account that benefits from the *receipt* of the goods must be that of an individual, so that individual's account must be debited (instead of the cash account, as it would be in the case of a cash sale). The corresponding entry must, therefore, be *credited* to some account. In this case it will be to the sales account.

You might also find it useful to remember another general rule used in double-entry book-keeping:

> **For every debit there must be a credit**
> and
> **For every credit there must be a debit.**

There are no exceptions to this rule. As this chapter develops, more practice will be obtained in deciding which account to debit and which account to credit. After some time, it becomes largely a routine exercise, and you will find yourself making the correct entries automatically.

It would now be helpful to illustrate the entry of a number of transactions in specific ledger accounts. We do so in the next section.

A LEDGER ACCOUNT EXAMPLE

This section illustrates the procedure adopted in entering various transactions in ledger accounts. The section brings together the basic material covered in the earlier part of this chapter. It demonstrates the use of various types, and the debiting and crediting effect of different types of transactions.

The example (shown in Exhibit 3.5) relates to a sole trader commencing business on his own account. As we explained in earlier chapters, while most non-accountants will not be involved in sole-trader entities, this type of entity is useful in illustrating the basic principles of double-entry book-keeping. Indeed, a more complex form of entity would only obscure those principles.

The example is also confined to a business that purchases and sells goods on cash terms. Businesses that buy and sell goods on credit terms will be a feature of later examples.

It is unnecessary for you as a non-accountant to spend too much time on detailed ledger account work, but before moving on to the next section, you are recommended to work through Exhibit 3.5 without reference to the answer. This exercise will help you to familiarize yourself with the dual aspect concept, and therefore enable you to understand much more clearly the basis on which accounting information is recorded.

Exhibit 3.5 Joe Simple: A sole trader

The following information relates to Joe Simple who started a new business on 1 January 19X1:

1	1.1.X1	Joe started the business with £5000 in cash.
2	3.1.X1	He paid £3000 of the cash into a business bank account.
3	5.1.X1	Joe bought a van for £2000 paying by cheque.
4	7.1.X1	He bought some goods, paying £1000 in cash.
5	9.1.X1	Joe sold some of the goods, receiving £1500 in cash.

Required:
Enter the above transactions in Joe's ledger accounts.

Answer to Exhibit 3.5

Joe Simple's books of account:

Cash Account

		£			£
1.1.X1	Capital (1)	5000	3.1.X1	Bank (2)	3000
9.1.X1	Sales (5)	1500	7.1.X1	Purchases (4)	1000

Capital Account

	£			£
1.1.X1			Cash (1)	5000

Bank Account

		£			£
3.1.X1	Cash (2)	3000	5.1.X1	Van (3)	2000

Van Account

		£	£
5.1.X1	Bank (3)	2000	

Purchases Account

		£	£
7.1.X1	Cash (4)	1000	

Sales Account

	£			£
		9.1.X1	Cash (5)	1500

Tutorial notes

1 The numbers in brackets after each entry refer to the exhibit notes; they have been inserted for tutorial guidance only.
2 The narration relates to that account in which the equal and opposite entry may be found.

After entering all the transactions for a particular period in appropriate ledger accounts, the next stage in the exercise is to calculate the balance on each account as at the end of each accounting period.

BALANCING THE ACCOUNTS

During a particular accounting period, some accounts (such as the bank and cash accounts) will contain a great many debit and credit entries. Some accounts may contain either mainly debit entries (e.g. the purchases account), or largely credit entries (e.g. the sales account). It would be somewhat inconvenient to allow the entries (whether mainly debits, credits, or a mixture of both) to build up without occasionally striking a balance. Indeed, the owner will almost certainly want to know not just what is in each account, but also what its overall or *net* balance is (i.e the total of all the debit entries less the total of all the credit entries). Thus, at frequent intervals, it will be necessary to calculate the balance on each account.

Balancing an account requires the book-keeper to add up all the respective debit and credit entries, take one total away from the other, and arrive at the net balance.

Accounts may be balanced fairly frequently, e.g. once a week or once a month, but some entities may only do so when they prepare their annual accounts. However, in order to keep a tight control on the management of the business, it is advisable to balance the accounts at reasonably short intervals. The frequency will depend upon the nature and the size of the entity, but once a month is probably sufficient for most entities.

The balancing of the accounts is part of the double-entry procedure, and the method is quite formal. In Exhibit 3.6 we show how to balance an account with a *debit* balance on it (i.e. when its total debit entries exceed its total credit entries).

Exhibit 3.6 Balancing an account with a debit balance

			Cash Account		
			£		£
1.1.X1	Sales (1)		2000	10.1.X1 Jones (1)	3000
15.1.X1	Rent received (1)		1000	25.1.X1 Davies (1)	5000
20.1.X1	Smith (1)		4000		
31.1.X1	Sales (1)		8000	31.1.X1 Balance c/d (2)	7000
		(3)	£15000	(3)	£15000
1.2.X1	Balance b/d (4)		7000		

Note: The number shown after each narration relates to the tutorial notes below.

Tutorial notes

1 The total debit entries equal £15000 (2000 + 1000 + 4000 + 8000). The total credit entries equal £8000 (3000 + 5000). The net balance on this account, therefore, at 31 January 19X1 is a *debit* balance of £7000 (15000 – 8000). Until both the debit entries and the credit entries have been totalled, of course, it will not usually be apparent whether the balance is a debit one or a credit one. However, it should be noted that there can never be a credit balance in a *cash* account, because it is impossible to pay out more cash than has been received.

2 The debit balance of £7000 is inserted on the *credit* side of the account at the time that the account is balanced (in the case of Exhibit 3.6, at 31 January

19X1). This then enables the total of the credit column to be balanced so that it agrees with the total of the debit column. The abbreviation 'c/d' means carried down. In this exhibit the debit balance is carried down in the account in order to start the new period on 1 February 19X1.

3 The £15 000 shown as a total in both the debit and the credit columns demonstrates that the columns balance (they do so, of course, because £7000 has been inserted in the credit column to make them balance). The totals are double-underlined with the currency sign placed in front of them in order to signify that they are a final total.

4 The balancing figure of £7000 is brought down ('b/d') in the account to start the new period on 1 February 19X1. The double-entry has been completed because £7000 has been debited *below* the line (i.e. below the £15 000 debit total), and the £7000 balancing figure credited *above* the line (i.e. above the £15 000 total).

Exhibit 3.6 demonstrates how an account with a debit entry is balanced. In Exhibit 3.7, we illustrate a similar procedure, but this time the account has a *credit* balance.

Exhibit 3.7 Balancing an account with a credit balance

Scott's Account

		£			£
31.1.X1	Bank (1)	20 000	15.1.X1	Purchases (1)	10 000
31.1.X1	Balance c/d (2)	5 000	20.1.X1	Purchases (1)	15 000
	(3)	£25 000		(3)	£25 000
			1.2.X1	Balance b/d (4)	5 000

Note: The number shown after each narration relates to the tutorial notes below.

Tutorial notes

1 Apart from the balance, there is only one debit entry in Scott's account: the bank entry of £20 000. The total credit entries amount to £25 000 (10 000 + 15 000). Scott has a credit balance, therefore, in his account as at 31 January 19X1 of £5000 (10 000 + 15 000 – 20 000). With many more entries in the account it would not always be possible to tell immediately whether the balance was a debit one or a credit one.

2 The credit balance of £5000 at 31 January 19X1 is inserted on the *debit* side of the account in order to enable the account to be balanced. The balance is then carried down (c/d) to the next period.

3 The £25 000 shown as the total for both the debit and the credit columns identifies the balancing of the account. This has been made possible because of the insertion of the £5000 balancing figure on the debit side of the account.

4 The balancing figure of £5000 is brought down (b/d) in the account in order to start the account in the new period beginning on 1 February 19X1. The

double-entry has been completed because the debit entry of £5000 above the £25 000 line on the debit side equals the credit entry below the £25 000 line on the credit side.

Exhibits 3.6 and 3.7 demonstrate the importance of always obeying the cardinal rule of double-entry book-keeping:

> **For every debit there must be a credit**
> and
> **For every credit there must be a debit.**

This rule must still be followed even if the two entries are made in the same account (as is the case when an account is balanced). If this rule is not obeyed, the accounts will not balance. This could mean that a lot of time is spent looking for an apparent error, or it could even mean that some incorrect information is given to the owner or managers of the business, since there is bound to be a mistake in at least one account.

The next stage after balancing each account is to check that the double-entry has been completed throughout the entire system. This is done by compiling what is known as a *trial balance*.

THE TRIAL BALANCE

A trial balance is a statement compiled at the end of a specific accounting period. It is a convenient method of checking that all the transactions and all the balances have been entered correctly in the ledger accounts. The trial balance is, however, a working paper, and it does not form part of the double-entry process.

A trial balance lists all of the debit balances and all of the credit balances extracted from each of the accounts throughout the ledger system. The total of all the debit balances is then compared with the total of all the credit balance. If the two totals agree, we can be reasonably confident that the book-keeping procedures have been carried out accurately.

We illustrate the preparation of a trial balance in Exhibit 3.8. We also take the opportunity of giving some more examples of how transactions are entered in ledger accounts. You are recommended to work through part (a) of Exhibit 3.8 before moving on to part (b). When you are confident that you understand the procedures involved, have a go at doing the question without looking at the solution.

Exhibit 3.8 Edward – compilation of a trial balance

Edward started a new business on 1 January 19X1. The following transactions took place during his first month in business:

19X1

1.1	Edward commenced business with £10 000 in cash.
3.1	He paid £8000 of the cash into a business bank account.
6.1	He bought a van on credit from Perkin's garage for £3000.
9.1	Edward rented shop premises for £1000 per quarter; he paid for the first quarter immediately by cheque.
12.1	He bought goods on credit from Roy Limited for £4000.
15.1	He paid shop expenses amounting to £1500 by cheque.
18.1	Edward sold goods on credit to Scott and Company for £3000.
21.1	He settled Perkin's account by cheque.
24.1	Edward received a cheque from Scott and Company for £2000; this cheque was paid immediately into the bank.
27.1	Edward sent a cheque to Roy Limited for £500.
31.1	Goods costing £3000 were purchased from Roy Limited on credit.
31.1	Cash sales for the month amounted to £2000.

Required:

(a) Enter the above transactions in appropriate ledger accounts, balance off each account as at 31 January 19X1, and bring down the balances as at that date; and

(b) extract a trial balance as at 31 January 19X1.

Cash Account

		£			£
1.1.X1	Capital (1)	10 000	3.1.X1	Bank (2)	8 000
31.1.X1	Sales (12)	2 000	31.1.X1	Balance c/d	4 000
		£12 000			£12 000
1.2.X1	Balance b/d	4 000			

Capital Account

		£			£
			1.1.X1	Cash (1)	10 000

Bank account

		£			£
3.1.X1	Cash (2)	8 000	9.1.X1	Rent payable (4)	1 000
24.1.X1	Scott and and		15.1.X1	Shop expenses (6)	1 500
	Company (9)	2 000	21.1.X1	Perkin's garage (8)	3 000
			27.1.X1	Roy Limited (10)	500
			31.1.X1	Balance c/d	4 000
		£10 000			£10 000
1.2.X1	Balance b/d	4 000			

Van Account

		£		£
6.1.X1	Perkin's Garage (3)	3 000		

Perkin's Garage Account

		£			£
21.1.X1	Bank (8)	3 000	6.1.X1	Van (3)	3 000

Rent Payable Account

		£		£
9.1.X1	Bank (4)	1 000		

Purchases Account

		£			£
12.1.X1	Roy Limited (5)	4 000			
31.1.X1	Roy Limited (11)	3 000	31.1.X1	Balance c/d	7 000
		£7 000			£7 000
1.2.X1	Balance b/d	7 000			

Roy Limited Account

		£			£
27.1.X1	Bank (10)	500	12.1.X1	Purchases (5)	4 000
31.1.X1	Balance c/d	6 500	31.1.X1	Purchases (11)	3 000
		£7 000			£7 000
			1.2.X1	Balance b/d	6 500

Shop Expenses Account

		£		£
15.1.X1	Bank (6)	1 500		

Sales Account

		£			£
			18.1.X1	Scott & Company (7)	3 000
31.1.X1	Balance c/d	5 000	31.1.X1	Cash (12)	2 000
		£5 000			£5 000
			1.2.X1	Balance b/d	5 000

Scott and Company Account

		£			£
18.1.X1	Sales (7)	3 000	24.1.X1	Bank (9)	2 000
			31.1.X1	Balance c/d	1 000
		£3 000			£3 000
1.2.X1	Balance b/d	1 000			

Tutorial notes

1 The number shown after each narration has been inserted for tutorial guidance only in order to illustrate the insertion of each entry in the appropriate account.
2 There is no need to balance an account and carry down the balance when there is only a single entry in one account (for example, Edward's Capital Account).
3 Note that some accounts have no balance in them at all as at 31 January 19X1 (for example, Perkin's Garage Account).

Answer to Exhibit 3.8 (b)

Trial Balance at 31 January 19X1

	Dr £	Cr £
Cash	4000	
Capital		10000
Bank	4000	
Van	3000	
Rent payable	1000	
Purchases	7000	
Roy Limited		6500
Shop expenses	1500	
Sales		5000
Scott and Company	1000	
	£21500	£21500

Tutorial notes

1 The total debit balance agrees with the total credit balance, and therefore the trial balance balances. This confirms that the transactions appear to have been entered in the books of account correctly.
2 The total amount of £21 500 shown in both the debit and credit columns of the trial balance does not have any significance, except to prove that the trial balance balances.

Did you manage to get your trial balance to balance? If not, re-read the earlier parts of this chapter, and then have another attempt at the exhibit.

It should be noted that there are some errors that do not affect the balancing of the trial balance. These errors may be summarized as follows:

1 **Omission:** a transaction could have been completely omitted from the books of account.
2 **Complete reversal of entry:** a transaction could have been entered in (say) Account A as a debit and in Account B as a credit, when it should have been entered as a credit in Account A and as a debit in Account B.

3 **Principle:** a transaction may have been entered in the wrong *type* of account, e.g. the purchase of a new delivery van may have been debited to the purchases account, instead of the delivery vans account.

4 **Commission:** a transaction may have been entered in the correct type of account, but in the wrong *personal* account, e.g. in Bill's Account instead of in Ben's Account.

5 **Compensating:** an error may have been made in (say) adding the debit side of one account, and an identical error made in adding the credit side of another account; the two errors would then cancel each other out.

6 **Original entry:** a transaction may be entered incorrectly in both accounts, e.g. as £291 instead of as £921.

Even allowing for the types of errors listed above, the trial balance still serves three useful purposes. These are as follows:

1 it enables the accuracy of the transactions entered in the accounts to be checked;

2 a summary of the balance on each account can be obtained; and

3 it provides the information needed in preparing the annual accounts.

We shall be dealing with the third purpose in some detail in the next two chapters.

CONCLUSION

As a non-accountant, it is most unlikely that you will become involved in having to write up ledger accounts or enter transactions into a computerized accounting system. In this chapter, we have avoided going into too much detail about double-entry book-keeping that is irrelevant for your purposes. As part of your managerial role, you will almost certainly be supplied with information which has been extracted from a ledger system. In order to assess its real benefit to you, we believe that it is most important that you should know something about where it has come from, what it means, and what reliability can be placed on it. Before leaving this chapter, therefore, we recommend that you make absolutely sure that you are familiar with the following features of a double-entry book-keeping system:

- the type of accounts generally used in practice;
- the meaning of the terms *debit* and *credit*;
- the definition of the terms *debtor* and *creditor*;
- the method of entering transactions in ledger accounts;
- the balancing of ledger accounts;
- the importance of the trial balance.

This chapter has provided you with the basic information necessary to become familiar with the six features listed above. If you are reasonably confident that you now have a basic grasp of double-entry book-keeping, you can move on to an examination of how financial accounts are prepared. Before doing so, however, you are recommended to test your understanding of the contents of this chapter by attempting some of the questions at the end of the chapter.

Key points

1 An account is an explanation, a record, or a history of a particular event.

2 A book of account is known as a ledger.

3 A page is referred to as a folio.

4 A transaction is the carrying out and the performing of any business.

5 All transactions have a twofold effect.

6 A double-entry system records that twofold effect.

7 A debit means a transaction is received into an account.

8 A credit means that a transaction is given by an account.

9 Debits are entered on the left-hand side of an account.

10 Credits are entered on the right-hand side of an account.

11 For every debit entry, there must be a credit entry.

12 Accounts are balanced periodically.

13 The accuracy of the book-keeping is tested by preparing a trial balance.

14 The trial balance does not reveal all possible book-keeping errors.

CHECK YOUR LEARNING

1 Fill in the missing blanks in the following sentence:
A debit entry goes on the _____ -hand side of a ledger account, and a _____ entry goes on the right-hand side.

2 Which two ledger accounts would you use in recording each of the following transactions?
(a) cash sales
(b) rent paid by cheque
(c) wages paid in cash
(d) a supplier of goods paid by cheque
(e) goods sold on credit to Ford.

3 State which account would be debited and which account would be credited in respect of each of the following items:

(a) cash paid to a supplier
(b) office rent paid by cheque
(c) cash sales
(d) dividend received by cheque.

4 Is there anything wrong with the following abbreviated bank account?

Debit		Credit	
	£000		£000
10.3.X6 Wages paid	1000	6.6.X6 Interest received	500

5 State whether each of the following errors would be discovered as as result of preparing a trial balance:
(a) £342 has been entered in both ledger accounts instead of £432.   Yes/No
(b) The debit column in Prim's account has been overstated by £50.   Yes/No
(c) £910 has been put in Anne's account instead of in Agnes's.   Yes/No

Answers

1 (a)   left; credit
2 (a)   cash; sales   (b) rent paid; bank   (c) wages; cash   (d) supplier's; bank
   (e)   Ford; sales
3   Debit   Credit
   (a)   Supplier   Cash
   (b)   Office rent   Bank
   (c)   Cash   Sales
   (d)   Bank   Dividends received
4 The entries are on the wrong side.
5 (a) no   (b) yes   (c) no

QUESTIONS

3.1
Adam has just gone into business. The following is a list of his transactions for the month of January 19X1:

1 Cash paid into the business by Adam.
2 Goods for resale purchased on cash terms.
3 Van bought for cash.
4 One quarter's rent for premises paid in cash.
5 Some goods sold on cash terms.
6 Adam buys some office machinery for cash.

Required:
State which account in Adam's books of account should be debited and which account should be credited for each transaction.

3.2
The following is a list of Brown's transactions for February 19X2:

1 Transfer of cash to a bank account.
2 Cash received from sale of goods.
3 Purchase of goods paid for by cheque.

4 Office expenses paid in cash.
5 Cheques received from customers from sale of goods on cash terms.
6 A motor car for use in the business paid for by cheque.

Required:
State which account in Brown's books of account should be debited and which account should be credited for each transaction.

3.3

Corby is in business as a retail distributor. The following is a list of his transactions for March 19X3:

1 Goods purchased from Smith on credit.
2 Corby introduces further capital in cash into the business.
3 Goods sold for cash.
4 Goods purchased for cash.
5 Cash transferred to the bank.
6 Machinery purchased, paid for in cash.

Required:
State which account in Corby's books of account should be debited and which account should be credited for each transaction.

3.4

Davies buys and sells goods on cash and credit terms. The following is a list of his transactions for April 19X4:

1 Capital introduced by Davies paid into the bank.
2 Goods purchased on credit terms from Swallow.
3 Goods sold to Hill for cash.
4 Cash paid for purchase of goods.
5 Dale buys goods from Davies on credit.
6 Motoring expenses paid by cheque.

Required:
State which account in Davies's books of account should be debited and which account should be credited for each transaction.

3.5

The following is a list of Edgar's transactions for May 19X5:

1 Goods purchased on credit from Gill.
2 Goods sold on credit to Ash.
3 Goods sold for cash to Crosby.
4 Goods purchased in cash from Lowe.
5 Cheque sent to Gill.
6 Cash received from Ash.

Required:
State which account in Edgar's books should be debited and which account should be credited for each transaction.

3.6

Ford buys and sells goods on cash and credit terms. The following is a list of his transactions for June 19X6:

1 Goods sold on cash terms to Orange.
2 Goods purchased from Carter on credit.
3 Goods sold to Holly on credit.
4 Goods bought on cash terms from Apple.
5 Holly returns some of the goods.
6 Goods returned to Carter.

Required:

State which account in Ford's books of account should be debited and which account should be credited for each transaction.

3.7

The following transactions relate to Gordon's business for the month of July 19X7:

1 Bought goods on credit from Watson.
2 Sold some goods for cash.
3 Sold some goods on credit to Moon.
4 Sent a cheque for half the amount owing to Watson.
5 Watson grants Gordon a cash discount.
6 Moon settles most of his account in cash.
7 Gordon allows Moon a cash discount that covers the small amount owed by Moon.
8 Gordon purchases some goods for cash.

Required:

State which accounts in Gordon's books of accounts should be debited and which account should be credited for each piece of information.

3.8

Harry started a new business on 1 January 19X8. The following transactions cover his first three months in business:

1 Harry contributed an amount in cash to start the business.
2 He transferred some of the cash to a business bank account.
3 He paid an amount in advance by cheque for rental of business premises.
4 Bought goods on credit from Paul.
5 Purchased a van paying by cheque.
6 Sold some goods for cash to James.
7 Bought goods on credit from Nancy.
8 Paid motoring expenses in cash.
9 Returned some goods to Nancy.
10 Sold goods on credit to Mavis.
11 Harry withdrew some cash for personal use.
12 Bought goods from David paying in cash.
13 Mavis returns some goods.
14 Sent a cheque to Nancy.
15 Cash received from Mavis.

16   Harry receives a cash discount from Nancy.

17   Harry allows Mavis a cash discount.

18   Cheque withdrawn at the bank in order to open a petty cash account.

Required:

State which accounts in Harry's books of account should be debited and which account should be credited for each transaction.

3.9

The following is a list of transactions which relate to Ivan for the first month that he is in business:

1.9.X9	Started the business with £10 000 in cash.
2.9.X9	Paid £8000 into a business bank account.
3.9.X9	Purchased £1000 of goods in cash.
10.9.X9	Bought goods costing £6000 on credit from Roy.
12.9.X9	Cash sales of £3000.
15.9.X9	Goods sold on credit terms to Norman for £4000.
20.9.X9	Ivan settles Roy's account by cheque.
30.9.X9	Cheque for £2000 received from Norman.

Required:

Enter the above transactions in Ivan's ledger accounts.

3.10

Jones has been in business since 1 October 19X1. The following is a list of his transactions for October 19X1:

1.10.X1	Capital of £20 000 paid into a business bank account.
2.10.X1	Van purchased on credit from Lang for £5000.
6.10.X1	Goods purchased on credit from Green for £15 000.
10.10.X1	Cheque drawn on the bank for £1000 in order to open a petty cash account.
14.10.X1	Goods sold on credit for £6000 to Haddock.
18.10.X1	Cash sales of £5000.
20.10.X1	Cash purchases of £3000.
22.10.X1	Miscellaneous expenses of £500 paid out of petty cash.
25.10.X1	Lang's account settled by cheque.
28.10.X1	Green allows Jones a cash discount of £500.
29.10.X1	Green is sent a cheque for £10 000.
30.10.X1	Haddock is allowed a cash discount of £600.
31.10.X1	Haddock settles his account in cash.

Required:

Enter the above transactions in Jones's ledger accounts.

3.11

The transactions listed below relate to Ken's business for the month of November 19X2:

1.11.X2	Started the business with £15 000 in cash.

2.11.X2	Transferred £14 000 of the cash to a business bank account.
3.11.X2	Paid rent of £1000 by cheque.
4.11.X2	Bought goods on credit from the following suppliers:

      Ace   £5000
      Mace   £6000
      Pace   £7000

10.11.X2 Sold goods on credit to the following customers:
      Main   £2000
      Pain   £3000
      Vain   £4000

15.11.X2 Returned goods costing £1000 to Pace.

22.11.X2 Pain returned goods sold to him for £2000.

25.11.X2 Additional goods purchased from the following suppliers:
      Ace   £3000
      Mace   £4000
      Pace   £5000

26.11.X2 Office expenses of £2000 paid by cheque.

27.11.X2 Cash sales for the month amounted to £5000.

28.11.X2 Purchases paid for in cash during the month amounted to £4000.

29.11.X2 Cheques sent to the following suppliers:
      Ace   £4000
      Mace   £5000
      Pace   £6000

30.11.X2 Cheques received from the following customers:
      Main   £1000
      Pain   £2000
      Vain   £3000

30.11.X2 The following cash discounts were claimed by Ken:
      Ace   £200
      Mace   £250
      Pace   £300

30.11.X2 The following cash discounts were allowed by Ken:
      Main   £100
      Pain   £200
      Vain   £400

30.11.X2 Cash transfer to the bank of £1000.

Required:

Enter the above transactions in Ken's ledger accounts.

3.12

The following transactions relate to Pat's business for the month of December 19X3:

1.12.X3 Started the business with £10 000 in cash.

2.12.X3 Bought goods on credit from the following suppliers:
      Grass   £6000
      Seed   £7000

10.12.X3 Sold goods on credit to the following customers:
      Fog   £3000

	Mist	£4000

12.12.X3 Returned goods to the following suppliers:

Grass	£1000
Seed	£2000

15.12.X3 Bought additional goods on credit from Grass for £3000 and from Seed for £4000.

20.12.X3 Sold more goods on credit to Fog for £2000 and to Mist for £3000.

24.12.X3 Paid office expenses of £5000 in cash.

29.12.X3 Received £4000 in cash from Fog and £6000 in cash from Mist.

31.12.X3 Pat paid Grass and Seed £6000 and £8000, respectively, in cash.

Required:
(a) Enter the above transactions in Pat's ledger accounts.
(b) Balance off the accounts as at 31 December 19X3.
(c) Bring down the balances as at 1 January 19X4.
(d) Compile a trial balance as at 31 December 19X3.

3.13

Vale has been in business for some years. The following balances were brought forward in his books of account as at 31 December 19X2:

	£	£
	Dr	Cr
Bank	5000	
Capital		20000
Cash	1000	
Dodd		2000
Fish	6000	
Furniture	10000	
	£22000	£22000

During the year to 31 December 19X3 the following transactions took place:

1   Goods bought from Dodd on credit for £30000.
2   Cash sales of £20000.
3   Cash purchases of £15000.
4   Goods sold to Fish on credit for £50000.
5   Cheques sent to Dodd totalling £29000.
6   Cheques received from Fish totalling £45000.
7   Cash received from Fish amounting to £7000.
8   Office expenses paid in cash totalling £9000.
9   Purchase of delivery van costing £12000 paid by cheque.
10   Cash transfers to bank totalling £3000.

Required:
(a) Compile Vale's ledger accounts for the year 31 December 19X3, balance off the accounts and bring down the balances as at 1 January 19X4.
(b) Extract a trial balance as at 31 December 19X3.

3.14

Brian started in business on 1 January 19X4. The following is a list of his transactions for his first month of trading:

1.1.X4 Opened a business bank account with £25 000 obtained from private resources.
2.1.X4 Paid one month's rent of £2000 by cheque.
3.1.X4 Bought goods costing £5000 on credit from Linda.
4.1.X4 Purchased motor car from Savoy Motors for £4000 on credit.
5.1.X4 Purchased goods costing £3000 on credit from Sydney.
10.1.X4 Cash sales of £6000.
15.1.X4 More goods costing £10 000 purchased from Linda on credit.
20.1.X4 Sold goods on credit to Ann for £8000.
22.1.X4 Returned £2000 of goods to Linda.
23.1.X4 Paid £6000 in cash into the bank.
24.1.X4 Ann returned £1000 of goods.
25.1.X4 Withdrew £500 in cash from the bank to open a petty cash account.
26.1.X4 Cheque received from Ann for £5500; Ann also claimed a cash discount of £500.
28.1.X4 Office expenses of £250 paid out of petty cash.
29.1.X4 Sent a cheque to Savoy Motors for £4000.
30.1.X4 Cheques sent to Linda and Sydney for £8000 and £2000, respectively. Cash discounts were also claimed from Linda and Sydney of £700 and £l00, respectively.
31.1.X4 Paid by cheque another month's rent of £2000.
31.1.X4 Brian introduced £5000 additional capital into the business by cheque.

Required:
(a) Enter the above transactions in Brian's ledger accounts for January 19X4, balance off the accounts and bring down the balances as at 1 February 19X4.
(b) Compile a trial balance as at 31 January 19X4.

3.15

The following balances have been extracted from Field's ledger accounts as at 28 February 19X5:

	£
Bank	13 000
Cash	2 000
Capital	15 000
Creditors	4 000
Debtors	10 000
Drawings	5 000
Electricity	4 000
Furniture	7 000
Office expenses	3 000
Purchases	50 000
Sales	100 000
Wages	25 000

Required:
Compile Field's trial balance as at 28 February 19X5.

3.16

An accounts clerk has compiled Trent's trial balance as at 31 March 19X6 as follows:

	Dr	Cr
	£	£
Bank (overdrawn)	2 000	
Capital	50 000	
Discounts allowed		5 000
Discounts received	3 000	
Dividends received	2 000	
Drawings		23 000
Investments		14 000
Land and buildings	60 000	
Office expenses	18 000	
Purchases	75 000	
Sales		250 000
Suspense (unexplained balance)		6 000
Rates		7 000
Vans	20 000	
Van expenses		5 000
Wages and salaries	80 000	
	£310 000	£310 000

Required:
Compile Trent's corrected trial balance as at 31 March 19X6.

3.17

The following balances have been extracted from Severn's books of account as at 30 April 19X7:

	£000
Purchases	300
Cash	8
Discounts received	2
Rents received	5
Wages	44
Discounts allowed	5
Creditors	12
Telephone	3
Sales	500
Capital	100
Sales returns	20
Bank interest received	1
Furniture and fittings	18
Bank (deposit)	50
Advertising	14
Motor cars	22
Bank (current)	5
Purchases returns	15
Land and buildings	40

	£000
Debtors	30
Plant and equipment	37
Drawings	45
Fees received	10
Motor car expenses	4

Required:
Compile Severn's trial balance at 30 April 19X7.

ADDITIONAL QUESTIONS (WITHOUT ANSWERS)

3.18

Donald's transactions for the month of March 19X9 are as follows:

	£
Cash receipts	
Capital contributed	6 000
Sales to customers	3 000
Cash payments	
Goods for sale	4 000
Stationery	500
Postage	300
Travelling	600
Wages	2 900
Transfers to bank	500

	£
Bank receipts	
Receipts from trade debtors:	
Smelt	3 000
Tait	9 000
Ure	5 000
Bank payments	
Payments to trade creditors:	
Craig	2 800
Dobie	5 000
Elgin	6 400
Rent and rates	3 200
Electricity	200
Telephone	100
Salaries	2 000
Miscellaneous expenses	600
Other transactions	
Goods purchased from:	
Craig	3 500
Dobie	7 500
Elgin	7 500

	£000
Goods returned to Dobie	400
Goods sold to:	
Smelt	4 000
Tait	10 000
Ure	8 000
Goods returned by Ure	900
Discounts allowed:	
Smelt	200
Tait	500
Ure	400
Discounts received:	
Craig	50
Dobie	100
Elgin	200

Required:

(a) Enter the above transactions in appropriate ledger accounts;

(b) balance each account as at 31 March 19X9; and

(c) extract a trial balance as at that date.

3.19

The following trial balance was extracted from Ryan's books of account as at 30 June 19X2:

	£ Dr	£ Cr
Bank		1 500
Capital		61 500
Cash	100	
Trade creditors:		
Arnot		2 000
Bain		3 000
Croft		4 000
Trade debtors:		
Xram	11 200	
Yousif	12 300	
Zlot	13 400	
Vehicles	35 000	
	£72 000	£72 000

During July 19X2, the following transactions took place:

(1) Cash and bank

	Receipts			Payments	
	Cash £	Bank £		Cash £	Bank £
Watt (sales)	2 000	4 000	Arnot		1 800
Xram		9 000	Bain		3 000
Yousif		10 000	Croft		2 500

	£	£		£	£
Zlot		12 000	Ducat (purchases)		6 000
Sales	1 500		Drawings	1 200	
			Heat and light		750
			Wages and salaries		3 400
			Office expenses		550
			Purchases	1 000	

(2) Other transactions

	Purchases	Purchases Returns	Sales	Sales Returns	Discounts
	£	£	£	£	£
Arnot	3 000	500			150
Bain	4 500	1 500			250
Croft	6 000	700			200
Ducat	7 000	600			100
Watt			9 000	300	450
Xram			8 000	400	50
Yousif			22 000	2 000	350
Zlot			26 000	1 000	650

Required:
(a) Enter the above transactions in appropriate ledger accounts;
(b) balance each account as at 31 July 19X2; and
(c) extract a trial balance as at that date.

DISCUSSION QUESTIONS

3.20

Do you think that non-accounting managers need to know anything about double-entry book-keeping?

3.21

'My accountant has got it all wrong,' argued Freda. 'She's totally mixed up all her debits and credits.'
'But what makes you say that?' queried Dora.
'Oh! I've only to look at my bank statement to see that she's wrong,' responded Freda. 'I know I've got some money in the bank, and yet she tells me I'm in debit when she means I'm in credit.'
Is Freda right?

3.22

'Double-entry book-keeping is a waste of time and money because everything has to be recorded twice.' Discuss.

CHAPTER 4

Basic financial accounts

Gemina approves balance sheet

By Andrew Hill, Milan

Shareholders in Gemina, the Italian investment company, have approved what the group's chairman described as 'this damned balance sheet' for 1995, despite the reservations of the internal auditors and sharp criticism from small shareholders. Saturday's six-hour shareholder meeting came a day after the latest adjustment to Gemina's full-year result for 1995, to cover new 'anomalies' discovered at two financial subsidiaries. Having increased its risk reserves, Gemina finally declared a consolidated loss of L694.5bn, against the loss of L631.6bn originally announced.

Paribas of France has sold its 2.1 per cent stake in Gemina, the meeting revealed. Gemina confirmed it had paid three former managers, including the former managing director, between Ll.7bn and L2.7bn each after they claimed L46bn (£19.36m) for 'biological damage' caused by the company's problems.

The Financial Times, 1 July 1996

Exhibit 4.0 Not everyone loves accounts

We suggested in Chapter 1 that the owners of a business want to know the answers to three fundamental questions:

1 What profit has the business made?
2 How much does the business owe?
3 How much is owed to it?

We finished the last chapter with an illustration of how to construct a trial balance. The trial balance not only enables us to check how accurate the book-keeping has been, but it also enables us to prepare the *basic financial accounts*. As can be seen from Exhibit 4.1, these normally include a trading account, a profit and loss account, and a balance sheet.

The information contained in the basic financial accounts will then enable us to answer the three questions asked by the owners of a business. In this chapter, we are going to show you how to prepare a set of basic financial accounts.

Exhibit 4.1 The basic financial accounts

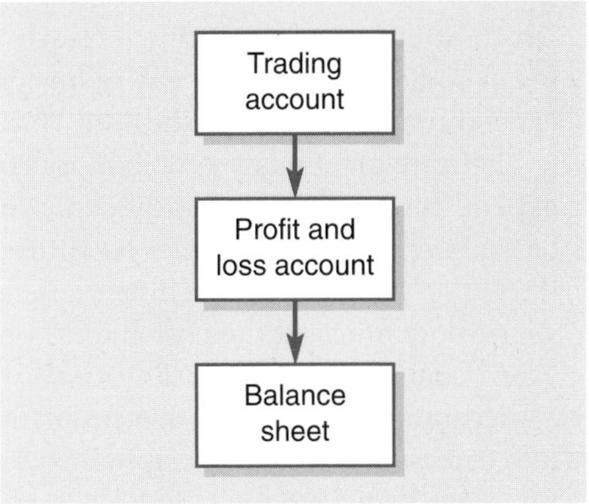

In the last chapter, we concentrated on sole-trader accounts. We shall be doing the same in this chapter, because a more complicated form of business organization would obscure the main points that we want to make. In the first section, we will have a look at what accountants mean by profit, before we move on to have a look at how financial accounts are constructed.

Learning objectives

By the end of this chapter, you will be able to:

● **describe what accountants mean by profit;**

● **prepare a basic set of financial accounts.**

CASH VERSUS PROFIT

The owners of a business often try to measure the profit that a business has made (i.e. how well it has done) by deducting the cash held at the end of a period from cash held at the beginning (after allowing for capital introduced or withdrawn during the period). It is then assumed that the difference represents profit (if the cash has increased) or loss (if the cash has decreased). This is *not* what accountants mean by profit.

As was outlined in Chapter 2, accounts are normally prepared by adopting a certain number of accounting rules. You will remember that the realization rule requires us to match the sales revenue for a particular period against the cost of selling those goods during the same period. The matching rule requires a similar procedure to be adopted for other types of incomes and expenses. It is unlikely that the difference between cash received and cash paid will be the same as the difference between *income* and *expenditure*. Cash transactions may relate to earlier or later periods, whereas incomes and expenditure (as defined in accounting) measure the *actual* economic activity which has taken place during a clearly defined period of time. By income we mean something that the entity has *gained* during a particular period, and expenditure as something the entity has *lost* during the same period.

There are great many problems, of course, in trying to measure income and expenditure in this way, rather than on a cash receipts and cash payments basis. In calculating profit, expenditure is especially difficult to determine. If the entity purchases a machine, for example, that has an estimated life of 20 years, how much of the cost should be charged against the income for (say) Year 1 compared with Year 20?

Accountants deal with this problem by attempting to classify *expenditure* into capital and revenue. Capital expenditure is expenditure that is likely to provide a benefit to the entity for more than one accounting period, and revenue expenditure is expenditure that is likely to provide a benefit for only one period. As the basic financial accounts are normally prepared on an annual basis, we can regard revenue expenditure as being virtually the same as annual expenditure. If a similar benefit is required the next year, then the service will have to be re-ordered and another payment made.

Examples of revenue expenditure include goods purchased for resale, electricity charges, rates paid to the local authority, and wages and salaries. Examples of capital expenditure include land and buildings, plant and machinery, motor vehicles, and furniture and fittings. Such items are described as *fixed assets*, because they are owned by the entity and they are intended for long-term use within it.

It is also possible to classify *income* into capital and revenue, although the terms capital income and capital revenue are not normally adopted. Income of a revenue nature would include the revenue from the sale of goods to customers, dividends and rents received. Income of a capital nature would include the resources invested by the owner in the business, and long-term loans made to it (such as bank loans).

In practice, it is not always easy to distinguish between capital and revenue items, and the distinction is often an arbitrary one. Some items of expenditure are particularly difficult to determine, although most transactions fall into recognizable categories.

The distinction between capital and revenue items is very important because, essentially, accounting profit is the difference between revenue income and revenue expenditure (see Exhibit 4.2). If capital and revenue items are not classified accurately, the accounting profit will be incorrectly calculated. This could be disastrous, especially if the amount was over-stated, because the owner might then draw too much out of the business, or have to pay more tax. Bearing in mind the prudence rule, it would be much less serious if the profit was under-stated, because it is likely that more cash would then have been retained within the business.

Exhibit 4.2 Accounting profit

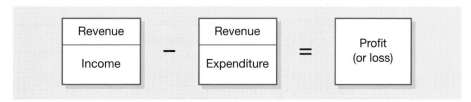

PREPARATION

We are now in a position to examine how the basic financial accounts are compiled, and hence how to calculate the amount of profit a business has made. We will assume that a trial balance has been prepared and that the books balance. There are then two main stages we have to take in order to compile the accounts. We will deal with each stage separately.

The trading and profit and loss account stage

Following the preparation of the trial balance, the first step we need to take in compiling the basic financial accounts is to prepare a trading account and a profit and loss account. In this chapter, we are going to use trading entities as examples, because we want to show you how to deal with the sale and purchase of goods, and the accounting problems that these can cause. In Chapter 6 we shall be dealing with manufacturing entities.

In order to compile a trading and profit and loss account, we need to extract from the trial balance all the revenue income and expenditure items. These are then matched against each other in the form of a statement called (as you would expect) a *trading and a profit and loss account*. By deducting the total of the revenue balances from the total of the revenue expenditure balances, we can determine the level of the profit (or loss) for the period. There are two important points to note. These are as follows:

1 The **trading account** comes before the profit and loss account. It matches the sales revenue for a certain period against the cost of goods sold (i.e. purchases) for the same period. The difference between the sales revenue and the cost of goods sold is known as *gross profit*. The gross profit is then transferred to the profit and loss account where it is added to the other revenue incomes of the business. That total is then matched against the other expenses of the business (such as heat and light, and wages and salaries). The difference between the gross profit plus other non-trading incomes, less the other expenses is known as *net profit* (or net loss). This all sounds very complicated, but we can express it in the form of two equations:
   (a) Sales revenue – cost of goods sold = gross profit;
   (b) (Gross profit + revenue income) – revenue expenditure = net profit (or net loss).

2 Both the trading account and the profit and loss account are accounts in their own right. This means that any transfer to or from them forms part of the double-entry procedure, and so a corresponding and equal entry has to be made in some other account.

The balance sheet stage

Once the trading account and profit and loss account balances have been extracted, the second stage in the preparation of the basic financial accounts is to summarize all the balances left in the trial balance in the form of a statement called a *balance sheet*. A balance sheet is simply a listing of all the remaining balances left in the ledger account system following the preparation of the trading and the profit and loss account. Unlike a trading and profit and loss account, a balance sheet does not form part of the double-entry: it is merely a listing of the remaining balances in the ledger system at the end of an accounting period. We could also describe it another way, and suggest that it is a listing of all the capital revenue and capital expenditure balances.

We are now in a position to show you how to prepare a set of basic financial accounts.

AN ILLUSTRATIVE EXAMPLE

In this section, we explain how to compile a trading account and a profit and loss account, and a balance sheet. This is illustrated in Exhibit 4.3.

Exhibit 4.3 Preparation of basic financial accounts

The following trial balance has been extracted from Bush's books of account as at 30 June 19X7:

Name of account		Dr £	Cr £
Bank (1)		5 000	
Capital (at 1 July 19X6) (2)			11 000
Cash (3)		1 000	
Drawings (4)		8 000	
Motor vehicle at cost (5)		6 000	
Motor vehicle expenses (6)	(R)	2 000	
Office expenses (7)	(R)	3 000	
Purchases (8)	(R)	30 000	
Trade creditors (9)			4 000
Trade debtors (10)		10 000	
Sales (11) (R)			50 000
		£65 000	£65 000

Notes: There were no opening or closing stocks.
             R = revenue items.

Required:
(a) Prepare Bush's trading and profit and loss account for the year to 30 June 19X7
(b) Prepare a balance sheet as at that date.

Answer to Exhibit 4.3 (a)

BUSH
Trading and profit and loss account for the year to 30 June 19X7

	£		£
Purchases (8)	30 000	Sales (11)	50 000
Gross profit c/d	20 000		
	£50 000		£50 000
Motor vehicle expenses (6)	2 000	Gross profit b/d	20 000
Office expenses (7)	3 000		
Net profit c/d	15 000		
	£20 000		£20 000
		Net profit b/d	15 000

Tutorial notes
1 The number shown in brackets after each narration refers to the account number of each balance extracted from the trial balance.
2 Both the trading account and the profit and loss account cover a period of time. In this exhibit it is for the year *to* (or alternatively, *ending*) 30 June 19X7.
3 It is not customary to keep the trading account totally separate from the profit and loss account. The usual format is the one shown above whereby the trading account balance (that is, the gross profit) is carried down straight into the profit and loss account.
4 Note that the proprietor's drawings [account (4)], are not an expense of the business. They are treated as an *appropriation*, i.e. an amount withdrawn by the proprietor in advance of any profit that the business might have made.

Answer to Exhibit 4.3 (b)

BUSH
Balance sheet at 30 June 19X7

	£	£		£	£
Capital			*Fixed assets*		
Balance at 1 July			Motor vehicle at		
19X6 (2)		11 000	cost (5)		6 000
Add: Net profit					
for the year*	15 000		*Current assets*		
c/f	15 000	11 000		c/f	6 000

	£	£		£	£
b/f	15 000	11 000	b/f		6 000
Less: Drawings (4)					
	8 000	7 000	Trade debtors (10)	10 000	
			Bank (1)	5 000	
			Cash (3)	1 000	16 000
Current liabilities					
Trade creditors (9)		4 000			
		£22 000			£22 000

*This balance has been obtained from the profit and loss account.

Note: The number in brackets shown after each narration refers to the account number of each balance listed in the trial balance on page 76.

Tutorial notes

1 The balance sheet is prepared at a particular moment in time. It depicts the balances as they were at a specific date. In this example, the balances are shown as at 30 June 19X7.

2 The format of this balance sheet shows the capital and liability balances on the left-hand side of the page, and the asset balances on the right-hand side.

3 The left-hand side of the balance sheet is divided into two main sections:
   (a) the capital section shows how the business has been financed (usually from a combination of the original capital contributed by the proprietor and the profit that has been left in the business); and
   (b) the current liabilities section shows the amounts owed to various parties outside the entity and due for payment within 12 months.

4 As far as the capital section is concerned, the net profit obtained from the profit and loss account must be added to it, because it is a remaining balance within the ledger system. In effect, it is a summary balance: it is merely a *net* balance obtained after matching the revenue income and expenditure balances. It is preferable to deduct any drawings that the proprietor may have made from the net profit for the year in order to show how much profit has been left in the business out of that year's profits.

5 The current liabilities should be listed in the order of those that are going to be paid last being placed before those that are going to be paid first, e.g. creditors should come before a bank overdraft.

6 The right-hand side of the balance sheet is also divided into two main sections:
   (a) the fixed assets section includes those assets that are intended for long-term use within the business; and
   (b) the current assets section includes assets that are constantly being turned over, for example, stocks, debtors and cash.

7 Fixed assets are usually shown at their original, i.e. at their *historic* cost. The fact that they are stated at cost should be noted on the balance sheet.

8 Both fixed assets and current assets should be listed with the least liquid (or realizable) asset being placed first, e.g. property should come before machinery, and stocks before debtors.

9 The total of fixed assets and current assets is known as *total assets*.

You are now recommended to work through Exhibit 4.3 again, but this time without reference to the answer.

FORMAT

In preparing the answer to Exhibit 4.3, we adopted what is known as the *horizontal* format. In the UK, it is now much more fashionable to prepare such statements in a *vertical* format so that the information can be read down the page on a line-by-line basis. There are three good reasons for adopting this method:

1 it does not presuppose any knowledge of double-entry book-keeping, since the information is not presented in the style of a ledger folio;
2 it highlights the various sections more clearly;
3 it is easier to read down a page than across it.

As you are probably more likely to meet financial accounts prepared in the vertical format, we shall be adopting it throughout the rest of this book.

The vertical format is illustrated in Exhibit 4.4 using the data obtained from Exhibit 4.3.

Exhibit 4.4 Vertical format of Exhibit 4.3

BUSH
Trading and profit and loss account for the year to 30 June 19X7

	£	£
Sales		50 000
Less: Cost of goods sold:		
Purchases		30 000
Gross profit		20 000
Less: Expenses:		
Motor vehicle expenses	2 000	
Office expenses	3 000	5 000
Net profit for the year		£15 000

BUSH
Balance sheet at 30 June 19X7

	£	£
Fixed assets		
Motor vehicle at cost		6 000
Current assets		
Trade debtors	10 000	
Bank	5 000	
Cash	1 000	
c/f	16 000	6 000

		£	£
	b/f	16 000	6 000
Less: Current liabilities:			
Trade creditors		4 000	12 000
			£18 000
Financed by:			
Capital			
Balance at 1 July 19X6			11 000
Add: Net profit for the year		15 000	
Less: Drawings		8 000	7 000
			£18 000

You are recommended to study Exhibit 4.4 carefully, noting how the information shown in Exhibit 4.3 has been rearranged. There are, in fact, very few changes, except that the information now reads down the page instead of across it.

CONCLUSION

In this next chapter we have examined the preparation and format of a basic trading and profit and loss account, and a basic balance sheet. In practice, once the trial balance has been agreed, a number of end-of-year adjustments would normally be made before the financial accounts are eventually finalized. These adjustments will be examined in the next chapter.

Key points

1 **A trial balance provides the data for the preparation of the basic financial accounts.**

2 **The basic financial accounts normally consist of a trading account, a profit and loss account and a balance sheet.**

3 **Revenue transactions are transferred to either the trading account or the profit and loss account, and capital items to the balance sheet.**

4 **The trading account and the profit and loss account form part of the double-entry system. The balance sheet is merely a listing of the balances that remain in the ledger system once the trading and profit and loss accounts have been prepared.**

5 **The basic financial accounts are normally prepared in a vertical format.**

CHECK YOUR LEARNING

1 Are the following statements true of false?
   (a) Accounting profit is normally the difference between cash
       received and cash paid.   True/False
   (b) Capital expenditure only provides a short-term benefit.   True/False
   (c) Fixed assets are normally written off to the trading account.   True/False

2 Name two stages in the preparation of the basic financial accounts.

3 What description is given to the balances on (a) the trading account; and (b) the
   profit and loss account?

4 What are the two main types of account formats?

Answers 1 (a) false (b) false (c) false
2 the trading and profit and loss account stages; and the balance sheet stage
3 (a) gross profit/loss (b) net profit/loss
4 horizontal and vertical

QUESTIONS

4.1

The following trial balance has been extracted from Ethel's books of accounts as at
31 January 19X1:

	Dr	Cr
	£	£
Capital		10 000
Cash	3 000	
Creditors		3 000
Debtors	6 000	
Office expenses	11 000	
Premises	8 000	
Purchases	20 000	
Sales		35 000
	£48 000	£48 000

Required:

Prepare Ethel's trading and profit and loss account for the year to 31 January 19X1
and a balance sheet as at that date.

4.2

Marion has been in business for some years. The following trial balance has been extracted from her books of account as at 28 February 19X2:

	Dr	Cr
	£000	£000
Bank	4	
Buildings	50	
Capital		50
Cash	2	
Creditors		24
Debtors	30	
Drawings	55	
Heat and light	10	
Miscellaneous expenses	25	
Purchases	200	
Sales		400
Wages and salaries	98	
	£474	£474

Required:

Prepare Marion's trading and profit and loss account for the year to 28 February 19X2 and a balance sheet as at that date.

4.3

The following trial balance has been extracted from the books of Garswood as at 31 March 19X3:

	Dr	Cr
	£	£
Advertising	2 300	
Bank	300	
Capital		55 700
Cash	100	
Discounts allowed	100	
Discounts received		600
Drawings	17 000	
Electricity	1 300	
Investments	4 000	
Investment income received		400
Office equipment	10 000	
Other creditors		800
Other debtors	1 500	
Machinery	20 000	
Purchases	21 400	
Purchases returns	1 400	
Sales		63 000
Sales returns	3 000	
Stationery	900	
Trade creditors		5 200
Trade debtors	6 500	
Wages	38 700	
	£127 100	£127 100

Required

Prepare Garswood's trading and profit and loss account for the year to 31 March 19X3 and a balance sheet as at that date.

ADDITIONAL QUESTIONS (WITHOUT ANSWERS)

4.4

The following trial balance has been extracted from Jody's books of account as at 30 April 19X4:

	Dr	Cr
	£000	£000
Capital (as at 1 May 19X3)		30
Cash	1	
Electricity	2	
Maintenance	4	
Miscellaneous expenses	7	
Purchases	40	
Rent and rates	6	
Sales		85
Vehicle (at cost)	30	
Wages	25	
	£115	£115

Required:

Prepare Jody's trading and profit and loss account for the year to 30 April 19X4 and a balance sheet as at that date.

4.5

Pete has extract the following trial balance from his books of account as at 31 May 19X5:

	Dr	Cr
	£000	£000
Bank		15
Building society account	100	
Capital (as at 1 June 19X4)		200
Cash	2	
Heat, light and fuel	18	
Insurances	10	
Interest received		1
Land and property (at cost)	200	
Long-term loan		50
Long-term loan interest paid	8	
Motor vehicles (at cost)	90	
Motor vehicle expenses	12	
Plant and equipment (at cost)	100	
c/f	540	c/f 266

	b/f 540	b/f 266
Property maintenance	7	
Purchases	300	
Repairs to machinery	4	
Rent and rates	65	
Sales		900
Wages and salaries	250	
	£1 166	£1 166

Required:
Prepare Pete's trading and profit and loss account for the year to 31 May 19X5 and a balance sheet as at that date.

DISCUSSION QUESTIONS

4.6
Explain why an increase in cash during a particular accounting period does not necessarily mean that an entity has made a profit

4.7
'The differentiation between so-called capital and revenue expenditure is quite arbitrary and unnecessary.' Discuss.

4.8
How far does a balance sheet tell users how much an entity is worth?

CHAPTER 5

Accounting for adjustments

Accounting change helps JAL show improvement

By Gerard Baker in Tokyo

Japan Airlines, the country's largest carrier, yesterday reported its first operating profit since 1991.

The company attributed the improvement in the 12 months to March to its extensive restructuring programme and strong demand in growing Asian markets. But a change in its method of accounting for depreciation also significantly improved JAL's results.

Operating profit for the year was Y15.4bn ($141.8m), compared with the previous year's loss of Y9.9bn. Recurring profit – before extraordinary items and tax – jumped 56 per cent to Y4.4bn. Net profit was Y500m, following last year's loss of Y1.3bn.

But JAL said that, as a result of significant new investments made in the past few years, the company had decided to change its method of depreciation accounting. In the past such investments would have been written off on a heavily front-loaded, declining balance, basis. But as from this year they would be accounted for by the straight-line method. The effect was to increase recurring profit by Y10.9bn compared with last year.

Although the move suggested the company would have recorded a large recurring loss for the year under the old principles, the company said the change was a fairer reflection of the costs and benefits of its big outlays on new airports and other facilities.

Total sales rose by almost 8 per cent to Y1,116bn. International passenger traffic grew by more than 13 per cent, helped by the strong yen, which increased demand for overseas travel by Japanese residents, and by a recovery in business traffic.

New routes and special excursion fares and packages had also contributed to international passenger growth. International cargo volumes grew by 2.5 per cent, also helped by the strong yen.

In the domestic market, new routes and a more competitive fare structure produced an increase in volumes, in spite of the continuing weakness of the Japanese economy. Domestic passenger traffic and domestic cargo volumes both registered increases of nearly 6 per cent.

The company's long-term restructuring programme, which aims to reduce staff numbers by 5000 in the five years to 1998, remained on course and had contributed to the improving business performance, JAL said.

For the current year the company expects domestic demand to remain sluggish, offset by continued growth in international traffic. Sales are forecast to rise by 4.5 per cent to Y1.167bn, with recurring profits up slightly at Y5bn.

The Financial Times, 30 May 1996

Exhibit 5.0 It is amazing what an adjustment to depreciation can do for profits!

In the last chapter, we explained how, once the trial balance had been compiled, it is possible to prepare a trading account, a profit and loss account, and a balance sheet. At the end of an accounting period, however, a number of various adjustments are usually required. These adjustments are not normally incorporated into the trial balance (although they can be). Instead, the financial accounts themselves will be amended, and it is only after they have been finalized that any post-trial adjustments will then be entered in the ledger accounts.

In this chapter, we shall be dealing with four main types of year-end adjustments. These are shown in Exhibit 5.1, and they may be summarized as follows:

1 closing stock adjustments;
2 depreciation adjustments;
3 accruals and prepayment adjustments;
4 adjustments for bad and doubtful debts.

Exhibit 5.1 Main adjustment made to the trading and profit and loss account after the compilation of the trial balance

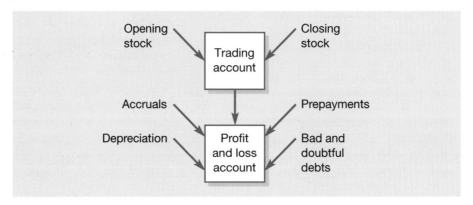

Learning objectives	**By the end of this chapter, you will be able to:**

● make post-trial balance adjustments for stock, depreciation, accruals and prepayments, and bad and doubtful debts;

● prepare a set of financial accounts incorporating such adjustments;

● list five main defects of conventional financial accounts.

STOCK

It is most unlikely that all of the purchases that have been made during a particular period will have been sold by the end of it, so some stock will almost certainly still be in the stores at the period end (in accounting terminology, purchases still on hand at the period end are referred to as *stock*).

In calculating the gross profit for the period, therefore, it is necessary to make some allowance for closing stock, since we want to match the cost of goods sold (and not the cost of all of those goods actually purchased during the period) with the sales revenue earned for the period. Consequently, we have to check the quantity of stock we have on hand at the end of the accounting period, and then put some value on it. In practice, this is an extremely difficult exercise, and we shall be examining it in more detail in Chapter 14. Most examples used in this part of the book assume that the value of the closing stock is readily available.

We also have another problem in dealing with stock. Closing stock at the end of one period becomes the opening stock at the beginning of the next period. In calculating the cost of goods sold, therefore, we have to allow for opening stock. In fact, the cost of goods sold can be quite easily calculated by adopting the following formula:

> **Cost of goods sold = (Opening stock + Purchases) – Closing stock**

The book-keeping entries are not quite as easy to understand, but they may be summarized as follows:

1 Enter the opening stock in the trading account. To do so, make the following entries: DEBIT the trading account; CREDIT the stock account; with the value of the opening stock as estimated at the end of the previous period (this should have been brought down as a debit balance in the stock account at the beginning of the current period).
2 Estimate the value of the closing stock (using one of the methods described in Chapter 14).
3 Enter the closing stock in the trading account. To do so, make the following entries: DEBIT the stock account; CREDIT the trading account; with the value of the closing stock as estimated in stage 2 above.

By making these adjustments the trading account should now appear as in Exhibit 5.2

Exhibit 5.2 Example of a trading account with stock adjustments

	£		£
Opening stock	1 000	Sales	4 000
Purchases	2 000	Closing stock	1 500
Gross profit c/d	2 500		
	£5 500		£5 500

		Gross profit b/d	2 500

Note: This format does not show clearly the cost of goods sold, so it is customary to *deduct* the closing stock from the total of opening stock and purchases. If the horizontal format is adopted the information will then be presented as follows:

	£		£
Opening stock	1 000	Sales	4 000
Purchases	2 000		
	3 000		
Less: Closing stock	1 500		
	1 500		
Gross profit c/d	2 500		
	£4 000		£4 000

		Gross profit b/d	2 500

If the vertical format is adopted, the trading account will look a little different:

	£	£
Sales		4 000
Less: Cost of goods sold		
Opening stock	1 000	
Purchases	2 000	
	3 000	
Less: Closing stock	1 500	1 500
Gross profit		2 500

Study this amended format very carefully, because it will be encountered frequently in subsequent examples.

DEPRECIATION

As we have already explained, expenditure which covers more than one accounting period is known as *capital expenditure*. Capital expenditure as such is not normally included in either the trading account or the profit and loss account, but it would be misleading to exclude it altogether from the calculation of profit.

Expenditure on fixed assets (such as plant and machinery, motor vehicles, and furniture) is necessary in order to help provide a general service to the business. The benefit received from the purchase of fixed assets must (by definition) extend beyond at least one accounting period. The cost of the benefit provided by fixed assets ought, therefore, to be charged to those accounting periods that benefit from such expenditure. The problem is in determining what charge to make. In accounting terminology, such a charge is known as *depreciation*.

There is also another reason why fixed assets should be depreciated. By *not* charging each accounting period with some of the cost of fixed assets, the level of profit will be correspondingly higher. Thus, the owner will be able to withdraw a higher level of profit from the business. If this is the case, insufficient cash may be left in the business, and the owner may then find it difficult to buy new fixed assets or replenish stocks.

In practice, it is not easy to measure the benefit provided to each accounting period by some groups of fixed assets. Most depreciation methods tend to be somewhat simplistic. The one method most commonly adopted is known as *straight-line depreciation*. This method charges an equal amount of depreciation to each accounting period that benefits from the purchase of a fixed asset. The annual depreciation charge is calculated as follows:

Annual depreciation charge =

$$\frac{\text{Original cost of the asset} - \text{estimated residual value}}{\text{Estimated life of the asset}}$$

You can see that in order to calculate the annual depreciation charge, it is necessary to work out (a) how long the asset is likely to last, and (b) what it can be sold for when its useful life is ended.

Although it is customary to include fixed assets at their historic (i.e. original) cost in the balance sheet, some fixed assets (such as property) may be revalued at regular intervals. If this is the case, then the depreciation charge will be based on the revalued amount, and not on the historic cost. It should also be noted that even if the asset is depreciated on the basis of its revalued amount, there is still no guarantee that it can be replaced at that amount. A combination of inflation and obsolescence may mean that the eventual replacement cost is far in excess of either the historic cost or the revalued amount. It follows that when the fixed asset eventually comes to be replaced, the entity may still not have sufficient cash available to replace it.

Besides straight-line depreciation, there are other methods that may be adopted. One such method that is sometimes used (although it is far less common than the straight-line method) is known as the *reducing balance method*. This method is similar to the straight-line one in that it is based on the historic cost of the asset. It also requires an estimate to be made of the life of the asset and of its estimated residual value. The depreciation rate is usually expressed as a percentage, and the rate is then applied to the *reducing* balance of the asset, i.e. after the depreciation charge in previous years has been deducted. The procedure is illustrated in Exhibit 5.3.

Exhibit 5.3 Illustration of the reducing balance method of depreciating fixed assets

Assume that an asset costs £1000, and that the depreciation rate is 50% of the reduced balance. The depreciation charge per year would then be as follows:

Year		£
1. 1. X1	Historic cost	1000
31.12.X1	Depreciation charge for the year (50%)	500
	Reduced balance	500
31.12.X2	Depreciation charge for the year (50%)	250
	Reduced balance	250
31.12.X3	Depreciation charge for the year (50%)	125
	Reduced balance	125

. . . and so on, until the asset has been written down to its estimated residual value.

The reducing balance depreciation rate can be calculated by using the following formula:

$$r = 1 - \sqrt[n]{\frac{R}{C}}$$

Where: r = the depreciation rate to be applied;
n = the estimated life of the asset;
R = its estimated scrap value; and
C = its historic cost.

The reducing balance method results in a much higher level of depreciation in the first few years of the life of an asset, and a much lower charge in later years. It is a suitable method to adopt when calculating the depreciation rate for such fixed assets as vehicles, because vehicles tend to have a high depreciation rate in their early years, and a low rate towards the end of their life. In addition, maintenance costs tend to be low initially, and become greater as the vehicles become older. Consequently, the combined depreciation charge plus the maintenance costs produce a more even pattern of total vehicle costs than does the straight-line method.

There are other methods of depreciating fixed assets, but since these are rarely used, we do not think that it is necessary for us to go into them in this book.

The ledger account entries for depreciation are quite straightforward. The annual charge for depreciation will be entered into the books of account as follows:

DEBIT Profit and loss account;
CREDIT Accumulated depreciation account
with the depreciation charge for the year.
(*Note*: Each group of fixed assets will normally have its own accumulated depreciation account.)

As far as the balance sheet is concerned, it is customary to disclose the following details for each group of fixed assets:

1 historic cost (or revalued amount), i.e. the gross book value (GBV);
2 accumulated depreciation;
3 net book value (NBV).

(In other words, line 1 less line 2 = line 3.)

We illustrate how this is normally shown in a balance sheet in Exhibit 5.4. The exhibit shows how the accumulated depreciation is deducted from the original cost for each group of assets, thereby arriving at the respective net book value for each group. The total net book value (£88 000 in Exhibit 5.4)

Exhibit 5.4 Balance sheet disclosure of fixed assets

Fixed assets	Historic cost £	Accumulated depreciation £	Net book value £
Buildings	100 000	30 000	70 000
Equipment	40 000	25 000	15 000
Furniture	10 000	7 000	3 000
	£150 000	£62 000	88 000
Current assets			
Stocks		10 000	
Debtors		8 000	
Cash		2 000	
			20 000
			£108 000

forms part of the balancing of the balance sheet. The total cost of the fixed assets and the total accumulated depreciation are shown purely for information. Such totals do not form part of the balancing process.

ACCRUALS AND PREPAYMENTS

We explained in Chapter 2 why, at the end of a particular accounting period, it is sometimes necessary to make an adjustment for accruals and prepayments. We will now examine this procedure in a little more detail.

Accruals

An accrual is an amount outstanding for a service provided during a particular accounting period which is still to be paid for at the end of it. It is expected that the amount due will normally be settled in cash in a subsequent accounting period. The entity may, for example, have paid the last quarter's electricity bill one week before the year end. In its accounts for that year, therefore, it needs to allow for (or *accrue*) the amount that it will owe for the electricity consumed during the last week of the year.

The accrual will be based on an estimate of the likely cost of one week's supply of electricity, or, as a proportion of the amount payable (if it has already received the invoice).

The ledger account entries are reasonably straightforward. It is not normal practice to open a separate account for accruals, the double-entry being completed within the account that relates to the particular service. Exhibit 5.5 illustrates the procedure.

Exhibit 5.5 Accounting for accruals

Electricity Account

		£			£
1.4.X1	Bank	400	1.4.X1	Balance b/d*	400
1.7.X1	Bank	300			
1.9.X1	Bank	100			
1.1.X2	Bank	500			
31.3.X2	Balance c/d**	600	31.3.X2	Profit and loss account	1500
		£1900			£1900
			1.4.X2	Balance b/d	600

* This balance is assumed to be an accrual made in the year to 31 March 19X1.

** This amount is an accrual for the year to 31 March 19X2.

You will note that in Exhibit 5.5, the balance on the electricity account at 31 March 19X2 is transferred to the profit and loss account. The ledger account entries are as follows:

DEBIT Profit and loss account;
CREDIT Electricity account
with the electricity charge for the year.

The double-entry has been completed for the accrual by debiting it in the accounts for the year to 31 March 19X2 (i.e. above the line), and crediting it in the following year's account (i.e. below the line). The accrual of £600 will be shown on the balance sheet at 31 March 19X2 in the current liabilities section under the sub-heading 'accruals'.

Prepayments

A prepayment is an amount paid in cash during an accounting period for a service that has not yet been provided. For example, if a company's year end is 31 December, and it buys a van half-way through (say) 1998 and licences it for 12 months, half of the fee paid will relate to 1998 and half to 1999. It is necessary, therefore, to adjust 1998's accounts so that only half of the fee is charged in that year. The other half will eventually be charged to the 1999 accounts. The book-keeping procedure is illustrated in Exhibit 5.6.

Exhibit 5.6 Accounting for prepayments

Van Tax Account

		£			£
1.1.X1	Balance b/d*	40	31.12.X1	Profit and	
1.7.X1	Bank	100		loss account	90
			31.12.X1	Balance c/d**	50
		£140			£140
1.1.X2	Balance b/d	50			

*   This balance is assumed to be a prepayment arising in the previous period.
** This amount is assumed to be a prepayment for the year to 31 December 19X1.

You will note from Exhibit 5.6 that the balance on the van tax account is transferred to the profit and loss account. The double-entry procedure is as follows:

DEBIT Profit and loss account;
CREDIT Van tax account
with the annual cost of the tax on the van.

The double-entry has been completed by debiting the prepayment in next year's accounts (i.e. below the line) and crediting it to this year's accounts (i.e. above the line).

The prepayment of £50 made at 31 December 19X1 will be shown in the balance sheet at that date in the current assets section under the sub-heading 'prepayments'.

BAD AND DOUBTFUL DEBTS

The fourth main adjustment made in finalizing the annual accounts relates to bad debts and provisions for bad and doubtful debts.

It was explained in Chapter 2 that the realization rule allows us to claim profit for any goods that have been sold, even if the cash for them is not received until a later accounting period. This means that we are taking a risk in claiming the profit on those goods in the earlier period, even if the legal title has been passed to the customer. If the goods are not eventually paid for, we will have over-estimated the profit for the period when we thought that we had sold them. The owner might already have taken the profit out of the business (e.g. by increasing his cash drawings), and it then might be too late to do anything about it.

Fortunately, there is a technique whereby we can build in an allowance for any possible *bad* debts (as they are called). This is quite a tricky operation, so we will need to explain in two stages: (a) how to account for bad debts; and (b) how to allow for the possibility that some debts may be *doubtful*.

Bad debts

Once it is clear that a debt is bad (in other words, if it is highly unlikely that it will ever be paid), then it must be written off immediately. This means that we have to charge it to the current year's profit and loss account, even though it may relate to an earlier period. We have to deal with it this way, because it is usually impractical to change accounts once they have been finalized as the owner may have long since drawn his share of the profits out of the business.

The double-entry procedure for writing off bad debts is quite straightforward. The entries are as follows:

DEBIT Profit and loss account;
CREDIT Trade debtor's account
with the amount of the bad debt to be written off.

Trade debtors will be shown in the balance sheet *after* deducting any bad debts that have been written off to the profit and loss account.

Provisions for bad and doubtful debts

The profit in future accounting periods would be severely distorted if the entity suffered a whole series of bad debts. It seems prudent, therefore, to allow for the possibility that some debts may become bad. In order to ensure that we do not overstate profit, we can set up a provision for bad and doubtful debts (a provision is simply an amount set aside for something that is highly likely to happen). This means that we have to open what we call a 'provision for bad and doubtful debts account'.

This involves estimating the likely level of bad debts. The estimate will normally be based on the experience that the entity has had in dealing with specific bad debts. In simple book-keeping exercises, the provision is usually expressed as a percentage of the outstanding trade debtors. The double-entry procedure is as follows:

DEBIT Profit and loss account;
CREDIT Provision for bad and doubtful debts account
with the amount of the provision needed to meet the expected level of bad and doubtful debts.

The procedure is illustrated in Exhibit 5.7.

Exhibit 5.7 Accounting for bad and doubtful debts

You are presented with the following information for the year to 31 March 19X3:

	£
Trade debtors at 1 April 19X2	20 000
Trade debtors at 31 March 19X3 (including £3000 of specific bad debts)	33 000
Provision for bad and doubtful debts at 1 April 19X2	1 000

Note: A provision for bad and doubtful debts is maintained equivalent to 5% of the trade debtors as at the end of the year.

Required:
(a) Calculate the increase required in the bad and doubtful debts provision account for the year to 31 March 19X3; and
(b) show how both the trade debtors and the provision for bad and doubtful debts account would be featured in the balance sheet at 31 March 19X3.

Answer to Exhibit 5.7

(a)	£
Trade debtors as at 31 March 19X3	33 000
Less: Specific bad debts to be written off to the profit and loss account for the year to 31 March 19X3	3 000
	30 000

Provision required: 5% thereof	1 500
Less: Provision at 1 April 19X2	1 000
Increase in the bad and doubtful debts provision account to be charged to the profit and loss account for the year to 31 March 19X3	500

Tutorial note

The balance on the provision for bad and doubtful debts account will be higher at 31 March 19X3 than it was at 1 April 19X2. This arises because the level of trade debtors is higher at the end of 19X3 than it was at the end of 19X2. The required increase in the provision of £500 will be *debited* to the profit and loss account. If it had been possible to reduce the provision (because of a lower level of trade debtors at the end of 19X3 compared with 19X2), the decrease would have been *credited* to the profit and loss account.

(b) Balance sheet extract at 31 March 19X3

	£	£
Current assets		
Trade debtors	30 000	
Less: Provision for bad and doubtful debts	1 500	
		28 500

The treatment of bad debts and doubtful debts in ledger accounts is a fairly complicated and technical exercise. However, as a non-accountant it is important for you to grasp just two essential points:

1 A debt should never be written off until it is absolutely certain that it is bad because once written off, no further attempt will probably ever be made to recover it.
2 It is prudent to allow for the possibility of some doubtful debts, although as sometimes happens, it is rather a questionable decision to reduce profit by an arbitrary amount, e.g. by guessing whether it should be 3% or 5% of outstanding debtors. Obviously, the level that you choose can make a big difference to profit!

We have covered a great deal of technical matter in this chapter, so it would now be helpful to bring all the material together in the form of a comprehensive example.

A COMPREHENSIVE EXAMPLE

In this section, we use a comprehensive example to cover all the basic procedures that we have outlined in both this chapter and the preceding one. The example used in Exhibit 5.8 is a fairly detailed one, so take your time in working through it.

Exhibit 5.8 Example of basic accounting procedures

Wayne has been in business for many years. His accountant has extracted the following trial balance from his books of account as at 31 March 19X5:

	£	£
Bank	1 200	
Capital		33 000
Cash	300	
Drawings	6 000	
Insurance	2 000	
Office expenses	15 000	
Office furniture at cost	5 000	
Office furniture: accumulated depreciation at 1 April 19X4		2 000
Provision for bad and doubtful debts at 1 April 19X4		500
Purchases	55 000	
Salaries	25 000	
Sales		100 000
Stock at 1 April 19X4	10 000	
Trade creditors		4 000
Trade debtors	20 000	
	£139 500	£139 500

Notes: The following additional information is to be taken into account:

1 Stock at 31 March 19X5 was valued at £15 000.
2 The insurance included £500 worth of cover which related to the year to 31 March 19X6.
3 Depreciation is charged on office furniture at 10% per annum of its original cost (it is assumed not to have any residual value).
4 A bad debt of £1000 included in the trade debtors balance of £20 000 is to be written off.
5 The provision for bad and doubtful debts is to be maintained at a level of 5% of outstanding trade debtors as at 31 March 19X5, i.e. after excluding the bad debt referred to in note 4 above.
6 At 31 March 19X5, there was an amount owing for salaries of £1000.

Required:
(a) Prepare Wayne's trading and profit and loss account for the year to 31 March 19X5;
(b) Prepare a balance sheet as at that date.

Answer to Exhibit 5.8

(a)
WAYNE
Trading and profit and loss account for the year to 31 March 19X5

	£	£	(Source of entry)
		100 000	(TB)
Sales			
Less: Cost of goods sold:			
Opening stock	10 000		(TB)
Purchases	55 000		(TB)
	65 000		
Less: Closing stock	15 000		(QN 1)
		50 000	
Gross profit		50 000	
Less: Expenses:			
Insurance (2000 – 500)	1 500		(Wkg 1)
Office expenses	15 000		(TB)
Depreciation: office furniture (10% × 5000)	500		(Wkg 2)
Bad debt	1 000		(QN 4)
Increase in provision for bad and doubtful debts	450		(Wkg 3)
Salaries (25 000 + 1000)	26 000		(Wkg 4)
		44 450	
Net profit for the year		£5 550	

(b)
WAYNE
Balance sheet at 31 March 19X5

Fixed assets	£ Cost	£ *Accumulated depreciation*	£ *Net book value*	(Source of entry)
Office furniture	5 000	2 500	2 500	(TB & Wkg 5)
Current assets				
Stock		15 000		(QN 1)
Trade debtors				
(20 000 – 1000)	19 000			(Wkg3)
Less: Provision for bad and				
doubtful debts	950	18 050		(Wkg 3)
	c/f	33 050	2500	

	£	£	£	(Source of entry)
b/f		33 050	2 500	
Prepayment		500		(QN2)
Cash at bank		1 200		(TB)
Cash in hand		300		(TB)
		35 050		
Less: Current liabilities				
Trade creditors	4 000			(TB)
Accrual	1 000			(QN 6)
	5 000		30 050	
			£32 550	
Financed by:				
Capital				
Balance at 31 March 19X4			33 000	(TB)
Add: Net profit for the year		5 550		(P&L A/c)
Less: Drawings		6 000	(450)	
			£32 550	

Key:
TB = from trial balance;
QN = extracted straight from the question and related notes;
Wkg = workings (see below);
P&L A/c = balance obtained from the profit and loss account.

Workings

1 Insurance:

As per the trial balance	2 000
Less: Prepayment (QN 2)	500
Charge to the profit and loss account	1 500

2 Depreciation:

Office furniture at cost	5 000
Depreciation: 10% of the original cost	500

3 Increase in provision for bad and doubtful debts:

Trade debtors at 31 March 19X5	20 000
Less: Bad debt (QN 4)	1 000
	19 000
Provision required: 5% thereof	950
Less: Provision at 1 April 19X4	500
Increase in provision: charge to profit and loss	450

4 Salaries:

As per the question	25 000
Add: Accrual (QN 6)	1 000
	26 000

5 Accumulated depreciation:

Balance at 1 April 19X4 (as per TB)	2 000
Add: Depreciation for the year (Wkg 2)	500
Accumulated depreciation at 31 March 19X5	2 500

After you have worked through Exhibit 5.8 as carefully as you can, try to do the question without referring to the answer.

We are nearly at the end of a difficult chapter, but before we move on to other matters, we ought to examine somewhat critically what we have done in both this chapter and the preceding one.

ESTIMATING ACCOUNTING PROFIT

As we have worked through the book, we have tried to point out that the calculation of accounting profit calls for a great deal of subjective judgement. Accounting involves much more than merely being very good at mastering some advanced arithmetical exercises, so we think that it will be helpful (indeed essential) for us to summarize the major defects inherent in the traditional method of calculating accounting profit.

As a non-accountant, it is most important that you appreciate one vital fact: the method that we have outlined results in an *estimate* of what the accountant thinks the profit should be. You must not place too much reliance on the *absolute* level of accounting profit. It can only be as accurate and as reliable as the assumptions upon which it is based. If you accept the assumptions, then you can be fairly confident that the profit figure is reliable. You will then not go too far wrong in using the information for decision-making purposes. But you must know what the assumptions are, and you must support them. The message can, therefore, be put as follows:

> **Always question accounting information before accepting it.**

A summary of the main reasons why you should not place too much reliance on the actual level of accounting profit (especially if you are unsure about the assumptions upon which it is based) is outlined below:

1 Goods are treated as being sold when the legal title to them changes hands, and not when the customer has paid for them. In some cases, the cash for some sales may never be received.

2 Goods are regarded as having been purchased when the legal title to them is transferred to the purchaser, although there are occasions when they may not be received or paid for (e.g. if a supplier goes into receivership).

3 Goods that have not been sold at the period end have to be quantified and valued. This procedure involves a considerable amount of subjective judgement.

4 There is no clear distinction between so-called capital and revenue items.

5 Estimates have to be made to allow for accruals and prepayments.

6 The cost of fixed assets is apportioned between different accounting periods using methods that are fairly simplistic and highly questionable.

7 Arbitrary reductions in profit are made to allow for bad and doubtful debts.

8 Historic cost accounting makes no allowance for inflation. In a period of inflation, for example, the value of £100 at 1 January 19X1 is not the same as £100 at 31 December 19X1. Hence, profit tends to be overstated (partly because of low closing stock values, and partly because depreciation charges will be based on the historic cost).

The above disadvantages of historic cost accounting are extremely serious (and you may even be able to think of some more). As yet, however, accountants have not been able to suggest anything better. If at this stage you are feeling pretty disillusioned, therefore, and you do not feel to have much confidence in accounting information, then take comfort in the old adage that 'it is better to be vaguely right than precisely wrong'!

CONCLUSION

In this chapter, we have examined in some detail the main adjustments made to the financial accounts at the end of an accounting period. You should now be in a far better position to assess the relevance and reliability of any accounting information that is presented to you.

The material that we have covered has provided a broad foundation for all the remaining chapters. It is essential that before moving on to the other chapters, you satisfy yourself that you really do understand the mechanics behind what amounts to the preparation of a set of some fairly basic financial accounts. To test your understanding of this subject, you are recommended to work through all of the Exhibits contained in this chapter and the preceding one once again, and then to attempt some of the following chapter exercises.

Key points

1 Following the completion of the trial balance, some last-minute adjustments have usually to be made to the financial accounts. The main adjustments are: closing stock, depreciation, accruals and pre-payments, and bad and doubtful debts.

2 Accounting profit is merely an estimate. The method used to calculate it is highly questionable, and it is subject to very many criticisms. Undue reliance should not be placed on the actual level of profit shown in the accounts. The assumptions upon which profit is based should be carefully examined, and it should be viewed merely as a guide to decision making

CHECK YOUR LEARNING

1 Are the following statements true or false?
   (a) A provision for bad and doubtful debts results in cash leaving the business.   True/False
   (b) An amount owing for rent at the year end is an accrual.   True/False
   (c) There is no such thing as the correct level of accounting profit.   True/False

2 Fill in the missing word(s) in each of the following statements:
   (a) opening stock + _____ – closing stock = gross profit.
   (b) gross profit + other incomes – total expenditure = _____ _____ .
   (c) _____ – liabilities = capital.

3 A company buys a machine for £12 000. It is expected to have a life of ten years, and an estimated residual value of £2000. If the company uses the straight-line method of depreciation what is the annual charge to the profit and loss account?
   (a) £12 000
   (b) £1000
   (c) £2000
   (d) none of these

4 List five basic defects of conventional accounting statements.

Answers

1 (a) false (b) true (c) true
2 (a) purchases (b) net profit (c) assets
3 £1000 (12 000 – 2000 ÷10)
4 (a) distinction between capital and revenue; (b) revenue recognition; (c) stock valuation problems; (d) depreciation calculations; (e) estimates for outstanding creditors and debtors. (In addition, conventional accounting statements use the historic cost concept which may be a major defect under inflationary conditions; Chapter 12 discusses this point.)

QUESTIONS

5.1

The following information has been extracted from Lathom's books of account for the year to 30 April 19X4:

	£
Purchases	45 000
Sales	60 000
Stock (at 1 May 19X3)	3 000
Stock (at 30 April 19X4)	4 000

Required:
(a) Prepare Lathom's trading account for the year to 30 April 19X4; and
(b) state where the stock at 30 April 19X4 would be shown on the balance sheet as at that date.

5.2

Rufford presents you with the following information for the year to 31 March 19X5:

	£
Purchases	48 000
Purchases returns	3 000
Sales	82 000
Sales returns	4 000
Stock at 1 April 19X4	4 000

He is not sure how to value the stock as at 31 March 19X5. Three methods have been suggested. They all result in different closing stock values, viz.:

Method 1	£8 000
Method 2	£16 000
Method 3	£4 000

Required:
(a) Calculate the effect on gross profit for the year to 31 March 19X5 by using each of the three methods of stock valuation; and
(b) state the effect on gross profit for the year to 31 March 19X6 if method 1 is used instead of method 2.

5.3

Standish has been trading for some years. The following trial balance has been extracted from his books of account as at 31 May 19X6:

	Dr £	Cr £
Capital		22 400
Cash	1 200	
Creditors		4 300
Debtors	6 000	
Drawings	5 500	
Furniture and fittings	8 000	
Heating and lighting	1 500	
c/f	22 200	26 700

		Dr	Cr
		£	£
	b/f	22 200	26 700
Miscellaneous expenses		6 700	
Purchases		52 000	
Sales			79 000
Stock (at 1 June 19X5)		7 000	
Wages and salaries		17 800	
		£105 700	£105 700

Note: Stock at 31 May 19X6: £12 000.

Required:
Prepare Standish's trading and profit and loss account for the year to 31 May 19X6 and a balance sheet as at that date.

5.4

Witton commenced business on 1 July 19X6. The following trial balance was extracted from his books of account as at 30 June 19X7:

	Dr	Cr
	£	£
Capital		3 000
Cash	500	
Drawings	4 000	
Creditors		1 500
Debtors	3 000	
Motor car at cost	5 000	
Office expenses	8 000	
Purchases	14 000	
Sales		30 000
	£34 500	£34 500

Additional information:
1 Stock at 30 June 19X7: £2000.
2 The motor car is to be depreciated at a rate of 20% per annum on cost; it was purchased on 1 July 19X6.

Required:
Prepare Witton's trading and profit and loss account for the year to 30 June 19X7 and a balance sheet as at that date.

5.5

Croxteth has been in the retail trade for many years. The following is his trial balance as at 31 July 19X8:

	Dr	Cr
	£	£
Bank	2 000	
Capital		35 000
Creditors		4 800
Delivery vans at cost	40 000	
Depreciation of delivery vans (at 1 August 19X7)		12 000
Shop equipment at cost	8 000	
Depreciation of equipment (at 1 August 19X7)		2 400
Drawings	8 000	
Purchases	70 000	
Sales		85 000
Shop expenses	7 200	
Stock (at 1 August 19X7)	4 000	
	£139 200	£139 200

Additional information:
1 Stock at 31 July 19X8: £14 000.
2 Depreciation on delivery vans at a rate of 30% per annum on cost, and on shop equipment at a rate of 10% per annum on cost.

Required:
Prepare Croxteth's trading and profit and loss account for the year to 31 July 19X8 and a balance sheet as at that date.

5.6
The following is an extract from Barrow's balance sheet at 31 August 19X8:

Fixed assets	*Cost*	*Accumulated depreciation*	*Net book value*
	£	£	£
Land	200 000	–	200 000
Buildings	150 000	60 000	90 000
Plant	55 000	37 500	17 500
Vehicles	45 000	28 800	16 200
Furniture	20 000	12 600	7 400
	£470 000	£138 900	£331 100

Barrow's depreciation policy is as follows:

1 a full year's depreciation is charged in the year of acquisition, but none in the year of disposal;
2 no depreciation is charged on land;
3 buildings are depreciated at an annual rate of 2% on cost;
4 plant is depreciated at an annual rate of 5% on cost after allowing for an estimated residual value of £5000;

5 vehicles are depreciated on a reduced balance basis at an annual rate of 40% on the reduced balance;

6 furniture is depreciated on a straight-line basis at an annual rate of 10% on cost after allowing for an estimated residual value of £2000.

Additional information:

1 During the year to 31 August 19X9, new furniture was purchased for the office. It cost £3000 and it is to be depreciated on the same basis as the old furniture. Its estimated residual value is £300.

2 There were no additions to or disposals of any other fixed assets during the year to 31 August 19X9.

Required:

(a) Calculate the depreciation charge for each of the fixed asset groupings for the year to 31 August 19X9; and

(b) show how the fixed assets would appear in Barrow's balance sheet as at 31 August 19X9.

5.7

Pine started business on 1 October 19X1. The following is his trial balance at 30 September 19X2:

	£	£
Capital		6 000
Cash	400	
Creditors		5 900
Debtors	5 000	
Furniture at cost	8 000	
General expenses	14 000	
Insurance	2 000	
Purchases	21 000	
Sales		40 000
Telephone	1 500	
	£51 900	£51 900

The following information was obtained after the trial balance had been prepared:

1 Stock at 30 September 19X2: £3000.

2 Furniture is to be depreciated at a rate of 15% on cost.

3 At 30 September 19X2, Pine owed £500 for telephone expenses, and insurance had been prepaid by £200.

Required:

Prepare Pine's trading and profit and loss account for the year to 30 September 19X2 and a balance sheet as at that date.

5.8

Dale has been in business for some years. The following is his trial balance at 31 October 19X3:

	Dr £	Cr £
Bank	700	
Capital		85 000
Depreciation (at 1 November 19X2):		
Office equipment		14 000
Vehicles		4 000
Drawings	12 300	
Heating and lighting	3 000	
Office expenses	27 000	
Office equipment, at cost	35 000	
Rates	12 000	
Purchases	240 000	
Sales		350 000
Stock (at 1 November 19X2)	20 000	
Trade creditors		21 000
Trade debtors	61 000	
Vehicles at cost	16 000	
Wages and salaries	47 000	
	£474 000	£474 000

Additional information (not taken into account when compiling the above trial balance) is as follows:

1 Stock at 31 October 19X3: £26 000.
2 Amount owing for electricity at 31 October 19X3: £1500.
3 At 31 October 19X3, £2000 had been paid in advance for rates.
4 Depreciation is to be charged on the office equipment for the year to 31 October 19X3 at a rate of 20% on cost and on the vehicles at a rate of 25% on cost.

Required:
Prepare Dale's trading and profit and loss account for the year to 31 October 19X3 and a balance sheet as at that date.

5.9

The following information relates to Astley for the year to 30 November 19X4:

Item	Cash paid during the year to 30 November 19X4	As at 1 December 19X3 Accruals/ Prepayments		As at 30 November 19X4 Accruals/ Prepayments	
	£	£	£	£	£
Electricity	26 400	5 200	–	8 300	–
Gas	40 100	–	–	–	4 900
Insurance	25 000	–	12 000	–	14 000
Rates	16 000	–	4 000	6 000	–
Telephone	3 000	1 500	–	–	200
Wages	66 800	1 800	–	–	–

Required:

(a) Calculate the charge to the profit and loss account for the year to 30 November 19X4 for each of the above items.

(b) Demonstrate what amounts for accruals and prepayments would be shown in the balance sheet as at 30 November 19X4.

5.10

Duxbury started in business on 1 January 19X3. The following is his trial balance as at 31 December 19X3:

	Dr £	Cr £
Capital		40 000
Cash	300	
Delivery van, at cost	20 000	
Drawings	10 600	
Office expenses	12 100	
Purchases	65 000	
Sales		95 000
Trade creditors		5 000
Trade debtors	32 000	
	£140 000	£140 000

Additional information:

1 Stock at 31 December 19X3 was valued at £10 000.

2 At 31 December 19X3, an amount of £400 was outstanding for telephone expenses, and the rates had been prepaid by £500.

3 The delivery van is to be depreciated at a rate of 20% per annum on cost.

4 Duxbury decides to set aside a provision for bad and doubtful debts equal to 5% of trade debtors as at the end of the year.

Required:

Prepare Duxbury's trading and profit and loss account for the year to 31 December 19X3 and a balance sheet as at that date.

5.11

Beech is a retailer. Most of his sales are made on credit terms. The following information relates to the first four years that he has been in business:

	19X4	19X5	19X6	19X7
Trade debtors as at 31 January:	£60 000	£55 000	£65 000	£70 000

The trade is one which experiences a high level of bad debts. Accordingly, Beech decides to set aside a provision for bad and doubtful debts equivalent to 10% of trade debtors as at the end of the year.

Required:

(a) Show how the provision for bad and doubtful debts would be disclosed in the respective balance sheets as at 31 January 19X4, 19X5, 19X6 and 19X7; and

(b) calculate the increase/decrease in provision for bad and doubtful debts transferred to the respective profit and loss accounts for each of the four years.

5.12
The following is Ash's trial balance as at 31 March 19X5:

	Dr £	Cr £
Bank		4 000
Capital		20 500
Depreciation (at 1 April 19X4): furniture		3 600
Drawings	10 000	
Electricity	2 000	
Furniture, at cost	9 000	
Insurance	1 500	
Miscellaneous expenses	65 800	
Provision for bad and doubtful debts (at 1 April 19X4)		1 200
Purchases	80 000	
Sales		150 000
Stock (at 1 April 19X4)	10 000	
Trade creditors		20 000
Trade debtors	21 000	
	£199 300	£199 300

Additional information:
1   Stock at 31 March 19X5: £15 000.
2   At 31 March 19X5 there was a specific bad debt of £6000. This was to be written off.
3   Furniture is to be depreciated at a rate of 10% per annum on cost.
4   At 31 March 19X5, Ash owes the electricity board £600, and £100 had been paid in advance for insurance.
5   The provision for bad and doubtful debts is to be made equal to 10% of trade debtors as at the end of the year.

Required:
Prepare Ash's trading and profit and loss account for the year to 31 March 19X5 and a balance sheet as at that date.

5.13
Elm is a wholesaler. The following is his trial balance at 30 June 19X6:

	Dr £	Cr £
Advertising	3 000	
Bank	400	
Capital		73 500
Cash	100	
c/f	3 500	73 500

		£	£
	b/f	3 500	73 500
Depreciation (at 1 July 19X5):			
furniture			1 800
vehicles			7 000
Discounts allowed		400	
Discounts received			500
Drawings		10 000	
Electricity		3 200	
Furniture, at cost		12 000	
General expenses		28 900	
Interest on investments			800
Investments, at cost		5 000	
Provision for bad and doubtful debts			
(at 1 July 19X5)			2 300
Purchases		645 000	
Purchases returns			2 000
Rates		6 000	
Sales			820 000
Sales returns		4 000	
Stock (at 1 July 19X5)		47 000	
Telephone		1 300	
Trade creditors			13 000
Trade debtors		42 000	
Vehicles, at cost		35 000	
Wages and salaries		77 600	
		£920 900	£920 900

Additional information:
1 Stock at 30 June 19X6: £50 000.
2 The provision for bad and doubtful debts is to be made equal to 5% of trade debtors as at 30 June 19X6.
3 Furniture is to be depreciated at a rate of 15% on cost, and the vehicles at a rate of 20% on a reducing balance basis.
4 At 30 June 19X6 amount owing for electricity, £300; rates paid in advance, £1000.

Required:
Prepare Elm's trading profit and loss account for the year to 30 June 19X6 and a balance sheet as at that date.

5.14
Lime's business has had liquidity problems for some months. The following trial balance was extracted from his books of account as at 30 September 19X7:

	Dr £	Cr £
Bank		15 200
Capital		19 300
Cash from sale of office equipment		500
Depreciation (at 1 October 19X6):		
office equipment		22 000
Drawings	16 000	
Insurance	1 800	
Loan (long-term from Cedar)		50 000
Loan interest	7 500	
Miscellaneous expenses	57 700	
Office equipment, at cost	44 000	
Provision for bad and doubtful debts		
(at 1 October 19X6)		2 000
Purchases	320 000	
Rates	10 000	
Sales		372 000
Stock (at 1 October 19X6)	36 000	
Trade creditors		105 000
Trade debtors	93 000	
	£586 000	£586 000

Additional information:
1 Stock at 30 September 19X7: £68 000.
2 At 30 September 19X7, accrual for rates of £2000 and insurance prepaid of £200.
3 Depreciation on office equipment is charged at a rate of 25% on cost. During the year, office equipment costing £4000 had been sold for £500. Accumulated depreciation on this equipment amounted to £3000. Lime's depreciation policy is to charge a full year's depreciation in the year of acquisition, and none in the year of disposal.
4 Specific bad debts of £13 000 are to be written off.
5 The provision for bad and doubtful debts is to be made equal to 10% of outstanding trade debtors as at 30 September 19X7.

Required:
Prepare Lime's trading, and profit and loss account for the year to 30 September 19X7, and a balance sheet as at that date.

5.15
Teak has extracted the following trial balance from his books of account as at 31 December 19X8:

	Dr	Cr
	£	£
Building society deposit	20 000	
Capital		66 500
Cash at bank and in hand	400	
Depreciation:		
Plant and equipment		
(at 1 January 19X8)		30 000
vehicles (at 1 January 19X8)		16 000
Dividends received (interim)		100
Interest received from building society		700
Interest received from Gray		500
Investments at cost	5 000	
Loan to Gray (repayable 1 October 19X9)	10 000	
Office expenses	39 000	
Plant and equipment at cost	50 000	
Purchases	83 000	
Sales		164 000
Stock (at 1 January 19X8)	2 800	
Trade debtors/trade creditors	13 200	22 200
Vehicles at cost	64 000	
Vehicle expenses	12 600	
	£300 000	£300 000

Additional information:
1 Stock at 31 December 19X8: £15 800.
2 During the year to 31 December 19X8, Teak had used some goods (purchased through the business) for his own personal consumption. At cost price these were estimated to be worth £6000. No entries had been made in the books of account to record this transaction.
3 At 31 December 19X8 there was an amount owing for office expenses of £1200. At the same date Teak was due to receive interest from the building society of £800, and a final dividend of £600 from a company in which he had some investments.
4 Depreciation is to be charged on plant and equipment at a rate of 30% per annum on cost, and on vehicles at a rate of 25% on the reduced balance.
5 Office expenses include Teak's drawings for the year of £9000.

Required:
Prepare Teak's trading and profit and loss account for the year to 31 December 19X8 and a balance sheet as at that date.

ADDITIONAL QUESTIONS (WITHOUT ANSWERS)

5.16

Daly's book-keeper has extracted the following trial balance as at 31 January 19X1:

	Dr	Cr
	£000	£000
Administrative expenses	63	
Capital		252
Cash at bank and in hand	9	
Creditors		8
Debtors	1	
Drawings	18	
Furniture and fittings at cost:	200	
accumulated depreciation		
(at 1 February 19X0)		90
Motor vehicles at cost:	800	
accumulated depreciation		
(at 1 February 19X0)		480
Purchases	500	
Rent, rates, heat and light	9	
Sales		760
Stock (at 1 February 19X0)	35	
Trade creditors		170
Trade debtors	70	
Wages and salaries	55	
	£1760	£1760

Additional information:
1 Stock at 31 January l9X1: £40 000.
2 Depreciation is charged on the fixed assets as follows:
    Furniture and fittings: 15% on cost;
    Motor vehicles: 60% on the reduced balance.
3 A trade debt of £10 000 is to be written off.
4 A provision for bad and doubtful debts is to be established equivalent to 5% of outstanding trade debtors as at the end of the year.

Required:
Prepare Daly's trading and profit and loss account for the year to 31 January 19X1, and a balance sheet as at that date.

5.17

Patsy Chan has been in business for several years. The following trial balance was extracted from her books of account as at 30 September 19X9:

	Dr £000	Cr £000
Bad debt	15	
Capital		653
Carriage inwards	10	
Carriage outwards	34	
Cash at bank and in hand	7	
Discounts allowed	18	
Discounts received		27
Dividends received		2
Drawings	12	
Investments at cost	20	
Motor vehicles at cost:	600	
accumulated depreciation (at 1 October 19X8)		300
Office expenses	35	
Plant and equipment at cost:	240	
accumulated depreciation (at 1 October 19X8)		144
Provision for bad and doubtful debts (at 1 October 19X8)		3
Purchases	570	
Salaries	105	
Sales		900
Stock (at 1 October 19X8)	200	
Trade creditors		71
Trade debtors	160	
Wages	74	
	£2100	£2100

Additional information:
1 Stock at 30 September 19X9: £180 000.
2 Depreciation is charged as follows:
    Motor vehicles: 25% on cost;
    Plant and equipment: 30% on cost.
3 Wages owing at 30 September 19X9: £2000.
4 Business rates paid in advance at 30 September 19X9: £5000.
5 A provision for bad and doubtful debts is maintained equivalent to $2\frac{1}{2}$% of outstanding trade debtors as at the end of the year.

Required:
Prepare Patsy Chan's trading and profit and loss account for the year to 30 September 19X9, and a balance sheet as at that date.

DISCUSSION QUESTIONS

5.18

'Depreciation methods and rates should be prescribed by law.' Discuss.

5.19

Explain why it is quite easy to manipulate the level of gross profit when preparing a trading account.

5.20

How far is it possible for an entity to build up secret reserves by making some adjustments in the profit and loss account for bad and doubtful debts?

CHAPTER 6

Manufacturing accounts

Stress is highest for teachers

Press Association

Teaching is the most stressful job, according to a survey by Guardian Financial Services, which questioned 1200 workers and managers. The least stressful industry is manufacturing, followed by accounting and finance, the poll found. It says ill health caused by work is increasing throughout industry and 90 per cent of employers are unaware of the extent of the problem, even though ill-health absenteeism is costing industry an estimated £10bn a year. Workers complained about management styles. Some said that their managers were aware of soaring stress but did nothing about it.

The Financial Times, 1 July 1996

Exhibit 6.0 Manufacturing – the least stressful industry

In the three previous chapters, we have been dealing almost entirely with trading entities. This means that we have assumed that when goods have been purchased, no further work needed to be done on them before they were sold.

There are, of course, many businesses whose main purpose is simply to buy and sell goods. We have referred to such businesses as *trading* entities. There are, however, other businesses who *manufacture* their own products, and so they may buy materials that require further work to be done on them before they are sold. Such materials are known as *raw materials*.

A manufacturing entity is not likely to have a purchases account within its ledger system, since it normally buys raw materials in order to work on them before they are eventually sold in a *finished goods* state. Before we can begin to compile the trading account, therefore, we have to calculate what it has cost the entity to put the goods or materials it has bought into a finished goods state. This cost is called the *manufacturing cost*, and it is the equivalent of a trading entity's purchases. In order to calculate the manufacturing cost, we need an additional account, and this account is called a *manufacturing account*.

In this chapter, we are going to examine what a manufacturing account contains, and how it is constructed. Manufacturing accounts are, in fact, similar to trading and profit and loss accounts in three respects:

1 they form part of the double-entry system;
2 they are used as periodic financial summary statements;
3 they can be presented in either the horizontal or the vertical format.

The chapter falls into two main parts. The first part examines the contents of a manufacturing account, and the second part explains how it is constructed.

By the end of this chapter, you will be able to:

● **describe the nature and purpose of the manufacturing account;**

● **prepare a basic manufacturing account.**

CONTENTS

A manufacturing account mainly records manufacturing costs, and it rarely includes any incomes. The costs which are debited to the account can be divided into two important categories. These are as follows:

1 direct costs, i.e. costs that can be traced directly to the product, such as materials and labour;
2 indirect costs, i.e. costs that are difficult to trace to individual products, e.g. canteen expenses and factory management.

Direct and indirect costs may be more formally defined as follows:

A **direct cost** is a cost which can be easily identified with a particular department, section, product or unit.

An **indirect cost** is a cost which cannot be easily identified with a particular department, section, product or unit.

The manufacturing account is usually broken down into three main categories, viz.:

1 materials;
2 labour;
3 indirect costs.

These categories are sometimes known as the *elements of cost*, and, using the vertical format, they are illustrated in a fairly simple example in Exhibit 6.1. A detailed explanation of the items in the account follows the exhibit.

Exhibit 6.1 Format of a basic manufacturing account

	£000	£000
Direct costs (1)		
Direct material (2)	20	
Direct labour (3)	70	
Other direct expenses (4)	5	
Prime cost (5)		95
Manufacturing overhead (6)		
Indirect material cost (7)	3	
Indirect labour cost (7)	7	
Other indirect expenses (7)	10	
Total manufacturing overhead incurred (8)		20
Total manufacturing costs incurred (9)		115
Work-in-progress (10)		
Opening work-in-progress	10	
Closing work-in-progress	(15)	(5)
Manufacturing cost of goods produced (11)		110
Manufacturing profit (12)		11
Market value of goods produced transferred to the trading account (13)		£121

Notes:
(a) The number shown after each item refers to the tutorial notes (see below). The amounts have been inserted purely for illustrative purposes.
(b) The term 'factory' or 'work' is sometimes substituted for the term *manufacturing*.

Tutorial notes

1 *Direct costs*. The exhibit relates to a *company's* manufacturing account. It is assumed that the direct costs listed for materials, labour and other expenses relate to those expenses which have been easy to identify with the specific products that the company manufactures.

2 *Direct materials*. The charge for direct materials will be calculated as follows:

Direct material cost = (Opening stock of raw materials + purchases of raw materials) – Closing stock of raw materials

The total of direct material cost is sometimes referred to as *materials consumed*. Direct materials will include all the raw material costs and component parts which have been easy to identify with particular products.

3 *Direct labour*. Direct labour will include all those employment costs that have been easy to identify with particular products.

4 *Other direct expenses*. Besides direct material and direct labour costs, there are sometimes other direct expenses that are easy to identify with particular products, for example, the cost of hiring a specific machine. Such expenses are relatively rare.

5 *Prime cost*. The total of direct material costs, direct labour costs and other direct expenses is known as prime cost.

6 *Manufacturing overhead*. Overhead is the collective term given to represent the total of all indirect costs, so any manufacturing costs that are not easy to identify with specific products will be classified separately under this heading.

7 *Indirect material cost*, *indirect labour cost* and *other indirect expenses*. Manufacturing overhead will probably be shown separately under these three headings.

8 *Total manufacturing overhead incurred*. This item represents the total of indirect material cost, indirect labour cost and other indirect expenses.

9 *Total manufacturing costs incurred*. The total of prime cost and total manufacturing overhead incurred equals the total manufacturing costs incurred.

10 *Work-in-progress*. Work-in-progress represents the estimated cost of incomplete work that is not yet ready to be transferred to finished stock. There will usually be some opening and closing work-in-progress.

11 *Manufacturing cost of goods produced*. The manufacturing cost of goods produced equals the total manufacturing costs incurred plus (or minus) the difference between the opening and closing work-in-progress.

12 *Manufacturing profit*. The manufacturing cost of goods produced is sometimes transferred to the finished goods stock account without any addition for manufacturing profit. If this is the case the double-entry effect is as follows:

DEBIT finished goods stock account,
CREDIT manufacturing account
with the manufacturing cost of goods produced.

The finished goods stock account is the equivalent of the purchases account in a trading organization.

Sometimes, however, a manufacturing profit is added to the manufacturing cost of goods produced before it is transferred to the trading account. The main purpose of this adjustment is to enable management to compare more fairly the company's total manufacturing cost inclusive of profit with outside prices (since such prices will also be normally inclusive of profit). The profit added to the manufacturing cost of goods produced may simply be an appropriate percentage, or it may represent the level of profit that the industry generally expects to earn. Any profit element added to the manufacturing cost (irrespective of how it is calculated) is an internal book-keeping arrangement, as the profit has not been *realized* or earned outside the business. The double-entry is affected as follows:

DEBIT manufacturing account,
CREDIT profit and loss account
with the manufacturing profit.

13 *Market value of goods produced*. As explained in 12 above, the market value of goods produced is the amount which will be transferred (that is, debited) to the trading account.

You are now recommended to study Exhibit 6.1 most carefully. If you are not sure about a particular item, then refer to the accompanying tutorial notes. Once you are clear about the basic structure of a manufacturing account, you can move on to the next section.

CONSTRUCTION

In this section, we are going to explain how to construct a manufacturing account. This can best be understood by reference to an example. We use one in Exhibit 6.2.

Exhibit 6.2 Constructing a manufacturing account

The following balances, *inter alia*, have been extracted from the Wren Manufacturing Company as at 31 March 19X5:

	Dr £
Carriage inwards (on raw materials)	6 000
Direct expenses	3 000
Direct wages	25 000
Factory administration	6 000
Factory heat and light	500
Factory power	1 500
Factory rent and rates	2 000
Factory supervisory costs	5 000
Purchase of raw materials	56 000
Raw materials stock (at 1 April 19X4)	4 000
Work-in-progress (at 1 April 19X4)	5 000

Additional information:
1 The stock of raw materials at 31 March 19X5 was valued at £6000.
2 The work-in-progress at 31 March 19X5 was valued at £8000.
3 A profit loading of 50% is added to the total cost of manufacture.

Required:
Prepare Wren's manufacturing account for the year to 31 March 19X5.

Answer to Exhibit 6.2

WREN MANUFACTURING COMPANY
Manufacturing account for the year to 31 March 19X5

	£	£	£
Direct materials			
Raw material stock at 1 April 19X4		4 000	
Purchases	56 000		
Carriage inwards (1)	6 000	62 000	
		66 000	
Less: Raw material stock at 31 March 19X5		6 000	
Cost of materials consumed			60 000
Direct wages			25 000
Direct expenses			3 000
Prime cost			88 000
Other manufacturing costs (2)			
Administration		6 000	
Heat and light		500	
Power		1 500	
Rent and rates		2 000	
Supervisory		5 000	
Total manufacturing overhead expenses			15 000
Total manufacturing costs incurred			103 000
Work-in-progress			
Add: Work-in-progress at 1 April 19X4		5 000	
Less: Work-in-progress at 31 March 19X5		(8 000)	(3 000)
Manufacturing cost of goods produced			100 000
Manufacturing profit (50%) (3)			50 000
Market value of goods produced (4)			£150 000

Tutorial notes

1 Carriage inwards (i.e. the cost of transporting goods to the factory) is normally regarded as being part of the cost of purchases.
2 Other manufacturing costs include production overhead expenses. In practice, there would be a considerable number of other manufacturing costs.
3 A profit loading of 50% has been added to the manufacturing cost (see Note 3 of the question). The manufacturing profit is a debit entry in the manufacturing account. The corresponding credit entry will eventually be made in the profit and loss account.
4 The market value of goods produced will be transferred to the finished goods stock account.

You are now recommended to work through Exhibit 6.2 again, but this time without reference to the answer.

LINKS WITH THE OTHER ACCOUNTS

Exhibit 6.2 deals with the manufacturing account in isolation. However, once the manufacturing account has been prepared it will then be linked with the trading account and the profit and loss account by transferring either the manufacturing cost of the goods produced or the market value of goods produced to the trading account. Thus the manufacturing cost or the market value of goods produced is the equivalent of the entry for 'purchases' which may be found in the trading account of a non-manufacturing entity. Apart from this slight amendment, the preparation of a trading account for a manufacturing entity is exactly the same as it is for a trading entity.

The relationship between a manufacturing account and the other main financial statements is shown in Exhibit 6.3.

Exhibit 6.3 The relationship between a manufacturing, trading and a profit and loss account and a balance sheet

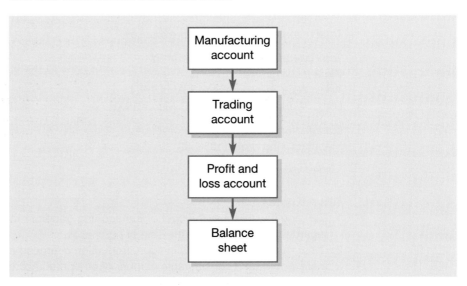

CONCLUSION

A manufacturing account is required for those businesses that undertake further work on goods purchased before they are sold to customers. Manufacturing accounts are normally prepared annually along with all of the other basic financial accounts.

Some entities may prepare a manufacturing account more frequently than once a year, but the traditional double-entry book-keeping system is not really designed to cope with short-term reporting requirements. As was explained in Chapter 1, many manufacturing entities now incorporate a cost and management accounting system into their reporting procedures. Such a system then gives them a lot more detailed information about their manufacturing costs than does one based on the procedures outlined in this chapter. Thus those entities that have a cost and management accounting system will not normally find it necessary to prepare a manufacturing account.

Key points	
	1 **Those entities that undertake further work on any goods purchased before offering them for resale may wish to prepare a manufacturing account.**
	2 **A manufacturing account is part of the double-entry system. It will usually be prepared annually along with the other basic financial accounts. It may be presented in either the horizontal or the vertical format, and it precedes the trading account.**
	3 **Its main elements include: direct materials, direct labour and various indirect manufacturing expenses.**
	4 **Direct cost means a cost that can be easily identified with a particular department, section, product or unit. An indirect cost cannot be easily identified in such a way.**
	5 **A separate manufacturing account will not always be needed, as many manufacturing entities now operate a cost and management accounting system. This system provides better and more frequent information than does a simple manufacturing account.**

CHECK YOUR LEARNING

1 State whether each of the following assertions is either true or false:
   (a) A manufacturing account will normally be required if an entity makes a product.   True/False
   (b) An indirect cost is a cost that can be easily identified with a specific department.   True/False
   (c) Opening work-in-progress has to be added to the total of manufacturing costs incurred.   True/False

2 Put the following items in the order that you would expect to find them in a manufacturing account:
   Closing work-in-progress
   Direct labour
   Direct materials

Indirect labour
Indirect materials
Opening work-in-progress

3 To which element of cost does the following definition refer?
'Goods purchased for incorporation into products for sale'

Answers 1 (a) true (b) false (c) true
2 Direct materials; direct labour; indirect materials; indirect labour; opening work-in-progress; closing work-in-progress
3 Raw material

QUESTIONS

6.1

The following information relates to Megg for the year to 31 January 19X1:

	£000
Stocks at 1 February 19X0:	
Raw material	10
Work-in-progress	17
Direct wages	65
Factory: Administration	27
Heat and light	9
Indirect wages	13
Purchases of raw materials	34
Stocks at 31 January 19X1:	
Raw material	12
Work-in-progress	14

Required:
Prepare Megg's manufacturing account for the year to 31 January 19X1.

6.2

The following balances have been extracted from the books of account of Moor for the year to 28 February 19X2:

	£
Direct wages	50 000
Factory indirect wages	27 700
Purchases of raw materials	127 500
Stocks at 1 March 19X1:	
Raw material	13 000
Work-in-progress	8 400
Stocks at 28 February 19X2:	
Raw material	15 500
Work-in-progress	6 300

Required:
Prepare Moor's manufacturing account for the year to 28 February 19X2.

6.3
The following balances have been extracted from the books of Stuart for the year to 31 March 19X3:

	£000
Administration: Factory	230
Direct wages	330
Purchases of raw materials	1123
Stocks at 1 April 19X2:	
Raw material	38
Work-in-progress	29

Additional information:
Stocks at 31 March 19X3:

Raw material	44
Work-in-progress	42

Required:
Prepare Stuart's manufacturing, account for the year to 31 March 19X3.

ADDITIONAL QUESTIONS (WITHOUT ANSWERS)

6.4
The following balances have been extracted from the books of the David and Peter Manufacturing Company as at 30 April 19X4:

	£000
Direct wages	70
Factory equipment: at cost	360
General factory expenses	13
Heat and light (factory 3/4; general 1/4)	52
Purchases of raw materials	100
Stocks at 1 May 19X3:	
Raw material	12
Work-in-progress	18
Rent and rates (factory 2/3; general 1/3)	42

Additional information:

1 Stocks at 30 April 19X4:	£000
Raw material	14
Work-in-progress	16

2 The factory equipment is to be depreciated at a rate of 15% per annum on cost.

Required:
Prepare the David and Peter Manufacturing Company's manufacturing account for the year to 30 April 19X4.

6.5

Jeffrey is in business as a manufacturer. The following balances have been extracted from his books of account as at 31 May 19X5:

	£000
Factory expenses:	
Direct wages	200
General expenses	60
Plant:	
at cost	160
Purchases of raw materials	180
Stocks at 1 June 19X4:	
Raw material	17
Work-in-progress	21

Additional information:

1 Stocks at 31 May 19X5:

Raw material	20
Work-in-progress	30

2 Goods manufactured by Jeffrey are transferred to finished stock at the cost of manufacture plus 20%.

3 Plant is to be depreciated at a rate of 20% per annum on cost.

Required:

Prepare Jeffrey's manufacturing, trading, and profit and loss account for the year to 31 May 19X5.

DISCUSSION QUESTIONS

6.6

Does a manufacturing account serve any useful purpose?

6.7

How far is it possible to classify cost on a direct and an indirect basis?

6.8

Should a manufacturing account include an adjustment for manufacturing profit?

CHAPTER 7

Company accounts

ASB's new proposals on fixed assets under fire

'Big bath' provisions could return to haunt company accounts if the Accounting Standards Board pushes ahead with its proposals for dealing with falls in the value of fixed assets, critics said last week.

The ASB's April discussion paper, *Impairment of Fixed Assets*, proposes a framework for determining the value at which assets should be carried, and how to account for any resulting falls in value. The ASB said that, in certain circumstances, impairment provisions could be reversed and put back through the profit and loss account.

But Ron Paterson, technical head at Ernst & Young, said the proposals opened the door to 'the kind of abuse that the ASB is trying to stamp out with provisions, that is, taking a loss now and a profit later'.

The ASB's November 1995 discussion paper on provisions aimed to stop companies manipulating results by taking a big hit through a large provision one year, only to release it back to profit later. Danielle Stewart, partner in the firm of Warrener Stewart and vice-chairman of the London Society of Chartered Accountants' technical committee, said the ASB's new proposals were ill-thought out and could lead to a form of 'negative depreciation' being credited to the profit and loss. 'This could introduce big bath provisions by the back door,' she warned.

Accountancy Age, 30 May 1996

Exhibit 7.0 All sorts of fascinating problems arise in company accounting

The last four chapters, have dealt mainly with sole trader types of entities. However, as was argued in Chapter 1, this term is not to be taken too literally. The term *sole trader* means that the entity is *owned* by one individual, although hundreds of employees may work for it. The owner can also be engaged in any kind of business, and not just one that relates to trading.

Sole-trader entities are quite common, especially among very small businesses (e.g. those employing less than perhaps 20 people), but there are two other main types of entities which are perhaps just as common. These are partnerships and limited liability companies.

A partnership entity is very similar to that of a sole trader, except that the business is owned and managed by more than one individual, and the profits and losses are shared among the partners in agreed proportions. As the basic financial procedures are also similar to those of a sole trader, it is not necessary to go into any further detail about partnerships in this book. Instead, we will concentrate on limited liability companies which, as a non-accountant, you are far more likely to come across in your day-to-day work.

Learning objectives	**By the end of this chapter, you will be able to:**
	● **describe the nature of limited liability;**
	● **distinguish between private and public limited companies;**
	● **prepare a basic set of company accounts.**

LIMITED LIABILITY

There is a great personal risk in operating a business as a sole trader or as a partnership. If the business runs short of funds, the owners may be called upon to settle the business's debts out of their own private resources. This type of risk can have an inhibiting effect on the development of new businesses. Hence the need for a different type of entity which will neither make the owners bankrupt nor inhibit new developments. This need became apparent in the nineteenth century as a result of the industrial revolution when, in order to finance the new and rapidly expanding industries (such as the railways and iron and steel), enormous amounts of capital were required.

These sorts of ventures were undertaken at great personal risk. By agreeing to become involved in them, investors often faced bankruptcy if the ventures were unsuccessful (as they often were). It became apparent that the development of industry would be severely restricted unless some means could be devised of restricting the personal liability of prospective investors.

Hence the need for a form of *limited liability*. In fact, the concept of limited liability was not entirely an innovation of the nineteenth century, although it did not receive legal recognition until the Limited Liability Act was passed in 1855. The Act only remained in force for a few months before it was repealed and incorporated into the Joint Stock Companies Act 1856.

By accepting the principle of limited liability, the 1855 Act also recognized the *entity* concept. By distinguishing between the private and public affairs of business proprietors, it effectively created a new form of entity. Since the 1850s, Parliament has passed a number of other Companies Acts, all of which have continued to give legal recognition to the concept of limited liability.

The important point about a limited liability company is that no matter what financial difficulties a company may get into, its members cannot be required to contribute more than an agreed amount of capital. Thus, there is no risk of members being forced into bankruptcy.

The concept of limited liability is often very difficult for business owners to understand, especially if they have formed a limited liability company out of what was perhaps a sole trader or a partnership. Unlike such entities, companies are bound by some fairly severe legal restrictions that affect their operations.

The legal restrictions can be somewhat burdensome, but they are necessary for the protection of all those parties who might have dealings with the company, such as creditors and employees, since if a limited liability company runs short of funds, the creditors and employees might not get paid. It is only fair, therefore, to warn all those people who might have dealings with the company that they run a risk in dealing with it. Consequently, companies have to be more open about their affairs than do sole traders and partnerships.

STRUCTURE AND OPERATION

In this section, the structure and operation of limited liability companies is briefly examined. In order to make it easier to follow, we have broken down our examination into a number of sub-sections.

Share capital

Although the law recognizes that limited liability companies are separate beings with a life of their own (i.e. separate from those individuals who collectively own and manage them), it also accepts that someone has to take responsibility for promoting the company, i.e. bringing it into being. Only one person is now required to form a private company (two for a public company), and that person (or persons, if there is more than one), agrees to make a capital contribution by buying a number of shares. The capital of a company is known as its *share capital*. The share capital will be made up of a number of shares of a certain denomination, such as 10p, 50p, and £1. A member may hold only one share, or many hundreds or thousands, depending upon the total share capital of the company, the denomination of the shares, and the amount that he wishes to contribute.

The maximum amount of capital that the company envisages ever raising has to be stated. This is known as its *authorized share capital*, although this does not necessarily mean that it will issue shares up to that amount. In practice, it will probably only issue sufficient capital to meet its immediate and foreseeable requirements. The amount of share capital that it has actually issued is known as the *issued share capital*. Sometimes when shares are issued, prospective shareholders are only required to contribute to them in instalments. Once all of the issued share capital has been received in cash, it is described as being *fully paid*.

There are two main types of shares: *ordinary* shares and *preference* shares. Ordinary shares do not usually entitle the shareholder to any specific level of dividend (see page 132), and the rights of other types of shareholders always take precedence over the rights of the ordinary shareholders, e.g. if the company goes into liquidation. Preference shareholders are normally entitled to a fixed level of dividend, and they usually have priority over the ordinary shareholders if the company is liquidated. Sometimes, the preference shares are classed as *cumulative*. This means that if the company cannot pay its preference dividend in one year, the amount due accrues until such time as the company has the profits to pay all of the accumulated dividends.

There are many other different types of shares, but in this book, we need only concern ourselves with ordinary shares and preference shares.

Types of companies

A prospective shareholder may invest in either a public company or a private company. A public company must have an authorized share capital of at least £50 000, and it becomes a public company merely by stating that it *is* a public company. In fact, most public limited companies have their shares listed on the Stock Exchange, and hence they are often referred to as *listed* companies.

As a warning to those parties who might have dealings with them, public companies have to include the term 'public limited liability company' after their name (or its abbreviation 'plc').

Any company that does not make its shares available to the public is regarded as being a *private* company. Like public companies, private companies must also have an authorized share capital, although no minimum amount is prescribed. Otherwise, they are very similar to public companies in respect of their share capital requirements.

Private companies also have to warn the public that their liability is limited. They must do so by describing themselves as 'limited liability companies', and attaching the term 'limited' after their name (or the abbreviation 'ltd').

Loans

Besides obtaining the necessary capital from their shareholders, companies often borrow money in the form of *debentures*. A company may invite the public to loan it some money for a certain period of time (although the period can be unspecified) at a certain rate of interest. A debenture loan may be secured on specific assets of the company, on its assets generally, or it might not be secured at all. If it is secured and the company cannot repay it on its due repayment date, the debenture holders may sell the secured assets and use the amount to settle the amount owing to them.

Debentures, like shares, may be bought and sold freely on the Stock Exchange. The nearer the redemption date for the repayment for the debentures, the closer the market price will be to their nominal (i.e. their face, or stated paper) value, but sometimes if they are to be redeemed at a premium (i.e. in excess of their nominal value), the market price may exceed the nominal value.

Debenture holders are not shareholders of the company, and they do not have voting rights. From the company's point of view, one further advantage of raising capital in the form of debenture loans is that for taxation purposes the interest can be charged as a business expense against the profit for the year (unlike dividends paid to shareholders).

Disclosure of information

It is necessary for both public and private companies to supply a *minimum* amount of information to their members. The detailed requirements will be examined in Part 4. You might find it surprising to learn that shareholders have neither a right of access to the company's premises, nor a right to receive any information that they demand. This might not seem fair, but it would clearly be difficult for a company's managers to cope with thousands of shareholders, all of whom suddenly all turned up one day demanding to be let into the buildings in order to inspect the company's books of account!

Instead, shareholders in both private and public companies have to be supplied with an annual report containing at least the minimum amount of information required by the Companies Act 1985. The company also has to file (as it is called) a copy of the report with the Registrar of Companies at Companies House (either in Cardiff or in Edinburgh). This means that, on payment of a small fee, the report is open for inspection by any member of the public who wants to consult it. Some companies (defined as small or medium-sized) are permitted to file an abbreviated version of their annual report with the Registrar, although the full report must still be sent to their shareholders.

Company accounts

Company accounts are very similar to those of sole traders (Exhibit 7.1 shows the basic stucture). They do, however, tend to be more detailed, and some modifications have to be made in order to comply with various legal requirements. We shall be looking at company accounts in more detail a little later on in the chapter.

Directors

It must be clearly understood that any limited liability company is regarded as being a separate entity, i.e. separate from those shareholders who own it collectively, and separate from anyone who works for it. This means that all those who are employed by it (no matter how senior) are its employees. Nonetheless, someone has to take responsibility for the management of the company, of course, so the shareholders usually delegate that responsibility to *directors*.

Directors are the most senior level of management. They are responsible for the day-to-day running of the company, and they answer to the shareholders. Directors are officers of the company, and any remuneration paid to them as directors is charged as an expense of the business. Directors may also be shareholders, but any payment that they receive as such is regarded as being a private matter, and it must not be confused with any income that they receive as directors.

The distinction between employees and shareholder-employees is an important one, although it is one that is not always understood. This is especially the case in very small companies where both employees and

Exhibit 7.1 A company's basic financial accounts

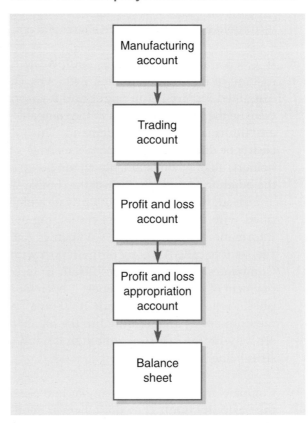

shareholders may be one and the same. As we have tried to emphasize, in law, the company is regarded as being a separate entity. Even if there are just two shareholders, for example, who both work full-time for the company, the company is still treated as distinct from that of the two individuals who happen to own it. They may take decisions which appear to affect no one else except themselves, but because they operate the company under the protection of limited liability, they have certain obligations as well as rights. Consequently, they are not as free to operate the company as they might if they ran it as a partnership.

Dividends Profits are usually distributed to shareholders in the form of a dividend. A dividend is usually calculated on the basis of so many pence per share. The actual dividend will be recommended by the directors to the shareholders. It will depend upon the amount of net profit earned during the year, and how much profit the directors want to retain in the business.

A dividend may have been paid during the year as an *interim* dividend. In effect, an interim dividend is a payment on account. In preparing the annual accounts, the directors recommend a proposed dividend (sometimes referred to as the *final* dividend). The proposed dividend has to be approved by the shareholders at a general meeting.

Taxation Taxation is another feature which clearly distinguishes a limited liability company from that of a sole-trader entity.

Sole-trader entities do not have tax levied on them as entities. Instead, tax is levied on the amount of profit the owner has made during the year. The tax that is then due for payment is a private matter, and in accordance with the entity rule, it lies outside the boundary of the entity. Any tax that appears to have been paid by the entity on the owner's behalf is treated as part of their drawings (i.e. an amount paid to them as part of their share of the profits).

Companies are treated quite differently. Companies are taxed in their own right, like individuals. They have their own form of taxation, known as *corporation tax*. Corporation tax was introduced in 1965, and all companies are eligible to pay it. It is based on the company's accounting profits for a particular financial year. The accounting profit has to be adjusted, however, because some items are treated differently for tax purposes, for example, the depreciation of fixed assets. The corporation tax based on a company's profits is then due for payment nine months after the company's year end.

The corporation tax due will normally be shown in the company's balance sheet at the year end under current liabilities as a creditor, and it should normally have all been paid by the time that the next balance sheet is prepared.

Corporation tax has sometimes to be paid in advance. This is known as *advance corporation tax* (ACT). ACT is due for payment each time that the company pays a dividend, and the amount due is based on the dividend. Any ACT paid is eventually deducted from the total corporation charge payable for the year. The net amount due (i.e. the total amount of corporation tax payable for the year less any ACT paid) is known as *mainstream* corporation tax. The book-keeping entries are extremely complex but, fortunately, we do not need to go into them in this book.

Now that the basic structure and operation of limited liability companies have been outlined, we can begin to examine company accounts in some detail. We start with the profit and loss account.

THE PROFIT AND LOSS ACCOUNT

As was suggested earlier, the preparation of a company's manufacturing, trading and profit and loss account is basically no different from that of sole-trader entities. Almost an identical format may be adopted, and it is only after the net profit stage that some differences become apparent. Company accounts usually include for example, a profit and loss appropriation account (although no clear dividing line is usually drawn between where the profit and loss account ends and the appropriation account begins). A company's profit and loss appropriation account is illustrated in Exhibit 7.2.

Exhibit 7.2 Example of a company's profit and loss appropriation account

	£000
Net profit for the year before taxation	1000
Taxation	(300)
Net profit for the year after taxation	700
Dividends	(500)
Retained profit for the year	200
Retained profits brought forward	400
Retained profits carried forward	£600

As can be seen from Exhibit 7.2, the company's net profit for the year is used (or appropriated) in three ways:

1 to pay tax;
2 to pay dividends;
3 for retention within the business.

THE BALANCE SHEET

The structure of a limited liability company's balance sheet is also very similar to that of a sole trader. The main differences arise because of the company's share capital structure. There are, however, some other features that are not usually found in non-company balance sheets.

We illustrate the main features of a company's balance sheet in Exhibit 7.3. Study this exhibit carefully, but please note that the information has been kept to a minimum. We have not given the full details where there are insignificant differences between a company's balance sheet and those of other entities.

Exhibit 7.3 Example of a company's balance sheet

EXHIBITOR LIMITED
Balance sheet at 31 March 19X1

	£000	£000	£000
Fixed assets			600
Investments (1)			100
Current assets		6000	
Less: Current liabilities			
Trade creditors	2950		
Accruals	50		
Corporation tax (2)	300		
Proposed dividend (3)	500	3800	2200
			£2900

Financed by:

Capital and reserves (4)	Authorized	Issued and fully paid
	£000	£000
Ordinary shares of £1 each (5)	2000	1500
Preference shares of £0.50 each (5)	500	500
	£2500	2000
Capital reserves (6)		200
Revenue reserves (7)		600
Shareholders' funds (8)		2800
Loans (9)		100
		£2900

Note: The number shown after each narration refers to the tutorial notes below.

Tutorial notes

1 *Investments*. This item usually represents long-term investments in the shares of other companies. Short-term investments (such as money invested in bank deposit accounts) would be included in current assets. The shares may be either in public limited liability companies or in private limited companies.

It is obviously more difficult to buy shares in private companies and to obtain current market prices for them. The market price of the investments should be stated, or where this is not available, a directors' valuation should be obtained.

2 *Corporation tax*. Corporation tax represents the tax due on the company's profits for the year. It is due for payment nine months after the company's year end, that is, in Exhibitor's case, on 1 January 19X2.

3 *Proposed dividend*. A proposed dividend will probably be due for payment very shortly after the year end, so it will usually be shown as a current liability.

4 *Capital and reserves*. Details of the authorized, issued and fully paid-up share capital should be shown.

5 *Ordinary shares and preference shares*. Details about the different types of shares that the company has issued should be shown.

6 This section may include several different reserve accounts of a capital nature, that is, amounts that are not available for distribution to the shareholders as dividend. It might include, for example, a share premium account, i.e. the extra amount paid by shareholders in excess of the nominal value of the shares. This extra amount does not rank for dividend, but sometimes shareholders are willing to pay a premium if they think that the shares are particularly attractive. Another asset may have been revalued, and the difference between the original cost and the revalued amount will be credited to this account.

7 *Revenue reserves*. Revenue reserve accounts are amounts which are available for distribution to the shareholders. Sometimes profits which could be distributed to shareholders are put into general reserve accounts, although no real purpose is served in classifying them in this way.

8 *Shareholders' funds*. The total amount available to shareholders at the balance sheet date is equal to the share capital originally subscribed, plus all the capital, reserve and revenue reserve account balances.

9 *Loans*. The loans section of the balance sheet will include all the long-term loans obtained by the company, i.e. those loans which do not have to be repaid for at least twelve months, such as debentures and long-term bank loans.

A COMPREHENSIVE EXAMPLE

In this section, the structure of a company's accounts is examined in a little more detail. Exhibit 7.4 is used as an example. The example assumes that the accounts are being prepared for internal management purposes (accounts for external purposes are dealt with in Part 4 of the book). Work through the answer to Exhibit 7.4 making sure that you understand each step in its construction.

Exhibit 7.4 Preparation of a company's accounts

The following information has been extracted from the books of Handy Limited as at 31 March 19X5:

	Dr £	Cr £
Bank	2 000	
Capital: 100 000 issued and fully paid ordinary		
shares of £1 each		100 000
50 000 issued and fully paid 8% preference		
shares of £1 each		50 000
Debenture loan stock (10%: repayable 19X9)		30 000
Debenture loan stock interest	3 000	
Discounts allowed	2 000	
Discounts received		5 000
Dividends received		700
Dividends paid: Ordinary interim	5 000	
Preference	4 000	
Freehold land at cost	200 000	
Investments (listed: market value at 31 March		
19X5 was £11 000)	10 000	
Office expenses	15 000	
Office salaries	35 000	
Motor van at cost	15 000	
Motor van: accumulated depreciation at 1 April 19X4		6 000
Motor van expenses	2 700	
Purchases	220 000	
Retained profits at 1 April 19X4		9 000
Sales		300 000
Share premium account		10 000
Stocks at cost (at 1 April 19X4)	20 000	
Trade creditors		50 000
Trade debtors	27 000	
	£560 700	£560 700

Additional information:
1 The stocks at 31 March 19X5 were valued at cost at £40 000.
2 Depreciation is to be charged on the motor van at a rate of 20% per annum on cost. No depreciation is to be charged on the freehold land.
3 Corporation tax (based on profits for the year at a rate of 35%) has been estimated at £10 000.
4 The directors propose a final ordinary dividend of 10p per share.
5 The authorized share capital of the company is as follows:
    (a) 150 000 ordinary shares of £1 each; and
    (b) 75 000 preference shares of £1 each.

Required:
Prepare (a) Handy Limited's trading and profit and loss account for the year to 31 March 19X5; and
    (b) a balance sheet as at that date.

Answer to Exhibit 7.4

(a)   **HANDY LIMITED**
Trading and profit and loss account for the year to 31 March 19X5

	£	£	£
Sales			300 000
Less: Cost of goods sold:			
Opening stocks		20 000	
Purchases		220 000	
		240 000	
Less: Closing stocks		40 000	200 000
Gross profit			100 000
Add: Incomes:			
Discounts received		5 000	
Dividends received		700	5 700
			105 700
Less: Expenditure:			
Debenture loan stock interest		3 000	
Discounts allowed		2 000	
Motor van depreciation (1)	3 000		
Motor van expenses	2 700	5 700	
Office expenses		15 000	
Office salaries		35 000	60 700
Net profit for the year future taxation			45 000
Less: Corporation tax (based on the profits for the year at a rate of 35%) (2)			10 000
Net profit future year after taxation			35 000
Less: Dividends (3):			
Preference dividend paid (8%)		4 000	
Interim ordinary paid (5p per share)		5 000	
	c/f	9 000	35 000

		£	£	£
	b/f		9 000	35 000
Proposed final ordinary dividend (10p per share)			10 000	19 000
Retained profit for the year				16 000
Retained profits brought forward				9 000
Retained profits carried forward (4)				£25 000

(b)

HANDY LIMITED
Balance sheet at 31 March 19X5

Fixed assets	Cost	Accumulated depreciation	Net book value
	£	£	£
Freehold land (5)	200 000	–	200 000
Motor van (6)	15 000	9 000	6 000
	£215 000	£9 000	206 000

Investments			
At cost (market value at 31 March 19X5: £11 000) (7)			10 000
Current assets			
Stocks at cost		40 000	
Trade debtors		27 000	
Bank		2 000	
		69 000	
Less: Current liabilities			
Trade creditors	50 000		
Corporation tax (due for payment on 1 January 19X6) (8)	10 000		
Proposed ordinary dividend (9)	10 000	70 000	
Net current assets			(1 000)
			£215 000

Financed by:	Authorized	Issued and fully paid
Capital and reserves		
Ordinary shares of £1 each (10)	150 000	100 000
Preference shares of £1 each (10)	75 000	50 000
	£225 000	150 000
Share premium account (11)		10 000
Retained profits (12)		25 000
Shareholders' funds (13)		185 000
Loans (14)		
10% debenture stock (repayable 19X9)		30 000
		£215 000

Note: The number shown after each narration refers to the following tutorial notes.

Tutorial notes

1 Depreciation has been charged on the motor van at a rate of 20% per annum, on cost as instructed in question note 2.

2 Question note 3 requires £10 000 to be charged as corporation tax. Note that the corporation tax rate of 35% is applied to the taxable profit, and not to the accounting profit of £45 000. The taxable profit has not been given in the question.

3 A proposed ordinary dividend of 10p has been included as instructed in question note 4.

4 The total retained profit of £25 000 is carried forward to the balance sheet (see tutorial note 12 below).

5 Question note 2 states that no depreciation is to be charged on the freehold land.

6 The accumulated depreciation for the motor van of £9000 is the total of the accumulated depreciation brought forward at 1 April l9X4 of £6000 plus the £3000 written off to the profit and loss account for the current year (see tutorial note 1 above).

7 Note that the market value of the investments has been disclosed on the face of the balance sheet.

8 The corporation tax charged against profit (question note 3,) will be due for payment on 1 January 19X6 (to be precise, nine months plus one day after the year end). It is, therefore, a current liability.

9 The proposed ordinary dividend will be due for payment shortly after the year end, so it is also a current liability. The interim dividend and the preference dividend have already been paid, so they are not current liabilities.

10 Details of the authorized, issued and fully paid share capital should be disclosed.

11 The share premium is a capital account: it cannot be used for the payment of dividends. This account will tend to remain unchanged in successive balance sheets, although there are a few highly restricted purposes for which it may be used.

12 The retained profits become part of a revenue account balance that the company could use for the payment of dividends. The total retained profits of £25 000 is the amount brought in to the balance sheet from the profit and loss account.

13 The total amount of shareholders' funds should always be shown.

14 The loans are long-term loans. Loans are not part of shareholders' funds, and they should be shown in the balance sheet as a separate item.

You are now recommended to work through Exhibit 7.4 again without reference to the answer.

CONCLUSION

This chapter has briefly examined the background to the legislation affecting limited liability companies. This was followed by some examples of how company accounts are prepared for *internal* purposes.

Although a great deal of information can be obtained from studying the annual accounts of a company, it is difficult to extract the most relevant and significant features. Some further guidance is needed, therefore, in how to make the best use of the financial accounting information presented to you. That guidance is provided in the next two chapters.

Key points

1 Company accounts have to be adapted in order to meet certain legal requirements. Basically, the structure of the annual accounts is similar to those of sole traders.

2 The profits of a company are taxed separately (like an individual). The tax is based on the accounting profit for the year, and any tax due at the year end will be shown in the balance sheet as a creditor.

3 The net profit after tax may be paid to shareholders in the form of a dividend (although some profit may still be retained within the business). Any proposed dividend (i.e. one recommended but not yet paid) should be shown in the balance sheet as a creditor.

4 As a result of paying a dividend, some corporation tax may be due for payment in advance. This is known as advance corporation tax (ACT).

CHECK YOUR LEARNING

1 Fill in the blank spaces in each of the following statements:
   (a) Limited liability is a _____ _____ concept.
   (b) The shares in a _____ _____ _____ company can be bought and sold on the Stock Exchange.
   (c) There are two main types of shares, _____ and _____.
   (d) Debentures are a form of _____ _____ _____.

2 Complete the following equations:
   (a) Sales – cost of goods sold = _____
   (b) Profit for the year after taxation – _____ = retained profit for the year
   (c) _____ – current liabilities = net current assets
   (d) Ordinary shares + share premium account + retained profits = _____
   (e) Retained profits brought forward + _____ = retained profits carried forward

3 State in which section of the balance sheet you are likely to find the following items:
   (a) amount owing for taxation
   (b) debenture stock
   (c) plant and machinery
   (d) preference shares
   (e) trade debtors

1 (a) nineteenth-century   (b) public limited liability   (c) ordinary; preference
   (d) long-term loan
   2 (a) gross profit (b) dividends (c) current assets (d) shareholders' funds
   (e) retained profits for the year
   3 (a) current liabilities (b) loans (c) fixed assets (d) share capital
   (e) current assets

QUESTIONS

7.1
The following balances have been extracted from the books of Margo Limited for the year to 31 January 19X1:

	Dr £000	Cr £000
Cash at bank and in hand	5	
Plant and equipment:		
At cost	70	
Accumulated depreciation (at 31.1.X1)		25
Profit and loss account (at 1.2.X0)		15
Profit for the financial year (to 31.1.X1)		10
Share capital (issued and fully paid)		50
Stocks (at 31.1.X1)	17	
Trade creditors	20	12
Trade debtors		
	£112	£112

Additional information:
1 Corporation tax based on the profits for the year is estimated at £3000.
2 Margo Limited's authorized share capital is £75 000 of £1 ordinary shares.
3 A dividend of 10p per share is proposed (ignore advance corporation tax).

Required:
Prepare Margo Limited's profit and loss account for the year to 31 January 19X1 (insofar as the information permits) and a balance sheet as at that date.

7.2

Harry Limited was formed in 1980. The following balances as at 28 February 19X2 have been extracted from the books of account after the trading account has been compiled:

	Dr £000	Cr £000
Administration expenses	65	
Cash at bank and in hand	10	
Distribution costs	15	
Dividend paid (on preference shares)	6	
Furniture and equipment:		
At cost	60	
Accumulated depreciation at 1.3.X1		36
Gross profit for the year		150
Ordinary share capital (shares of £1 each)		100
Preference shares (cumulative 15% of £1 shares)		40
Profit and loss account (at 1.3.X1)		50
Share premium account		20
Stocks (at 28.2.X2)	130	
Trade creditors		25
Trade debtors	135	
	£421	£421

Additional information:

1 Corporation tax based on the profits for the year is estimated at £24 000.
2 Furniture and equipment is depreciated at an annual rate of 10% of cost and it is all charged against administrative expenses.
3 A dividend of 20p per ordinary share is proposed (ignore advance corporation tax).
4 All of the authorized share capital has been issued and is fully paid.

Required:

Prepare Harry Limited's profit and loss account for the year to 28 February 19X2 and a balance sheet as at that date.

7.3

The following balances have been extracted from the books of Jim Limited as at 31 March 19X3:

	Dr £000	Cr £000
Advertising	3	
Bank	11	
Creditors		12
Debtors	118	
Furniture and fittings:		
At cost	20	
Accumulated depreciation (at 1.4.X2)		9
Directors' fees	6	
Profit and loss account (at 1.4.X2)		8
c/f	158	29

		£000	£000
	b/f	158	29
Purchases		124	
Rent and rates		10	
Sales			270
Share capital (issued and fully paid)			70
Stock (at 1.4.X2)		16	
Telephone and stationery		5	
Travelling expenses		2	
Vehicles:			
At cost		40	
Accumulated depreciation (at 1.4.X2)			10
Wages and salaries		24	
		£379	£379

Additional information:
1 Stock at 31 March 19X2 was valued at £14 000.
2 Furniture and fittings and the vehicles are depreciated at a rate of 15% and 25%, respectively, on cost.
3 Corporation tax based on the year's profits is estimated at £25 000.
4 A dividend of 40p per share is proposed (ignore advance corporation tax).
5 The company's authorized share capital is £100 000 of £1 ordinary shares.

Required:
Prepare Jim Limited's trading and profit and loss account for the year to 31 March 19X3, and a balance sheet as at that date.

7.4
The following trial balance has been extracted from Cyril Limited as at 30 April 19X4:

		Dr	Cr
		£000	£000
Advertising		2	
Bank overdraft			20
Bank interest paid		4	
Creditors			80
Debtors		143	
Directors' remuneration		30	
Freehold land and buildings:			
At cost		800	
Accumulated depreciation at 1.5.X3			102
General expenses		15	
Investments at cost		30	
Investment income			5
Motor vehicles:			
At cost		36	
Accumulated depreciation (at 1.5.X3)			18
Preference dividend paid		15	
	c/f	1075	225

		£000	£000
	b/f	1075	225
Preference shares (cumulative 10% shares of £1 each)			150
Profit and loss account (at 1.5.X3)			100
Purchases		480	
Repairs and renewals		4	
Sales			900
Share capital (authorized, issued and fully paid ordinary shares of £1 each)			500
Share premium account			25
Stock (at 1.5.X3)		120	
Wages and salaries		221	
		£1900	£1900

Additional information:
1 Stock at 30 April 19X4 was valued at £140 000.
2 Depreciation for the year of £28 000 is to be provided on buildings and £9 000 for motor vehicles.
3 A provision of £6 000 is required for the auditors' remuneration.
4 £2 000 had been paid in advance for renewals.
5 Corporation tax based on the year's profits is estimated at £60 000.
6 The directors propose an ordinary dividend of 10p per share.
7 The market value of the investments at 30 April 19X4 was £35 000.
8 Ignore advance corporation tax.

Required:
Prepare Cyril Limited's trading and profit and loss account for the year to 30 April 19X4 and a balance sheet as at that date.

7.5
Nelson Limited was incorporated in 1980 with an authorized share capital of 500 000 £1 ordinary shares, and 200 000 5% cumulative preference shares of £1 each. The following trial balance was extracted as at 31 May 19X5:

	Dr	Cr
	£000	£000
Administrative expenses	257	
Auditor's fees	10	
Cash at bank and in hand	5	
Creditors		85
Debentures (12%)		100
Debenture interest paid	6	
Debtors	225	
Directors' remuneration	60	
Dividends paid:		
Ordinary interim	20	
Preference	5	
c/f	588	185

		£000	£000
	b/f	588	185
Furniture, fittings and equipment:			
At cost		200	
Accumulated depreciation at 1.6.X4			48
Investments at cost (market value at 31.5.X5:			
£340 000)		335	
Investment income			22
Ordinary share capital (issued and fully paid)			400
Preference share capital			200
Profit and loss account (at 1.6.X4)			17
Purchases		400	
Sales			800
Share premium account			50
Stock at 1.6.X4		155	
Wages and salaries		44	
		£1722	£1722

Additional information:
1 Stock at 31 May 19X5 was valued at £195 000.
2 Administrative expenses owing at 31 May 19X5 amounted to £13 000.
3 Depreciation is to be charged on the furniture and fittings at a rate of 12½% on cost.
4 Salaries paid in advance amounted to £4000.
5 Corporation tax based on the profit for the year is estimated at £8000.
6 Provision is to be made for a final ordinary dividend of 1.25p per share.
7 Ignore advance corporation tax.

Required:
Prepare Nelson Limited's trading and profit and loss account for the year to 31 May 19X5 and a balance sheet as at that date.

7.6
The following trial balance has been extracted from the books of Keith Limited as at 30 June 19X6:

		Dr	Cr
		£000	£000
Advertising		30	
Bank		7	
Creditors			69
Debentures (10%)			70
Debtors (all trade)		300	
Directors' remuneration		55	
Electricity		28	
Insurance		17	
Investments (quoted)		28	
Investment income			4
	c/f	465	143

		£000	£000
	b/f	465	143
Machinery:			
At cost		420	
Accumulated depreciation at 1.7.X5			152
Office expenses		49	
Ordinary share capital (issued and fully paid)			200
Preference shares			50
Preference share dividend		4	
Profit and loss account (at 1 July 19X5)			132
Provision for bad and doubtful debts			8
Purchases		1240	
Rent and rates		75	
Sales			2100
Stock (at 1.7.X5)		134	
Vehicles:			
At cost		80	
Accumulated depreciation (at 1.7.X5)			40
Wages and salaries		358	
		£2825	£2825

Additional information:
1. Stock at 30 June 19X6 valued at cost amounted to £155 000.
2. Depreciation is to be provided on machinery and vehicles at a rate of 20% and 25%, respectively, on cost.
3. Provision is to be made for auditors' remuneration of £12 000.
4. Insurance paid in advance at 30 June 19X6 amounted to £3000.
5. The provision for bad and doubtful debts is to be made equal to 5% of outstanding trade debtors as at 30 June 19X6.
6. Corporation tax based on the profits for the year of £60 000 is to be provided.
7. An ordinary dividend of 10p per share is proposed.
8. The investments had a market value of £30 000 at 30 June 19X6.
9. The company has an authorized share capital of 600 000 ordinary shares of £0.50 each and of 50 000 8% cumulative preference shares of £1 each.
10. Ignore advance corporation tax.

Required:
Prepare Keith Limited's trading and profit and loss account for the year to 30 June 19X6 and a balance sheet as at that date.

ADDITIONAL QUESTIONS (WITHOUT ANSWERS)

7.7

Muir Limited's trial balance for the year to 30 November 19X1 is shown below:

	Dr	Cr
	£000	£000
Administrative expenses	210	
Called up share capital (£1 ordinary shares)		720
Cash at bank and in hand	40	
Distribution costs	580	
Dividends received		4
Fixed asset investments (at cost)	20	
Land and property at cost	200	
Accumulated depreciation (at 1 December 19X0)		16
Profit and loss account (at 1 December 19X0)		160
Purchases	1360	
Sales		2480
Stock (at 1 December 19X0)	260	
Trade creditors		120
Trade debtors	430	
Vans at cost:	700	
Accumulated depreciation		
(at 1 December 19X0)		300
	£3800	£3800

Additional information:

1 Stock at 30 November 19X1: £250 000.
2 Depreciation is to be charged as follows:
   Property: 4% on cost (land at cost = £100 000)
   Vans: 25% on cost.
3 At 30 November 19X1:
   £10 000 was owing for office salaries
   £5000 had been paid in advance for van licences.
4 Corporation tax based on the profit for the year at a rate of 35% is estimated to be £55 000.
5 The directors propose to pay an ordinary dividend of 10p per share.
6 Advance corporation tax may be ignored.

Required:

Prepare Muir's profit and loss account for the year to 30 November 19X1, and a balance sheet as at that date.

7.8

The following trial balance has been extracted from the books of account of McAdam Limited as at 31 December 19X2:

	Dr £000	Cr £000
Administrative expenses	2 370	
Bank overdraft		130
Called up share capital:		
Ordinary shares of £1 each		800
10% cumulative preference shares		200
Creditors		600
Debtors	570	
Deferred taxation		500
Distribution costs	900	
Fixed asset investments:		
Dividends received		120
Investments at cost	700	
Furniture and fittings at cost	100	
Accumulated depreciation (at 1 January 19X2)		40
Interim dividend paid (10p per ordinary share)	80	
Plant and equipment at cost	7 000	
Accumulated depreciation (at 1 January 19X2)		4 000
Preference dividend paid	10	
Profit and loss account		3 000
Purchases	8 000	
Sales		13 200
Share premium account		380
Stock at 1 January 19X2	2 000	
Trade creditors		980
Trade debtors	2 220	
	£23 950	£23 950

Additional information:

1 Stock at 31 December 19X2: £2 400 000.
2 Depreciation is to be charged as follows:
   Furniture and fittings: 10% on cost
   Plant and equipment (all relating to distribution activities): 50% on the reduced balance.
3 Corporation tax based on the profit for the year at a rate of 35%: £530 000.
4 The directors propose to pay a final ordinary dividend of 20p per ordinary share.
5 Advance corporation tax may be ignored.

Required:

Prepare McAdam's profit and loss account for the year to 31 December 19X2, and a balance sheet as at that date.

DISCUSSION QUESTIONS

7.9

'The concept of limited liability is an out-of-date nineteenth-century concept.' Discuss.

7.10

Do you think that there should be different accounting requirements for small and large companies?

7.11

How far do you think that the information presented in a limited liability company's profit and loss account and balance sheet is useful to the owners of the business?

PART 3

Financial performance

CHAPTER 8

Cash flow statements

BTR to face pressure over cash flow

By Ross Tieman

BTR's senior management will today face tough questions from analysts about the speed and scale of its disposal programme amid mounting concern that the diversified industrial group may be obliged to cut its dividend.

At lunchtime meetings with analysts today and tomorrow, Ms Kathleen O'Donovan, BTR finance director, will be pressed to explain how the group will address the widening gap between its shrinking cash flow and the £600m annual dividend bill.

Mr Ian Strachan, who took over as chief executive in January, has already signalled his plan to sell BTR's plastics manufacturing operations in Taiwan.

It is now believed in the City that the businesses, which are small players in notoriously tough markets, may prove difficult to divest. The disposal could raise about £290m, analysts estimate.

BZW, broker to BTR, has already forecast that the 1997 dividend may be pegged at 15.5p, but some analysts are predicting a cut

The City believes Mr Strachan might need to accelerate BTR's restructuring by widening his divestment programme radically. ABN Amro, the broker, says BTR could raise up to £1.6bn by selling its US aggregates businesses, other polymer producers, and a range of peripheral subsidiaries. Such a programme would reduce BTR's £10bn of annual sales by some £4bn.

To clear the path for the sale of Taiwanese companies BTR bought the 38 per cent minorities in BTR Nylex, its Australian subsidiary, for $2bn last December. Ten years ago, BTR Nylex acquired a controlling interest in the China General Plastics Group set up by entrepreneur Mr James Chao.

China General has three main operating subsidiaries. BTR has 41 per cent of the China General Plastics at Tourfen which makes PVC; 51 per cent of Asia Polymer Corporation at Kaosiung making low-density polyethylene; and 51 per cent of Taita Chemical Company, which makes styrene-based plastics. BTR runs all three.

BTR must find a buyer willing to reach a deal with its partner, and enter head-to-head competition with Formosa Plastics, which dominates plastics production in Taiwan.

Although Formosa could be a buyer, it has generally preferred to set up its own greenfield sites. Another company mentioned as a possible buyer is Sumitomo of Japan, which has a small joint venture with China General the US.

Mr Strachan's strategy is to concentrate BTR's energy and investment upon activities where it can be a global player, or at least dominate regional markets. But after a 25 per cent slump in BTR's share price since last August, to just 255½p on Friday, the City is keen to see him deliver.

Unless the share price recovers, BTR will find itself deprived of a £240m inflow of funds which had been expected this year as investors converted warrants into shares.

The shares are now trading below the conversion price. BZW, joint broker to BTR along with Cazenove, last week cut its forecast for 1996 pre-tax profits by £45m to £1.45bn. The broker blamed weakness in polymer prices and delays in new model programmes at Ford and Chrysler in the US, which hit BTR's automotive business.

The Financial Times, 24 June 1996

Exhibit 8.0 A company needs to keep an eagle eye on its cash flow

In previous chapters, we have been dealing with manufacturing, trading, profit and loss accounts, and balance sheets, and we have prepared them using the accounting rules laid down in Chapter 2. The accounts that we have prepared have provided us with some basic information about the profitability of a particular entity (i.e. how well it has performed), but we have been much less concerned about its *liquidity* (i.e. how much cash it has got). In fact, the type of basic accounts with which we have been dealing tell us very little about an entity's *cash* position.

This is rather curious, because such information is vital. An entity is technically insolvent (i.e. it is unlawful for it to carry on in business) if it cannot pay its creditors. We can, of course, always check the cash position by having a look at the balance sheet, but it tells us very little. What we really need is a statement that gives us some detail about the movement in the entity's cash position during a particular period. Since 1991, such a statement has been a professional requirement. It is known as a *cash flow statement*, and it forms the subject of this chapter.

The chapter falls into two main sections. In the first section, we will have a closer look at the relationship between accounting profit and cash flow, and, in the second section, we will examine the construction of a detailed cash flow statement.

Learning objectives	**By the end of this chapter, you will be able to:**
	● **make a distinction between profitability and liquidity;**
	● **prepare a basic cash flow statement.**

PROFIT AND CASH FLOW

Experience has taught accountants that it is unwise to rely entirely upon the profit and loss account and the balance sheet to monitor an entity's liquidity (i.e. cash) position. The opening and closing cash and bank balances can be obtained from the balance sheet, but this does not provide us with any information about the source and disposition of the cash. Such information is vital if we are to know how successful the entity has been in monitoring its cash position, and whether it has got enough cash to cover its future activities.

It is also important to provide some additional evidence about the cash position to those owners of a business for which it is thought that profit is calculated by taking cash receipts away from cash payments. If the owners think this way, then as long as the profit appears acceptable, they might pay very little attention to how much cash is available. If sales are expanding rapidly, for example, the owners and managers may be entirely misled into believing that the entity is doing very well. No wonder that they are completely mystified when the entity suddenly goes into liquidation!

This rather paradoxical situation is known as *over-trading*, and it arises because credit sales get out of step with cash receipts and cash payments. In order to avoid over-trading, it is important to ensure that the entity's daily cash receipts and payments are closely monitored.

You will recall that in an earlier chapter we suggested that owners want to know the answers to three important questions, i.e.:

1 What profit has the business made?
2 How much does the business owe?
3 How much is owed to it?

In view of the importance of keeping a tight control over cash, there ought perhaps to be a fourth question:

4 What is the cash position?

We have stressed throughout the book that accounting profit does not necessarily lead to an automatic increase in cash. This is because accounting statements are normally prepared on the basis of the realization and matching rules. These rules require us to adjust the cash received and the cash paid to reflect the operational activity for a particular accounting period. Thus neither the sales (and other incomes), nor purchases (and other expenses) will necessarily cause an immediate change in the cash position. Furthermore, capital items (such as the purchase of fixed assets and the issue of shares and debentures) are not, of course, included in the profit and loss account.

For these reasons it is very difficult to assess an entity's liquidity position from the information normally disclosed in traditional financial accounting statements. We need another type of statement that will give us a lot more information about what has happened to the cash position during a particular accounting period. This is what a cash flow statement is all about.

CONSTRUCTION

It might occur to you that we are making an awful lot of fuss over something that is very simple. Surely, if we want to know more about the cash position, all we need to do is look in the cash book? If we have access to it, of course, there is no reason why we cannot do this. However, it must be remembered that, even in the smallest of businesses, the cash book is likely to contain a great many entries. It might be relatively easy to prepare a simplified summary of the data contained is the cash book, and sometimes a cash flow statement is prepared in this way. However, it is also possible to compile such a statement by working backwards from information extracted from the profit and loss account and the balance sheet. Exhibit 8.1 shows how this can be done.

Exhibit 8.1 Preparation of a cash flow statement

You are presented with the following information:

DURTON LIMITED
Trading and profit and loss account for the year to 31 December 19X8

	£000	£000
Sales		1 000
Less: Cost of goods sold:		
Opening stock	200	
Purchases	700	
	900	
Less: Closing stock	300	600
Gross profit		400
Operating expenses		250
Net profit		150
Taxation		50
Net profit after tax		100
Dividends		60
Retained profit for the year		£40

DURTON LIMITED
Balance sheet at 31 December 19X8

	19X7		19X8	
	£000	£000	£000	£000
Fixed assets at cost	900		1 050	
Less: Accumulated depreciation	150	750	255	795
Current assets				
Stock	200		300	
Trade debtors	120		150	
Cash	20		45	
	340		495	
Less: Current liabilities				
Trade creditors	70		90	
Taxation	40		50	
Proposed dividend	30		60	
	140	200	200	295
		£950		£1 090
Capital and reserves				
Ordinary shares of £1 each		750		750
Profit and loss account		200		240
		950		990
Loans				
Debenture stock (10%: issued		–		100
1 January 19X8)		£950		£1 090

Required:
Prepare a cash flow statement for the year to 31 December 19X8.

Answer to Exhibit 8.1

DURTON LIMITED
Cash flow statement for the year to 31 December 19X8

	£000
Cash receipts	
Sale of goods (1)	970
Issue of debenture stock (2)	100
	1 070
Cash payments	
Purchases of goods (3)	(680)
Operating expenses (4)	(145)
Taxation (5)	(40)
Dividends (6)	(30)
Purchases of fixed assets (7)	(150)
	(1 045)

	£000
Increase in cash during the year (8)	25
Cash at 1 January 19X8	20
Cash at 31 December 19X8	45

Note: The number shown after each narration refers to the tutorial notes below.

Tutorial notes

1 The cash received from the customers has been calculated by taking the sales figure of £1 000 000, adding the opening trade debtors of £120 000, and then deducting the closing trade debtors of £150 000.

2 The issue of debenture stock equals the closing balance of £100 000 as at 31 December 19X8. As there was no opening balance, all of the debenture stock must have been issued during the year.

3 The cash payments to suppliers has been calculated as follows: purchases + opening trade creditors – closing trade creditors, i.e £700 000 + 70 000 – 90 000.

4 The other cash payments relate to the operating expenses of £250 000 less the depreciation on the fixed assets of £105 000 (i.e. the closing accumulated balance of £255 000 less the opening accumulated depreciation balance of £150 000). As there were no opening or closing debtors or creditors for operating expenses, the whole of the £145 000 must have been paid during the year.

5 The tax paid of £40 000 represents the taxation due for payment at 1 January 19X8, since the amount outstanding at 31 December 19X8 of £50 000 is the same as the figure for tax shown in the profit and loss account.

6 The dividend paid is the same as the proposed dividend at 1 January 19X8, because the dividends shown in the profit and loss account as £60 000 had not been paid at 31 December 19X8.

7 Purchase of fixed assets equals the closing balance of £1 050 000 less the opening balance of £900 000.

8 The increase in cash during the year of £25 000 plus the opening balance of £20 000 equals the closing balance of £45 000.

You are now recommended to work through Exhibit 8.1 again, but this time without reference to the answer.

In Exhibit 8.1, we have shown that there is an obvious close relationship between the profit and loss account, the balance sheet, and a cash flow statement. Exhibit 8.2 shows this relationship in diagrammatic format.

Unfortunately, although the format adopted in preparing the answer to Exhibit 8.1 shows that there is a very close *relationship* between the profit and loss account, the balance sheet, and the cash flow statement, the actual links

Exhibit 8.2 The inter-relationship between the main financial statements

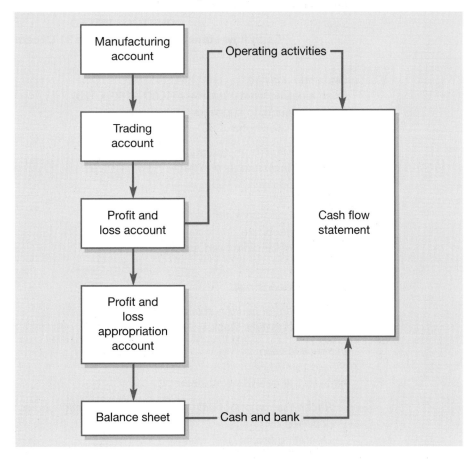

are somewhat difficult to trace. In fact, only two items (the opening and closing cash and bank figures) can be traced without too much difficulty. While the same can also be done for the taxation and dividends figures, this would not necessarily be the case in a more advanced example. Indeed, they would then almost certainly require some fairly complicated adjustments.

DIRECT AND INDIRECT METHODS

It would also be helpful if cash flow statements were produced in a standardized format so that it would be easier to make comparisons between different entities. In Financial Reporting Standard 1 (Revised 1996), the ASB has indicated that there are two acceptable methods for presenting cash flow information: a direct method and an indirect method. Using the data contained in Exhibit 8.l, these methods are illustrated in Exhibits 8.3 and 8.4, respectively.

Exhibit 8.3 The direct method of preparing cash flow statements

DURTON LIMITED
Cash flow statement for the year to 31 December 19X8

	£000
Operating activities	
Cash received from customers (1000 − 150 + 120)	970
Cash payments to suppliers (700 − 90 + 70)	(680)
Other cash payments (250 − 105 − 10)	(135)
Net cash inflow from operating activities	155
Return on investments and servicing of finance	
Interest paid (10% × 100)	(10)
Taxation	
UK corporation tax paid	(40)
Capital expenditure	
Purchase of tangible fixed assets	(150)
	(45)
Equity dividends paid	(30)
	(75)
Management of liquid resources and financing	
Issue of debenture stock	100
Increase in cash	25

Note to the cash flow statement:

Reconciliation of operating profit to net cash inflow from operating activities (1)	£000
Operating profit (2)	160
Depreciation changes (3)	105
Increase in stock (4)	(100)
Increase in debtors (5)	(30)
Increase in creditors (6)	20
	155

Movement in cash	At 1.1.X8	Cash flows	At 31.12.X8
	£000	£000	£000
Cash	20	25	45

Tutorial notes

1 This note is identical to a note which has also to be disclosed if the indirect method is adopted. This means that even if the direct method is preferred, certain characteristics of the indirect method cannot be avoided.

2 The operating profit figure is extracted from the profit and loss account. It is shown before the deduction of debenture interest, taxation and dividends.

3 The depreciation charge of £105 000 is the closing accumulated depreciation balance of £255 000 less the opening accumulated depreciation balance of £150 000.

4 The increase in stocks is the difference between the closing figure of £300 000 and the opening balance of £200 000. An *increase* in stocks represents an *outflow* of cash, whereas a *decrease* in stocks represents an *inflow* of cash.

5 The increase in debtors is the difference between the closing trade debtor figure of £150 000 and the opening figure of £120 000. An *increase* in debtors represents an *outflow* of cash. A *decrease* in debtors represents an *increase* in cash because presumably some cash has been received from debtors, thereby reducing the total amount that they owe.

6 The increase in creditors is the difference between the closing and opening balances of £90 000 and £70 000, respectively. An *increase* in creditors represents an *inflow* of cash (because less cash has been paid out). A *decrease* in creditors represents a cash *outflow* because more cash would appear to have been spent on paying off some of the creditors.

Exhibit 8.3 illustrates the basic format for a cash flow statement for an individual company as recommended by FRS 1 (Revised 1996). The standard also requires the statement to be accompanied by a number of reconciliations (including the one shown) and a series of notes. In order to ensure that the procedure explained here remains relatively straightforward, the other various reconciliations and notes have not been attached to the Exhibit. Exhibit 8.3 shows the direct method of presenting a net cash flow statement. Exhibit 8.4 illustrates the indirect method.

Exhibit 8.4 The indirect method of preparing cash flow statements

DURTON LIMITED
Cash flow statement for the year to 31 December 19X8

	£000
Net cash inflow from operating activities	155
Return on investments and servicing of finance	
Interest paid	(10)
Taxation	
Corporation tax paid	(40)
Capital expenditure	
Payments to acquire tangible fixed assets	(150)
	(45)
Equity dividends paid	(30)
	(75)
Management of liquid resources and financing	
Issue of debenture stock	100
Increase in cash	25

Tutorial notes
1 A note reconciling the operating profit to the net cash inflow from operating activities should be attached to the statement. The note is identical to the one required for the direct method (see Exhibit 8.3).

2 Other reconciliations (including a reconciliation of the movement in cash in the period) and various notes would normally be attached to the statement.

The various reconciliations and notes that are normally attached to the cash flow statement are identical, irrespective of whether the direct or the indirect method is adopted. In practice, both the actual statement itself and the formal notes are likely to contain more items than are shown in Exhibits 8.3 and 8.4. By comparing the two exhibits, it can be seen that the cash flow statements are identical apart from the 'operating activities' section. Which method, therefore, should you adopt: the direct or the indirect method?

In the original FRS 1, the ASB thought that for same companies there might be some extra costs involved if they insisted upon the use of the direct method, because not all companies would have the required information readily available. FRS 1 (Revised 1996) still permits a choice. The direct method would appear to be the most obvious one to adopt for a cash flow statement since it shows the total cash received from customers and the total cash paid to suppliers. Even so, even if the direct method is adopted, FRS 1 (Revised 1996) requires a reconciliation to be made between the operating profit and the net cash inflows/outflows from operating activities. In effect, this means that the indirect method cannot be avoided, and as most companies appear to have opted for it, you are recommended to do likewise.

CONCLUSION

The preparation of a cash flow statement is a complex operation. As a non-accountant, it is most unlikely that you will ever have to prepare one for yourself. It is our view, however, that in order to make the best possible use of such a statement, it is necessary for you to know something about its construction. In this chapter we have attempted to give you sufficient information so that you can construct your own cash flow statements, and in the process learn more about them

A cash flow statement (especially one constructed using the indirect method) links directly with the profit and loss account and the balance sheet. It contains some extremely useful information since, unlike the traditional financial statements, it gives a lot more detail about the movement in the cash position. This is vital, because it is possible for an entity to be profitable without necesssarily having the cash resources to keep it going. Strict control over cash resources is absolutely essential, and a cash flow statement can help in this respect.

This chapter is closely linked with the next one which deals with the interpretation of accounts. Before moving on, however, you are recommended to test your understanding of cash flow statements by attempting some of the chapter questions.

1 Entities may have a long-term profitable future, but in the short term they may be short of cash. This may curb their activities, and in extreme cases, they may be forced out of business.

2 To avoid this happening, owners and managers should be supplied with information about the cash movement and resources of the entity, i.e. about its liquidity. This can be done by preparing a cash flow statement.

3 A cash flow statement can be presented in any format, but most companies are required to adopt the recommendations contained in FRS 1 (Revised 1996).

4 FRS 1 (Revised 1996) permits the cash flow statement to be presented in either: (a) a direct method format, or (b) an indirect method format. The indirect method is preferred, because it can be more easily linked directly to the profit and loss account and the balance sheet.

CHECK YOUR LEARNING

1 State whether each of the following assertions is either true or false:
   (a) Accounting profit is the difference between cash received
       and cash paid.   True/False
   (b) Depreciation reduces the cash position.   True/False
   (c) Tax paid decreases the cash position.   True/False
   (d) A proposed dividend increases the cash position.   True/False
   (e) A decrease in debtors increases the cash position.   True/False
   (f) An increase in creditors decreases the cash position.   True/False

2 Fill in the missing blanks in each of the following statements:
   (a) There are _____ main sections in a cash flow statement.
   (b) If stocks go up, cash goes _____.
   (c) If accruals go up, cash goes _____.
   (d) If the opening cash was £15 000, and the closing cash was £20 000, there
       was a _____ _____ _____ of £5000.

Answers 1 (a) false (b) false (c) true (d) false (e) true (f) false
         2 (a) seven (b) down (c) up (d) net cash inflow

QUESTIONS

8.1

You are presented with the following information:

DENNIS LIMITED
Balance sheet at 31 January 19X2

	31 January 19X1		31 January 19X2	
	£000	£000	£000	£000
Fixed assets				
Land at cost		600		700
Current assets				
Stock	100		120	
Debtors	200		250	
Cash	6		10	
	306		380	
Less: Current liabilities				
Creditors	180	126	220	160
		£726		£860
Capital and reserves				
Ordinary share capital		700		800
Profit and loss account		26		60
		£726		£860

Required:

Prepare Dennis Limited's cash flow statement for the year ended 31 January 19X2.

8.2

The following balance sheets have been prepared for Frank Limited:

Balance sheets at:	28.2.X1		28.2.X2	
	£000	£000	£000	£000
Fixed assets				
Plant and machinery at cost		300		300
Less: Depreciation		80		100
		220		200
Investments at cost		–		100
Current assets				
Stocks	160		190	
Debtors	220		110	
Bank	–		10	
	380		310	
Less: Current liabilities				
Creditors	200		160	
Bank overdraft	20		–	
	220	160	160	150
		£380		£450

	£000	£000	£000	£000
Capital and reserves				
Ordinary share capital		300		300
Share premium account		50		50
Profit and loss account		30		40
		380		390
Shareholders' funds				
Loans				
Debentures		–		60
		£380		£450

Additional information:
There were no purchases or sales of plant and machinery during the year.

Required:
Prepare Frank Limited's cash flow statement for the year ended 28 February 19X2.

8.3
You are presented with the following information:

STARTER
Profit and loss account for the year to 31 March 19X3

	£	£
Sales		10 000
Less: Cost of goods sold:		
Purchases	5 000	
Less: Closing stock	1 000	4 000
Gross profit		6 000
Less: Depreciation		2 000
Net profit for the year		£4 000

Balance sheet at 31 March 19X3

	£	£
Van		10 000
Less: Depreciation		2 000
		8 000
Stock	1 000	
Trade debtors	5 000	
Bank	12 500	
	18 500	
Less: Trade creditors	2 500	16 000
		£24 000
Capital		20 000
Add: Net profit for the year		4 000
		£24 000

Note: Starter commenced business on 1 April 19X2.

Required:

Using the indirect method, compile Starter's cash flow statement for the year ended 31 March 19X3.

8.4

The following is a summary of Gregory Limited's accounts for the year ended 30 April 19X4:

Profit and loss account for the year ended 30 April 19X4

	£000
Net profit before tax	75
Taxation	25
	50
Dividend (proposed)	40
Retained profit for the year	£10

Balance sheet at 30 April 19X4

	30.4.X9		30.4.X4	
	£000	£000	£000	£000
Fixed assets				
Plant at cost		400		550
Less: Depreciation		100		180
		300		370
Current assets				
Stocks	50		90	
Debtors	70		50	
Bank	10		2	
	130		142	
Less: Current liabilities				
Creditors	45		55	
Taxation	18		25	
Proposed dividend	35		40	
	98	32	120	22
		£332		£392
Capital and reserves				
Ordinary share capital		200		200
Profit and loss account		132		142
		332		342
Loans		–		50
		£332		£392

Additional information:

There were no sales of fixed assets during the year ended 30 April 19X4.

Required:

Prepare Gregory Limited's cash flow statement for the year ended 30 April 19X4.

8.5

The following summarized accounts have been prepared for Pill Limited:

Profit and loss account for the year ended 31 May 19X5

	19X4 £000	19X5 £000
Sales	2 400	3 000
Less: Cost of goods sold	1 600	2 000
Gross profit	800	1 000
Less: Expenses:		
Administrative expenses	310	320
Depreciation: vehicles	55	60
furniture	35	40
	400	420
Net profit	400	580
Taxation	120	150
	280	430
Dividends	200	250
Retained profits for the year	£80	£180

Balance sheet at 31 May 19X5

	31.5.X4 £000	31.5.X4 £000	31.5.X5 £000	31.5.X5 £000
Fixed assets				
Vehicles at cost	600		800	
Less: Depreciation	200	400	260	540
Furniture	200		250	
Less: Depreciation	100	100	140	110
Current assets				
Stocks	400		540	
Debtors	180		200	
Cash	320		120	
	900		860	
Less: Current liabilities				
Creditors	270		300	
Corporation tax	170		220	
Proposed dividends	150		100	
	590	310	620	240
		£810		£890
Capital and reserves				
Ordinary share capital		500		550
Profit and loss account		120		300
Shareholders' funds		620		850
Loans				
Debentures (10%)		190		40
		£810		£890

Additional information:
There were no sales of fixed assets during the year ended 31 May 19X5.

Required:
Compile Pill Limited's cash flow statement for the year ended 31 May 19X5.

8.6
The following information relates to Brian Limited for the year ended 30 June 19X6:

Profit and loss account for the year to 30 June 19X6

	£000	£000
Gross profit		230
Administrative expenses	76	
Loss on sale of vehicle	3	
Increase in provision for doubtful debts	1	
Depreciation on vehicles	35	115
Net profit		115
Taxation		65
		50
Dividends		25
Retained profit for the year		£25

Balance sheet at 30 June 19X6

	19X5		19X6	
	£000	£000	£000	£000
Fixed assets				
Vehicle at cost		150		200
Less: Depreciation		75		100
		75		100
Current assets				
Stocks		60		50
Trade debtors	80		100	
Less: Provision for bad and doubtful debts	4	76	5	95
Cash		6		8
		142		153
Current liabilities				
Trade creditors	(60)		(53)	
Taxation	(52)		(65)	
Proposed dividend	(20)	(132)	(25)	(143)
		£85		£110
Capital and reserves				
Ordinary share capital		75		75
Profit and loss account		10		35
		£85		£110

Additional information:

1 The company purchased some new vehicles during the year for £75 000.
2 During the year the company sold a vehicle for £12 000 in cash. The vehicle had originally cost £25 000, and £10 000 had been set aside for depreciation.

Required:
Prepare a cash flow statement for Brian Limited for the year ended 30 June 19X6.

ADDITIONAL QUESTIONS (WITHOUT ANSWERS)

8.7

The following summarized information relates to Weir Limited for the year ended 30 September 19X9:

Profit and loss account

	£000
Profit before taxation	320
Taxation	100
Profit after taxation	220
Dividends	80
Retained profit for the year	£140

Balance sheets at 30 September

	19X8	19X9
	£000	£000
Fixed assets		
At cost	2 130	2 560
Less: Accumulated depreciation	740	930
	1 390	1 630
Current assets		
Stocks	470	535
Trade debtors	540	620
Prepayments	45	40
	1 055	1 195
Current liabilities		
Bank overdraft	(95)	(110)
Trade creditors	(145)	(180)
Accruals	(50)	(30)
Taxation	(200)	(50)
Dividends	(60)	(70)
	(550)	(440)
Debenture loans (10%)	(580)	(630)
	£1 315	£1 755

	£000	£000
Capital and reserves		
Called up share capital	350	615
Share premium account	15	30
Revaluation reserve	130	150
Profit and loss account	820	960
	£1 315	£1 755

Additional information:

1 A provision for bad and doubtful debts is maintained. At 1 October 19X8, the balance was £30 000, and at 30 September 19X9 it was £40 000.
2 During the year to 30 September 19X9, fixed assets originally costing £65 000 (and on which depreciation of £40 000 had been charged) were sold for £30 000 in cash.

Required:

Prepare Weir's cash flow statement for the year ended 30 September 19X9.

8.8

The following summarized information relates to Conway Limited:

Profit and loss account for the year ended 31 October 19X9

	£000
Gross profit	2 400
Distribution costs	(190)
Administration expenses	(900)
Profit before taxation	1 310
Taxation	(200)
Profit after taxation	1 110
Dividends	(170)
Retained profit for the year	£940

Balance sheets at 31 October

	19X8	19X9
	£000	£000
Fixed assets		
At cost	3 400	5 800
Less: Accumulated depreciation	1 400	2 100
	2 000	3 700
Current assets		
Stocks	700	100
Trade debtors (net of provision)	2 000	6 000
Other debtors	200	250
Bank and cash	950	–
	3 850	6 350
c/f	5 850	10 050

		19X8	19X9
		£000	£000
	b/f	5 850	10 050
Current liabilities			
Bank overdraft		–	(400)
Trade creditors		(300)	(1 200)
Other creditors		(400)	(210)
Taxation		(350)	(450)
Dividend		(100)	(150)
		(1 150)	(2 410)
Long-term loans (15% debenture stock)		–	(2 000)
		£4 700	£5 640
Capital and reserves			
Called up share capital		2 500	3 500
Share premium account		500	500
Profit and loss account		1 700	1 640
		£4 700	£5 640

Additional information:

1 During the year to 31 October 19X9, fixed assets originally costing £650 000 were sold for £300 000 in cash. The accumulated depreciation on these fixed assets was £400 000.

2 The company maintains a provision for bad and doubtful trade debtors. The provision at 1 November 19X8 was £100 000 and at 31 October 19X9 it was £500 000.

3 During the year to 31 October 19X9, a bonus issue of two shares for every five shares held was made to the company's shareholders.

Required:
Prepare Conway's cash flow statement for the year ended 31 October 19X9.

DISCUSSION QUESTIONS

8.9 'Proprietors are more interested in cash than profit.' Discuss.

8.10 It has been argued by some academic accountants that the traditional historic cost accounting model should be replaced by a system of cash flow accounting. How far do you agree?

8.11 Does a cash flow statement serve any useful purpose?

CHAPTER 9

Interpretation of accounting data

Late payment worsens for smaller businesses

Average payment times to smaller businesses have increased for the first time, according to a survey published last week by Grant Thornton.

Michael Rogerson, a senior partner with Grant Thornton, said businesses could improve their payment times by ensuring that terms were clearly set out at the start of the week. He added that a statutory right to interest, which some firms have called for, would not solve the problem.

Rogerson said the new draft British Standard on prompt payment was the best solution to the late payment problem for smaller businesses.

This point was echoed by Giles Wintle, head of business law at the English ICA. 'Legislation on statutory interest may work against smaller businesses as they will also have to pay interest on their own late paid debts,' he said.

The Confederation of British Industry is now collecting comments from businesses on the draft British Standard which is meant to improve commercial payment practice.

The CBI will release a final set of recommendations during the summer.

The problem of late payments to smaller companies has also been highlighted by the Trade Indemnity Group's latest quarterly financial survey. It shows that smaller companies are 10 times more likely to have their invoices left unpaid for more than 30 days after the due date.

Accountancy Age, 29 February 1996

Exhibit 9.0 Debt collection can be a problem for all companies

In previous chapters, we have shown that a set of basic financial accounts can tell you a great deal about an entity's performance. In this chapter, we are going to explain how you can use those accounts to an even greater effect, i.e. how to squeeze out the maximum possible amount of information. Accountants call this process 'interpretation', and it forms the subject of this chapter.

In order to understand the importance of this topic, we need to review some of the material covered in the earlier part of the book. We do so in the next section.

By the end of this chapter, you will be able to:

● **explain the usefulness and importance of ratio analysis;**

● **calculate at least nine basic accounting ratios;**

● **apply those ratios in interpreting a set of accounts.**

BACKGROUND

You will recall that, in Chapter 1, we suggested that owners want to know the answers to three basic questions. We keep coming back to these questions, and as they are so important we will repeat them once again. They are as follows:

1 How much profit has the business made?
2 How much does the business owe?
3 How much is owed to the business?

In Chapters 3 to 7 we described how an accountant would go about trying to answer these questions, but as we have seen, the method is far from satisfactory. The profit and loss account provides only an *estimate* of an entity's profitability, while the balance sheet is a mishmash of different costs and values.

If such results are used in isolation, the owner could be misled by the apparent long-term trend of his profits, and by his current liquidity (i.e. cash) position. For example, his debtor and creditor balances do not tell him very much: are they too high or too low? A debtor's balance of £200 000 would appear be a very large amount for a small business, but it would be insignificant for a large international company.

The results, therefore, need to be put into context, and we need to go into them in much greater detail.

It might also be necessary to do this in order to satisfy the demand for information from other groups of interested parties, e.g. analysts, creditors, employees, the general public, the government, investors, journalists, management, shareholders, and trade unions. All of these groups will have some interest in how an entity performs (especially if it is a public company), and the information contained within the basic statements may not tell them what they want to know.

If you are asked to interpret a set of accounts, therefore, the amount of work you will have to undertake will depend upon the reasons for your investigation. For example, if you are asked to examine a company's accounts because your own company is considering making a take-over bid, you will probably need all the information that you can get. However, if you are a creditor, your main interest will be in finding out whether the company is in a position to pay what it owes you.

It might be helpful if we give you some general guidance that you can follow in carrying out your investigation, but obviously you will need to adapt it to suit the circumstances.

Obtaining information

You are recommended to look at the economic environment in which the company operates. In which countries is it based? What is the state of their economies? What are the prospects for the economic sector in which the company is placed? How does it compare with other companies in the same sector?

Then try to obtain as much information about the company as you can. It is not usually difficult to obtain information if you search for it. You can start with the company's annual report and accounts, and the company's own public relations department may be willing to supply you with additional information about the company. There are also a number of commercial agencies that specialize in obtaining company information, and you may be able to find some information in newspaper and journal articles.

You will find that by assimilating information about the company from such a wide range of sources, you will already have got some idea of its performance.

Calculating trends and ratios

It is desirable to look at the company's progress over a number of years. As a general rule, it is recommended that you think in terms of a three- to a five-year period. Anything less than three years does not enable you to plot much of a trend, and beyond five years the data can become somewhat out of date.

Once you have collected some data, you can use them to establish some trends and to calculate some statistics. The exact number and type will depend upon the purpose of your investigation, and some of them may need to be fairly specialist. For example, if you were dealing with a hotel's accounts, you might want to calculate the rooms occupied as a proportion of the total number of rooms in the hotel, or in the case of a retailing organization, the staff salaries of the sale personnel as a proportion of sales revenue.

You can begin to assess the trends and calculate the ratios by using a number of different techniques, but they all have one overriding purpose: they attempt to put the accounting information into context. The four main techniques are shown in Exhibit 9.1, and they may be summarized as follows:

1 **Horizontal analysis**. This technique involves making a line-by-line comparison of the company's accounts for each accounting period that you have chosen to investigate. You might observe, for example, that the sales were £100m in 1996, £110m in 1997, and £137.5m in 1998. Thus, they have increased by 10% in 1997, and by 25% in 1998. This type of comparison is something that we tend to do naturally when we look at a set of accounts, although if you are going to calculate the percentage changes, you will probably need a calculator.

2 **Trend analysis**. Trend analysis is similar to horizontal analysis, except that the first set of accounts in the series is given a weighting of 100. Subsequent accounts are then related to the base of 100. In the example used above, the 1996 sales would be expressed as 100, the 1997 sales as 110, and the 1998 sales as 137.5. This method enables us to see what changes have taken place much more easily than by inspecting the absolute amounts. For example, it is much easier to grasp the significance of, say, 159 than it is £323 739 392.

3 **Vertical analysis**. This technique requires all of the profit and loss account, and all of the balance sheet items to be expressed as a percentage of their respective totals. For example, if trade debtors in 1998 were £20m and the balance sheet total was £50m, trade debtors would be expressed as 40%, compared (say) with 35% in 1997, and 30% in 1996. Again, the reason for adopting this method is that it is much easier to grasp the significance of the figures.

4 **Ratio analysis**. We are shortly going to deal with ratio analysis in some detail, but for the moment, all you need note is that a ratio attempts to relate one item to another item, e.g. 20 to 40, and then perhaps express the relationship as a percentage, i.e. 50% ($\frac{20}{40} \times 100$).

If you had adopted all of the above techniques in your analysis, you would already have a great deal of information about the company, so you could now begin a detailed assessment of it. It is likely, however, that you would be selective in adopting the above four techniques. For example, in trend analysis, you probably would not need to calculate a trend for literally every line in the accounts: you would be much more likely to choose only the most significant items.

There is one further point that we need to make before moving on to the next section. It is probable that the annual accounts have not been adjusted for inflation, so to make a fairer comparison between different accounting periods, you should make some allowance for inflation. We return to this subject in Chapter 12, but we suggest that for the moment, you could use the Retail Price Index (RPI) as a rough guide.

In the next section, we take a closer look at ratio analysis.

Exhibit 9.1 Main analytical techniques used in interpreting accounts

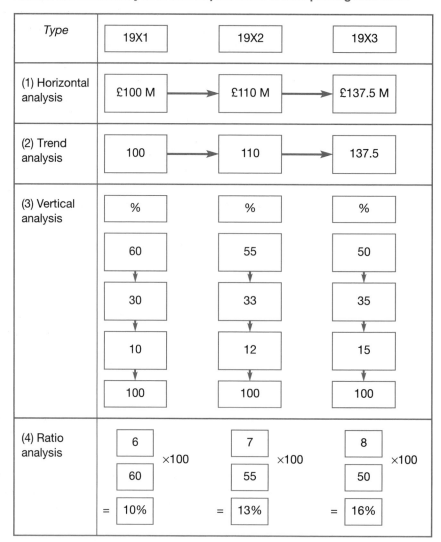

RATIO ANALYSIS

In this section we are going to deal with ratio analysis in some detail. We need to do so, otherwise it is unlikely that you will understand it! But don't be put off! You will find that the time spent studying this topic will be well worth while: you will find it useful in both your business and your private life, e.g. if you ever want to buy some shares.

We will start our study by examining what is meant by a *ratio*. Data may be extracted from accounting statements and converted into statistics. These statistics can then be used to examine an entity's performance over a given period of time. They may also be used to compare the current year's performance with previous years, or with similar entities. Such comparisons may be done on a percentage basis or by using simple factors. For example, we might report that the net profit is 7% of the annual sales, or that the dividend for the year represents three times the profit for that year. In order to make such statistics easier to understand, we will refer to them all as *ratios*.

In order to establish clearly the concept underpinning a ratio, we will assume that you have put £1000 in a building society account on 1 January 1994. During the year to 31 December 1994, you leave the £1000 in your account. You do not withdraw any of it, and you do not add to it. At the end of the year, the building society credits you with £100 of interest. If we express the interest received as a *ratio*, the calculation will be as follows:

$$\frac{£100}{1000} \times 100 = \underline{\underline{10\%}}$$

This might all seem quite obvious, but it is worth labouring the point. The £100 received represents 10% of the £1000 invested. In other words, there is a clear relationship between the interest earned and what it took to earn it.

You will find that as we go through this chapter we are going to express many other accounting relationships in the form of percentages. Make sure, therefore, that you always establish a clear, meaningful relationship between the numerator (the £100 in the above example), and the denominator (the £1000 in the example). This is not always easy, so be careful, and make sure that you do not try to link some quite spurious relationships, such as dividends received to the cost of goods sold.

It would be possible to produce hundreds of recognized accounting ratios, but for the purposes of this book, we will limit ourselves to just a small number of key ones. We do so for three main reasons:

1 we do not need to use very many ratios in demonstrating the *principles* of ratio analysis;
2 a select number of ratios will give sufficient information;
3 experience suggests that in analysing the ratios, it is difficult to deal with more than just a select few.

For convenience, we will examine the main ratios under four main headings: (a) profitabililty ratios; (b) liquidity ratios; (c) efficiency ratios; and (d) investment ratios. This classification is, however, somewhat arbitrary, and some ratios could be included in another grouping. A diagrammatic version of the classification adopted is shown in Exhibit 9.2.

Exhibit 9.2 Classification of accounting ratios

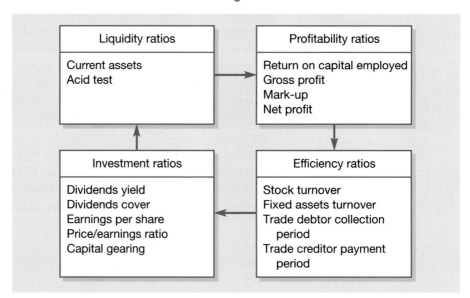

PROFITABILITY RATIOS

Users of accounts will want to know how much profit a business has made, and then to compare it with previous periods or with other entities. The absolute level of accounting profit will not be of much help, because it needs to be related to the size of the entity, and how much capital it has got invested in it. There are four main profitability ratios, and they are examined in the following sections.

Return on capital employed ratio

The best way of assessing profitability is to calculate a ratio known as the *return on capital employed* (ROCE) ratio. It can be expressed quite simply as:

$$\frac{\text{Profit}}{\text{Capital}} \times 100 = \text{X\%}$$

This ratio (like most other ratios) is usually expressed as a percentage, and it is one of the most important. Even so, there is no common agreement about how it should be calculated. The problem is that both 'profit' and 'capital' can be defined in several different ways. As a result, a variety of ROCE ratios can be produced merely by changing the definitions of either profit or capital. The main definitions are listed below:

Profit

1 Operating profit
2 Net profit before interest and taxation
3 Net profit before taxation
4 Net profit after taxation
5 Net profit after taxation and preference dividend

Capital

1 Total assets
2 Total assets less intangible assets
3 Total assets less current liabilities
4 Shareholders' funds
5 Shareholders' funds less preference shares
6 Shareholders' funds plus long-term loans
7 Shareholders' funds plus total liabilities (this might be the same as total assets)

Which definitions should you adopt? Provided that the numerator and denominator are compatible, that really depends upon your purpose. If you are looking at profit from the point of view of the entity as a whole, we would suggest that you should select the *net profit before interest and taxation*. This should then be related to the total amount of capital needed to generate it, i.e. *shareholders' funds plus long-term loans* (long-term loans are included because we have taken the profit *before* interest). However, if we were looking at profit from only an ordinary shareholder's point of view, we might define profit as being the *net profit after taxation and preference dividends* (i.e. the amount available for distribution to ordinary shareholders), and capital as *shareholders' funds less preference shares* (i.e. the total amount of capital that the ordinary shareholders have invested in the business). Does this latter relationship make sense to you? Net profit after taxation and preference dividends reflects what *could* be distributed to ordinary shareholders. Shareholders' funds less preference shares gives the total amount of capital contributed (or financed) by the ordinary shareholders (ordinary shares + capital reserves + revenue reserves + other reserves + retained profits).

Irrespective of the definitions, ROCE is often calculated using the capital as at the year end. However, as profit builds up during the year, we really ought to take the *average* capital invested in the entity during the year. If so, it is customary to take a simple average, i.e. ½ (opening capital + closing capital).

You may need to calculate ROCE for different purposes, so it would be useful if we summarize the main methods used in calculating this most important ratio. Here they are:

$$1 \quad \frac{\text{Net profit before taxation}}{\text{Average shareholders' funds}} \times 100 = X\%$$

$$2 \quad \frac{\text{Net profit after taxation}}{\text{Average shareholders' funds}} \times 100 = X\%$$

3
$$\frac{\text{Net profit after taxation and preference dividends}}{\text{Average shareholders' funds less preference shares}} \times 100 = X\%$$

4
$$\frac{\text{Profit before taxation and interest}}{\text{Average shareholders' funds plus long-term loans}} \times 100 = X\%$$

By calculating the return on capital employed, we can get a far better idea of the entity's profitability than we can by merely looking at the absolute level of profit. ROCE means that we can avoid making sweeping assertions about (say) a profit of £500 million being high (it might be thought rather poor if the capital employed was £10 billion), or a profit of £500 being low (it might be acceptable if the capital invested was £2000). High and low in this context can only be viewed in a relative sense.

There are a number of other important profitability ratios which we ought to consider. One is the *gross profit ratio*.

Gross profit ratio

This ratio enables us to judge how successful the entity has been at trading. It is calculated as follows:

$$\frac{\text{Gross profit}}{\text{Total sales revenue}} \times 100 = X\%$$

The gross profit ratio measures how much profit the entity has earned in relation to the amount of sales that it has made. The definition of gross profit does not usually cause any problems. Most entities adopt the definition which we have used in this book, viz. sales less the cost of goods sold, so meaningful comparisons can usually be made between different entities.

Mark-up ratio

The gross profit ratio complements another main trading ratio: for convenience, we will refer to it as the *mark-up ratio*. The mark-up ratio is calculated as follows:

$$\frac{\text{Gross profit}}{\text{Cost of goods sold}} \times 100 = X\%$$

Mark-up ratios measure the amount of profit added to the cost of goods sold [i.e. cost of goods sold = (opening stock + purchases) – closing stock], and the cost of goods sold plus profit equals the sales revenue. The mark up may be reduced to stimulate extra sales activity, but this will have the effect of reducing the gross profit. However, if extra goods are sold, there may be a greater volume of sales. This will help to compensate for the reduction in the mark up on each unit.

180

Net profit ratio

Owners sometimes like to compare their net profit with the sales revenue. This can be expressed in the form of the net profit ratio. The *net profit ratio* is calculated as follows:

$$\frac{\text{Net profit before taxation}}{\text{Total sales revenue}} \times 100 = X\%$$

It is difficult to compare fairly the net profit ratio for different entities. Individual operating and financing arrangements vary so much that entities are bound to have different levels of expenditure, no matter how efficient one entity is compared with another. Thus it may only be realistic to use the net profit ratio in making *internal* comparisons. Over a period of time, a pattern may emerge, and it might then be possible to establish a trend. If you do use the net profit ratio to make inter-company comparisons, make sure you allow for different circumstances.

We can now turn to our second main category of accounting ratios: liquidity ratios.

LIQUIDITY RATIOS

Liquidity ratios measure the extent to which assets can be quickly turned into cash. In other words, they try to assess how much cash the entity has available in the short term (this usually means within the next twelve months). For example, it is easy to extract the total amount of trade debtors and trade creditors from the balance sheet, but are they perhaps too high? We cannot really tell until we put them into context. We can do this by calculating two liquidity ratios known as the *current assets ratio* and the *acid test ratio*.

Current assets ratio

The current assets ratio is calculated as follows:

$$\frac{\text{Current assets}}{\text{Current liabilities}}$$

It is usually expressed as a factor, e.g. 3 to 1, or 3 : 1, although you will sometimes see it expressed as a percentage.

In most circumstances we can expect that current assets will be in excess of current liabilities. The current assets ratio will then be at least 1 : 1. If this is not the case, the entity may not have sufficient liquid resources available (i.e. current assets that can be quickly turned into cash) to meet its immediate financial commitments. Some textbooks argue that the current ratio must be at least 2 : 1, but there is no evidence to support this assertion. You are not, therefore, advised to accept that a 2 : 1 relationship is required.

The term 'current' means receivable or payable within the next twelve months, so the entity may not always have to settle all of its current debts within the next week or even the next month. Be careful, then, before you assume that a factor of (say) 1 : 2 suggests that the company will be going into immediate liquidation! For example, corporation tax may not have to be paid for at least nine months, and it may be several months before a proposed dividend is actually paid. In the meantime, the company may receive regular receipts of cash from its debtors, and it may be able to balance these against what it has to pay to its creditors. In other instances, some entities (such as supermarkets), do not do much trade on credit terms, so it is not uncommon for them to have a current assets ratio of less than 2 : 1. This is not likely to be a problem for them, because they are probably collecting large amounts of cash daily through the check-outs. In some cases, however, a current assets ratio of less than 2 : 1 may signify a serious financial position, especially if the current assets consist of a very high proportion of stocks. This leads us on to the second liquidity ratio: the acid test ratio.

Acid test ratio

It may not be easy to dispose of stocks in the short term as they cannot always be readily turned into cash, but in any case, the entity would then be depriving itself of those very assets that enable it to make a trading profit. It seems sensible, therefore, to see what would happen to the current ratio if stocks were not included in the definition of current assets. This ratio is called the acid test (or quick) ratio. It is calculated as follows:

$$\frac{\text{Current assets} - \text{stocks}}{\text{Current liabilities}}$$

Like the current ratio, the acid test ratio is usually expressed as a factor (or occasionally as a percentage). It is probably a better measure of the entity's immediate liquidity position than the current assets ratio because it excludes stocks since they cannot always be readily sold. Do not assume, however, that if current assets less stocks are less than the current liabilities, then the entity's cash position is vulnerable. As we explained above, some of the current liabilities may not be due for payment for some months. As with the current assets ratio, some textbooks suggest that the acid test ratio must be at least 1 : 1, but once again there is no evidence to support this view, so you are advised not to accept it.

EFFICIENCY RATIOS

Traditional accounting statements do not tell us how *efficiently* an entity has been managed, that is, how well its resources have been looked after. Profit may, to some extent, be used as a measure of efficiency, but as we have explained in earlier chapters, accounting profit is subject to too many arbitrary adjustments to be entirely reliable. What we need to do, therefore, is put what evidence we do have into context, and then to compare it with earlier accounting periods and with other similar entities.

There are very many different types of ratios that we can use to measure the efficiency of an entity, but in this book we will cover only the more common ones.

Stock turnover ratio

The stock turnover ratio may be calculated as follows:

$$\frac{\text{Cost of goods sold}}{\text{Average stock}} = \times \text{ times}$$

The average stock is usually calculated as follows:

$$\frac{\text{Opening stock} + \text{closing stock}}{2}$$

The stock turnover ratio is normally expressed as a number (e.g. 5 or 10) and not as a percentage. Note that there are also various other ways in which this ratio can be calculated.

Sometimes the sales revenue is substituted for the cost of goods sold, but it should not be used if it can be avoided because the sales contain a profit loading which can cause the ratio to become distorted. Many accountants also prefer to substitute a more accurate average stock level than the simple average shown above (particularly if goods are purchased at irregular intervals). It is also quite common to compare the *closing* stock with the cost of sales in order to gain a clearer idea of the stock position at the end of the year. This may be misleading, however, if the company's trade is seasonal, and the year end falls during a quiet period.

The greater the turnover of stock, the more efficient the entity would appear to be in purchasing and selling goods. A stock turnover of 2, for example, would suggest that the entity has about six months of sales in stock. In most circumstances, this would appear to be high, whereas a stock turnover of (say) 12 would mean that the entity had only a month's normal sales in stock.

Fixed assets turnover ratio

Another important area to examine from the point of view of efficiency, relates to fixed assets. Fixed assets (such as plant and machinery) enable the business to function more efficiently, so a high level of fixed assets ought to generate more sales. We can check this by calculating a ratio known as the *fixed assets turnover ratio*. This may be done as follows:

$$\frac{\text{Total sales revenue}}{\text{Fixed assets at net book value}} = X$$

The fixed assets turnover ratio may also be expressed as a percentage. The more times that the fixed assets are covered by the sales revenue, the greater the recovery of the investment in fixed assets.

This ratio is really only useful if it is compared with previous periods or with other entities. In isolation, it does not mean very much. For example, is a turnover of 5 good and 4 poor? All we can suggest is that if the trend is upwards, then the investment in fixed assets is beginning to pay off, at least in terms of increased sales. Note also that the ratio can be strongly affected by the entity's depreciation policies. There is an argument, therefore, for taking the gross book value of the fixed assets, and not the net book value.

Trade debtor collection period

Investing in fixed assets is all very well, but there is not much point in generating extra sales if the customers do not pay for them. Customers might be encouraged to buy more by a combination of lower selling prices and generous credit terms. If the debtors are slow at paying, the entity might find that it has run into cash flow problems. It is important, therefore, for it to watch its trade debtor position very carefully. We can check how successful it has been by calculating the *average trade debtor collection period*. The ratio is calculated as follows:

$$\frac{\text{Average trade debtors}}{\text{Total credit sales}} \times 365 = X \text{ days}$$

The average trade debtors are usually calculated by using a simple average [i.e. ½ (opening trade debtors + closing trade debtors)]. The closing trade debtor figure is sometimes substituted for average trade debtors. This is acceptable, provided that the figure is representative of the overall period.

It is important to relate trade debtors to credit sales if possible, so cash sales should be excluded from the calculation. The method shown above for calculating the ratio would relate the average trade debtors to X days' sales, but it would be possible to substitute weeks or months for days. It is not customary to express the ratio as a percentage.

An acceptable debtor collection period cannot be suggested, as much depends upon the type of trade in which the entity is engaged. Some entities expect settlement within 28 days of delivery of the goods, or on immediate receipt of the invoice. Other entities might expect settlement within 28 days following the end of the month in which the goods were delivered. On average, this adds another 14 days (half a month) to the overall period of 28 days. If this is the case, a company would appear to be highly efficient in collecting its debts if the average debtor collection period was about 42 days (in the United Kingdom, the *median* debtor collection period is 50 days).

Like most of the other ratios, however, it is important to establish a trend, and if the trend is upwards, then it might suggest that the company's credit control was beginning to weaken.

Trade creditor payment period

A similar ratio can be calculated for the average trade creditor payment period. The formula is as follows:

$$\frac{\text{Average trade creditors}}{\text{Total credit purchases}} \times 365 = X \text{ days}$$

The average trade creditors would again be a simple average of the opening and closing balances, although it is quite common to use the closing trade creditors. The trade creditors must be related to credit purchases, and weeks or months may be substituted for the number of days. Like the trade debtor collection period, it is not usual to express it as a percentage.

An upward trend in the average level of trade creditors would suggest that the entity is having some difficulty in finding the cash to pay its creditors. Indeed, it might be a sign that it is running into financial difficulties.

INVESTMENT RATIOS

The various ratios examined in the previous sections are probably of interest to all users of accounts, such as creditors, employees, and managers, as well as shareholders. There are, however, some other ratios which are primarily (although not exclusively) of interest to prospective investors. These ratios are known as *investment* ratios.

Dividend yield

The first investment ratio which you might find useful is the dividend yield. It usually applies to *ordinary* shareholders, and it may be calculated as follows:

$$\frac{\text{Dividend per share}}{\text{Market price per share}} \times 100 = X\%$$

The dividend yield measures the rate of return an investor gets by comparing the cost of his shares with the dividend receivable (or paid). For example, if an investor buys 100 £1 ordinary shares at a market rate of 200p per share, and the dividend was 10p, his yield would be 5% (10/200 × 100). As far as the company is concerned, while he may have invested £200 (100 × £2 per share), he will be registered as holding 100 shares at a nominal value of £1 each (100 shares × £1). He would be entitled, therefore, to a dividend of £10 (10p × 100 shares), but from the shareholder's individual point of view, he will only be getting a return of 5%, i.e. £10 for his £200 invested.

Dividend cover

Another useful investment ratio is called dividend cover. It is calculated as follows:

$$\text{Divided cover} = \frac{\text{Net profit after taxation and preference dividend}}{\text{Paid and proposed ordinary dividends}} = X \text{ times}$$

This ratio shows the number of times that ordinary dividend could be paid out of current earnings. The dividend is usually described as being X times covered by the earnings. Thus, if the dividend is covered twice, the company would be paying out half of its earnings as an ordinary dividend.

Earnings per share

Another important investment ratio is that known as earnings per share (EPS). This ratio enables us to put the profit into context, and to avoid looking at it in simple absolute terms. It is usually looked at from the ordinary shareholder's point of view, and it may be calculated as follows:

$$\frac{\text{Net profit after taxation and preference dividend}}{\text{Number of ordinary shares in issue during the year}} = Xp$$

It is customary to calculate this ratio by taking the net profit after taxation (although there is no reason why it could not be taken before taxation). Preference dividends are deducted because they are usually paid before ordinary shareholders receive a dividend.

EPS enables a fair comparison to be made between one year's earnings and another by relating the earnings to something tangible, i.e. the number of shares in issue.

Price/earnings ratio

Another common investment ratio is the price earnings ratio (or P/E ratio). It is calculated as follows:

$$\frac{\text{Market price per share}}{\text{Earnings per share}} = X$$

The P/E ratio enables a comparison to be made between the earnings per share (as defined above) and the market price. It tells us that the market price is X times the earnings. It means that it would take X years before we recovered the market price paid for the shares out of the earnings (assuming that they remained at that level, and that they were all distributed). Thus the P/E ratio is a multiple of earnings, and a high or low ratio can only be judged in relation to other companies in the same sector of the market.

Capital gearing ratio

We come finally to our last investment ratio: the *capital gearing ratio*. This is usually a most difficult one for students to understand, possibly because (like ROCE) there are so many ways of calculating it.

As we outlined in an Chapter 7, companies are financed out of a mixture of share capital, retained profits and borrowings. Borrowings may be long term (such as debentures), or short term (such as credit given by trade creditors). In addition, the company may have set aside all sorts of provisions (e.g. for taxation) which it expects to meet sometime in the future. These may also be regarded as 'borrowings'. From an ordinary shareholder's point of view, even preference share capital can be classed as 'borrowings', because the preference shareholders may have priority over ordinary shareholders, both in respect of dividends and upon liquidation.

If a company, therefore, finances itself from a high level of borrowings, there is obviously a higher risk in investing in it. This arises for two main reasons:

1 the higher the borrowings, the more interest that the company will have to pay, and that may affect the company's ability to pay an ordinary dividend;
2 if the company cannot find the cash to repay its borrowings, the ordinary shareholders may not get any money back if the company goes into liquidation.

As far as item 1 is concerned, there will be no real problem if income is rising, because the interest on borrowings will become a smaller and smaller proportion of the total income. But it could become a problem if income is falling and the interest is having to be paid out of a continuing decline in income. It might then be difficult to pay out any ordinary dividend.

There are many different ways of calculating capital gearing, so the first point we need to establish is: what is our objective? The objective can be expressed as follows:

To calculate the proportion of the entity financed out of borrowings.

But how should it be calculated? There are three factors involved in the relationship: (a) the amount financed by the ordinary shareholders; (b) the amount financed out of borrowings; and (c) the total amount of financing. This may be put in the form of an equation:

Shareholders' funds + borrowings = total amount financed

This equation is normally expressed in the form of a ratio. There are several ways of calculating it, the two most common being as follows:

1
$$\frac{\text{Borrowings}}{\text{Shareholders' funds} + \text{borrowings}}$$

$$2 \qquad \frac{\text{Borrowings}}{\text{Shareholders' funds}}$$

We prefer the first method, since if we express it as a percentage, it appears clearer, i.e. 'X% of the company has been financed by borrowings'. The second method tells us the borrowings represent a certain proportion of the shareholders' funds (including preference shares). You might not agree with our reasoning, and if you prefer the second method, there is no reason why you should not use it.

Irrespective of which method we adopt, we now have to decide what we mean by 'shareholders' funds' and 'borrowings'. It is not too difficult to define shareholders' funds. They include the following items:

- Ordinary share capital
- Preference share capital (see below)
- Share premium account
- Capital reserves
- Revenue reserves
- Other reserves
- Profit and loss account.

Borrowings may (but will not necessarily) include the following items:

- Preference share capital (see above)
- Debentures
- Loans
- Overdrafts
- Provisions
- Accruals
- Current liabilities
- Other amounts due for payment.

Note that in a complex group structure, you might also come across other items that could be classed as 'borrowings', but the above analysis is sufficient for our purposes.

There is not much doubt about what to include in shareholders' funds. Some accountants might exclude preference share capital because that is a form of borrowing. Borrowings are a little trickier to determine, but we will not complicate the calculation of the ratio by getting involved in too much technical detail. We recommend, therefore, that you go for a fairly straightforward approach and adopt the following definition of capital gearing:

$$\frac{\text{Preference shares} + \text{long-term loans}}{\text{Shareholders' funds} + \text{long-term loans}} \times 100 = X\%$$

A company that has financed itself out of a high proportion of borrowings (e.g. in the form of a combination of preference shares and long-term loans) is known as a high geared company. Conversely, a company with a low level of borrowing is regarded as being low geared. Note that high and low in this context are relative terms. As we indicated above, a high geared company is potentially a higher risk investment, as it has to earn sufficient profit to cover the interest payments and the preference dividend before it can pay out any ordinary dividend. This should not be a problem when profits are rising, but if they are falling, then they may not be sufficient to cover even the preference dividend.

We have now defined 18 common accounting ratios, and there are many others that could also have been included! However, the 18 selected are enough for you to be able to interpret a set of accounts. If the ratios are used in isolation, many of them are not particularly helpful, but you will find that as part of a detailed analysis they are invaluable.

AN ILLUSTRATIVE EXAMPLE

In this section, we use the ratios outlined above to interpret a set of accounts. In order to establish a reasonable trend, we really need to adopt something like a three- to a five-year period. It would also be useful to compare our results with the ratios obtained from similar entities (there are some commercial organizations that provide such comparative data). However, for our purposes, such a long period would be impractical, and it would also obscure the basic procedures that we want to illustrate. Consequently, we shall limit our data to a single company for a two-year period. We do so in Exhibit 9.3.

Exhibit 9.3 Interpreting company accounts

You are provided with the following summarized information relating to Gill Limited for the year to 31 March 19X3:

GILL LIMITED
Trading and profit and loss account for the year to 31 March 19X3

		19X2		19X3	
		£000	£000	£000	£000
Sales			160		180
Less: Cost of goods sold:					
Opening stock		10		14	
Purchases		100		130	
		110		144	
Less: Closing stock		14	96	24	120
Gross profit	c/f		64		60

		£000	£000	£000	£000
Gross profit	b/f		64		60
Less: Expenses:					
Administration		18		24	
Loan interest		1		1	
Selling and distribution		12	31	16	41
Net profit before taxation			33		19
Taxation			15		6
Net profit after taxation			18		13
Dividends: preference (paid)		2		2	
ordinary (proposed)		8	10	5	7
Retained profit for the year			8		6
Retained profit brought forward			4		12
Retained profit for the year			£12		£18

GILL LIMITED
Balance sheet at 31 March 19X3

	Cost	19X2 Depreci-ation	Net book value	Cost	19X3 Depreci-ation	Net book value
	£000	£000	£000	£000	£000	£000
Fixed assets						
Freehold property	60	–	60	60	–	60
Vehicles	42	14	28	48	22	26
	£102	£14	88	£108	£22	86
Current assets						
Stocks		14			24	
Trade debtors		20			60	
Bank		3			1	
		37			85	
Less: Current liabilities						
Trade creditors	10			62		
Taxation	15			6		
Proposed dividend	8	33	4	5	73	12
			£92			£98
Capital and reserves						
Authorized, issued and fully paid ordinary shares of £1 each			40			40
Preference shares (10%)			20			20
Profit and loss account			12			18
Shareholders' funds	c/f		72			78

	£000	£000	£000	£000	£000
Shareholders' funds	b/f 72				78
Loans					
Debenture stock (5%)	20				20
	£92				£98

Additional information:

1 Purchases and sales are made evenly throughout the year.
2 All purchases and all sales are made on credit terms.
3 You may assume that price levels are stable.
4 The company only sells one product: in 19X2 it sold 40 000 units and in 19X3 60 000 units.
5 There were no sales of fixed assets during the year.
6 The market value of the ordinary shares was estimated to be worth £2.30 per share at 31 March 19X2 and £1.80 per share at 31 March 19X3.

Required:

(a) Compute significant ratios for the two years to 31 March 19X2 and 19X3 respectively; and

(b) using the ratios which you have calculated in part (a) of the question, comment upon the results for the year to 31 March 19X3.

Answer to Exhibit 9.3

(a) Significant ratios   **GILL LIMITED**

	19X2	19X3

Profitability ratios:

● Return on capital employed (ROCE):

$$\frac{\text{Net profit before taxation}}{\text{Shareholders' funds*}} \times 100 = \frac{33\,000}{72\,000} \times 100 = \frac{19\,000}{78\,000} \times 100$$

$$= 45.83\% \qquad = 24.36\%$$

* The opening balance for shareholders' funds for 19X2 has not been given, so the closing balance has been used.

● Gross profit:

$$\frac{\text{Gross profit}}{\text{Total sales revenue}} \times 100 = \frac{64\,000}{160\,000} \times 100 = \frac{60\,000}{180\,000} \times 100$$

$$= 40.00\% \qquad = 33.33\%$$

● Mark up:

$$\frac{\text{Gross profit}}{\text{Cost of goods sold}} \times 100 = \frac{64\,000}{96\,000} \times 100 = \frac{60\,000}{120\,000} \times 100$$

$$= 66.67\% \qquad = 50.00\%$$

191

		1992	1993

- Net profit:

$$\frac{\text{Net profit before taxation}}{\text{Total sales revenue}} \times 100 \quad = \frac{33\,000}{160\,000} \times 100 \quad = \frac{19\,000}{180\,000} \times 100$$

$$= \; 20.63\% \qquad\qquad = \; 10.56\%$$

Liquidity ratios:

- Current assets:

$$\frac{\text{Current assets}}{\text{Current liabilities}} \quad = \frac{37\,000}{33\,000} \quad = \frac{85\,000}{73\,000}$$

$$= \; 1.12 \text{ to } 1 \qquad\qquad = \; 1.16 \text{ to } 1$$

- Acid test:

$$\frac{\text{Current assets – stocks}}{\text{Current liabilities}} \quad = \frac{37\,000 - 14\,000}{33\,000} \quad = \frac{85\,000 - 24\,000}{73\,000}$$

$$= \; 0.70 \text{ to } 1 \qquad\qquad = \; 0.84 \text{ to } 1$$

Efficiency ratios:

- Stock turnover:

$$\frac{\text{Cost of goods sold}}{\text{Average stock*}} \quad = \frac{96\,000}{\frac{1}{2}(10\,000 + 14\,000)} = \frac{120\,000}{\frac{1}{2}(14\,000 + 24\,000)}$$

$$= \; 8.0 \text{ times} \qquad = \; 6.3 \text{ times}$$

* $\frac{1}{2}$ (Opening stocks + closing stocks)

- Fixed assets turnover:

$$\frac{\text{Total sales revenue}}{\text{Fixed assets at net book value}} \quad = \frac{160\,000}{88\,000} \quad = \frac{180\,000}{86\,000}$$

$$= \; 1.82 \text{ times} \qquad = \; 2.09 \text{ times}$$

- Trade debtor collection period:

$$\frac{\text{Closing trade debtors*}}{\text{Total credit sales}} \quad = \frac{20\,000}{160\,000} \times 365 \quad = \frac{60\,000}{180\,000} \times 365$$

$$= \; 46 \text{ days} \qquad = \; 122 \text{ days}$$

*Opening trade debtors have not been given for 19X2, so closing trade debtors have been used.

- Trade creditor payment period:

$$\frac{\text{Closing trade creditors*}}{\text{Total credit purchases}} \times 365 \quad = \frac{10\,000}{100\,000} \times 365 \quad = \frac{62\,000}{130\,000} \times 365$$

$$= \; 37 \text{ days} \qquad = \; 175 \text{ days}$$

*Opening trade creditors have not been given for 19X2, so closing trade creditors have been used.

Investment ratios:		1992	1993

- Dividend per share:

$$\frac{\text{Dividend}}{\text{Ordinary share capital}} \times 100 \quad = \frac{8000}{40\,000} \times 100 \quad = \frac{5000}{40\,000} \times 100$$

$$= \underline{\underline{20\text{p}}} \qquad\qquad = \underline{\underline{12.5\text{p}}}$$

- Dividend yield:

$$\frac{\text{Dividend per share}}{\text{Market price per share}} \times 100 \quad = \frac{20}{230} \times 100 \quad = \frac{12.5}{180} \times 100$$

$$= \underline{\underline{8.70\%}} \qquad\qquad = \underline{\underline{6.94\%}}$$

- Dividend cover:

$$\frac{\text{Net profit after taxation and preference dividend}}{\text{Paid and proposed ordinary dividends}} = \frac{18\,000 - 2000}{8000} \quad = \frac{13\,000 - 2000}{5000}$$

$$= \underline{\underline{2.00\text{ times}}} \qquad = \underline{\underline{2.20\text{ times}}}$$

- Earnings per share (EPS):

$$\frac{\text{Net profit after taxation and preference dividend}}{\substack{\text{Number of ordinary shares} \\ \text{in issue during the year}}} = \frac{18\,000 - 2000}{40\,000} \quad = \frac{13\,000 - 2000}{40\,000}$$

$$= \underline{\underline{40.00\text{p}}} \qquad\qquad = \underline{\underline{27.50\text{p}}}$$

- Price/earnings (P/E) ratio:

$$\frac{\text{Market price per share}}{\text{Earnings per share}} = \frac{2.30}{0.40} \qquad = \frac{1.80}{0.275}$$

$$= \underline{\underline{5.75}} \qquad\qquad = \underline{\underline{6.55}}$$

- Capital gearing:

$$\frac{\substack{\text{Preference shares +} \\ \text{long-term loans}}}{\substack{\text{Shareholders' funds +} \\ \text{long-term loans}}} \times 100 = \frac{20\,000 + 20\,000}{72\,000 + 20\,000} \times 100 = \frac{20\,000 + 20\,000}{78\,000 + 20\,000} \times 100$$

$$= \underline{\underline{43.48\%}} \qquad\qquad = \underline{\underline{40.82\%}}$$

(b) Comments on the ratios

Profitability

1 The selling price of the product in 19X2 must have been £4.00 per unit since the company sold 40 000 units and its total sales revenue was £160 000 (£160 000 ÷ 40 000). In 19X3 the company sold 60 000 units and its total sales revenue was £180 000. The selling price per unit must, therefore, have been £3.00. It would appear that Gill Limited deliberately reduced its selling price per unit by 25% (1 × 100/4 = 25%). There was thus a 50% increase in sales volume (from 40 000 units to 60 000), but its total sales revenue only increased by £20 000 (or 12.5%).

2 The relatively modest increase in sales revenue did not help to increase the gross profit (down from £64 000 to £60 000), largely because the reduction in mark up (down from 66.67% to 50%) did not generate sufficient extra sales.

3 The large increase in sales volume also affected overall profitability. The net profit on sales was reduced from 20.63% to 10.56%, partly because of the reduction in gross profit and partly because other expenses increased by £10 000. Consequently, the return on capital employed was much reduced: from 45.83% to 24.36%. This is still a favourable rate of return when compared with alternative forms of investment, but the company's management must view the downward trend with some concern.

Liquidity

1 Gill's current assets position does not appear to have been greatly affected by the overall decline in profitability. In fact the current assets ratio has improved slightly, from 1.12 to 1 to 1.16 to 1. The current assets are in excess of current liabilities in both years, so provided that receipts from trade debtors can be kept in step with payments to trade creditors, the company would appear not to have an immediate liquidity problem.

2 If stocks are excluded from current assets, however, the position is a little more worrying. The acid test ratio was 0.71 to 1 in 19X2, and 0.84 to 1 in 19X3, so there has been an improvement in Gill's immediate liquidity position. Even so, by the end of 19X3 the company did not have sufficient cash to pay its proposed dividend, so it was dependent on either being able to obtain overdraft facilities from the bank, or on cash receipts from its trade debtors (note that there was a similar situation in 19X2). Fortunately, the tax would probably not have to be paid until 1 January 19X4 (i.e. nine months after the year end).

Efficiency

1 Gill was not as efficient at trading in 19X3 as it had been in 19X2. Its stock turnover was down from 8.0 to 6.3, which means that it was not turning over its stocks as quickly in 19X3 as it did in 19X2.

2 The company's investment in fixed assets (as measured by its sales activity) has improved from 1.82 times in 19X2 to 2.09 times in 19X3. This arose largely because the purchase of new assets only increased the gross book value of its fixed assets by £6000, whereas the depreciation charge for the year reduced the total net book value by £8000, a net difference of £2000.

3 The extra sales generated during 19X3 were made at some cost to its potential liquidity position. At the end of 19X3 its outstanding trade debtors represented 46 days' sales, but at the end of 19X3, they represented 122 days' sales. This suggests that Gill encouraged a greater sales volume by reducing both its selling prices and by offering more generous credit terms. It is also possible that the company was so busy coping with the increased operational activity that it did not have time to control its debtor position.

4 Gill appears to have been fortunate in 19X3 in not having to pay its trade creditors as promptly as it did in 19X2. At the end of 19X2, its trade creditors represented about 37 days' purchases. If Gill had had to pay its creditors as quickly in 19X3 as it had done in 19X2, its total trade creditors at the end of 19X3 would have amounted to about £13 000 (130 000 × 37/365), instead of

the £62 000 actually owing at that date. By paying its trade creditors more quickly, Gill would probably have had a bank overdraft of some £48 000 [(62 000 – 13 000) = 49 000 – 1000], instead of the favourable balance of £1000.

Investment

1 Gill Limited is a private company, so its shares would not be freely available on a recognized stock exchange. The market price of the shares given in the question is bound to be rather a questionable one, and it probably does not reflect the earnings potential of the company.

2 The dividend yield has fallen from 8.7% in 19X2 to 6.94% in 19X3. Compared with the yield currently available from other investments, these yields are about average, although the reduction in the dividend for 19X3 could be the start of a downwards trend.

3 Whilst the reduction in the dividend from 20p per share in 19X2 to 12.5p per share in 19X3 is worrying, the dividend is well covered by the earnings. Indeed, the company could have paid the same dividend in 19X3 as it did in 19X2, and the dividend would still have been covered 1.38 times (13 000 – 2000/8000). It would appear that the company's policy is to pay less than half of its earnings as dividend, even if it means reducing the dividend. This would not matter as much to a private company as it would to a public one. In a public company a reduction in dividend can result in a fall in the market value of its shares, thus reflecting the reduction in confidence that the market has in the company.

4 No new shares were issued during the year. Thus, as a result of the reduction in profits, the earnings per share declined from 40.00p to 27.50p.

5 The increase in the price earnings ratio (up from 5.75 to 6.55) is surprising. It was probably caused by the market's view (albeit a rather restricted one) that the company's future is a reasonably good one, notwithstanding the reduction in the company's profit. However, this company is a private one, so we cannot be certain how the market price of its shares has been determined.

6 Gill Limited is a fairly high geared company. In 19X2, nearly 44% of its financing had been raised in the form of fixed interest stock, but in 19X3 this was reduced to just under 41%. By financing itself in this way, the company is committed to making annual payments of £3000 (£2000 of preference dividend + £1000 of debenture interest). In absolute terms, this amount is not large, and so although it is a relatively high geared company, its earnings should be sufficient to cover its interest commitments.

Summary

1 In 19X3 Gill Limited achieved its presumed objective of increasing its sales. It did this partly by reducing its unit selling price, and partly by offering extended credit terms to its customers. The effect of this policy has been to reduce gross profit by £4000 and its net profit by £14 000.

2 The new policy did not affect its liquidity position, largely because the extended credit terms (leading to delays in the settlement of its trade debts) were offset by similar delays in paying its trade creditors.

3 As a result of the reduction in its profits for 19X3, the company reduced its dividend, although its earnings would still have enabled it to maintain the same dividend as in 19X2.

4 The market (such as it is) does not seem to agree that the reduction in the profit or of the dividend is serious. Indeed, it can be argued the company's future is healthy provided that it can persuade its trade debtors to pay their debts more promptly.

You are now advised to go through Exhibit 9.3 again most carefully. Make sure that you know how to calculate the ratios, and that you know what they mean. Then try to list your own views on Gill Limited's progress during 19X3. The comments listed above are only brief ones, and much more could have been written about the company. However, we hope that we have been able to demonstrate that ratio analysis enables us to extract a great deal more information about the company than could be obtained merely by attempting to 'read' the profit and loss account and the balance sheet.

Although ratios help us to put the information into context, they must then be used as part of a detailed overall analysis. Think of ratios as signposts. They point us in the right direction, but they are not a substitute for the journey itself. We now need to undertake that journey. In other words, we must look a little closer at what we mean by 'interpretation'.

INTERPRETATION

Once you have collected all the data that you need about a company, and you have established a considerable number of trends and calculated innumerable ratios, you have to write a story. This means that you have to use the date to *interpret* what has happened, and possibly predict what *will* happen. It is important that you appreciate that ratios themselves are not particularly useful unless they are incorporated into an overall analysis. What can you do to make some sense out of all the information that you have got? Much depends, of course, upon the reason for your investigation, but the following questions might help help you to come to some provisional conclusions:

1 **The market for the company's products**. Has this expanded or contracted in recent years? How has the company coped with the changes in market conditions? What is the market likely to be like over (say) the next five years? How will it be affected by general demographic, economic, political, and social factors? Does the company seem attuned to these possible changes?

2 **Sales and profits**. Have these increased or decreased over the period? If there has been any growth, has it been because of internal expansion or because of acquisition? Does the management seem keen enough to pursue growth, or is the company stagnating?

3 **Capital investment**. What capital investment has there been and what is planned? How would future investments be financed? What retained reserves has the company built up?

4 **Management**. What is the record of the management? Are the senior managers near retirement? Are they young enough to want change? Are they ambitious? How well do they seem to have managed the company's resources? Is its liquidity position secure? How good are they at portraying a favourable public image for the company?

5 **Employees and industrial relations**. Does the company appear to have a stable workforce? Has it had any industrial disputes? What is its attitude and relationship as far as the trade unions are concerned? How does the output and profit record per employee compare with other companies?

6 **Generally**. The 'feel good' factor. Having found out a great deal about the company, does it inspire you with some confidence about its future? Is it likely to expand in the short term and survive in the long term ? Overall, do you feel good about the company?

The above questions are not exhaustive, but they should be a help to you in your analysis. There is no doubt that having extensively researched a company's history and examined its future, you will already have formed a provisional view before you come to make your recommendations. All that remains for you to do is to commit your thoughts to paper. You might have to produce only a *brief* report, so you then will have the difficult task of summarizing all that you have learned about the company in just a few pages. You may well find that this is almost as difficult as carrying out the original investigation!

CONCLUSION

This chapter concludes the first three parts of the book. By now, you should know something about the nature of accounting information, where it comes from, and how it can be of help to both owners and managers.

As has been argued throughout this book, the techniques adopted by accountants are open to some fairly serious criticisms, so it is only right that we should have expressed some reservations about the reliability of accounting information. Nonetheless, no one has yet devised a better method of accounting, and, until they do, we have to make the best of the present one. We would argue that by being fully aware of the deficiencies of financial accounting, the non-accountant can make allowances for them when faced with such information.

The chapter has expained how you can go about interpreting a set of accounts by using a variety of techniques, viz. horizontal analysis, trend analysis, vertical analysis, and ratio analysis. The use of these techniques can help to put all the data that you have obtained about a particular company into perspective, but remember that the ratios that you do produce are based on accounting information which is somewhat questionable. Furthermore, remember to use the ratios as signposts: they are not a substitute for an analytical assessment of the company's performance.

Key points	
	1 The interpretation of accounts involves examining accounts in some detail so as to be able to explain what has happened and to predict what is likely to happen.
	2 The examination can be undertaken by using a number of techniques such as horizontal analysis, trend analysis, vertical analysis, and ratio analysis.
	3 Ratio analysis, in particular, is a popular method of interpreting accounts. It involves comparing one item in the accounts with another closely related item. Ratios are normally expressed in the form of a percentage or a factor. There are literally hundreds of recognized accounting ratios (the main ones are summarized at the very end of the chapter), as well as those that relate only to specific industries.
	4 When relating one item to another item, and then expressing it in the form of a ratio, be careful to make sure that there is a close and logical correlation between the two items.
	5 Remember that, in the case of some ratios, different definitions can be adopted. This applies particularly to ROCE and capital gearing. In other cases, remember that sometimes only year-end balances are used, and not an annual average. This applies especially to ratios relating to stocks, debtors, and creditors.

CHECK YOUR LEARNING

1 State whether the following assertions are true or false:
  (a) Ratio analysis aims to put the financial results of an entity into
      perspective.   True/False
  (b) Ratio analysis is only one form of analysis that can be used in
      interpreting accounts.   True/False
  (c) Ratio analysis helps establish whether or not an entity is a
      going concern.   True/False

2 Fill in the missing blanks in the following equations:
  (a) $\dfrac{\text{gross profit (50)}}{\text{sales (200)}} \times \underline{\hspace{1cm}} \% = 25\%.$

  (b) $\dfrac{\text{profit}}{\text{capital}} \times 100 = \underline{\hspace{2cm}}.$

  (c) $\underline{\text{trade debtors}} \times 365 = \text{trade debtor collection period.}$

  (d) $\dfrac{\underline{\hspace{2cm}}}{\text{average stock}} = \text{stock turnover ratio.}$

(e) $\dfrac{\text{net profit after taxation and preference dividend}}{\rule{6cm}{0.4pt}} = \text{dividend cover.}$

(f) $\dfrac{\text{preference shares} +}{\text{shareholders' funds} + \text{long-term loans}} \times 100 = \text{capital gearing.}$

3 State how each of the following ratios would normally be classed:
  (a) gross profit ratio: 70%   High/Low/Neither
  (b) net profit ratio: 3%   High/Low/Neither
  (c) return on capital employed: 30%   High/Low/Neither
  (d) trade debtors collection period: 125 days   High/Low/Neither
  (e) capital gearing: 40%   High/Low/Neither

Answers 1 (a) true (b) true (c) true
               2 (a) 100 (b) return on capital employed (c) credit sales (d) cost of goods sold
                  (e) ordinary dividends (f) long-term loans
               3 (a) high (b) low (c) high (depends upon the business concerned) (d) high
                  (e) neither

SUMMARY OF THE MAIN RATIOS

Profitability ratios

$$\text{ROCE} = \dfrac{\text{Net profit before taxation}}{\text{Average shareholders' funds}} \times 100$$

$$\text{ROCE} = \dfrac{\text{Net profit after taxation}}{\text{Average shareholders' funds}} \times 100$$

$$\text{ROCE} = \dfrac{\text{Net profit after taxation and preference dividends}}{\text{Average shareholders' funds less preference shares}} \times 100$$

$$\text{ROCE} = \dfrac{\text{Profit before taxation and interest}}{\text{Average shareholders' funds} + \text{long-term loans}} \times 100$$

$$\text{Gross profit ratio} = \dfrac{\text{Gross profit}}{\text{Total sales revenue}} \times 100$$

$$\text{Mark-up ratio} = \dfrac{\text{Gross profit}}{\text{Cost of goods sold}} \times 100$$

$$\text{Net profit ratio} = \dfrac{\text{Net profit before taxation}}{\text{Total sales revenue}} \times 100$$

Liquidity ratios

$$\text{Current assets ratio} = \frac{\text{Current assets}}{\text{Current liabilities}}$$

$$\text{Acid test ratio} = \frac{\text{Current assets} - \text{stocks}}{\text{Current liabilities}}$$

Efficiency ratios

$$\text{Stock turnover} = \frac{\text{Cost of goods sold}}{\text{Average stock}}$$

$$\text{Fixed assets turnover} = \frac{\text{Total sales revenue}}{\text{Fixed assets at net book value}}$$

$$\text{Trade debtor collection period} = \frac{\text{Average trade debtors}}{\text{Total credit sales}} \times 365$$

$$\text{Trade creditor payment period} = \frac{\text{Average trade creditors}}{\text{Total credit purchases}} \times 365$$

Investment ratios

$$\text{Dividend yield} = \frac{\text{Dividend per share}}{\text{Market price per share}} \times 100$$

$$\text{Dividend cover} = \frac{\text{Net profit after taxation and preference dividend}}{\text{Paid and proposed ordinary dividends}}$$

$$\text{Earnings per share} = \frac{\text{Net profit after taxation and preference dividend}}{\text{Number of ordinary shares in issue during the year}}$$

$$\text{Price/earnings ratio} = \frac{\text{Market price per share}}{\text{Earnings per share}}$$

$$\text{Capital gearing} = \frac{\text{Preference shares} + \text{long-term loans}}{\text{Shareholders' funds} + \text{long-term loans}} \times 100$$

QUESTIONS

9.1

The following information has been extracted from the books of account of Betty for the year to 31 January 19X1:

Trading and profit and loss account for the year to 31 January 19X1

	£000	£000
Sales (all credit)		100
Less: Cost of goods sold:		
Opening stock	15	
Purchases	65	
	80	
Less: Closing stock	10	70
Gross profit		30
Administrative expenses		16
Net profit		£14

Balance sheet at 31 January 19X1

	£000	£000
Fixed assets (net book value)		29
Current assets		
Stock	10	
Trade debtors	12	
Cash	3	
	25	
Less: Current liabilities		
Trade creditors	6	19
		£48
Financed by:		
Capital at 1 February 19X0		40
Add: Net profit	14	
Less: Drawings	6	8
		£48

Required:
Calculate the following accounting ratios:
1 gross profit;
2 net profit;
3 return on capital employed;
4 current ratio;
5 acid test;
6 stock turnover; and
7 debtor collection period.

9.2

You are presented with the following summarized accounts:

JAMES LIMITED
Profit and loss account for the year to 28 February 19X2

	£000
Sales (all credit)	1200
Cost of sales	600
Gross profit	600
Administrative expenses	(500)
Debenture interest payable	(10)
Profit on ordinary activities	90
Taxation	(30)
	60
Dividends	(40)
Retained profit for the year	£20

JAMES LIMITED
Balance sheet at 28 February 19X2

	£000	£000	£000
Fixed assets (net book value)			685
Current assets			
Stock		75	
Trade debtors		200	
		275	
Less: Current liabilities			
Trade creditors	160		
Bank overdraft	10		
Taxation	30		
Proposed dividend	40	240	35
			£720
Capital and reserves			
Ordinary share capital			600
Profit and loss account			20
Shareholders' funds			620
Loans:			
10% debentures			100
			£720

Required:
Calculate the following accounting ratios:
1 return on capital employed;
2 gross profit;
3 mark up;
4 net profit;
5 acid test;
6 fixed assets turnover;
7 debtor collection period; and
8 capital gearing.

9.3
You are presented with the following information for each of three companies:

Profit and loss accounts for the year to 31 March 19X3

	Mark Limited £000	Luke Limited £000	John Limited £000
Profit before tax	£64	£22	£55

Balance sheet (extracts) at 31 March 19X3

	Mark Limited £000	Luke Limited £000	John Limited £000
Capital and reserves			
Ordinary share capital of £1 each	100	177	60
Cumulative 15% preference shares of £1 each	–	20	10
Share premium account	–	70	20
Profit and loss account	150	60	200
Shareholders' funds	250	327	290
Loans			
10% debentures	–	–	100
	£250	£327	£390

Required:
Calculate the following accounting ratios:
1 return on capital employed; and
2 capital gearing.

9.4

The following information relates to Helena Limited:

Trading account year to 30 April

	19X1	19X2	19X3	19X4	19X5	19X6
	£000	£000	£000	£000	£000	£000
Sales (all credit)	–	130	150	190	210	320
Less: Cost of goods sold:						
Opening stock	–	20	30	30	35	40
Purchases (all in credit terms)	–	110	110	135	145	305
	–	130	140	165	180	345
Less: Closing stock	–	30	30	35	40	100
	–	100	110	130	140	245
Gross profit	–	£30	£40	£60	£70	£75
Trade debtors at 30 April	£40	£45	£40	£70	£100	£150
Trade creditors at 30 April	£20	£20	£25	£25	£30	£60

Required:
Calculate the following accounting ratios for each of the five years from 30 April 19X2 to 19X6 inclusive:
1 gross profit;
2 mark-up;
3 stock turnover;
4 trade debtor collection period; and
5 trade creditor payment period.

9.5

You are presented with the following information relating to Hedge public limited company for the year to 31 May 19X5:

(a) The company has an issued and fully paid share capital of £500 000 ordinary shares of £1 each. There are no preference shares.
(b) The market price of the shares at 31 May 19X5 was £3.50.
(c) The net profit after taxation for the year to 31 May 19X5 was £70 000.
(d) The directors are proposing a dividend of 7p per share for the year to 31 May 19X5.

Required:
Calculate the following accounting ratios:
1 dividend yield;
2 dividend cover;
3 earnings per share; and
4 price/earnings ratio.

9.6

The following information relates to Style Limited for the two years to 30 June 19X5 and 19X6, respectively:

Trading and profit and loss accounts for the years

	19X5		19X6	
	£000	£000	£000	£000
Sales (all credit)		1500		1900
Less: Cost of goods sold:				
Opening stock	80		100	
Purchases (all on credit terms)	995		1400	
	1075		1500	
	100	975	200	1300
Gross profit		525		600
Less: Expenses		250		350
Net profit		£275		£250

Balance sheet at 30 June

	19X5		19X6	
	£000	£000	£000	£000
Fixed assets (net book value)		580		460
Current assets				
Stock	100		200	
Trade debtors	375		800	
Bank	25		–	
	500		1000	
Less: Current liabilities				
Bank overdraft	–		10	
Trade creditors	80		200	
	80	420	210	790
		£1000		£1250
Capital and reserves				
Ordinary share capital		900		900
Profit and loss account		100		350
Shareholders' funds		£1000		£1250

Required:

(a) Calculate the following accounting ratios for the two years 19X5 and 19X6 respectively:

1 gross profit;
2 mark-up;
3 net profit;
4 return on capital employed;
5 stock turnover;
6 current ratio;
7 acid test;
8 trade debtor collection period; and
9 trade creditor payment period.

(b) Comment upon the company's performance for the year to 30 June 19X6.

ADDITIONAL QUESTIONS (WITHOUT ANSWERS)

9.7

The following summarized information relates to Turnbull public limited company.

Year to 31 October	19X2	19X3	19X4	19X5	19X6
	£000	£000	£000	£000	£000
Profit and loss accounts:					
Sales (all credit)	5500	5600	5700	6000	9300
Cost of sales	(3030)	(3050)	(3000)	(3250)	(5400)
Gross profit	2470	2550	2700	2750	3900
Distribution costs	(520)	(550)	(600)	(600)	(900)
Administration expenses	(1500)	(1500)	(1500)	(1500)	(2000)
Profit before taxation	450	500	600	650	1000
Taxation	(60)	(90)	(120)	(150)	(200)
Profit after taxation	390	410	480	500	800
Dividends	(90)	(90)	(100)	(150)	(150)
Transferred to reserves	300	320	380	350	650
Balance sheets at 31 October					
Fixed assets at cost	3100	3200	3900	4600	6000
Less: Accumulated depreciation	200	300	400	500	600
	2900	2900	3500	4100	5400
Current assets:					
Stocks	600	700	750	750	2400
Trade debtors	800	800	900	900	1600
Cash and bank	100	100	100	150	260
	1500	1600	1750	1800	4260
Current liabilities:					
Trade creditors	(2390)	(2140)	(2470)	(2690)	(5750)
Taxation	(60)	(90)	(120)	(150)	(200)
Dividend	(90)	(90)	(100)	(150)	(150)
	(2540)	(2320)	(2690)	(2990)	(6100)
	£1860	£2180	£2560	£2910	£3560
Capital and reserves:					
Called up share capital (ordinary shares of £1 each)	500	500	500	500	500
Profit and loss account	1360	1680	2060	2410	3060
	£1860	£2180	£2560	£2910	£3560

Notes:

1 Stock at 1 November 19X1: £550 000

2 All purchases are obtained on credit terms.

Required:
Prepare a report for the Board of Directors of Turnbull plc examining the financial performance of the company during the five-year period 1 November 19X1 to 31 October 19X6.

9.8
The following information relates to three companies all operating in the same industry.

	Begg plc £000	Chow plc £000	Doyle plc £000
Profit and loss accounts for the			
year to 30 November 19X1			
Turnover	11 200	11 500	13 000
Cost of sales	(5 600)	(4 800)	(7 100)
Gross profit	5 600	6 700	5 900
Operating expenses	(4 000)	(3 300)	(4 700)
Profit before taxation	1 600	3 400	1 200
Taxation	(600)	(1 100)	(550)
Profit after taxation	1 000	2 300	650
Dividends	(600)	(200)	(300)
Retained profit	400	2 100	350
Balance sheets at 30 November 19X1			
Fixed assets at cost	2 600	2 700	2 800
Less: Accumulated depreciation	1 000	700	1 400
	1 600	2 000	1 400
Current assets:			
Stocks	1 700	1 300	1 300
Trade debtors	2 900	5 200	2 000
Debtors	300	1 800	300
Cash and bank	400	50	2 200
	5 300	8 350	5 800
Current liabilities:			
Trade creditors	(1 300)	(1 200)	(1 500)
Other creditors	(1 000)	(1 400)	(1 450)
Taxation	(600)	(1 100)	(550)
Dividends	(600)	(200)	(300)
	(3 500)	(3 900)	(3 800)
	£3 400	£6 450	£3 400

Capital and reserves:

Called up share capital			
(ordinary shares of £1 each)	500	2 000	750
Profit and loss account	2 900	4 450	2 650
	£3 400	£6 450	£3 400

Market price of shares at			
30 November 19X1	£22.20	£1.90	£7.40

Required:

Assume that you are a trainee investment analyst in a firm of stockbrokers.

Prepare a report for your section manager comparing and contrasting the financial performance of the three companies.

DISCUSSION QUESTIONS

9.9

'Accounting ratios are only as good as the data on which they are based.' Discuss.

9.10

How far do you accept the argument that the return on capital employed ratio can give a misleading impression of an entity's profitability?

9.11

Is ratio analysis useful in understanding how an entity has performed?

Not so secure

Learning objectives

By the end of this case study, you will be able to:

- **analyse financial statements;**
- **extract additional information from a set of financial statements;**
- **summarize information contained within them;**
- **prepare a report based on your observations.**

Background

LOCATION   Security Systems Limited: the Head Office

PERSONNEL   Alan Pymn: Joint Managing Director
             Frank Lynch: Joint Managing Director

Synopsis

Some years ago, Alan Pymn and Frank Lynch went into partnership marketing and installing security alarm systems. Both Alan and Frank had previously worked at the local brewery, Alan in plant maintenance, and Frank in the sales office.

They lived in Stutfield, a quiet north country town of about 80 000 inhabitants. Stutfield was within easy travelling distance of several major cities. At that time, the town was suffering from an increasing amount of crime and vandalism, and house owners were extremely worried by the number of houses being burgled.

The two partners were neighbours. They were also both keen members of the local squash club. Talking at the bar one night about the latest burglary, they had the idea of forming their own security system business. The idea appealed to them, especially as neither of them wanted to work for someone else for the rest of their lives.

They thought about the idea for a little while. In the meantime, by working for a friend at the weekend, Alan was able to gain some experience of installing security systems, and Frank learned something about the administrative and marketing side of the security business. Financial backing was promised from various friends and relatives, and within just a few months, they were able to set up their business.

The business was an instant success as everyone in the town seemed to want some form of protection. After a few years of rapid growth they decided to convert the partnership into a limited liability company called 'Security Systems Limited'.

The charge for installing a security system was based partly on the size of the property and partly on the complexity of the installation. The policy of the company was to invoice customers 30 days after a job had been satisfactorily completed.

After the first year, a fixed annual maintenance charge became payable. This charge covered all further inspections and repairs. Customers were contracted to pay this charge for five years, but after that time only a nominal annual charge was made. All contracts had a maximum life of ten years.

Following the formation of the company, the business continued to grow, although at a slower rate than had previously been experienced. By the time that Security Systems was formed, most householders in Stutfield had obtained a burglar alarm, so the company began to conduct more of its business in the nearby cities.

It proved to be much more difficult to operate outside Stutfield. Although there was quite a demand for such services, the competition was extremely tough. Furthermore, city customers always argued about the effectiveness of the system, and both operative and office staff spent a great deal of time persuading customers to settle their accounts.

An additional worrying feature first became apparent in 19X4. Contrary to expectations, those security systems installed in the earlier years of the business proved increasingly expensive to maintain, and the operative staff spent more and more of their time repairing old systems instead of installing new ones. Under the terms of the contract, it was not possible to increase the annual maintenance charge.

The company's accounting policy had always been to claim any profit made on the installation of a system in the year of installation, and to credit maintenance fees receivable to each year's profit and loss account. Separate records were not kept of installation expenses and maintenance costs, and no provision had been made for maintenance and repairs.

Required:
1 Inspect the summarized financial statements for Security Systems Limited for the five-year period 1 April 19X3 to 31 March l9X8 (Appendix A). Make a note of any obvious changes or features that become apparent as you read through the accounts.
2 Using *selected* data for the five-year period 1 April 19X3 to 31 March 19X8, prepare the following analyses:

- a horizontal analysis;
- a trend analysis;
- a vertical analysis;
- a ratio analysis.

3 Using the information obtained in completing 1 and 2 above, prepare a report for the Board of Directors of Security Systems Limited examining the company's efficiency, liquidity and profitability during the five-year period 1 April 19X3 to 31 March 19X8 inclusive.

Note: Be careful to state what recommendations you would make to the Board of Directors in order to enable the company to continue in business.

Appendix A

PROFIT AND LOSS ACCOUNTS (EXTRACTS) FOR THE YEAR TO 31 MARCH

	19X4 £000	19X5 £000	19X6 £000	19X7 £000	19X8 £000
INCOME					
Installation fees	1250	1500	2100	2400	2500
Maintenance fees	1000	1500	1920	2340	2600
	2250	3000	4020	4740	5100
EXPENDITURE					
Direct materials	250	306	437	528	575
Direct labour	795	1254	1753	2182	3060
Direct expenditure	40	40	70	90	120
Operational overheads	140	200	280	370	470
	1225	1800	2540	3170	4225
OPERATING PROFIT	1025	1200	1480	1570	875
Directors' emoluments	80	100	130	150	150
Loan interest	–	–	–	75	75
Office expenses	675	780	995	1040	1085
Office salaries	120	140	155	180	210
	875	1020	1280	1445	1520
NET PROFIT (LOSS)	150	180	200	125	(645)
Taxation	45	60	65	70	–
	105	120	135	55	(645)
Dividends	100	115	115	120	–
RETAINED PROFIT/(LOSS)	£5	£5	£20	£(65)	£(645)

BALANCE SHEET (EXTRACTS) AT 31 MARCH

	19X4	19X5	19X6	19X7	19X8
	£000	£000	£000	£000	£000
FIXED ASSETS					
At cost	1400	1450	1500	1550	1900
Less: Accumulated					
depreciation	275	355	440	530	695
	1125	1095	1060	1020	1205
CURRENT ASSETS					
Stocks at cost (19X3					
£15 000)	20	25	40	50	80
Trade debtors	200	240	363	434	806
Other debtors	25	25	30	40	50
Cash and bank	–	–	–	278	–
	245	290	433	802	936
	£1370	£1385	£1493	£1822	£2141
CAPITAL AND RESERVES					
Ordinary shares of					
£1 each	1000	1000	1000	1000	1000
Retained profits/(losses)	55	60	80	15	(630)
	1055	1060	1080	1015	370
DEBENTURE LOANS (15%)	–	–	–	500	500
CURRENT LIABILITIES					
Trade creditors	26	31	43	52	66
Other creditors	40	50	60	65	80
Bank overdraft	104	69	130	–	1125
Taxation	45	60	65	70	–
Proposed dividend	100	115	115	120	–
	315	325	413	307	1271
	£1370	£1385	£1493	£1822	£2141

Notes:

1 There were no sales of fixed assets during the period 1 April 19X3 to 31 March 19X8 inclusive.

2 Advance corporation tax may be ignored.

CASH FLOW STATEMENTS FOR THE YEAR TO 31 MARCH

	19X5 £000	19X6 £000	19X7 £000	19X8 £000
NET CASH INFLOW/(OUTFLOW)FROM OPERATING ACTIVITIES	230	164	213	(788)
RETURNS ON INVESTMENTS AND SERVICING OF FINANCE				
Interest paid	–	–	(75)	(75)
TAXATION				
Corporation tax paid	(45)	(60)	(65)	(70)
CAPITAL EXPENDITURE				
Payments to acquire tangible fixed assets	(50)	(50)	(50)	(350)
NET CASH INFLOW/(OUTFLOW)				
	135	54	23	(1283)
EQUITY DIVIDENDS PAID	(100)	(115)	(115)	(120)
	35	(61)	(92)	(1403)
MANAGEMENT OF LIQUID RESOURCES AND FINANCING	–	–	500	–
INCREASE/(DECREASE) IN CASH	35	(61)	408	1403

RECONCILIATION OF OPERATING PROFIT TO NET
CASH INFLOW/OUTFLOW FROM OPERATING ACTIVITIES

Operating activities (net profit/(loss)				
and loan interest)	180	200	200	(570)
Depreciation charges	80	85	90	165
Increase in stocks	(5)	(15)	(10)	(30)
Increase in debtors	(40)	(128)	(81)	(382)
Increase in creditors	15	22	14	29
NET CASH INFLOW/(OUTFLOW) FROM OPERATING ACTIVITIES	230	164	213	(788)

PART 4

Financial reporting

CHAPTER 10

Disclosure of information

The DTI's consultative paper on accounting simplifications for small companies contains much promise but as yet there are no promises of significant change to the existing regime, the Institute of Chartered Accountants of Scotland (ICAS) said.

ICAS's Business Legislation Unit supports the proposed amendment or deletion for small companies of the bulk of the specific 50 accounting disclosure requirements facing both them and large companies, and for raising the size thresholds for small and medium-sized companies – indeed, ICAS would prefer the maximum increase subject to shareholder approval or veto.

ICAS said it would also favour reformatting the Companies Act to specify clearly the requirements for most companies, with separate additional requirements for larger ones; simplifying and rationalising the exemption thresholds; and introducing a standard format for small company accounts so that all accounts and returns could be prepared from one master document.

Among other suggestions, ICAS said dormant companies should be automatically exempted from filing accounts so long as a set was filed in the first year of being dormant and dormancy is confirmed in subsequent annual returns.

The Institute of Chartered Accountants in England and Wales (ICAEW) also went for the maximum increase in the size threshold and the bottom-up approach to setting out Companies Act requirements. But it differed with ICAS, which suggested small companies in general should not be required to send reports and accounts to all shareholders but shareholders should be able to opt-in to receive them. And standard formats for accounts 'would tend to discourage innovation and development', the ICAEW said.

CA Magazine, October 1995

Exhibit 10.0 Should all companies disclose the same amount of information?

In previous chapters, we have been mainly concerned with collecting and summarizing information for *internal* management purposes. In order to illustrate some of the basic principles of accounting, we have also concentrated on problems dealing with sole traders and companies. In addition, these problems have largely been related to profit-making entities, often of a manufacturing or of a trading nature. It would be as well to remind you again at this stage that the accounting principles with which we have been dealing can similarly be applied to non-profit-making entities (such as a local authority or a hospital), or to service industries (such as an electrical contractor or a chain of garages).

However, irrespective of the nature of the entity (whether it is involved in manufacturing or providing a service, or whether it is profit-making or non-profit making), if it is constituted as a limited liability company, it also has a statutory duty to disclose some information about its financial affairs to parties external to the company. This requirement relates mainly to its shareholders.

The main aim of this chapter is, therefore, to explore the background to the requirement for limited liability companies to publish some information about their affairs to external parties.

Learning objectives	**By the end of this chapter, you will be able to:** ● list seven user groups of financial information; ● state the main sources of authority for company disclosure of information.

USER GROUPS

In Chapter 1, it was indicated that there were seven main user groups of accounting information. These groups were identified in an influential report published in 1975 by the ASC called *The Corporate Report*. More recently, a similar (although not entirely identical) list of user groups has been recognized by the ASB in an Exposure Draft (*Statement of Principles for Financial Reporting*) published in 1995. Both reports listed seven user groups, and in summary the Exposure Draft's groupings are as follows (they are are also shown in Exhibit 10.1):

1. Investors. This is the most obvious grouping. Investors provide the risk capital, and as shareholders they are, of course, also the owners of the company. Nonetheless, the law has always regarded it as being impractical for every shareholder (in some large companies, there could be hundreds of thousands of individual shareholders) to have an automatic right of access to the company's premises to inspect the books of account, and to demand an unrestricted amount of information. Thus, since shareholders' rights are legally defined, they may be regarded as one of the main *external* user groups.

Exhibit 10.1 The main users of financial accounts

The public

Suppliers
and
other creditors

Employees

Investors

Lenders

Customers

Government
and
their agencies

Source: Statement of Principles for Financial Reporting, Exposure Draft, ASB, 1995

2 Lenders. Lenders are groups of people who have loaned funds to the business under some formal agreement, for example, by buying debentures in the company. It is considered that they need to be supplied with some information about the company's affairs in order to be reassured that the company will be able to continue paying interest on their debt, and that their loans will eventually be repaid.

3 Suppliers and other creditors. This group is similar to the lender group. Suppliers and creditors need some information about the company in order to decide whether to trade with it. Thereafter, they need some reassurance that they will be paid for what they have supplied to the company.

4 Employees. Without an appropriate amount of *financial* capital, a company could not be formed, but it would soon go out of business without the input of some *human* capital, that is, without someone to manage and operate it. It follows that employees must be a potentially important user group of financial information, because they need some assurance about the stability and profitability of the company. It could be argued, of course, that employees are hardly an *external* group since they work within the company. However, this does not necessarily mean that they have ready access to the type of information about the company that would be of interest to them.

5 Customers. Customers often have a long-term involvement with a company, and like many of the other groupings, therefore, they too need some reassurance about its long-term future.

6 The public. A company does not work in isolation, and its success or otherwise does have an indirect impact on many other people with whom it comes into contact. A company that happens to be a major employer in a small town, for example, helps to generate employment outside the company itself, since other entities develop to provide services to the company's employees and their families. Hence the public, in the form of the local community, has an interest in a company's performance and future prospects.

7 Government and their agencies. Government and their agencies (as the Exposure Draft puts it) is another important user group that is interested in a company's progress, whether this is in respect of employment prospects, the collection of taxes (such as value added tax or corporation tax), or the compilation of statistics.

It should be noted that not all observers accept the above groupings. It could be argued, for example, that the public's interest is too remote for a company to be required to inform the local community about its affairs (although it may be good public relations to do so). Similarly, the government can obtain all the information it wants about a company by other means, without necessarily having to establish a separate reporting system.

Nonetheless, the above analysis is a useful starting point for a discussion about the disclosure of information, and it leads on to a debate about the current minimum disclosure requirements.

SOURCES OF AUTHORITY

In the United Kingdom, the reporting of information to parties external to a limited liability company is governed by three main sources of authority:

1 those covered by Acts of Parliament referred (to as 'statutory requirements');
2 those determined by the business community acting in conjunction with the accountancy profession (referred to as 'professional requirements'); and
3 those laid down by the capital market (referred to as 'stock exchange requirements').

Statutory requirements

For well over 150 years, the United Kingdom has adopted what might be called a *permissive* system of financial reporting. This means that Parliament lays down a body of general accounting law, but the detailed implementation of it is left mainly to those parties who have a direct interest in the legislation. Until recently, this was left largely to the accountancy profession, but more recently the wider business and professional community has also become involved. The permissive system is in marked contrast to the *prescriptive* system of financial reporting which is found in most continental countries (such as France and Germany). In a prescriptive system, some very detailed accounting rules and regulations are laid down in law, and hence there is not the same opportunity for individual interpretation of it as there is in a permissive system.

Unfortunately, the permissive system as operated in the United Kingdom has given rise to what has become known as *creative accounting*. Loosely translated, this means that it is possible for a company to report its results within some very wide limits and still be within the law. This form of accounting has not enhanced the accountancy profession's reputation, because it is difficult, for example, for the public to see how one firm of accountants can argue that a company has made a profit, while another firm of accountants (using exactly the same data) can assert that it has made a loss. Fortunately, as will be discussed shortly, steps have now been taken to reduce the opportunity for producing such conflicting results.

The present British statutory requirements are contained in an Act of Parliament known as the *Companies Act 1985*. This Act is a consolidating measure and it includes the earlier Companies Acts of 1948, 1967, 1976, 1980, and 1981, respectively, but some provisions have now been amended by the Companies Act of 1989. However, when you come across an auditor's report, it will simply state that the accounts have been prepared in accordance with 'the Companies Act 1985', as the 1985 Act remains the main legislative source.

Companies Act legislation since 1981 has been brought about mainly by the UK's membership of the European Union, and so, strictly speaking, it is no longer British law but European law which has been adopted in the United Kingdom.

The Companies Act 1985 lays down the *minimum* disclosure requirements which companies must disclose to their shareholders. (Apart from some brief references to creditors and employees, the other user groups discussed earlier in this chapter are barely mentioned.) Although the Act lays down the minimum requirements, the inclusion of additional professional and stock exchange requirements means that shareholders are now supplied with a considerable amount of detailed information about a company's affairs.

In effect, the statutory disclosure of information to parties external to a company takes two forms:

1 Shareholders are automatically supplied with a copy of the company's annual report of which they can elect to receive a summary version (see Chapter 12 for more detail).
2 The annual report has also to be 'filed' with the Registrar of Companies. This means that anyone can go along to Companies House in either Cardiff or Edinburgh in order to have a look at it. 'Large' companies must file the full annual report, but 'medium' and 'small' companies may file a modified version. The terms 'large', 'medium', and 'small' are defined in the Act, but they can be amended from time-to-time by means of a 'statutory instrument'. The definitions are based on a combination of size criteria, viz. turnover, gross assets, and number of employees.

Professional requirements

As mentioned in Chapter 2, the professional requirements that govern the disclosure of information by limited liability companies are issued by a body called the Accounting Standards Board (ASB). The ASB was set up in 1990. It succeeded an earlier body known as the Accounting Standards Committee (ASC) which was created in 1970 (originally as the Accounting Standards Steering Committee, or ASSC).

The main aim of the ASC was to narrow the areas of difference in accounting practice. As explained above, it has been traditional in the UK for only broad principles of company law to be laid down by Parliament, and accountants and other interested parties have then been relatively free to interpret the law quite broadly. This meant that different accountants quite often adopted different methods, even when using the same data as other accountants. In the late 1960s this resulted in a number of well-publicized accounting 'scandals', and the profession was forced into taking some action. This resulted in the setting up of the ASSC by the accountancy profession, although it was not until 1976 that all the six main professional accountancy bodies had become members of it.

The ASC issued what were known as 'Statements of Standard Accounting Practice' (SSAPs). SSAPs laid down some fairly general guidelines which professionally-qualified accountants were expected to follow in preparing financial accounts (in theory, they could be disciplined by their respective professional body if they did not do so). Such accountants were also expected to encourage their clients and their employers to adopt and abide by the spirit of the standards' programme.

By the time of its demise in 1990, the ASC had issued 25 SSAPs (although three had been withdrawn). The ASC fell into disrepute, partly because many of the standards enabled a great deal of interpretation (hence defeating their objective), and partly because the ASC was perceived to be very slow in reacting to events. This was caused largely because all the six bodies had to approve a draft standard before it could be issued.

The ASB's position is somewhat different. It is one of the main committees of the *Financial Reporting Council* (FRC). The FRC comprises members from industry, commerce, and the public sector, and unlike the ASC its membership is not dominated by the accountancy profession. The ASB issues what are called 'Financial Reporting Standards' (FRSs), but at its inception in 1990 it also adopted the 22 SSAPs that were still outstanding. It is the intention of the ASB to replace all the SSAPs with FRSs, and indeed by mid-1996 eight FRSs had been issued. Unlike SSAPs, FRSs do not need to be approved by all six professional bodies before they are issued. Hence, in theory, the ASB can react to events much more quickly than did the ASC, although in practice a great deal of discussion and argument is still required.

Like SSAPs, FRSs are meant to give guidance on how certain matters should be dealt with in preparing financial reports. Some FRSs permit various options, whereas others prescribe a specific method. They normally also include a great deal of information to be disclosed. Most of the FRSs that have been issued so far deal with some extremely complex issues, and they are very difficult to understand.

The ASB's job is also supported by an *Urgent Issues Task Force* (UITF). No doubt at this stage you are finding all of these initials somewhat confusing, but since you are likely to come across them, it is necessary to refer to them. However, in order to help you sort them out, the standard-setting process in the United Kingdom (through the FRC) is shown in diagrammatic format in Exhibit 10.2.

The UITF's role is to react quickly to any new or emerging financial reporting issue that requires some immediate response to be given. In other words, it acts as a 'fire-fighting' body.

As can be seen from Exhibit 10.2, besides the ASB, the FRS has another main arm attached to it. This is known as the Financial Reporting Review Panel (FRRP). The FRRP's job is to examine apparent defects in published accounts, and to decide what it should do about them. It is usually successful in persuading companies to accept its recommendations, but if this were not the case, it has the power to ask for the accounts to be re-issued. If a company refuses to accede to the FRRP's wishes, then it is possible for court proceedings to be instituted.

This possibility arises because the Companies Act 1985 (as amended by the 1989 Companies Act) requires companies (other than small and medium-sized ones) to state whether their accounts have been prepared in accordance with applicable accounting standards. If this is not the case, then details have to be given for all material departures from such standards. If a company has not abided by a particular standard, it is possible for the court to ask the directors of the company for an explanation, and they might then be ordered to comply with that standard. This is the first time in British law that accounting standards have been given some legal recognition, so that it can be argued that accounting standards now have semi-statutory status.

Exhibit 10.2 The structure of standard setting in the United Kingdom

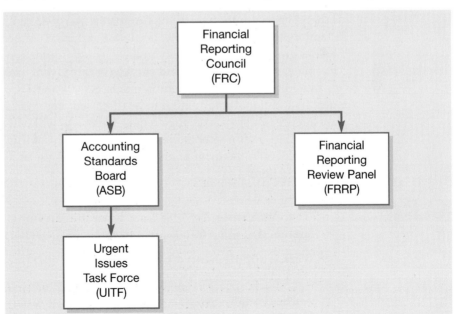

However, the Companies Act 1985 also has an overriding clause that requires accounts to give 'a *true and fair view* of the state of affairs of the company'. As no one is quite sure what is meant by the phrase 'true and fair', directors can always argue that they have not followed a particular standard because to do so would not present a 'true and fair view'. Although this phrase has been enshrined in company law for some 50 years, its meaning has never been tested in a court of law, and no one has ever been taken to court if they have adopted it as an overriding rule. It is also interesting to note that the phrase has been incorporated into European law, but the other member states have tended to translate it literally, and hence it is open to quite different interpretations in all 15 member countries.

Stock exchange requirements

The stock exchange regulations covering disclosure of information no longer carry the same significance that they once did, primarily because most of what used to be required is now contained within either statutory or professional requirements. However, for certain categories of companies (such as those that are listed), there are a few additional disclosure requirements, e.g. some extra information has to be provided about creditors, and an interim report has to be issued.

CONCLUSION

In this chapter, we have provided you with some background information about the external disclosure requirements relating to limited liability companies. Although it is possible to recognize at least seven user groups of published financial information, the Companies Act 1985 (which contains the main statutory disclosure requirements) almost exclusively concentrates on the shareholder group. Indeed, it is only in the event of liquidation of the company that two other groups (creditors and employees) are given some recognition.

In addition to statutory requirements, SSAPs and FRSs also require a great deal of additional information to be disclosed, and for listed companies there are a few extra stock exchange requirements. As will be seen in the next chapter, all these requirements mean that the amount of information supplied to shareholders in the form of an *Annual Report* results in a document of daunting proportions.

Key points	
	1 **The Companies Act 1985 lays down the minimum amount of information that must be supplied to company shareholders.**
	2 **This is supplemented by professional requirements issued by the ASB in the form of SSAPs and FRSs.**
	3 **Such accounting standards have semi-statutory status.**

> 4 Listed companies are also bound by a number of additional stock exchange requirements.
>
> 5 Accounts should be prepared in such a way that they represent a true and fair view of the company's affairs. This is an overriding rule of the Companies Act, and it takes precedence over other legislative, professional, and stock exchange requirements.

CHECK YOUR LEARNING

1 What are the three main sources of authority for the disclosure of information to shareholders?

2 What is the main source of company legislation in the UK?

3 What do the following initials mean:
   (a) ASC
   (b) SSAP
   (c) FRC
   (d) ASB
   (e) FRS?

4 What statutory rule overrides all other disclosure requirements?

Answers
1 legislation; professional requirements; stock exchange requirements
2 Companies Act 1985
3 (a) Accounting Standards Committee (b) Statement of Standard Accounting Practice (c) Financial Reporting Council (d) Accounting Standards Board (e) Financial Reporting Standard
4 the true and fair view rule

DISCUSSION QUESTIONS

10.1
What type of information should a company disclose to its shareholders?

10.2
Should Parliament lay down rigid accounting procedures for supplying information to company shareholders?

10.3
'Accounting standards should become enshrined in company law.' Discuss.

10.4
Do you think that the true and fair view rule should be abandoned?

CHAPTER 11

The annual report

Finance directors set less store by annual reports

By Jim Kelly,
Accountancy Correspondent

Finance directors at Britain's top companies think informal talks with analysts and preliminary, interim, and final results announcements are far more important in communicating with the City than the annual report and accounts.

The finance directors, representing 50 per cent of the value of the FTSE 100 companies, believe informal communication with the City helps underpin a 'no surprises' culture in which the share price is protected by disclosing good and bad news.

But Mr Richard Barker, the academic who interviewed 40 finance directors at top companies, believes the report and accounts are valued as helping to underpin the credibility of financial information. 'It is the dog that doesn't bark,' he said.

Mr Barker said that his research surprisingly revealed that finance directors held 'leading analysts' in high regard and that as a whole the City was not seen as short-termist. Finance directors believe shares are fairly accurately valued as a result.

Mr Barker, of the faculty of economics and politics at the University of Cambridge, said that he was surprised by the amount of time and effort finance directors and chief executives spent after results announcements in talks with institutional investors and analysts.

In spite of the apparent lack of interest in the report and accounts Mr Barker found that finance directors considered it an 'anchor', providing stability, and important for wider communication especially with individual shareholders.

He said that he had found a 'strategic interaction' between finance directors and the City in which it was understood that credibility was vital to the share price and that it was therefore impossible, and damaging, to obscure bad news for any period.

'If you didn't have the report and accounts there the credibility game wouldn't work in the same way. It needs to be there but plays a negative role rather than a positive one,' said Mr Barker, whose research was funded by the Economic and Social Research Council.

As a result of the perceived importance of accounting information the work of the Accounting Standards Board was widely seen in a positive light.

Finance directors thought that the accounting treatment of goodwill was important to the market's perception of value – in spite of the fact that theoretically the treatment had no impact on earnings. He concluded that it was possible that communications with the City were based on an 'over-focus' on set parameters rather than a 'full understanding of value'.

The Financial Times, 17 May 1996

Exhibit 11.0 Maybe annual reports are not all that important?

The annual accounts of a company must be supplied to shareholders at least 21 days before the accounts are due to be considered at a general meeting of the company. The accounts comprise the *company's* balance sheet, and a profit and loss account, the directors' report, the auditors' report, and if required, *group* accounts. However, 'the accounts' are often accompanied by other types of reports and reviews. In this chapter, we are going to examine the contents of what, for convenience, will be called 'the annual report'.

<table>
<tr><td>**Learning objectives**</td><td>

By the end of this chapter, you will be able to:

- **identify the main sections of an annual report;**

- **list the main contents of a chairman's statement, an auditor's financial report, and a directors' report;**

- **locate the major items contained in a group profit and loss account, a statement of total recognized gains and losses, a group balance sheet, a group cash flow statement, and notes to the accounts;**

- **trace the notes to the accounts back to the main financial statements.**

</td></tr>
</table>

BACKGROUND

An annual report received from a large multi-national company can be somewhat off-putting, especially to those shareholders who have had no training in basic accounting. It will usually arrive in a large brown/white envelope, and it will feel very heavy. Assuming that the envelope is opened and the pages flicked through, the average shareholder is likely to be totally bewildered by what is inside the report. Some reports may be as long as 100 pages, they will usually be printed in a wide variety of print sizes and colours, and they will contain a great many narrative reports as well as many pages of statistical data. Fortunately, the sheer off-putting nature of such information is often relieved by a series of eye-catching glossy diagrams and photographs.

Nonetheless, it is difficult for even experienced and trained users of annual reports to make much sense of them, so it is probably almost impossible for the average shareholder to do so, unless they have had some training in accounting. In this chapter we aim to offer you some clear guidance about the contents of annual reports so that you will be able to find your way round them relatively easily. However, you will appreciate that, as not all annual reports necessarily follow the same format and structure, we can only offer you some *general* guidance, although by the end of the chapter you will have sufficient confidence to be able to adapt the knowledge that you have gained so as to be able to cope with different types of annual reports.

For convenience, our study of annual reports will be divided into four main sections, although in practice no such clear differentiation will normally be apparent. These sections will be referred to as *introductory material*, *operational reports and reviews*, *the accounts*, and *shareholder information*. They are shown in diagrammatic format in Exhibit 11.1.

INTRODUCTORY MATERIAL

Many annual reports begin with a brief summary of the history of the company and its objectives. These may then be followed by a review of the year's financial and operating results which may be supported by a series of charts, graphs, photographs, and statistical tables comparing the year's achievements with previous years.

None of this information is statutory or professionally required, and sometimes it is presented in a somewhat misleading fashion. A carefully constructed graph, for example, can often disguise the fact that an apparent rise in sales has not been particularly spectacular.

OPERATIONAL REPORTS AND REVIEWS

This section will nearly always contain a report from the chairman, and it may also contain a report from the chief executive, as well as individual reports from other senior officers of the company. These various reports are often accompanied by many pages detailing the company's operational activities, especially those relating to production and marketing. They are frequently accompanied by a series of vivid photographs proclaiming the virtues of the company's products.

This section of an annual report might, therefore, be regarded as more in the nature of a public relations exercise than an attempt to communicate financial information. Indeed, such material is normally a fairly blatant form of advertising, and it is especially prominent in consumer-orientated companies, since it is to the company's advantage, of course, to encourage the shareholders to buy the company's own products.

The above comments might now, however, be a little unfair, because in the ASB issued a statement of good practice that supported the idea of companies including an *Operating and Financial Review* (OFR) in their annual report. The suggestion had come from the *Cadbury Report* which was published in 1992 by the Committee on the Financial Aspects of Corporate Governance. This Committee was set up in 1991 by the FRC, the London Stock Exchange and the

Exhibit 11.1 The main sections of an annual report

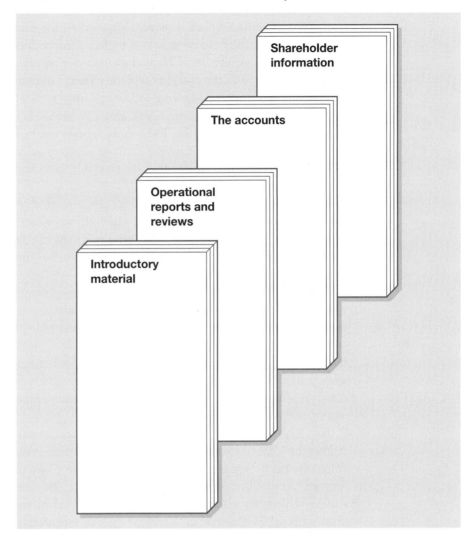

accountancy profession to examine the ways in which companies were governed. An OFR is supposed to cover, *inter alia*, the business as a whole, discuss individual aspects of the business, give an insight into matters that underpin the financial results, and consider factors that might affect the company's future performance.

It follows that the operational report and review section of an annual report may contain some interesting information, e.g. about the development of a new product. However, because such promotional material can take up many pages, the financial reports may have less impact. This is unfortunate because, after all, the main reason for publishing an annual report is to report to shareholders on the financial performance of the company.

In this context, probably the most interesting report contained in this section is the chairman's report. Indeed, from the research undertaken into the usefulness of annual reports, it would appear that the chairman's report is the one that is most likely to be read. As there are no statutory, professional, or stock exchange requirements for a chairman to prepare a report, there is no specified format, and the contents will vary from company to company. Some chairman's reports are very long (although most chairmen manage to limit their comments to one or two pages), and a chairman is quite free to include almost anything that they like. They should, however, be mindful of the effect that their remarks may have on the company's share price, and a great deal of trouble could be stored up for the company if the chairman is too optimistic about its future prospects.

A typical chairman's report will, *inter alia*, review the results for the year, give some details about the dividend, highlight the major changes in the company's activities for the year, and comment on the achievements of the directors and other employees. It may also give an indication of how the chairman views the company's future.

The chairman's report will normally be found within the first few pages of most annual reports, but in order to find its exact position you may need to consult the contents page of the annual report (assuming that there is one).

One other narrative report that may be included in this section is a brief biography of each of the company's directors. Such a report will not tell you very much, and each biography will probably give you no more than the director's age, profession, their specific company responsibilities, and the directorships held in other companies.

Two interesting points to note at this stage are (a) whether the Chairman is also the Chief Executive (the Cadbury Committee recommended that the roles should be separate); and (b) whether the company has a number of 'non-executive directors' (i.e. those without specific operational managerial duties within the company). The Cadbury Committee considered that a strong group of non-executive directors was essential if a company was to set and maintain high standards of corporate governance. This kind of information will, therefore, give you a strong indication of the type of company with which you are dealing. For example, is it one that has a strong sense of responsibility to all those groups that have an interest in the company, i.e its 'stakeholders'?

THE ACCOUNTS

This is the main section of the actual report. It contains the statutory and professionally-required information which is the reason for issuing the report in the first place. Such information is both detailed and complex, and so we will break it down into a number of sub-sections to make it easier for you to follow. This breakdown is also shown in diagrammatic format in Exhibit 11.2.

As the exact position of the various sub-sections within an overall annual report will vary from company to company, each of them will be dealt with in alphabetical order.

Exhibit 11.2 The accounts section of an annual report

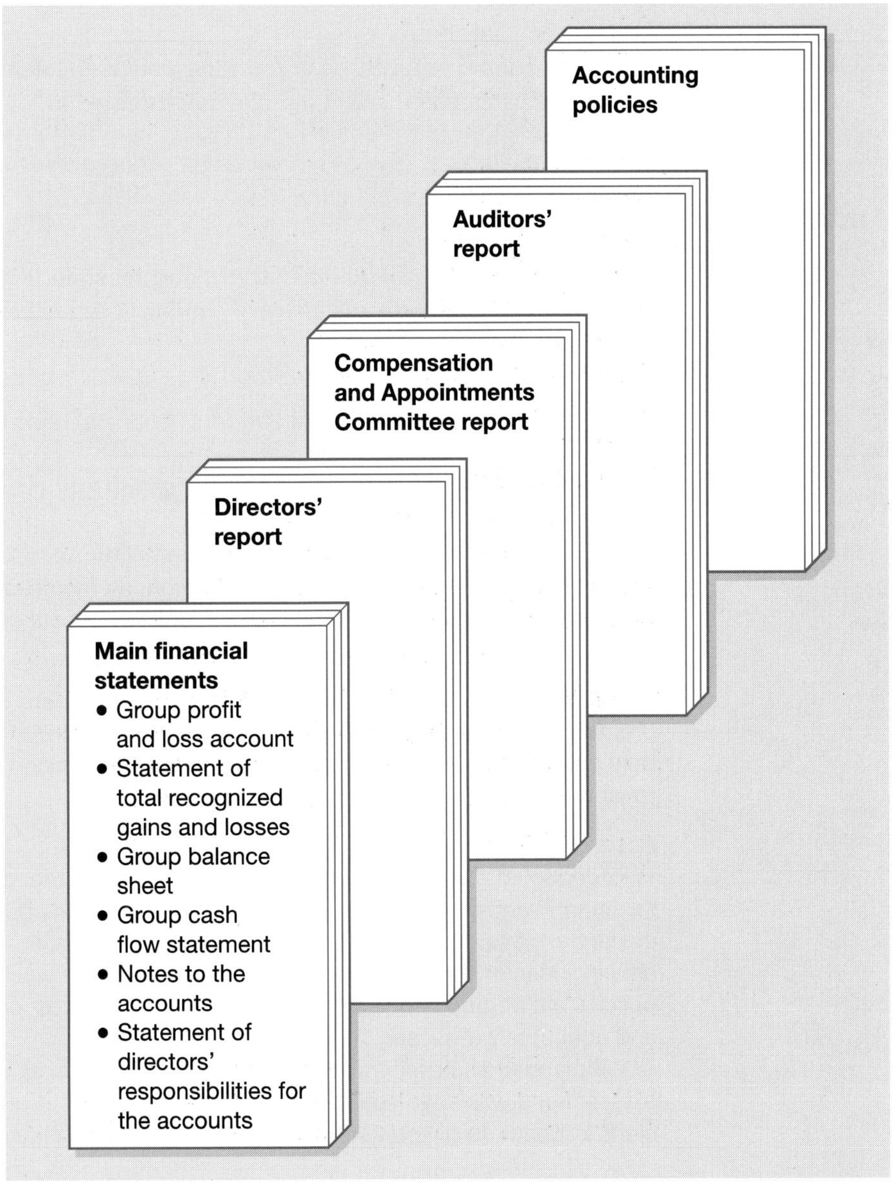

Accounting policies

Auditors' report

Compensation and Appointments Committee report

Directors' report

Main financial statements
- Group profit and loss account
- Statement of total recognized gains and losses
- Group balance sheet
- Group cash flow statement
- Notes to the accounts
- Statement of directors' responsibilities for the accounts

Accounting policies

This is a statement required by SSAP 2. It is important to digest it thoroughly in order to gain a fundamental understanding of the financial result for the year. As the term suggests, it lays down the accounting policies the company has adopted in compiling the financial accounts. It should state, for example, which accounting model has been adopted in preparing the accounts (normally historic cost, but it could be replacement cost), as well as the various methods adopted in dealing with such matters as consolidation policies, foreign currency translations, the definition of turnover, the treatment of research and development expenditure, the method and rates used for depreciating fixed assets, the stock valuation method, and the treatment of taxation and pension contributions.

In some annual reports, the accounting policies' statement is not prepared as a separate statement, and it may be incorporated in 'Notes to the accounts' (see below).

Auditors' report

The auditors' report will be fairly short, and most auditors' reports that you are likely to come across will be very similar. A typical example is shown in Exhibit 11.3.

Exhibit 11.3 Example of a typical auditors' financial report

REPORT OF THE AUDITORS TO THE MEMBERS OF ENERGY PLC

We have audited the financial statements on pages XX to XX which have been prepared under the historical cost convention, as modified by the revaluation of certain fixed assets and the accounting policies set out on page XX.

Respective responsibilities of Directors and Auditors
As described on page XX, the Company's Directors are responsible for the preparation of financial statements. It is our responsibility to form an independent opinion, based on our audit, on those statements, and to report our opinion to you.

Basis of opinion
We conducted our audit in accordance with Auditing Standards issued by the Auditing Practices Board. An audit includes examination, on a test basis, of evidence relevant to the amounts and disclosures in the financial statements. It also includes an assessment of the statements, and of whether the accounting policies are appropriate to the company's circumstances, consistently applied, and adequately disclosed.

We planned and performed our audit so as to obtain all the information and explanations which we considered necessary in order to provide us with sufficient evidence to give reasonable assurance that the financial statements are

---

free from material mis-statement, whether caused by fraud or other irregularity or error. In forming our opinion we also evaluated the overall adequacy of the presentation of information in the financial statements.

Opinion
In our opinion the financial statements give a true and fair view of the state of the Company's and the Group's affairs at 31 March 19X5 and the profit and cash flows of the Group for the (year then ended) and have been properly prepared in accordance with the Companies Act 1985.

Cope & Co.,   31 May 19X5
Chartered Accountants and Registered Auditors
London

Besides the auditors' report dealing with the financial statements, you might also find another type of auditors' report. Under a 'Code of Best Practice' which was another recommendation in the *Cadbury Report*, listed companies are recommended to include in their annual report a statement of compliance with the Code. This *statement of compliance* must be reviewed by the company's auditors.

There is no formal requirement for auditors to report publicly on their review. However, the Auditing Practices Board (APB) considers it desirable that auditors should publish a report that is separate from the one relating to financial statements. (The APB was set up in 1991 by the six major professional accountancy bodies in order to advance standards of auditing and associated review activities in the United Kingdom and Eire.)

Auditors' reports relating to corporate governance matters may take two forms: (a) where in the auditors' opinion the company has complied with the Code of Best Practice; or (b) where in the auditors' opinion the company has not (at least in part) complied with what is required by the Code. An example of the first form is shown in Exhibit 11.4.

Exhibit 11.4 Example of an auditors' report on corporate governance matters

REPORT OF THE AUDITORS TO THE MEMBERS OF ENERGY PLC

In addition to our audit of the financial statements, we have reviewed the directors' statement on page XX concerning the company's compliance with the paragraphs of the Code of Best Practice specified for our review by the London Stock Exchange. The objective of our review is to draw attention to non-compliance with those paragraphs of the Code which are not disclosed.

We carried out our review having regard to the Bulletin 1995/1 *Disclosures Relating to Corporate Governance*, issued by the Auditing Practices Board. That Bulletin does not require us to perform the additional work necessary to, and we do not, express any opinion on the effectiveness of either the company's system of internal financial control or its corporate governance procedures nor on the ability of the company to continue in operational existence.

▶

> *Opinion*
>
> With respect to the directors' statement on internal (financial) controls on page XX, in our opinion the directors have provided the disclosures required by paragraphs 4.5 and 4.6 of the Code (as supplemented by the related guidance for directors) and such statements are not inconsistent with the information of which we are aware from our audit work on the financial statements.
>
> Based on enquiry of certain directors and officers of the company, and examination of relevant documents, in our opinion the directors' statement on page XX appropriately reflects the company's compliance with the other paragraphs of the Code specified for our review.
>
> Cope & Co.,   31 May 19X5
> Chartered Accountants and Registered Auditors,
> London

Referring to Exhibit 11.4, if the auditors were of the opinion that the directors had not complied with the Code of Best Practice, then the auditors would refer to this fact in the last two paragraphs of their report.

Compensation and appointments committee report

Another aspect of the *Cadbury Report* was the recommendation that companies should institute formal procedures for the appointment and remuneration of directors. Some companies now include, therefore, either a separate 'compensation and appointments committee report' (the actual title may vary from company to company), or they may insert some comments within the directors' report.

A compensation and appointments committee report will include such matters as the membership of the committee, its terms of reference, the company's remuneration policy for directors and senior managers, and details of remuneration paid to them during the year.

Directors' report

The directors' report is a statutory requirement, and a copy must be attached to the accounts sent to shareholders. It contains a great deal of information, such as details of the company's activities, its auditors, some information about the directors, charitable and political donations paid, the proposed dividend, the company's employment policy, a note about any major changes or values affecting its fixed assets, and a reference to any changes in its share capital. Following the recommendations of the *Cadbury Report* (which has been referred to frequently throughout this chapter), the report will also now include a section on 'corporate governance'. The section will include some details about the Board and its Committees, and the company's system of internal control.

Main financial statements

You will normally find six main financial statements contained within a listed company's annual report: a profit and loss account, a statement of total recognized gains and losses, a balance sheet, a cash flow statement, some notes to the accounts, and a statement of directors' responsibilities. Most of these statements are extremely complex and quite hard to understand. However, based on the knowledge gained in the earlier part of this book, and by working carefully through this chapter, you should not have much difficulty in extracting the information you need.

The main parts of the financial statements will be dealt with in each of the following sub-sections. However, there are three points that we need to cover before we do so. They are as follows:

1 Differing formats. Companies do have slightly different ways of presenting the required information, so you must not expect to find accounts that are necessarily identical to the ones that are used as examples in this chapter.

2 Groups. The published accounts of most large listed companies will relate to a *group* of companies. A group of companies is like a family. One company (say Company A) may buy shares in another company (say Company B). When Company A owns more than 50% of the voting shares in Company B, B becomes a *subsidiary* of A. If A owned more than 20% but less than 50% of the voting shares in B, B would be known as an *associated* company of A. In effect, B is considered to be the offspring of A. Of course B might have children of its own), say Company C and Company D, and thus C and D become part of the family, i.e. part of the A group of companies. It is also the case that sometimes one company is in a position to *control* the affairs of another company, even if it does not necessarily own a substantial number of shares in the other company. If this is the case, then companies that are perhaps *controlled* by other companies will be included as part of the group. An example of this type of group structure is shown in Exhibit 11.5.

The Companies Act 1985 actually uses the term *group undertaking* for a subsidiary company, and *undertakings in which the company has participating interest* to describe an associated company. This is because the Companies Act 1989 brought in a requirement to include other types of entities (and not just companies) in the group accounts.

The main significance of these relationships is that the Companies Act 1985 then requires the accounts to be published for the *group*, i.e. in effect, as though it was one entire entity, thereby ignoring any inter-group activities, such as sales made or transfers of funds between group companies.

Thus, when inspecting a set of published accounts for a listed company, you can normally expect to see a *group* profit and loss account, a *group* balance sheet, and a *group* cash flow statement. The Companies Act 1985 does permit group accounts to be presented in several ways. The most common method

Exhibit 11.5 Example of a group of companies

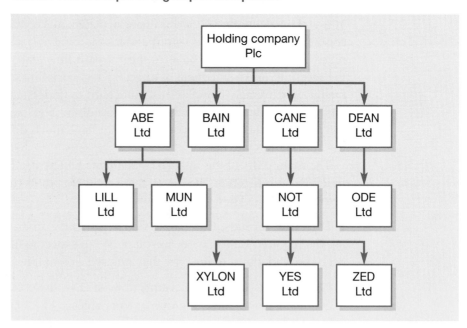

of satisfying the statutory requirements is to prepare a group profit and loss account and a group balance sheet, accompanied by a balance sheet for the *holding* company (i.e. Company A in the example used on page 235). Cash flow statements are not required by law, but professional requirements also normally expect large companies to prepare a group cash flow statement.

In order to prepare group accounts, it is necessary to add together, i.e. *consolidate*, all of the company accounts within the group. As a result, the subsidiary company results are absorbed into the *holding* company's accounts (the treatment is slightly different for associated companies). This may sound a fairly routine arithmetical task, but in practice (especially in the case of large multi-national companies), it is extremely complicated. Hence it has become somewhat of a specialism even among accountants.

3 Comparative figures. The Companies Act 1985 requires the previous year's accounts to be included alongside the current year's results. This adds to the amount of information given in the accounts, although there is some advantage in being able to make comparisons between the two years. However, it does appear to make the accounts even more complicated!

With the above points in mind, we can now begin to examine the main published financial statements in some detail.

The group profit and loss account

In presenting the profit and loss account, the Companies Act 1985 allows a choice to be made between two formats:

1 **Horizontal**. In this format, expenditures are listed on the left-hand side of the page, and incomes on the right-hand side.
2 **Vertical**. This format presents the income and expenditure on a line-by-line basis.

The vertical format should be familiar to you. It has been used almost exclusively throughout this book, mainly because as many UK companies have adopted it in their accounts, you are likely to come across it.

The Companies Act 1985 also permits expenditure to be disclosed according to *type*. Again, there is a choice between: (a) the operational format; and (b) the type of expenditure format. These formats are shown in Exhibit 11.6.

Exhibit 11.6 Examples of the vertical profit and loss account expenditure formats

(a) Operational	£000	(b) Type of expenditure	£000	£000
Turnover	9000	Turnover		9000
Cost of sales	(5500)	Change in stocks of finished goods and work-in-progress		200
Gross profit	3500	Own work capitalized		50
		Other operating income		100
				9350
Distribution costs	(1000)	Raw materials and consumables	(4000)	
Administrative expenses	(1600)	Other external charges	(400)	
Operating profit	900	Staff costs	(3000)	
		Depreciation and other amounts written off tangible and intangible fixed assets	(900)	
Other operating income	100	Other operating charges	(50)	(8350)
Operating profit	1000	Operating profit		1000

Notes:
1 The exhibit contains dummy information.
2 After the operating profit profit stage the two fomats are identical.

As can be seen from Exhibit 11.6, the type of expenditure format is very much more detailed than the operational format. Both types are used in the UK, but the operational format is very popular, probably because it is a little easier to follow. It is, in fact, basically the same format that we have used throughout the book. However, there is also another good reason for adopting it, which is that the type of expenditure format is much more difficult to adapt to the requirements of FRS 3 (Reporting Financial Performance).

Following this introduction, we can now examine a published profit and loss account in some detail. This is done in Exhibit 11.7.

Exhibit 11.7 Example of a published profit and loss account

ENERGY PUBLIC LIMITED COMPANY
Group profit and loss account for the year to 31 March 19X2

	19X2 £000	19X2 £000
Turnover (1)		
Continuing operations	44 000	
Acquisitions	2 000	
	46 000	
Discontinued operations	3 000	49 000
Cost of sales (2)		(40 000)
Gross profit (3)		9 000
Distribution costs (4)		(4 000)
Administrative expenses (5)		(2 000)
Other operating income (6)		20
Operating profit (7)		
Continuing operations	2 740	
Acquisitions	250	
	2 990	
Discontinued operations	30	
Profit on ordinary activities before interest		3 020
Other interest receivable and other income (8)		295
Interest payable and similar charges (9)		(260)
Profit on ordinary activities before taxation (10)		3 055
Tax on profit on ordinary activities (11)		(145)
Profit on ordinary activities after taxation (12)		2 910
Minority interests (13)		(110)
Profit for the financial year (14)		2 800
Dividends paid and proposed (15)		(2 400)
Retained profit for the year (16)		£400
Earnings per share (17)		2.85p

Notes:
(a) The numbers in brackets after each item refer to the tutorial notes below.
(b) Reference to the formal notes, and the notes themselves, are not included.
(c) Comparative figures have been ignored.
(d) The Exhibit contains dummy information.

Tutorial notes

1 Turnover is usually defined as being sales to customers outside the group less returns by customers, exclusive of trade discounts and value added tax. You will notice that turnover has been analysed between continuing operations, acquisitions and discontinued operations. In other words, sales from entities taken over during the year, and sales arising from activities prior to their disposal during the year. FRS 3 (Reporting Financial Performance) requires this breakdown of turnover.

2 The detailed calculation for the cost of sales does not have to be disclosed. The term is not defined in the Companies Act 1985.

3 The gross profit may not be identical to that shown in the internal accounts because of the definition used for the cost of sales.

4 The Companies Act 1985 does not define what is meant by distribution costs.

5 Similarly, administrative expenses are not defined in the Act.

6 Other operating income will include income from rentals and royalties.

7 Operating profit. This is the point at which the operational and type of expenditure formats become identical. Note that FRS 3 requires the operating profit to be broken down into operating profit from continuing operations, acquisitions, and discontinued operations.

8 Other interest receivable and similar income includes interest received on loans.

9 Interest payable and similar charges will include interest payable on bank and other short-term borrowings.

10 The profit on ordinary activities before taxation will require a detailed formal note to the accounts. It will include such information as the auditors' remuneration, directors' emoluments (as they are called), details of wages and salaries (in total), depreciation charges (in total), and social security and pension costs.

11 The tax on the profit on ordinary activities will consist largely of the company's corporation tax, but it may also include a number of technical accounting adjustments affecting taxation.

12 The amount shown for profit on ordinary activities after taxation is simply a sub-total.

13 A proportion of the after-tax profits may be due to shareholders outside the group if the holding company has not purchased all of the shares in a subsidiary company.

14 The profit for the financial year is the total amount of net profit for the year that could be distributed to group members.

15 The dividends paid and proposed to be paid will include dividends paid or payable on all types of shares.

16 The retained profit for the year will be transferred to the revenue reserves shown in the balance sheet. The retained profit will be used to help finance the future expansion of the company.

17 The formal definition of earnings per share is quite complex, but basically it is calculated by taking the after-tax earnings less preference dividends, and dividing them by the number of issued ordinary shares.

Statement of total recognized gains and losses

FRS 3 now requires companies to prepare a statement called a *statement of total recognized gains and losses*. This statement will normally be presented immediately after the profit and loss account. It should include *all* the gains and losses that the company has made during the year, and not just those that are debited/credited to the profit and loss account. It is possible for some gains/losses (such as deficits/surpluses arising from the revaluation of fixed assets, and foreign currency exchange gains/losses) to be taken straight to a balance sheet reserve account, and hence they may never appear in the profit and loss account. An example of a statement of total recognized gains and losses as shown in Exhibit 11.8.

Exhibit 11.8 Example of a statement of total recognized gains and losses

	19X2 £000
Profit for the financial year (1)	2800
Unrealized surplus on revaluation of properties (2)	100
Unrealized loss/gain on trade investments (3)	(30)
Currency translation difference on foreign currency net investments (4)	(10)
Total recognized gains relating to the year (5)	2860

Tutorial notes
1 These figures are extracted from the profit and loss account.
2 Revaluation surpluses on properties will be added to the revaluation reserve account shown on the balance sheet.
3 Trade investment losses and gains will be dealt with similarly.
4 Currency translation differences will be adjusted against the profit and loss account balance shown on the balance sheet.
5 These figures show the total gain (or loss) from all sources that the company has made during the year.
6 Comparative figures are not shown.

Group balance sheet

The Companies Act 1985 allows a choice to be made between two different balance sheet formats:

1 **Horizontal**. This format requires the assets to be laid out on the left-hand side of the page, and the capital on the right-hand side.

2 **Vertical**. Here, the assets are listed first on a line-by-line basis, followed by the liabilities.

The vertical format will be most familiar to you, as it has been adopted almost exclusively throughout this book. It is also popular among many UK companies which also adopt this format, although occasionally you may come across examples of the horizontal type.

Published balance sheets do not look very different from those prepared for internal purposes. The main differences are that they will normally be prepared for a group of companies, they will be far more detailed than a sole trader's balance sheets, they will include comparative figures, and a great many pages of formal notes will be attached to them.

An example of a group balance sheet is shown in Exhibit 11.9 (comparative figures are not disclosed).

Exhibit 11.9 Example of a published balance sheet

ENERGY PUBLIC LIMITED COMPANY
Group balance sheet at 31 March 19X2

	Group 19X2 £000	Company 19X2 £000
Fixed assets (1)		
Intangible assets (2)	90	–
Tangible assets (3)	1 400	1 300
Investments (4)	70	1 300
(5)	1 560	2 600
Current assets (6)		
Stocks (7)	6 500	3 300
Debtors (8)	7 500	4 800
Investments (9)	60	–
Cash in bank and in hand (10)	700	20
(11)	14 760	8 120
Creditors: Amounts falling due within one year (12)	(8 500)	(7 000)
Net current assets (13)	6 260	1 120
Total assets less current liabilities (14)	7 820	3 720
Creditors: Amounts falling due after more than one year (15)	(3 000)	–
Provisions for liabilities and charges (16)	(1 200)	–
(17)	£3 620	£3 720

241

	£000	£000
Capital and reserves (18)		
Called up share capital (19)	1 000	1 000
Share premium account (20)	500	500
Revaluation reserve (21)	600	900
Other reserves (22)	360	300
Profit and loss account (23)	1 040	1 020
(24)	3 500	3 720
Minority interests (25)	120	–
(26)	£3 620	£3 720

Approved by the board on XX June 19X2

——————————————— Director (27)

Notes:
(a) The numbers in brackets after each item refer to the tutorial notes below.
(b) Reference to the formal notes, and the notes themselves, are not included.
(c) Comparative figures have been ignored.
(d) The Exhibit contains dummy information.

Tutorial notes
1 The net book value of the fixed assets must be shown under three headings: (a) intangible assets; (b) tangible assets; and (c) investments.
2 Intangible assets are those assets that are not of a physical nature, such as goodwill, patents, and development costs.
3 Tangible assets include land and buildings, plant and machinery, fixtures, fittings, tools, and equipment.
4 Fixed assets investments are those that are intended to be held for the long term, i.e. in excess of 12 months.
5 This line is the total of all the fixed assets.
6 Current assets have also to be analysed into a number of categories (see 7 to 10 below).
7 Stocks must be disclosed under a number of categories, e.g. raw materials and consumables, work-in-progress, finished goods and payments on account. The detail will be shown in a formal note.
8 Debtors have also to be analysed under headings such as trade debtors, other debtors, prepayments, and accrued income. These will be included in a formal note.
9 Current asset investments are those investments held for the short term, i.e. normally for less than 12 months.
10 Cash at bank and in hand. This will be the same amount that will be included in the balance sheet prepared for internal purposes.
11 This line represents the total of current assets.
12 Creditors have to be analysed between short-term creditors (i.e. those payable within the next 12 months), and long-term creditors (i.e. those that do not have to be paid for at least 12 months). Both short- and long-term creditors have to be analysed into a number of categories, such as trade creditors, other creditors, and accruals and deferred income. The details will be found in a formal note.

13 The net current assets line is a sub-total of (Current Assets) (11) less Creditors: amounts falling due within one year (12).

14 This is another sub-total: Fixed assets (1) plus net current assets (13).

15 See 12 above.

16 Provisions for liabilities and charges include provisions for pensions and similar obligations, taxation (including deferred taxation), as well as other provisions which are not specified in the Companies Act 1985.

17 This line represents the balance sheet total.

18 The capital and reserves section is the other main part of the balance sheet. It explains how the net assets (17) have been financed.

19 The called up share capital represents all of the shares that have been issued, details of which will be shown in a formal balance sheet note.

20 The share premium account records the extra amount on top of the nominal value of their shares which shareholders were willing to pay when they bought their shares. It does not attract a dividend, and the Companies Act permits only a few, highly selected uses.

21 Some fixed assets, such as land and buildings, may be revalued. The difference between the revalued amount and the net book value will be credited to a revaluation reserve account. The balance cannot be distributed to shareholders.

22 Other reserves. This balance may include a number of other reserve accounts both of a capital nature (i.e. reserves that cannot be distributed to shareholders) and of a revenue nature (i.e. amounts that may be distributed to shareholders).

23 This is the total of all the profits that have not been distributed to shareholders, less those that have been put into special reserve accounts.

24 This is the total of the capital and reserves' section of the balance sheet. It represents shareholders' funds.

25 The minority interests represent that proportion of the net assets of subsidiary companies which is owned by shareholders outside the group.

26 This line should balance with line 17.

27 The balance sheet should be signed by one director.

Group cash flow statement

The construction of a cash flow statement (CFS) has already been examined in some detail in Chapter 8. Apart from reflecting the activities of a group of companies and the inclusion of comparative figures, published CFSs differ little from the format that was adopted in that chapter.

Unlike the profit and loss account and the balance sheet, CFSs do not have any statutory backing, although they are now considered so important that they are usually regarded as being one of the main financial statements. Indeed, FRS 1 (Revised 1996) requires most companies (small companies are the notable exception) to prepare a CFS, and it is highly unlikely that you will come across published accounts that do not include one.

An example of a group CFS is shown in Exhibit 11.10.

Exhibit 11.10 Example of a group cash flow statement

ENERGY PUBLIC LIMITED COMPANY
Group cash flow statement for the year ended 31 March 19X2

	£000	£000
Cash flow from operating activities		2820
Returns on investments and servicing of finance		(680)
Taxation		(660)
Capital expenditure and		
financial investment		(410)
Acquisitions and disposals		(180)
Equity dividends paid		(1000)
Cash outflow before use of liquid		
resources and financing		(110)
Management of liquid resources		100
Financing – Issue of shares	100	
Increase in debt	490	590
Increase in cash in the period		580

Tutorial notes

1 The exhibit contains dummy information.
2 The formal notes that would normally be attached to the statement have not been included. Such notes (along with various reconciliations) give details about the make-up of each heading.
3 The above format is only a guide: it is not mandatory.
4 Apart from some items that relate only to a group, e.g. dividend received from associated undertakings, and purchase of subsidiary undertakings, the statement is very similar to the one used in Chapter 8.
5 Comparative figures have not been included.

Exhibit 11.10 is based upon the example given in FRS (Revised 1996), but it is likely that you will come across other slightly amended formats. Some can be a little confusing, especially when some figures are shown in brackets. It might help to remember that the basic idea of a CFS is to show where the cash has come from and where it has gone to. In fact, irrespective of the precise format, it should be broken down into eight main sections:

1 operating activities
2 returns on investments and servicing of finance
3 taxation
4 capital expenditure and financial investment
5 acquisitions and disposals
6 equity dividends paid
7 management of liquid resources
8 financing.

Most of the above sections will contain both cash received and cash paid. It is usual to put brackets around amounts *paid* in cash, but sometimes the opposite is the case. This is somewhat confusing, so do not be alarmed if you might have to spend a little time working out exactly what the brackets mean!

Notes to the accounts

The profit and loss account, the balance sheets, and the cash flow statement are usually supported by a great deal of additional information in what is known as 'Notes to the accounts'. Such notes serve two main purposes: (a) they avoid too much detail being shown on the face of the accounts; and (b) they make it easier to provide supplementary information.

One important point to remember is that the notes form an integral part of the accounts and that they are an essential element in the total amount of information that has to be disclosed. However, it is only fair to warn you that it is sometimes difficult to understand how some of the information fits into the overall accounts (such as the movement of the various reserve accounts). By contrast, some information is straightforward, e.g. a note giving details about the company's profit before taxation will include such items as the depreciation charged to the profit and loss account for the year, the auditors' remuneration, and the amount of research and development expenditure.

Statement of directors' responsibilities for the accounts

The Cadbury Committee recommended that directors should explain the nature of their responsibility for preparing the accounts, so you should find a statement to that effect somewhere within the accounts. Normally, it will appear immediately before the auditors' report. It should include information relating to the directors' legal requirements to prepare financial statements, their responsibility to maintain adequate accounting records, the adoption of suitable accounting policies, and the applicable accounting standards adopted in preparing the accounts.

SHAREHOLDER INFORMATION

Towards the end of an annual report you might find some additional data. For convenience, we will refer to this as 'shareholder information'. Shareholder information may include some details about the financial results of the company over a five- or ten-year period, an analysis of the different types of shareholders, the company's financial calendar, notice of the annual general meeting, various names and addresses, and some information about the company's share price.

CONCLUSION

You are now recommended to study the contents of a published annual report with great care (most companies will supply you with a copy if you write to the Company Secretary). Work through the report and see if it does break down broadly into the various sections that we have used in this chapter, viz.:

1 introductory material;
2 operational reports and reviews;
3 the accounts; and
4 shareholder information.

As far as the accounts are concerned, first read through the various reports, e.g. the auditors' report, the statement of directors' responsibilities, and the compensation and appointments committee report, and then work your way through the statement of accounting policies. You will then be ready to tackle the main financial statements (the profit and loss account, the balance sheet, and the cash flow statement) along with the accompanying notes to the accounts.

The amount of time that you will need to spend on perusing the various accounts, statements, and reports will depend partly upon the size of the company, and partly upon your own objectives. If you are thinking of investing in the company, for example, it may be necessary for you to take some of the data contained in the accounts and convert them into the types of accounting ratios covered in Chapter 9. However, if you are only interested in an overview of the company's results, you may need to check only the earnings per share, the liquidity position, and gearing.

Irrespective of your purpose, do not be put off by the sheer volume of information contained in an annual report. GKN's annual report for 1995, for example, was some 85 pages long, but only 32 pages actually related to the accounts section. Nonetheless, even in those 32 pages, there was a great deal of information, so be warned: it normally takes a considerable amount of time to work out what all the information means!

Key points

1 An annual report contains a great many statements and reports. Some of these reports are not required either by statute or by professional requirements.

2 A typical annual report may be divided into four main sections: some introductory material, a number of operational reports and reviews, the main accounts, and some shareholder information.

3 The accounts of a group company will include a group profit and loss account, a statement of total recognized gains and losses, a group balance sheet (including the holding company's balance sheet), and a group cash flow statement. These statements will be supported by many pages of notes.

4 The accounts section will also include a statement of accounting policies, an auditors' report (plus one perhaps relating to corporate governance), a compensation and appointments committee report, a directors' report, and a statement outlining the directors' responsibilities for the preparation of the accounts.

CHECK YOUR LEARNING

1 What is the main section of an annual report?

2 Name four financial statements contained in the main section of an annual report.

3 Name six other statements that you might find in an annual report.

4 What report/statement is regarded as being the one that is most likely to be consulted?

Answers

1 the accounts

2 profit and loss account; balance sheet; cash flow statement; notes to the accounts

3 auditors' report (on the financial statements); compensation and appointments committee report; directors' report; statement of total recognized gains and losses; statement of directors' responsibilities for the accounts; chairman's report

4 chairman's report

DISCUSSION QUESTIONS

11.1
'A limited liability company's annual report should be made comprehensible to the average shareholder.' Discuss.

11.2
Examine the argument that annual reports are a costly irrelevance because hardly anyone refers to them.

11.3
Should companies be banned from including non-financial data in their annual report?

ASSIGNMENT

Objectives:
1 to enable you to familiarize yourself with what is contained in a company's annual report; and
2 to know where to look for information within it.

Required:
(a) Obtain a copy of the annual report of a public limited liability company.

Note: You are encouraged to choose a manufacturing company or a retail company, and to avoid banks, insurance companies, and investment trusts, as they produce somewhat specialist reports.

(b) Using the report that you have obtained, complete the following schedule:

NAME OF COMPANY

YEAR END

MAIN OPERATING ACTIVITIES

CHAIRMAN'S NAME

CHIEF EXECUTIVE'S NAME

CHAIRMAN'S STATEMENT
    Tone of the Chairman's statement in respect of the company's future:
      highly optimistic ☐ optimistic ☐ neutral ☐ pessimistic ☐
      highly pessimistic ☐

DIRECTORS' REPORT

Amount of the recommended final dividend
Charitable donations
Political donations
Job title of officer signing the report

ACCOUNTING POLICIES

Accounting convention
Depreciation rates for each major class of fixed assets

CONSOLIDATED PROFIT AND LOSS ACCOUNT

Turnover
Gross profit
Net profit before taxation
Net profit after taxation
Dividends paid and proposed
Retained profits
Earnings per share

CONSOLIDATED BALANCE SHEET

Total of all fixed assets
Cash at bank and in hand
Current assets total
Creditors: Amounts falling due within one year total
Net current assets/(liabilities) total
Creditors: Amounts falling due after more than one year total
Provisions for liabilities total
Shareholders' funds total

CONSOLIDATED CASH FLOW STATEMENT

Opening balance of cash in hand, and at bank
Increase/(decrease) in cash in the period
Closing balance of cash in hand, and at bank

NOTES TO THE ACCOUNTS

Geographical analysis of turnover:

Total operating profit
Geographical analysis of operating profit:

Total of tangible fixed assets' depreciation
Auditors' remuneration
Total of directors' emoluments
Average number of employees during the year

Debtors receivable after more than one year
Bank loans and overdrafts:
  in one year or less
  between one and two years
  between two and five years
  after five years
Total of the issued share capital
Profit and loss account balance

AUDITORS' REPORT
List any qualifications:

OTHER REPORTS AND STATEMENTS
List:

ACCOUNTING RATIOS
Calculate the following accounting ratios for the current year and (if possible) the previous year:
  Current ratio
  Acid test ratio
  Gearing
  Gross profit ratio
  Net profit before tax
  Net profit after tax
  Return on capital employed
  Stock turnover
  Trade debtor collection period
  Trade creditor payment period
  Fixed assets ratio

OVERALL ASSESSMENT
Liquidity
  very strong ☐ strong ☐ neutral ☐ weak ☐ very weak
Profitability
  very healthy ☐ healthy ☐ neutral ☐ sick ☐ very sick
Efficiency
  very efficient ☐ efficient ☐ neutral ☐ inefficient ☐
  highly inefficient ☐

CONCLUSION

Insert below your conclusions on the overall financial strength of the company:

Elizabeth Lo and friends

Learning objectives

After preparing this case study, you will be able to:

- **state the desirable characteristics of financial reports;**
- **design a questionnaire;**
- **interview the users of accounts**
- **write up the results of your survey.**

Background

LOCATION   The University of East Cheshire: The Main Lecture Theatre

PERSONNEL   Dale Galloway: Accounting Lecturer
Heather Watt: Student
Elizabeth Lo: Student

Synopsis   Elizabeth Lo was a first-year student in Business Studies at the University of East Cheshire. She had been born and brought up in Lighton, a small market town in the Midlands. Elizabeth was an attractive, bright and popular girl, and she had many sports and activities in which she was involved. She had been hoping to go to one of the ancient universities to read Philosophy, but her 'A' level results had been disappointing. In desperation, and somewhat at the last minute, her father had managed to get her a place at East Cheshire.

To begin with, Elizabeth had no more interest in Business Studies than she had in going to the moon, but the course was quite a varied one and she got on well with her fellow students. Although there were one or two subjects that some of the class hated, everyone found accounting to be the most boring.

Dale Galloway, their accounting lecturer, did his best, but it was hard going for all of them. During the first term, they ploughed through the mechanics of double-entry book-keeping, and it took a long time before it began to make sense. The one golden rule in accounting seemed to be that the answer to any question was the opposite of whatever you first thought.

In the spring term, the class began to study the format and structure of published financial statements. There were lots of rules to learn that were based partly on the Companies Act and partly on what were called 'financial reporting standards'.

251

As it was a degree class, Dale was very keen to be critical of such procedures. Elizabeth was not alone in finding it very difficult to understand what he was talking about. It was not easy to remember all that they were supposed to learn, and it was almost impossible to criticize something that was not very clear to you in the first place.

As the term went by, Elizabeth began to realize that accounting was not like simple arithmetic. She came to appreciate that, although you were supposed to follow a lot of accounting rules, it was possible to interpret them in any way you wished. It was quite a shock to find out that accountants were just as fallible as anybody else. You could, in fact, *fix* accounting statements so that they showed what you wanted, and yet you could still be following the rules! It was all very confusing.

Dale was even more scathing about the contents of an annual report. 'Just get hold of an annual report,' he invited the class. 'You have now done some accounting. Tell me honestly: does it mean anything to you?' Heather Watt, one of Elizabeth's friends, *did* get hold of an annual report, and they both had a good look at it. They quite agreed with Dale: it did appear to be meaningless.

By this time the class was thoroughly disillusioned. Although the students found the subject boring, they had understood that accountancy was a highly regarded profession, and yet it now appeared to be nothing more than a gigantic confidence trick.

Fortunately, Dale was a very experienced lecturer. He realized that some of the class did not understand him, while the remainder had been put off accounting for life. He tried to argue that while the current method of reporting financial results was open to question, neither the accountancy profession nor anyone else had anything better to put in its place. In other words, he stated, 'It's better to be vaguely right, than precisely wrong.'

'Well, why doesn't your profession try to do something about making it precisely *right*?', asked Heather (who was one of the bolder elements in the class). 'Why, for example, don't you ask people, such as shareholders, what they want, instead of supplying all this information that you say is rubbish?'

'Now that's a very good question,' replied Dale without a trace of sarcasm in his voice. 'Perhaps we *should* be able to design financial reports that will be useful to those who want to use them.' A thought struck him.

'I tell you what, we'll make this the subject of a tutorial exercise. I think it would be a lot more interesting for you, and it might either prove or disprove my point. How about it?' The class agreed, and Dale began preparing a suitable assignment.

By the next week he had come up with a few ideas. 'I want you to work in your respective tutorial groups,' he said. Elizabeth was pleased, because she was in a good tutorial group of only eight students. 'As part of a group exercise I want you to do two things: first, find out from looking at books in the library what are the desirable characteristics of financial reports. Now, I think you will find that, while it is relatively easy to put them down on paper, it is less easy to apply them in practice.'

'And that takes me on to the second part of the exercise. I want you to do a survey of what use shareholders make of their annual reports. I want each group to prepare a report on its findings, and then to present it to the rest of the class. There are one or two suggestions on how you should go about doing this exercise in the hand-out I circulated at the beginning of the lecture. Now, I think that four weeks should be long enough for the project, particularly as we shall not be holding any accounting lectures or tutorials during that time.'

The class cheered, and Elizabeth became quite excited. This seemed a lot more interesting than sitting in an uncomfortable lecture theatre taking notes from dozens of overhead slides.

Required:
1   Desirable characteristics of financial reports:
    (a) Consult a number of books on financial reporting in your library. List the desirable characteristics of financial reports as outlined in such books.
    (b) Obtain a selection of limited liability companies' annual reports. Most companies will let you have a copy of their latest report if you write to the Company Secretary.

        Examine such reports, and then assess them to see how far in your view they appear to contain the desirable characteristics of financial reports as outlined in the textbooks.

2   Shareholders' information needs and requirements:
    It would be interesting to find out what use shareholders make of a company's annual report, and what improvements they would like to see in its presentation.
    (a) Prepare a questionnaire suitable for surveying a number of shareholders in limited liability companies. You may need to consult a book on questionnaire design, but some idea of the type of questions that you might ask are listed in the Appendix overleaf.
        Note: Be careful that you do not ask questions that suggest a particular answer.
    (b) The next stage of the exercise is even more difficult. It perhaps would not be wise to stop people in the street and ask them if they would be prepared to answer some questions about their shareholdings! But you could ask family and friends who are shareholders in public limited liability companies whether they would be prepared to answer your questions.
        You will not have the time to survey a totally representative group of shareholders, but try and survey about ten people.
    (c) Prepare a written report on your findings, and present it to your tutorial group. In your conclusions, try to answer the following questions:

    ● To what extent do shareholders use their annual reports?
    ● What particular items are they interested in?
    ● Can they follow the structure of them?
    ● Do they understand the terminology used in the report?
    ● Would they like a different type of annual report, and if so, what?

Appendix SHAREHOLDERS' QUESTIONNAIRE: THE TYPE OF QUESTIONS TO ASK

1 Would you mind answering a few questions?
2 Do you have any shares in a company?
3 Did you buy the shares on the Stock Exchange?
4 Have you received an annual report from the company?
5 Can you tell from the envelope that it is an annual report?
6 Do you take it out of the envelope?
7 Do you look at the report at all?
8 Do you flick through it?
9 Do you look at the pictures?
10 Do you look at the advertising material?
11 Do you look at the other pages?
12 Do you read through the Chairman's report?
13 Do you read through the Directors' report?
14 Do you have a look at the profit and loss account?
15 Do you go through the profit and loss account notes?
16 Do you have a look at the balance sheet?
17 Do you go through the balance sheet notes?
18 Do you go through the cash flow statement?
19 Do you look at anything else in the report?
20 Is there anything else you would like to see given in the report?
21 Have you any knowledge of book-keeping or accounting?

CHAPTER 12

Contemporary issues in financial reporting

Out on a limb

Nearly one in four FT-SE 100 companies publishes a separate 'green' report – a growing trend among leading companies which recognise the impact their businesses have on the environment. Most explain why the report is needed. The chief executive of BAA, for example, says: 'With seven airports that account for 73 per cent of the UK's passenger air traffic and 83 per cent of air cargo, ours is a complex business. Our operations ... can affect the environment in many different ways.'

While most such reports give data on the big issues – pollution, use of the landscape, global warming, waste and recycling – Company Reporting's survey reveals many other types of disclosure. For example, 5 per cent of the sample discussed the use of live animals in testing programmes, and 14 per cent the effect of their activities on the quality of the public water supply.

More that four out of 10 told users of the report – which can include a wide range of interested parties beyond the shareholders – about the visual impact of building programmes on the landscape or townscape. And nearly half the sample looked at the noise generated by business operations.

Such reports, when comprehensive, give users an insight in the environmental risks taken by a company – and the risks society faces as a result of the business. This fits a growing trend in which financial reporting aids general risk management.

The Financial Times, 17 April 1996

Exhibit 12.0 'Green' issues – a new development in accounting

In the preceding chapter, we outlined the contents of an annual report published by a listed company. It is unlikely that you will come across an annual report that is identical to the one described in that chapter, and you will have to make allowances for slightly different formats, layout, presentation, contents, and the scheduling of the various reports and statements. You may also find that some companies include some additional reports beyond the ones covered in Chapter 11, while others may be omitted altogether. nonetheless, sufficient guidance was given in the chapter for you to find your way round most kinds of annual reports.

This means that we can now move on to have a brief look at a number of contentious financial reporting issues that are of current concern and interest to members of the accountancy profession. There is not sufficient space to deal with every issue, so we aim to cover just five important topics. In alphabetical order, these are: changing prices, goodwill and brands, international accounting, social and environmental reporting, and summary financial statements.

ACCOUNTING FOR CHANGING PRICES

In recent years, the accountancy profession has produced a number of proposals which would require financial reports to reflect the effects of inflation. So far in this book, we have assumed that the monetary unit remains stable, and that we can ignore inflation.

As yet, all of the proposals that have been put forward for producing inflation-adjusted reports have got nowhere, and current financial reporting in the UK is still based on the notion of price stability. This means that it is assumed that the original price (i.e. the historic cost) at which goods and services are exchanged retains its original value, but as you will know from your own experience, you need more pounds sterling to buy your weekly groceries today than you did last month.

Inflation and its effects

There is no satisfactory definition of inflation, but for our purposes we can regard it as either an upward movement in prices, or a downward movement in the purchasing power of the monetary unit. This means that, during a period of inflation, £100 available in cash in 19X1 will purchase fewer goods in 19X2 than it did in 19X1. Thus, in order to purchase the same amount of goods in 19X2 as we did in 19X1, we will have to pay more than £100. Prices in the United Kingdom over the last 30 years have been anything but stable, and in 1975, for example, the increase over the previous year reached the unprecedented level of 24.4%.

As far as accounting is concerned, the effect of inflation on traditional historic cost accounts can be stated quite simply: it tends to overstate the amount of profit. By over-stating profit, the proprietors may withdraw more cash from the business, and this may adversely affect the entity's liquid resources. Eventually, it may find that it does not have enough cash to replace its fixed assets or its stocks, and it may have to cut back on what it is doing, or even go out of business. The main effects of inflation can be summarized as follows:

1 The closing stock tends to have a higher value than goods purchased in earlier periods, thereby over-stating the gross profit (because the closing stock is *deducted* from the opening stock + purchases). However, when the stock is eventually sold, it will probably cost more to replace than it did when it was purchased.

2 Depreciation is under-stated, as it is usually based on the historic cost of the fixed assets. The fixed assets will eventually have to be replaced at a greater cost than was originally paid, so not enough cash may have been set aside to replace them if the depreciation charge is based on the historic cost.

3 There is a loss on loans. If the entity has put some of its funds into short- or long-term loans (such as in a bank deposit account or into debenture stock), such loans will lose value in a period of inflation. The entity might have invested (say) £10 000 in debenture stock in 19X1 which will be repaid in 19X5. In 19X5 it will be repaid the £10 000, but £10 000 received in 19X5 will not purchase the same amount of goods as £10 000 did in 19X1. Thus the entity loses by putting its cash into investments which are fixed in monetary terms. It also loses by allowing credit to its customers. Such debts will be fixed in money terms, so when the cash is eventually received (even if it is only a few months later), it will purchase fewer goods.

4 Gains on borrowings. An entity does not always lose during a period of inflation. If it borrows money on a short- or a long-term basis it will benefit. Goods purchased on credit terms, for example, will be settled in *money* terms, but the monetary payment will not be worth as much as it was when the goods were purchased. An entity gains similarly by borrowing on a long-term basis. By borrowing money through issuing debentures, for example, it will eventually have to pay back less money in purchasing power (or *real*) terms than it actually borrowed.

So what has the accountancy profession done to help overcome these problems? We try to answer this question below.

The accountancy profession's answer

In trying to cope with the effects of inflation on historic cost accounts, two main schools of thought have evolved (see Exhibit 12.1).

The purchasing power school

This school of thought recommends that the historic cost accounts should be adjusted by adopting some suitable inflation index. In the UK, the index that is usually adopted is the *retail price index* (RPI). This index is generally well known and understood. While this is an advantage, the RPI suffers from two main disadvantages:

1 it measures the effect of inflation on retail consumption;
2 it does not necessarily measure the effect of inflation on specific entities.

However, this method of allowing for inflation is relatively easy to adopt. The procedure is as follows:

1 take the historic cost (HC) accounts;
2 measure each transaction (or collection of transactions) in the HC accounts against the index at the time that it took place, and compare it with the index at the end of the relevant accounting period;
3 adjust the historic cost of the transaction by multiplying it by the closing index and dividing it by the opening index.

An example should help to make this procedure a little clearer. Suppose that we are presented with the following information:

	£	RPI
Fixed asset purchased on 1.01.X1:	1000	100
Historic cost accounts prepared on		
31.12.X1		120

∴ in the 'current purchasing power' accounts, the fixed asset would be shown as £1200 (£1000 × 120)/100).

Exhibit 12.1 Accounting for changing prices: the two schools of thought

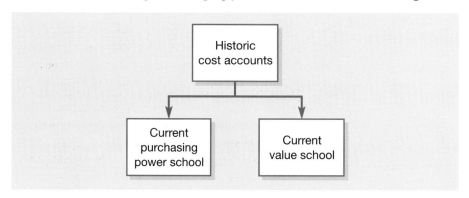

You may find that some tables and charts in an annual report have been adjusted on a current purchasing power (CPP) basis. In presenting the main financial statements, however, most companies adopt the historic cost principle.

The current value school

The current purchasing power (CPP) school of thought was much in favour until about 1975, but since then it has lost ground to the current value school. There are several versions of current value accounting. Basically, the current value school (of whatever dimension) requires fixed assets and stocks to be included in the accounts at their *current* value, rather than at their historic cost. In the vast majority of cases, current cost is the same as the *replacement* cost, i.e. what it would now cost to purchase an asset identical to one purchased in the past.

The main version of current value accounting used in the UK is known as *current cost accounting* (CCA). CCA became the subject of an accounting standard in 1980 (SSAP 16). Like all standards, it was supposed to be mandatory, but it became so unpopular that it was abandoned in 1985.

SSAP 16 was a very complicated statement (probably one reason for its unpopularity). In essence, what it tried to do was to reduce the level of the historic cost profit so that some allowance was made for the effects of inflation. Thus, the entity would always be able to retain sufficient cash in the business in order to continue operating at the same level that it had done in the past. In the jargon of accounting, this is known as 'maintaining an entity's operating capability'.

The statement required four main adjustments to be made to the historic cost profit and loss account, and two to the balance sheet (see Exhibit 12.2).

We will describe each of these adjustments separately, so that you can judge for yourself whether you think they cope with the inflation accounting problems we outlined earlier. We will start with the profit and loss account adjustments.

1 **A cost of sales adjustment (COSA).** This adjustment required both the opening and closing stock to be adjusted (normally by choosing a suitable index and applying it to the historic cost of the stocks) to a value which represented the average value of stock for the period. Hence, both the opening and the closing stocks were put on the same price basis as any purchases made during the period.

2 **An additional depreciation adjustment (ADA).** This adjustment meant that the depreciation charge for the year was normally based on the replacement cost of the asset, rather than on its historic cost.

3 **A monetary working capital adjustment (MWCA).** Monetary working capital was defined basically as the difference between trade debtors and trade creditors. SSAP 16 required an adjustment to be made to monetary working capital, the reasons being very similar to the ones that we outlined earlier, viz. in times of inflation, entities gain by borrowing and lose by lending. The MWCA, therefore, makes an allowance for short-term borrowing and

Exhibit 12.2 Current cost accounting: adjustments to the profit and loss account and the balance sheet

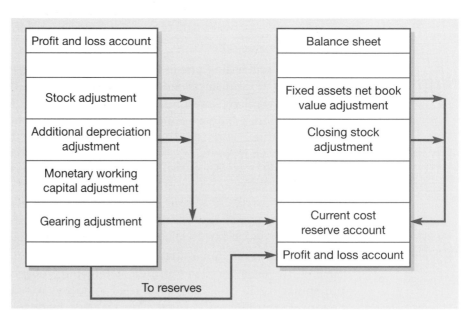

lending. The adjustment could be made by indexing both the opening net monetary working capital and closing net monetary capital so that they were measured on the same price basis. The opening and closing values are usually indexed in such a way that they both represent the average value for the year. The calculation is very similar to that adopted for the cost of sales adjustment.

4   **A gearing adjustment (GA)**. It is quite customary for a company to finance some of its operations from long-term borrowings. As indicated earlier, if it has borrowed money during a period of inflation, it will benefit by being able to repay the loan in monetary terms, although, by the time that it does so, the purchasing power of the original loan will have declined. The cost of sales adjustment, the additional depreciation adjustment, and the monetary working capital adjustment will all normally reduce the profit available for distribution to the shareholders. It seems only fair, therefore, that an adjustment should also be made if shareholders *benefit* from inflation (as they do if the company finances itself through borrowings).

  This is what the gearing adjustment is about. It tries to measure the extent of the shareholders' gain through borrowing. The method advocated by SSAP 16 was highly complex and very controversial, but basically it was calculated by taking the total of the three other profit and loss adjustments (COSA, ADA, and MWCA) and reducing it by an amount based on the extent of the company's borrowings.

  Suppose, for example, the total of COSA + ADA + MWCA = £10 000, and that the *gearing proportion* was estimated to be 20% (i.e. 20% of the company was financed out of borrowings), then £2000 (£10 000 X 20%) would be *credited* to the profit and loss account. The net extra cost charged to the profit and loss account to allow for inflation would be £8000 (£10 000 – £2000).

It is only necessary for non-accountants to understand the reasoning behind the gearing adjustment, and there is no need for you to know how to calculate it.

We move on now to look at the two balance sheet adjustments required under SSAP 16. These were as follows:

1 **Fixed assets**. Fixed assets would normally be included at their net *replacement* cost, i.e. their gross replacement cost less the accumulated depreciation based on that replacement cost. In effect, the gross replacement cost would be what the company would have to pay for similar fixed assets if the original fixed assets were to be replaced as at the date of the balance sheet.
2 **Closing stocks**. The closing stocks were also to be included in the balance sheet at their replacement cost. This would be based on their value as at the balance sheet date.

It will be appreciated, of course, that these six adjustments (four in the profit and loss account, and two in the balance sheet) alter the balancing of the accounts, and some sub-totals and totals also need to be changed. SSAP 16 allowed for the double-entry effect of the changes in an account called the *current cost reserve account*. This account was simply a balancing account, e.g. debit the profit and loss account, credit the current cost reserve account; or debit the current cost reserve account, credit the profit and loss account.

The current position As a result of the abandonment of SSAP 16, most companies do not now publish current cost accounts, or even make any sort of adjustment to their historic cost accounts in order to allow for inflation. However, some companies do produce summaries of their historic cost accounts that have been adjusted. They do this usually in one of two ways:

1 **A CPP approach**. Some of the historic cost inflation is indexed, using the RPI or some other suitable index.
2 **A CCA approach**. The fixed assets and stocks may be included at their replacement cost, and in the case of the fixed assets, depreciated on that basis.

Such price-adjusted information may be included in the formal notes, or in a separate statement.

As a non-accountant, you need not be unduly concerned with the technicalities of accounting for inflation, although you should be aware of the misleading impression gained by referring to accounting reports that have not been adjusted. As we have stated before, with inflation at a rate of only 5% per annum, prices double over something like a 15-year period. Thus, accounting information is significantly distorted even if it covers only a five-year period. If you are presented with only historic cost information, you ought to make some allowance for inflation. We would suggest that the retail price index can be used as a rough guide to the effects of inflation.

We have dealt with inflation and its effect on historic cost accounts at some length, because we believe that it is still one of the major problem areas in financial reporting. Furthermore, at the time of writing, the ASB has published some proposals which would include the incorporation of some of the ideas behind CCA in annual reports. As they are still at the discussion stage, however, we need not pursue them any further.

GOODWILL AND BRANDS

In the last chapter, we examined the format and structure of group accounts. As we mentioned in that chapter, the consolidation (i.e. the adding together) of the accounts of different entities is a formidable task, particularly if some of the entities are based overseas. The old ASC issued four accounting standards dealing with group accounting, and of the first eight FRSs issued by the ASB, three dealt with this very important topic.

Many of the issues with which these standards deal are highly technical, and as a non-accountant you do not need to be too concerned with the fine details. However, accounting information does have an impact on how your company is perceived, so you must be very careful how you present your accounts to the world. You must be prepared to question your accountants about what they are doing and why. One particular issue that arises out of group accounting is the problem of how to deal with goodwill and brands. In order to illustrate the problem we will use a simple example.

Let us assume that Company A buys a controlling interest in Company B (i.e it buys more than 50% of the voting shares). Company A may pay more for the net tangible (i.e. physical) assets of B than they are worth. The difference between what A pays and what the assets are worth is called *goodwill*. In other words, A pays a premium. It may be willing to do so because B is a long-established company with ready markets, a good product, reliable customers, and an efficient workforce.

If A and B's accounts are consolidated, the consolidated balance sheet will show an item for goodwill: after all, the company has bought something that it considers valuable in just the same way that it did for land and buildings. However, goodwill is referred to as an *intangible* fixed asset, because it does not have a physical presence. Hence A may not be confident that it can retain the goodwill: customers may go elsewhere, for example, and employees may leave. It seems prudent, therefore, to write it off (i.e. eliminate it from the group accounts) as soon as possible.

This is exactly what SSAP 22 (Accounting for goodwill) suggests: goodwill should be written off immediately when acquired. But how? SSAP 22 prefers that it should be immediately written off against reserves (it does not specify which reserves), but it may be amortized. This means that it will be depreciated (like tangible fixed assets), and an amount will be charged against each year's profit and loss account.

This procedure might be seen as a rather routine accounting adjustment, but think of the consequences! The goodwill may reduce the reserves to such a level that it might affect the company's ability to distribute its profits (there are some highly technical legal conditions affecting distribution of profits), but what happens if the goodwill is in excess of all the reserves? The company might then have to amortize the goodwill, and this will reduce the net profit for the year. This means that it will reduce the company's earnings per share, it may reduce the dividend payable and, in turn, affect the share price on the Stock Exchange.

Thus, an apparent minor book-keeping adjustment may result in some unwelcome consequences for the company. Indeed, as a result of this problem, some companies have tried to inflate their balance sheet figures by inserting a value for their 'brands', such as well-known chocolate bars, or popular beers. Unless the brand name is purchased, such procedures are purely a book exercise, i.e. they are entirely an internal arrangement, since they do not involve any outside parties. Thus, the value of the fixed assets is automatically increased, and a corresponding figure has to be included in the reserves in order to get the balance sheet to balance. This means that goodwill can then be written off against the reserves without any adverse effects either on the reserves themselves, or on the annual profit and loss account.

The problem is that no one knows how to put an objective value on brands for balance sheet purposes, and so it is anybody's guess as to what it should be. As yet, the issue is unresolved. The recommendation of the ASB is that brand values should not be separated from goodwill as the goodwill figure will include something for any brand value.

INTERNATIONAL ACCOUNTING

Accountants in the UK do not work entirely in a vacuum. They are influenced by what is happening in other countries, not least because many entities now operate on a global basis. Although we have concentrated almost exclusively on UK statutory and professional requirements, it is a fact that what is happening in the UK has been (and is being) strongly influenced by the experiences of other countries. The necessity to adapt UK requirements is coming from two main sources. We discuss each of them briefly below:

European Union (EU)

As a member of the EU, the UK is subject to directives approved by the Council of Ministers. A directive has to be incorporated into the national law of each member state. There have been three directives so far that influence UK accounting practice:

1 **The Fourth Directive**. The UK built this directive into the Companies Act 1981, the most notable feature being the introduction of standardized formats for presenting accounts.

2 **The Seventh Directive**. This was incorporated into the Companies Act 1989, and it basically tightened up the accounting requirements relating to group accounts.

3 **The Eighth Directive**. This directive dealt with the qualifications of auditors. It has not had the same impact in the UK as in some other countries, because the UK auditing profession was already strongly organized and highly trained.

International Accounting Standards Committee (IASC)

Besides national accounting standards, financial reports are supposed to incorporate international standards. The IASC was formed in 1973, and the UK was a founder member. It is a private body, financed largely by its members. The IASC aims to make financial statements more comparable on a world-wide basis. Its method of working is similar to that of the ASB. To date, it has issued 32 accounting standards, some on issues not dealt with by UK standards. As economic, financial, legal, and political conditions differ so markedly in various countries, IASC requirements tend to be much more general than are UK standards. This usually means that where UK FRS/SSAPs cover similar topics to the international accounting standards, observance of the UK ones normally ensures compliance with the IASC's requirements.

As countries become more inter-dependent. and as they operate more and more on a global basis, international accounting is becoming an important branch of accounting in its own right. There are enormous accounting problems to be solved in this area, covering such matters as accounting for groups, foreign currency translation methods, the treatment of taxation in accounts, the prices to charge between different segments of entities operating in different parts of the world (known as *transfer pricing*), and the reporting of segmental activities.

SOCIAL AND ENVIRONMENTAL REPORTING

Many accountants believe that traditional accounting is too narrowly based. There are two main reasons why there might be some merit in this view (a) emphasis is placed on reporting to shareholders, and much less weight is given to reporting to other groups, such as the ones identified in Chapter 10; and (b) there is too much of a focus given to the reporting of the *financial* results of an entity, and this is at the expense of other matters, such as social and environmental concerns.

Accordingly, there has been some thought given in recent years to the prospect of expanding the nature of the annual report so that it includes matters that would perhaps be of interest to a much wider audience than that of just shareholders.

As yet, there is no standardized definition of this expanded form of reporting, but it is often described as 'social reporting' or 'social and environmental reporting'. Gray, Owen and Maunders (in *Corporate Social Reporting: Accounting and Accountability*, London: Prentice-Hall, 1987) define social reporting (or corporate *social reporting*) as 'the process of providing information designed to discharge social accountability' (p.4). *Social accountability* they regard as 'the responsibility to account for actions for which one has social responsibility under an established contract' (p.4). We are in danger of getting into too deep water for a book of this nature, but in simple terms Gray *et al* argue that social responsibilities are 'the responsibilities for actions which do not have purely financial implications and which are demanded of an organization under some (implicit or explicit) identifiable contract' (p.4).

Hence an entity may include under the heading of 'social reporting' the donations that it gives to charities, the support that it gives to the general educational development of the community (e.g. by sponsoring concerts and festivals), and the contribution that it makes to the development of sport.

Similarly, activities that might be listed under 'environmental reporting' could include such matters as the health and safety of customers, employees, and the general public; the entity's accident record; the attention that it gives to pollution control, and the impact that its activities have on the overall environment.

As social and environmental reporting is at an early stage of development, there are no guidelines on what, where, and how social and environmental matters should be reported. However, there are some companies (e.g. The Body Shop) that are proud of their record in this respect, and you will find that their annual reports, plus a number of supplementary reports, contain a great deal of social and environmental information. You are recommended to obtain copies of such reports, therefore, so that you can judge for yourself the importance and significance of such information. Then, if you are in employment, ask yourself whether your company/entity should be reporting along similar lines. If the answer to this question is 'yes', then try to work out what you perhaps ought to report, what form it should be in, and where it should be published (e.g. in the annual report, or perhaps by issuing a specific social and environmental report).

SUMMARY FINANCIAL STATEMENTS

Instead of the detailed annual accounts, the Companies Act 1989 permits fully listed companies to supply (in certain circumstances), a *summary financial statement* (SFS) to shareholders. This move came about largely as a result of the privatization of some industries, such as British Telecom and the Trustee Savings Bank. In the ensuing privatization, literally millions of people took the opportunity of becoming shareholders in these new companies. Some companies then felt it would be too costly to send the traditional annual report to so many shareholders. The government agreed with this point of view, and so it was decided to make some allowance in the Act.

It is still too early to judge whether this move has been successful. There seems to be some evidence to suggest that it is very expensive to issue both a full report (if requested), and a summarized version of it. Similarly, there is little evidence to confirm that shareholders are better informed. This is not really surprising, because the format laid down in the regulations (the Department of Trade and Industry takes responsibility for this) is still far from easy for the lay-person to follow.

SFSs are certainly shorter than the full version. On average they are about four pages long, compared with an average of twenty-two pages for the full version. It is more likely, therefore, that they will be read. However, we believe that if they are to become readable, they will need to be even shorter, better designed, and absolutely free from jargon.

Most companies will require you to let them know which report you want, but some companies will automatically supply you with a copy of both the full annual report and an SFS.

CONCLUSION

In this chapter we have examined five current financial reporting issues. The first issue examined, *accounting for changing prices*, is not exercising the attention that it once did, mainly because of the relative low rate of inflation that most countries are currently enjoying. In dealing with changing prices, two main schools of thought can be identified: the CPP school, which advocates an index approach to changing prices, and a current value school. The latter is of particular interest in the UK because the ASB is at present considering replacing historic cost accounting with a form of current value accounting.

An important issue which is still unresolved is the treatment of *goodwill* and *brands* in financial accounts, and this problem can be seen in the increasing *internationalization* of accounting practices. Similarly, another exciting new branch of accounting has arisen in recent years, that known as *social and environmental reporting*, and this too may have international repercussions.

Finally, in recognition of the increasing complexity and size of annual reports, there is now a statutory provision for companies to issue a *summary financial statement*.

Key points	
	1 **Historic cost accounting assumes that the monetary unit is stable. Thus, in times of inflation, profits tend to be over-stated.**
	2 **In order to counteract the impact of changing prices (usually of an inflationary nature), historic cost accounts may be indexed (the CPP school of thought), or current values substituted for historic cost (the current value school of thought).**

3 The current value approach has now become more generally accepted, although there is fierce resistance on the part of many accountants to the idea of abandoning HCA.

4 The most appropriate method of dealing with goodwill and brands in consolidated accounts is still an unresolved issue. The UK preferred approach is to write off goodwill arising on consolidation immediately against reserves, and NOT to recognize the value of brands separately.

5 Financial reporting is now becoming more international. In the UK, EU directives are of some significance, and regard has also to be paid to international accounting standards.

6 Social and environmental reporting is now beginning to develop as a sub-branch of accounting, although it is currently at a very early stage of development.

7 Instead of issuing a full annual report to their shareholders, companies may now substitute a summary financial statement.

CHECK YOUR LEARNING

1 Identify two items in the profit and loss account that may need adjusting for inflation.

2 Name two main approaches adopted in accounting for inflation.

3 What adjustment required by SSAP 16 was the most controversial?

4 State two ways in which goodwill arising on consolidation can be dealt with in group accounts.

5 What does IASC stand for?

6 Does an annual report contain a statutory-required social and environmental report?

7 Do companies have to supply a summary financial statement to their shareholders?

Answers
1 stock; depreciation
2 current purchasing power; current value
3 the gearing adjustment
4 write off immediately against reserves; amortize

5   International Accounting Standards Committee
6   No
7   No – it is an option open to them

DISCUSSION QUESTIONS

12.1

'Now that inflation has fallen throughout the world, there is no need for the accountancy profession to worry about introducing inflation accounting.' Discuss.

12.2

Examine the argument that summary financial statements have proved to be a damp squib.

12.3

Do you think that a separate figure for 'brands' should be included in a company's balance sheet?

12.4

Should accounting practices in different countries be harmonized or standardized?

PART 5

Cost accounting

Cost accounting procedures

Exhibit 13.0 Trouble with costs – among other things

In the first four parts of this book, we have been mainly concerned with *financial accounting*. In this part of the book, we are going to deal with another important branch of accounting: *cost accounting*. In this chapter, we examine the background to cost accounting. The chapter falls into four main sections. The first section outlines the nature and purpose of cost accounting. The second section reviews the historical development of the subject. The third section examines what is meant by planning and control. The fourth section explains how accountants go about implementing a costing system. We start by describing what is meant by cost accounting.

By the end of this chapter, you will be able to:

● describe the nature and purpose of cost accounting;

● outline the five main procedures involved in implementing a costing system.

NATURE AND PURPOSE

Cost accounting is a branch of *management accounting*. According to the Chartered Institute of Management Accountants (CIMA), management accounting may be defined as follows:

Management accounting: the process of identification, measurement, accumulation, analysis, preparation, interpretation and communication of information used by management to plan, evaluate and control within an entity and to assure appropriate use of and accountability for its resources. Management accounting also comprises the preparation of financial reports for non-management groups such as shareholders, creditors, regulatory agencies and tax authorities.

This definition enables at least six major functional areas to be identified in which management accountants may become involved. These are as follows:

1 formulation of plans to meet objectives (strategic planning);
2 formulation of short-term operational plans (budget/profit planning);
3 acquisition and use of finance (financial management) and recording of transactions (financial accounting and cost accounting);
4 communication of financial and operating information;
5 corrective action to bring plans and results into line (financial control);
6 reviewing and reporting on systems and operations (internal audit, management audit).

This functional analysis is shown in Exhibit 13.1.

Exhibit 13.1 Elements of management accounting

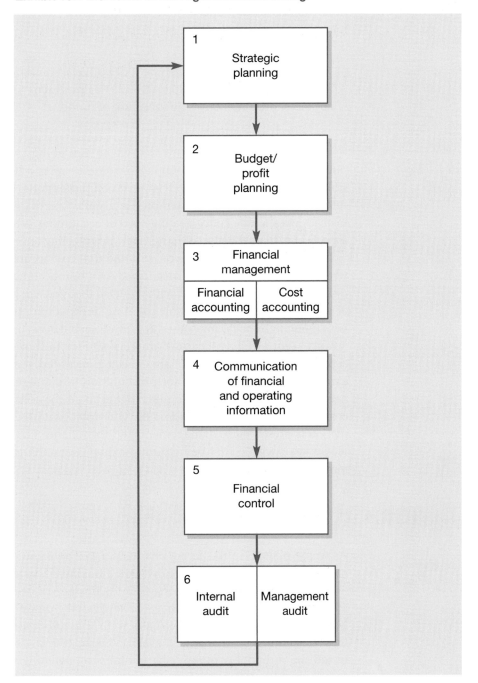

It will be noted that the recording of transactions (function 3) includes both financial accounting and cost accounting. CIMA defines cost accounting as follows:

> Cost accounting: the establishment of budgets, standard costs and actual cost of operations, processes, activities or products; and the analysis of variances, profitability or the social use of funds.

You will be relieved to know that we are not going to deal with all of the functions of management accounting, as some are more advanced than it is possible to cover in this book. Indeed, even on professional accounting courses, financial management, for example, is usually taught only at the final level. Instead, we shall be concentrating on cost accounting, along with some other aspects of management accounting, such as budgeting and financial control.

Like financial accounting, you will find that cost accounting is also riddled with some quite arbitrary procedures. As a non-accountant, therefore, it is essential that you are familiar with them, so that you can question the validity of any subsequent *management* accounting information put before you. Otherwise, you might be taking some very questionable decisions!

Cost accounting procedures are very similar to those found in financial accounting. Thus certain data are collected, recorded, stored, and eventually extracted in a form suitable for presentation to management. It will not be necessary for us to go into too much detail about the collection and storage of cost accounting data, as we are more concerned with the way that the information is presented to management, and the reliance that can be placed on it. However, it would first be helpful to explain something about the development of the subject.

HISTORICAL REVIEW

As was explained in the earlier chapters of this book, accounting evolved out of a need for information on how well a business was doing, how much it owed, and how much was owing to it. As businesses became more complex, and as ownership gradually became separated from managerial control, it became necessary to supply owners with some documentary information. Indeed, so much so, that over the last 150 years, the law has increasingly protected the rights of company shareholders by insisting that they should be supplied with a certain amount of information.

The information supplied is usually extracted from company records kept specially for that purpose, but these records may also be used to supply the management of the company (or any other entity) with information in order to help run it. Sometimes the records are kept mainly for external reporting purposes, and these may be the only major documentary source of information for internal purposes.

If such a situation applies, management's only source of information will be the annual accounts. The management may only then be aware that urgent action needed to be taken several months earlier, perhaps, for example, to avoid a cash crisis. By then, of course, it may be too late. In theory, the management ought to have known that some problems were beginning to build up, but in practice they may not have been aware of just how serious these had become. This is because managers can sometimes become so involved in dealing with day-to-day matters that, unless they are advised otherwise, they assume there are no problems. By the time they are warned, it may be too late to do anything. It should also be remembered that the annual accounting procedure is not designed for internal reporting purposes, so the records may not reflect the type of information the management needs.

You will not be surprised to learn that with increasing industrialization and specialization, managers began to demand information that was designed specially for *them*. In responding to this demand, accountants sometimes set up quite different recording systems from those required for financial reporting purposes (even though much of the data were common to both systems). These are known as *interlocking* systems, but nowadays it is much more common to find that only one single system is kept. This is known as an *integral* system.

Cost accounting (as it is known today) is a relatively new branch of accounting. It was rarely practised in the UK before 1914, but the increased industrial activity caused by the First and Second World Wars created a greater demand for management information. However, it was not until about 1960 that cost accounting systems became common, although even in the 1990s there are still very many entities who do not have even a rudimentary costing system. Hence the management of such companies have to rely on some highly unsatisfactory data for decision-making purposes. We would argue very strongly for better information to be supplied to managers so that they can direct the entity's activities more effectively.

PLANNING AND CONTROL

If an entity is to be run effectively and efficiently, managers must know what it is that they are trying to do. It is important, therefore, that some basic objectives are laid down for the entity. These might be quite straightforward. For example, a company might aim to achieve a return of (say) 20% on its capital employed, or a hospital may lay down maximum waiting periods for different types of operations.

Once the objectives have been established, the managers have then to work out the best way of achieving them. In other words, they have to prepare some plans, and then put them into action. From time to time, the managers will want to check what is actually happening against what they planned to happen. If there is a divergence between planned and actual results, then they will want to take some action that will bring future activities back into line with the plans. This is known as taking corrective action. In other words, they will want to *control* what is happening. Control is a word that you will come across frequently in management accounting, so we had better give you a formal definition obtained from FRS 8 (Related Party Disclosures). It is as follows:

> The ability to direct the financial and operating policies of an entity with a view to gaining economic benefits from its activities.

Cost accounting information can play a most important part in directing the financial and operating policies of an entity, but unlike a financial accounting system, it is *specially* designed to help management in planning and controlling the company's activities. It has, therefore, the following advantages over a financial accounting system:

1 information can be produced regularly and frequently;
2 it is very detailed;
3 it is as up to date as it possibly can be;
4 it does not depend exclusively on historical data;
5 it encourages a forward-looking approach.

These are substantial claims, but we hope to convince you of them in subsequent chapters. In the meantime, we will outline the stages involved in implementing a cost accounting system.

IMPLEMENTATION PROCEDURE

The implementation of a cost accounting system involves five basic stages, which can be summarized as follows:

1 the creation of an organizational structure;
2 the adoption of a documentary coding system;
3 the selection of a suitable product costing system;
4 the treatment of fixed production overheads;
5 the choice of a suitable cost control method.

An outline of the basic procedure is also shown in Exhibit 13.2.

Exhibit 13.2 Stages in implementing a product costing system

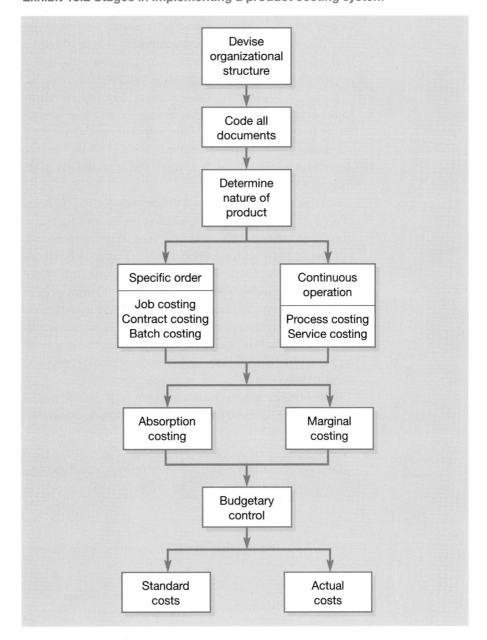

A basic outline of each of these stages is provided in the following sub-sections.

Stage 1: Create an organizational structure

Organizational planning and control can best be achieved by establishing clear lines of managerial responsibility. This may require a careful examination of the way in which the company is structured, and what specific responsibility is given to individuals within it.

In large organizations this may involve setting up a considerable number of inter-related departments and sub-departments. These may range from various production departments at the factory level through to a number of selling departments located in the head office. This might be described as the pyramid format and it is shown in diagrammatic form in Exhibit 13.3.

In large companies, it is not uncommon for the organizational structure to be of a *divisional* nature, perhaps based on the products it makes, or on the geographical areas in which it operates. Within each division there may be a number of factories (or works). Each factory may be divided into functions (e.g. administration, distribution, and production), and each function into departments (e.g. machine shop, stores control, and wages). The organization structure of a typical manufacturing company is shown in Exhibit 13.4.

The organizational structure within a manufacturing company can be quite complex. It is likely, for example, that there will be hundreds of departments within each function, and even in small companies there could well be several dozens.

Accountants use the term *cost centre* to describe what is often referred to as a department. CMIA provides the following definition:

> **Cost centre:** a production or service location, function, activity or item of equipment for which costs are accumulated.

Exhibit 13.3 The organizational structure of a company: the pyramid format

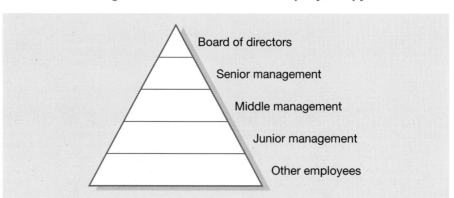

Exhibit 13.4 The organizational structure of a manufacturing company

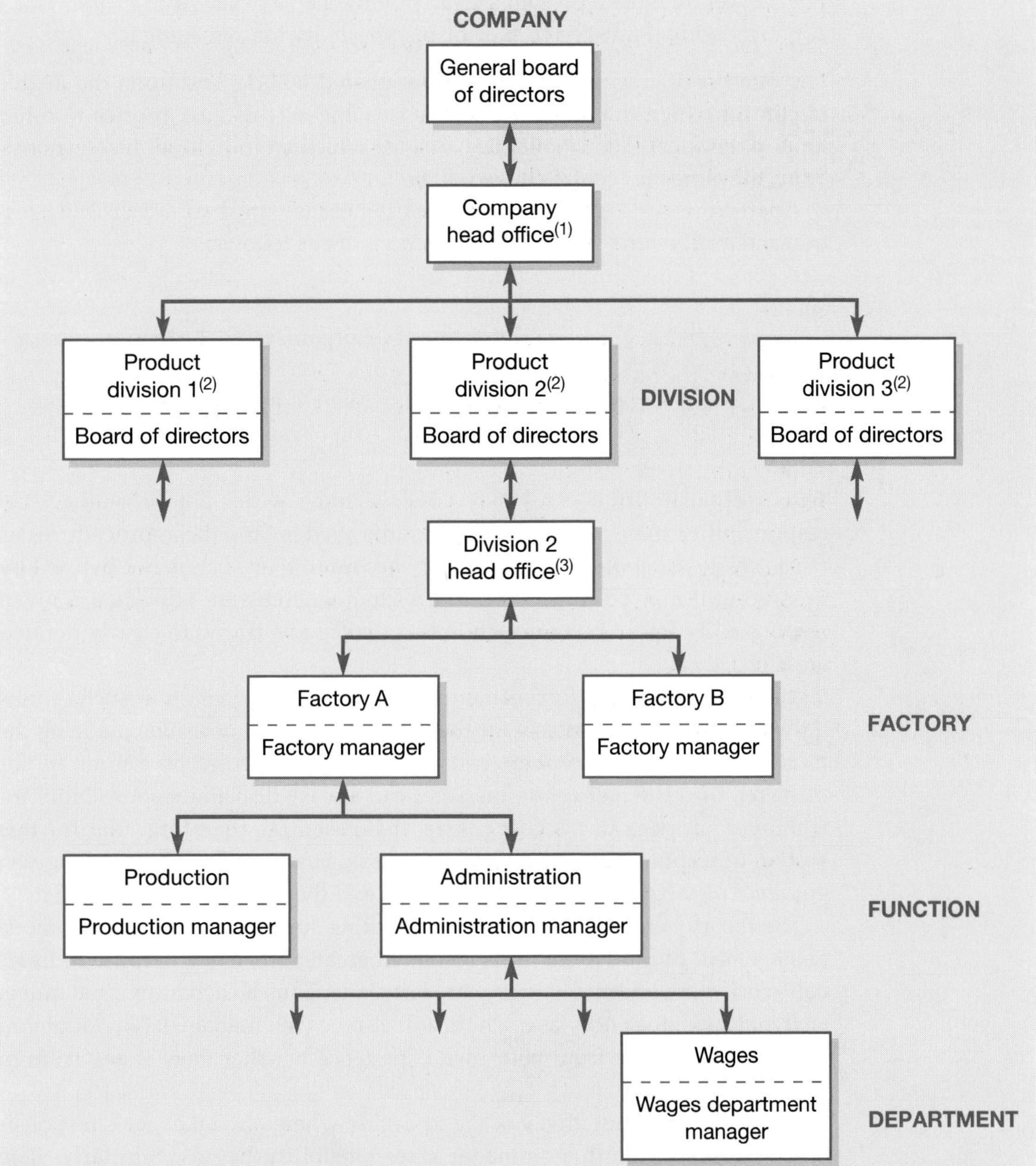

Notes:
1 The company's head office co-ordinates overall company policy. It also provides assistance and guidance generally throughout the company. The head office itself will be divided into a number of functions, such as accounting, marketing and personnel. Within each function there will probably be a number of departments, such as cash, taxation and salaries.
2 Divisions will usually be managed by a divisional board of directors, the board being answerable to the general board. Divisions often operate as separate limited liability companies in their own right (although all their shares may be owned by the main company).
3 Divisional head offices provide services for their respective divisions, similar to those provided by the company head office for the company as a whole. Divisional head offices will also be divided into a number of functions, and each function into departments.

Before a cost centre can be delineated, two main criteria must be met:

1 a cost centre must represent a clearly defined area of activity;
2 one individual must have specific responsibility for managing it.

The number of cost centres actually designated will depend upon the degree of control which the company wants to achieve (this also applies to other types of entities). The smaller the area for which an individual has responsibility, the more cost centres there will be.

Apart from cost centres, accountants sometimes speak of *responsibility centres*, and *profit centres*. The CIMA definitions are as follows:

> **Responsibility centre:** a department or organisational function whose performance is the direct responsibility of a specific manager.
> **Profit centre:** a part of a business accountable for both costs and revenues.

Thus responsibility centres may cover a much wider area of managerial responsibility than cost centres. Accountants describe these procedures as *responsibility accounting*. Responsibility accounting as such is not defined by CIMA, but it may be considered as a system whereby an individual is given responsibility for all revenues and costs that can be traced to clearly defined areas of activity.

Managers can only be expected to answer for what goes on in such centres if they are clearly responsible for them. For example, if decisions made by the manager of a cost centre were constantly being overruled by a more senior manager, then the cost centre manager can always disclaim responsibility for whatever happens in his cost centre. It is essential, therefore, that for this system of responsibility accounting to work, cost centre managers be given guidance on what they are expected to do, and then be left to get on with it.

The theory behind responsibility accounting suggests that the autonomous management of individual units results in greater efficiency, because individuals work more effectively if they are left alone. Thus if each individual unit is well managed, the entity as a whole will also be well managed. No doubt you will be able to judge from your own experience whether there is any truth in this argument.

In practice, it is not always easy to decide where one manager's responsibility ends and another manager's responsibility begins. Similarly, it is sometimes difficult to know which manager should take responsibility for certain types of costs. In order to illustrate this point, we will use business rates as an example of the problems involved.

Business rates are a form of local authority taxation. They are levied on property located in a particular local authority area. They cannot easily be identified with specific departments within a particular entity. Thus no one cost centre manager will have obvious responsibility for business rates. So which cost centre manager should it be?

It might be tempting to charge the rates to a sundry cost centre, but accountants do not recommend the use of such centres, because such cost centres tend to get charged with increasing amounts of cost, since that is often the easy way out of a difficult decision. Hence the sundry cost centres tend to defeat one of the main objectives of responsibility accounting, i.e. to ensure that all costs (as well as incomes) do become the responsibility of one specific manager.

In the case of business rates, therefore, the best advice that we can give is to suggest that they are charged to the legal department cost centre, since that department is likely to be involved in dealing with any dispute that may arise. However, it must be clearly recognized that the legal department manager does not have any control over the rates, and this must be taken into account when he has to answer for his departmental costs.

Stage 2: Adopt a documentary coding system

Clearly, the type of organizational structure described above is highly complex. There are formidable problems in managing an entity as a whole if it consists of a considerable number of largely autonomous units. A great deal of administrative effort, for example, is involved in ensuring that each cost centre is charged with its fair share of the entity's total costs.

It is necessary, therefore, to ensure that all the relevant accounting data are carefully documented, and that the cost of each transaction is charged to the correct cost centre. If this is not done, it is possible that a cost centre manager could take a decision based on some quite misleading data. In order to ensure that mistakes are minimized, it is recommended that the following procedure be adopted (although modern communication and computer systems of transmitting data may not always make the entire procedure necessary):

1 all transactions should be documented;
2 verbal instructions should be discouraged; telephone messages should be confirmed later in writing;
3 all documents should be specially designed to suit the particular transactions;
4 there should be a separate document for each type of transaction;
5 designated documents should only be supplied to authorized users;
6 all transactions should be approved and signed only by authorized personnel.

A cost accounting system normally involves a great deal of documentation so, in order to make sure that cost centres are charged correctly, it is usually necessary to adopt some formal coding system (this will almost certainly be necessary if the company uses computers). Unfortunately, codes can become very cumbersome, and it is very easy to make a mistake when coding a document (just as it is when dialling a telephone number). Furthermore, coding may be done by relatively junior members of staff who often do not understand why it is important to code the document correctly.

In a large organization, it may be necessary to adopt quite a complicated code consisting of a considerable number of digits. Such a code, for example, may be built up as follows:

Responsibility centre	Number of digits required
Division	000
Factory	000
Cost centre	000
Type of expense	0000
Total digits required	13

For example, let us assume that the fibres division (code 015) has a factory in Glasgow (code 123), and that the factory has a maintenance department (code 666). During a particular period, some raw materials are purchased (code 5432). Thus when the invoice is eventually received from the supplier, it will be coded as follows: 015/123/666/5432.

It would be possible, of course, to reduce the number of digits if there were only a small number of responsibility centres and a detailed analysis was not required. If possible, codes of just a few digits should be introduced, as mistakes can very easily be made even when a code has less than six digits.

Another point that must be emphasized is that a cost accounting system will not work properly unless its purpose has been explained to *all* staff and they understand its importance. This applies particularly to those who are coding the documents, since experience suggests that they do not always appreciate the importance of what they are doing. Operating a cost accounting system is expensive. There is no point having one if the information cannot be relied on, or for that matter, if it is not wanted. A cost accounting system should never be imposed on staff: it should only be introduced after there has been considerable consultation, and when it is generally agreed that there will be some obvious benefits.

Stage 3: Select an appropriate product costing system

The third stage in implementing a cost accounting system is to choose a method that is suitable for the type of goods produced or services administered by the entity. The CIMA definition of a product cost is:

> **Product cost:** the cost of a finished product built up from its cost elements.

In a book of this nature, it is not necessary to go into very much detail about specific product costing methods. Basically, the choice depends upon the *nature* of the product. Thus the costing method used in a chemical company, for example, will not be the same as one used in a hospital.

There are two broad groupings of costing methods, and each group contains a number of specific types. The main ones are as follows:

Specific order costing

1 **Job costing**: for use when specific units are produced, e.g. parts produced in an engineering works, or a customer's car repaired in a garage.
2 **Contract costing**: used in large, specific construction jobs, such as building bridges, hospitals, power stations, roads, schools, and shops.
3 **Batch costing:** used when specific units are produced in batches, e.g. nuts and bolts, boots and shoes.

Continuous operation costing

1 **Process costing:** for use in industries where there is a continuous or repetitive operation during the manufacture of products, e.g. cement manufacture, chemicals, glass, iron and steel, oil, paint and textiles.
2 **Service costing**: used in entities where the basic function is to provide a service, e.g. education, health and legal services.

The CIMA definition of a product cost quoted above included the term 'cost elements'. CIMA again provides a helpful definition. It is as follows:

> **Elements of cost:** the constituent parts of costs according to the factors upon which expenditure is incurred, namely, materials, labour and expenses.

The elements of cost are shown in diagrammatic form in Exhibit 13.5.

Exhibit 13.5 Unit cost structure: the elements of cost

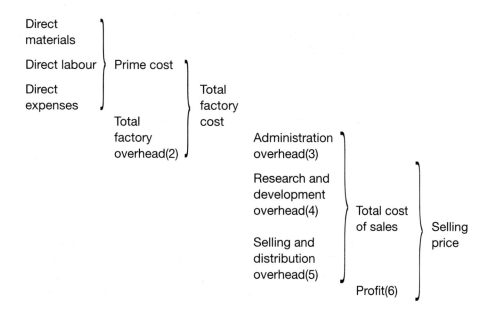

Notes:
1 The structure of the elements of cost is very similar to the structure used in Chapter 6 for manufacturing accounts. The chart assumes that the cost accounting system is based on absorption costing.
2 Factory overhead includes indirect production costs and other factory costs that are not easy to identify with production.
3 Administration overhead will include the non-factory cost of operating the company.
4 Research expenditure includes the cost of working on new products and processes. Development costs relate to costs incurred in developing existing products and processes.
5 Selling and distribution overhead includes the cost of promoting the company's products and the cost of distributing them to its customers.
6 A profit loading may be added to the total cost of sales in order to arrive at the unit's selling price.

Exhibit 13.5 may be somewhat misleading. For example, the selling price appears to be derived by adding a profit element to the total cost of sales. It is rare for selling prices to be derived in this way. They are usually determined by the market, i.e. prices charged by the entity's competitors. However, the diagram does help to establish the point about controlling costs. If the entity cannot fix its own selling prices, then in order to make a profit it has to ensure its total costs are less than its total sales revenue.

Another point about Exhibit 13.5 is the way that it depicts the treatment of overheads. This is another problem an entity faces when installing a cost accounting system. We outline the problem in the next sub-section, and we will also be returning to it in subsequent chapters.

Stage 4: Determine the treatment of fixed production overheads

The fourth main stage in implementing a cost accounting system concerns the treatment of fixed production overheads. Overheads refer to those costs that cannot be economically identified with specific units, and fixed means that they are unlikely to increase (or decrease) irrespective of how many units are produced. The entity can deal with such overheads in one of two ways:

1 it can share them out among specific units by using some agreed apportionment method; or
2 it can write them off in total.

The method of dealing with overheads is important, because it will determine what type of accounts will need to be kept within the ledger system, and the nature of the information that can be extracted from it.

The first method is known as *absorption costing*, and it will be dealt with in Chapter 15. The second method is known as *marginal costing*, and it will be examined in Chapter 16. The two techniques are shown in diagrammatic format in Exhibit 13.6.

Exhibit 13.6 Absorption costing versus marginal costing

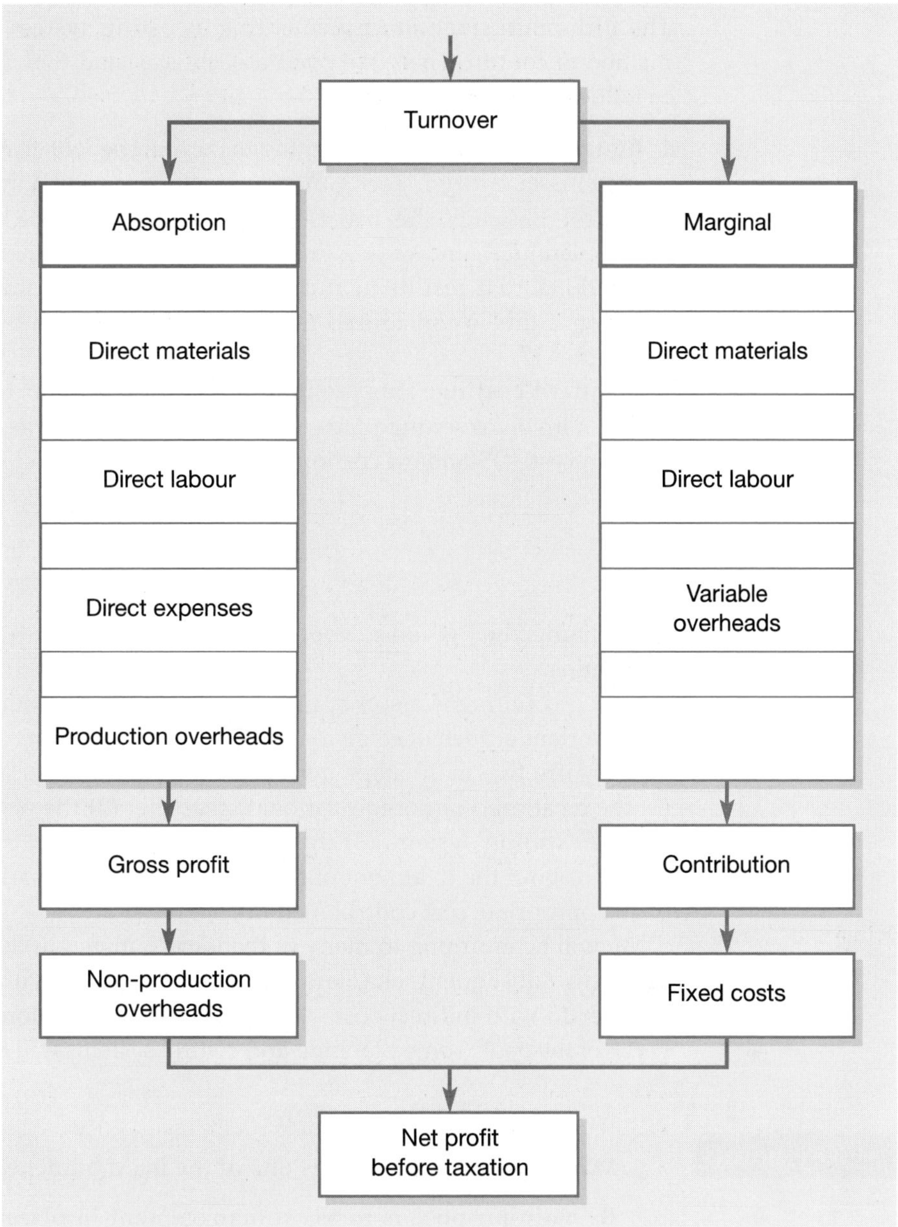

Stage 5: Choose a cost control method

The fifth main stage in implementing a costing system is to decide on the method of control. There are two basic choices, and they may be summarized as follows:

1 **Budgetary control**. To obtain the maximum benefit from a cost accounting system, an entity is recommended to incorporate a system of budgetary control. Basically, this involves working out what the entity intends to do (i.e. planning), and what it will cost. The control element involves comparing the actual results against the plans, and then taking any corrective action if this is considered necessary. We deal with budgetary control in Chapter 17.

2 **Standard costing**. This method of control is similar to budgeting except that it involves setting plans and controlling the results for individual units or processes. Standard costing is discussed in further detail in Chapter 18.

CONCLUSION

This chapter has given a brief outline of the nature and purpose of cost accounting.

Cost accounting is a sub-branch of management accounting, which is now an important branch of *accounting*.

There are five main steps involved in installing a cost accounting system: (1) the creation of an organizational structure; (2) the installation of a documentary coding system; (3) the selection of a product costing system; (4) a decision about the treatment of fixed production overheads; and (5) the choice of an appropriate cost control method.

We will be returning to many of the ideas outlined in this chapter in greater detail in subsequent chapters. Chapter 14 deals with direct costs, and Chapter 15 with indirect costs. Marginal costing is explored in Chapter 16. In Part 6 of the book, some planning and control systems will be examined.

Key points

1 Management accounting is one of the main branches of accounting.

2 Its main purpose is to assist management in planning and controlling an entity.

3 Important elements involved in this work involve devising plans, and monitoring their progress.

4 Cost accounting is an important sub-branch of management accounting.

> 5 Its main aim is to record data, and to summarize them in a form that will assist in managerial decision making.
>
> 6 Cost accounting requires an organizational structure, coded documents, a suitable product costing system, a decision about the treatment of overheads, and the selection of a cost control method.

CHECK YOUR LEARNING

1 Fill in the missing blanks in each of the following statements:
   (a) Financial accounting is more concerned with reporting to parties _____ the business.
   (b) _____ accounting is more concerned with internal reporting.
   (c) Planning and controlling is essential in an entity in order to ensure that it is run _____ and _____.

2 How many main stages are there in implementing a cost accounting system?

3 List three main elements of cost.

4 Which two main methods of cost accounting may be chosen in order to deal with overheads?

5 What are the two main cost control techniques?

Answers
1 (a) outside (b) management (c) effectively; efficiently
2 five
3 materials; labour; overheads
4 absorption costing; marginal costing
5 budgetary control; standard costing

QUESTIONS

13.1
Briefly describe the differences between financial accounting and management accounting.

13.2
List at least five categories of cost.

13.3
List the five main categories into which the organizational structure of a manufacturing entity might be classified.

13.4

What is a cost centre?

13.5

Distinguish between absorption costing and marginal costing.

ADDITIONAL QUESTIONS (WITHOUT ANSWERS)

13.6

Write a report for your managing director examining the main types of information that may be obtained from a cost accounting system.

13.7

Business organizations are usually based on some form of authoritative organizational structure.

Required:
(a) Outline the main principles to be adopted in developing a business organizational structure.
(b) Explain why such a structure is necessary for the successful implementation of a cost accounting system.

DISCUSSION QUESTIONS

13.8

'Responsibility accounting is a myth.' Discuss.

13.9

How far do you agree with the statement that while cost accounting may be of some relevance to the manufacturing industry, it can be of little relevance to the health service, where saving lives is more important?

13.10

'Cost accounting information supplied to management largely excludes non-financial data.' If this statement is true, how relevant, therefore, is a cost accounting system to managerial decision-making?

CASE STUDY

No problem

Learning objectives

After preparing this case study, you will be able to:

- **describe the nature and purpose of a cost accounting system;**
- **list the benefits of such a system;**
- **state the problems inherent in quantifying the benfits;**
- **prepare a report for management on cost accounting systems.**

Background

LOCATION   Yewtree Limited: the Managing Director's office.

PERSONNEL   Mark Pope: Managing Director
Alison Webster: Senior Auditor, Simey and Simey,
Chartered Accountants

Synopsis

Following the completion of the audit for the year to 30 June 19X1, a meeting had been arranged between Mark Pope, the Managing Director of Yewtree Limited, and Alison Webster, a Senior Auditor in Simey and Simey, the company's auditors.

After the usual pleasantries, Mark got down to business. As befitted his army training, he did not believe in wasting time. 'Now, what was it you wanted to see me about, Alison?' he enquired.

'Well, as you will recall, Mark, we usually hold a post-audit meeting. The audit has gone very well this year, and we're quite happy with the accounts. This time, what we really wanted to do was to have a close look at the future of the company.'

Mark immediately pricked up his ears. 'You mean you think we've got problems?' he queried, the alarm registering in his voice.

'Not in the immediate future,' responded Alison, 'but there are one or two matters that we would like to advise you about.'

Mark was not easily placated. 'What on earth do you mean?' he asked somewhat aggressively. 'We seem to be doing all right. Surely there can't be a problem?'

'No real problem,' replied Alison. 'I agree that everything seems fine, but be honest now. We did an interim audit towards the end of the financial year, and you were having some problems then, weren't you?'

'Yes,' admitted a somewhat reluctant Managing Director, 'but once you pointed them out, we took immediate action.'

Alison smiled to herself. Mark had walked right into a fairly obvious trap. 'Oh yes,' she said, 'but only when the year was almost over. It's probably only because you had good results up until December that the overall results for the year appear satisfactory.'

'I don't see how you can say that,' muttered Mark. 'You can't be sure.'

'That's exactly the point I am making,' said Alison. 'You don't really know, and neither, for that matter, do we.'

'Well, we pay you to tell us these things,' Mark snapped back. 'And if I may say so, we pay you rather a lot.'

'Actually, you don't,' replied Alison. 'I mean, you don't pay us to advise on such matters. Your shareholders pay us to do the audit. Advice about the management of the company is outside the audit, and it is not strictly part of our function.'

Mark backtracked a little. 'Be that as it may, what are you trying to tell me?'

Alison consulted her notes. 'Basically, Mark, we think that you and your senior staff have found it more and more difficult in the last few years to control the company. The company has grown considerably, and now you all spend most of your time at your desks, and less time on the shop floor seeing what's going on.'

'Yes, I know,' Mark murmured. 'It certainly wasn't like that in the old days, still less so in the army, but I do my best.' He had a feeling that he was not going to like what he was about to hear.

'Of course, Mark. I appreciate that. But it does mean that you don't *really* know what's gone on until the annual accounts are ready. When the company was small, you were always wandering around the place. You knew everybody. Everybody knew you, and you could tell if something was not quite right.'

'I must admit, I preferred the old days. But what are we to do? We can't turn the clock back.'

'I'm not suggesting you should, Mark. What I think you should do now, is to install what we call a "cost accounting system".'

'What! Even more book-keeping,' glared a somewhat revitalized Managing Director. 'More staff. More office space. More paper work. I thought that you had always warned us against too much administration.'

'Well, there would be an extra cost,' admitted Alison, 'although I would expect the benefits to outweigh the costs.'

'What benefits?' queried Mark.

'I should think substantial,' parried Alison. 'At the moment you get most information from the annual accounts. That's a long time since some of the events took place. That means you have little idea anything's gone wrong until it's too late. And even worse, you just guess when you are asked to quote a price for an order.'

'I've always been very good at that,' replied Mark, very much on the defensive.

'Yes, but you've less time for that now, and, frankly, your staff are not as good at it as you were.'

Mark noted the past tense and, in his heart of hearts, he knew that Alison was right. It was not easy to take such criticism about yourself and the company that you had founded. After his army service, the company became Mark's only love, and now here was this jumped up book-keeper daring to criticize the only thing that mattered to him.

Mark broke the silence. 'I suppose this company has prospered because I've always been willing to consider new ideas, and I'm not going to stop now. I will think about this "cost accounting system" you've mentioned, but I'm not having more administration just for the sake of it. I know that there are fashions in accounting, just as there are in anything else. If I buy it, it will have to pay for itself.'

'I agree with you Mark, although frankly it is difficult to prove on paper that such a system pays for itself.'

'Well, there you are,' said Mark. 'But I've said I would consider it, and I will. Can you look into it for me?'

'Actually, Mark, that's a bit difficult for my firm to do. You see, we are your company's auditors, and we cannot get too involved in such work. But I tell you what I can do in the meantime. I will get one of my colleagues to prepare a report for you. If you like it, maybe our Management Consultancy firm could take over. Would that arrangement suit you?'

Mark said that it suited him fine, and at that point, the meeting was concluded.

Required:

1 Yewtree's problem is probably not unique. There is a great deal of evidence that many British companies still depend almost entirely on their financial accounting system for management control purposes. Check this assertion by undertaking the following tasks:
   (a) refer to a number of articles in your library that report on studies undertaken into the use made of management accounting systems;
   (b) undertake a survey of local industry into the use made of such systems.
   Note: You may be able to do this task either by personal contact with some firms that you know, or by circulating a questionnaire.

2 Many accounting texts list the benefits of installing a cost accounting system, but they do not say much about what such systems cost to install and to operate. Consult a number of articles and textbooks in your library. Note whether they make any attempt to quantify in monetary terms the benefits of such systems.

3 Assume that you are employed by Alison Webster's firm and that you have been asked to draw up a preliminary report suitable for presentation to Mark Pope. Prepare such a report, and then present it to your tutorial group.

CHAPTER 14

Direct costs

Exhibit 14.0 Wages – a problem in any industry

It was suggested in the last chapter that the principal aims of cost accounting are to help management (a) plan and (b) control an entity's activities. This may be achieved by establishing a number of clear objectives, creating an organizational structure based on responsibility accounting, laying down plans in accordance with the overall objectives, and then leaving individual managers to get on with working towards achievement of those plans. The control element is achieved by a constant comparison of the actual results against the plans. If the actual results are unfavourable, then action will be taken to bring them into line with the plans. This process requires managers to be fed regular and frequent information about the progress of their respective cost centres.

In the case of a production unit cost centre, this procedure will almost certainly require a comparison to be made of the actual cost of each unit against the planned cost. As indicated in Chapter 13, unit costs comprise two main elements: direct costs and indirect costs. CIMA defines these terms as follows:

> **Direct cost:** expenditure which can be economically identified with and specifically measured in respect to a relevant cost object.

> Indirect cost: expenditure on labour, materials or services which cannot be economically identified with a specific saleable cost unit.

These definitions are fairly imprecise. For example, what is meant by 'economically identified'? All we can suggest is that it depends on the circumstances (like much else in accounting): what is economic in one case may not be economic in another. Ultimately, it becomes a matter of judgement. This means that it is possible to calculate a wide range of different costs for a specific unit (or a process or a service) depending upon the definition adopted of 'economically identifiable'. In practice, it is usually possible (from an economic point of view) to identify some material and labour costs with specific units of production, but it is not usually possible for other types of expenses to be similarly identified. This point is returned to later.

You will appreciate, therefore, that a great deal of subjective judgement is involved in identifying direct costs, although, as we shall see in the next chapter, there is even more subjectivity in dealing with indirect costs! As a result, the entire process of building up the total cost of a particular unit is based on a number of arguable assumptions. This means that it is difficult to calculate the exact cost of any one unit, because the cost of that unit will depend upon the assumptions adopted in calculating it.

In this chapter, the problems involved in dealing with *direct* costs are examined. It is assumed that we are dealing with a manufacturing company that makes a specific unit. It is recognized that not all manufacturing companies produce such units, and that not all entities are manufacturing. Nonetheless, it will enable us to establish a number of basic principles of cost accounting which are valid for all types of entities. We begin our examination of direct costs by having a look at *materials*.

Learning objectives	**By the end of this chapter, you will be able to:**
	● **identify costs that can be traced to particular activities;**
	● **describe four main methods of charging direct material costs to production;**
	● **recognize direct labour costs and other direct expenses.**

293

DIRECT MATERIAL COSTS

Materials consist of raw materials and component parts. CIMA defines raw materials as 'goods purchased for incorporation into products for sale'. The CIMA terminology does not define component parts, but we can assume that they include those miscellaneous items of ready-made parts purchased for the assembly of a finished unit. Before we examine the treatment of 'direct' material cost we must first offer some explanation of what is perhaps meant by 'economically identifiable'.

As an example, let us assume that we are making a table. We can observe that it is made of wood. It might be relatively easy to quantify the amount of wood used, simply because it is substantial enough to be recognized. However, the screws needed to hold this table together may be so insignificant that it is not worthwhile identifying them separately from screws used in making other tables. In other words, it is just not worth the expense involved in trying to work out the cost of (say) six screws. Thus, the wood would probably be treated as a direct material cost, while the screws would be classed as indirect.

In practice, it is often relatively easy to identify the *physical* quantity of goods used in manufacturing a particular unit (as we could do with the screws in the above example), but it is not always easy to determine what they cost. This is often the case with liquids, for example, because they are usually stored in containers. The containers will be topped up from time to time with additional purchases, but all of the contents of the container will become mixed. As the price paid for the various batches of liquid will almost certainly vary, what then is the cost of issuing (say) one litre of liquid to production? There is no way of knowing. Hence, although it may be relatively easy to identify the actual quantity of material issued to production, it may be difficult to cost it.

If the amount of material used in production is significant enough, the accountant would estimate the cost. Of course, if he can work out the actual cost of materials, he would use that cost. Not surprisingly, this is known as the *specific identification method*. If it cannot be used, then he will have to choose one of a number of other recognized accounting methods. We outline some of them in the following sub-sections.

First-in, first-out (FIFO)

It is sensible to issue the oldest stock to production first, followed by the next oldest, and so on, and this should be done wherever possible. This method of storekeeping means that old stock is not kept in store for very long, thus avoiding the possibility of deterioration or obsolescence. However, as out-lined above, some materials (such as grains and liquids) may be stored in such a way that they become a mixture of old and new stock, and it is then not possible to identify each separate purchase. Nonetheless, in pricing the issue of stock to production, it would still seem logical to follow the first-in, first-out procedure, and charge production with the oldest price first, fol-lowed by the next oldest price, and so on.

FIFO is a very common method used in charging out materials to produc-tion. The procedure is as follows:

1 Start with the price paid for the oldest material in stock, and charge any issues to production at that price.
2 Once all of the goods originally purchased at that price have been issued, use the next oldest price until all of that stock has been issued.
3 The third oldest price will be used next, then the fourth, and so on.

The prices attached to the issue of goods to production are not, of course, neces-sarily the same as those that were paid for the actual purchases of those goods. Indeed, they cannot be, for if it had been possible to identify specific receipts with *specific* issues, the *specific* identification method would have been used.

The use of the the FIFO pricing method is illustrated in Exhibit 14.1.

Exhibit 14.1 The FIFO pricing method of charging direct materials to production

The following information relates to the receipts and issue of material X into stock during January 19X1:

Date	Receipts into stores			Issue to production
	Quantity	Price	Value	Quantity
	Units	£	£	Units
1.1.X1	100	10	1000	
10.1.X1	150	11	1650	
15.1.X1				125
20.1.X1	50	12	600	
31.1.X1				150

Required:
Using the FIFO (first-in, first-out) method of pricing the issue of goods to produc-tion, calculate the following:
(a)   the issue prices at which goods will be charged to production; and
(b)   the closing stock value at 31 January 19X1.

Answer to Exhibit 14.1

(a)   The issue price of goods to production:

Date of issue	Tutorial note		Calculation	£
5.1.X1	(1)	100	units × £10=	1000
	(2)	25	units × £11=	275
		125		£1275
31.1.X1	(3)	125	units × £11=	1375
	(4)	25	units × £12=	300
		150		£1675

(b) Closing stock:

25 units × £12=	£300

Check:

Total receipts (1000 + 1650 + 600)	3250
Total issues (1275 + 1675)	2950
Closing stock	£300

Tutorial notes
1 The goods received on 1 January 19X1 are now assumed to have all been issued.
2 This leaves 125 units in stock out of the goods received on 10 January 19X1.
3 All the goods purchased on 10 January 19X1 are assumed to have been issued.
4 There are now 25 units left in stock out of the goods purchsed on 20 January 19X1.

Although Exhibit 14.1 is a simple example, it can be seen that if the amount of material issued to production includes a number of batches purchased at different prices, the FIFO method involves using a considerable number of different prices.

Last-in, first-out (LIFO)

Instead of FIFO, we could use LIFO. LIFO adopts the *latest* prices, and these are then used to charge the issue of goods to production. Once the physical quantity of the issue has been identified, the goods are priced to production at the price paid for the last receipt of goods. If more goods are being issued than had been purchased at that price, the next oldest price will be used, and so on. This means that if there has been a large number of issues of goods to production, the total value of the issue could comprise a considerable number of prices.

The LIFO method is illustrated in Exhibit 14.2.

Exhibit 14.2 The LIFO pricing method of charging direct materials to production

The same data are used as in Exhibit 14.1.

Required:
Using the LIFO (last-in, first-out) method of pricing the issue of goods to production, calculate the following:
(a) the issue prices at which goods will be issued to production; and
(b) the value of closing stock at 31 January 19X1.

Answer to Exhibit 14.2

(a) The issue price of goods to production:

Date of issue	Tutorial note		Calculation	£
15.1.X1	(1)	125	units × £11=	1375
31.1.X1	(2)	50	units × £12=	600
		25	units × £11=	275
		75	units × £10=	750
		150		£1625

(b) Closing stock value:

25 units × £10=	£250

Check:
Total receipts (1000 + 1650 + 600)	3250
Total issues (1375 + 1625)	3000
Closing stock	£250

Tutorial notes
1 This was the latest price at 15 January 19X1.
2 The latest price at 31 January 19X1 was £12, but only 50 units were purchased. The next oldest price, therefore, is used, but only 25 units are left at £11, because 125 units were priced out at £11 on 15 January 19X1. The balance is made up of goods purchased for £10 per unit, which also leaves 25 units in stock at that price.

Like the FIFO method, LIFO can involve a great deal of tedious arithmetic, but there is a certain logic to it. By using the latest prices, production is being charged with current economic prices. Thus the closing stock will be valued at much older prices, and this means that by using LIFO in times of rising prices, the gross profit tends to be lower than it does under FIFO (thereby allowing, to some extent, for inflation).

The lower profit arises because of a combination of a higher charge to production, and a lower value placed on closing stock (a lower closing stock figure reduces the cost of goods sold, because a smaller amount is being deducted from the total of opening stock plus purchases). The reverse applies, of course, when prices are falling.

In the UK, FIFO is an acceptable method of valuing stock for taxation purposes, but LIFO is not permitted. A company could still use LIFO for internal purposes if it wanted, but a different method would then have to be adopted in computing its tax charge. As this would involve more work, LIFO tends not to be used (although this is not the case in the United States of America).

Weighted average

In order to avoid the detailed arithmetical calculations which are involved in using both the FIFO and LIFO methods, it is possible to substitute an *average* pricing method. There are two main types, and they are as follows:

1 periodic weighted average method;
2 continuous weighted average method.

The *periodic* weighted average method involves calculating an average issue price based on all the prices paid for materials purchased during a particular period. The goods issued to production during that period are all then charged out at that average price. By using this method, it is not possible to charge out goods to production until after the end of the period, because the issue price cannot be calculated until all the purchase prices for the period are known. This method is illustrated in Exhibit 14.3.

Exhibit 14.3 The periodic weighted average pricing method of charging direct material to production

The same data are used as in Exhibit 14.1.

Required:
Using the periodic weighted average method of pricing the issue of goods to production, you are required to calculate the following:
(a) the issue price of goods to production for January 19X1; and
(b) the closing stock value as at 31 January 19X1.

Answer to Exhibit 14.3

(a) The issue price of goods to production:

Total value of receipts (1000 + 1650 + 600) =	£3250
Total number of units received (100 + 150 + 50) =	300
∴ Periodic weighted average price =	£10.83
∴ Issue on 15.1.X1: 125 units × £10.83 =	£1354
∴ Issue on 31.1.X1: 150 units × £10.83 =	£1625

(b) Value of closing stock:

	£	£
Total receipts		3250
Less: Issues – 15.1.X1	1354	
– 25.1.X1	1625	2979
∴ Closing stock value =		£271

The *continuous* weighted average method necessitates frequent changes to be made in calculating issue prices. Although it appears a very complicated method, it is the easiest one to use provided that the receipts and issues of goods are recorded in a stores ledger account. An example of a stores ledger account in shown in Exhibit 14.4.

Exhibit 14.4 Example of a stores ledger account

	Stores ledger account									
	Material: Maximum:							Code: Minimum:		
Date	Receipts				Issues				Stock		
	GRN No.	Quantity	Unit price	Amount	Stores Req. No.	Quantity	Unit price	Amount	Quantity	Unit price	Amount
			£	£			£	£		£	£

Notes:
GRN = Goods received note
Stores Req. No. = Stores requisition number

You will note that the stores ledger account shows both the quantity and the value of the stock in store at any one time. The *continuous weighted average price* is obtained by dividing the total value of the stock by the total quantity. A new price will be struck each time new purchases are taken into stock. Unlike the periodic weighted average price, it is not necessary to wait until the end of the period before calculating a new price.

The continuous weighted average price method is illustrated in Exhibit 14.5. We use the same data that we have used in the earlier exhibits, but we have taken the opportunity to present a little more information, so that we can explain more clearly how to calculate a continuous weighted average price.

Exhibit 14.5 The continuous weighted average pricing method of charging direct materials to production

You are presented with the following information relating to the receipt and issue of material X into stock during January 19X1:

Date	Receipts into stores			Issues to production			Stock balance	
	Quantity Units	Price £	Value £	Quantity Units	Price £	Value £	Quantity Units	Value £
1.1.X1	100	10	1000				100	1000
10.1.X1	150	11	1650				250	2650
15.1.X1				125	10.60	1325	125	1325
20.1.X1	50	12	600				175	1925
31.1.X1				150	11.00	1650	25	275

Note:
The company uses the continuous weighted average method of pricing the issue of goods to production.

Required:
Check that the prices of goods issued to production during January 19X1 have been calculated correctly.

Answer to Exhibit 14.5

The issue prices of goods to production during January 19X1 using the continuous weighted average method have been calculated as follows:

15.1.X1 $\quad\dfrac{\text{Total stock value at 10.1.X1}}{\text{Total quantity in stock at 10.1.X1}} = \dfrac{2650}{250} = \underline{\underline{£10.60}}$

25.1.X1 $\quad\dfrac{\text{Total stock value at 20.1.X1}}{\text{Total quantity in stock at 20.1.X1}} = \dfrac{1925}{175} = \underline{\underline{£11.00}}$

Other methods

There are a considerable number of other methods that may be considered suitable for determining the pricing of material issues to production. Many of them are are examined in some detail in accounting textbooks, but they have little practical importance. However, there is one other method which we ought to mention. This is the *standard cost method* (which we will be meeting again in Chapter 18).

The standard cost method involves estimating what materials are likely to cost in the future. Instead of the actual price, the estimated cost (or *planned cost*, as it is known) would then be used to charge out the cost of materials. Of course, any substantial difference between actual and planned costs would have to be investigated, and it might mean there had been a considerable under- (or over-) charging of materials to production. Any difference would be written off in total to the profit and loss account for the period in which the difference occurred.

The standard cost method is usually adopted as part of a standard costing system. Such a system adopts standard costs for all elements of cost. Frequent comparisons have to be made with actual costs and immediate action taken if there are any discrepancies between them.

SELECTING A METHOD

It would be helpful at this stage if we summarized the advantages and disadvantages of each of the pricing methods outlined in the previous section in order to make it easier for you to decide which one you prefer. The summary is shown in Exhibit 14.6.

Exhibit 14.6 Summary of the advantages and disadvantages of different material pricing methods

Method	Advantages	Disadvantages
1 FIFO	(a) it is logical (b) it may match the physical issue of goods (c) the closing stock is closer to the current economic value (d) the stores ledger account is self-balancing: there are no balancing adjustments to be written off to the profit and loss account (e) it is acceptable for tax purposes	(a) it is arithmetically cumbersome (b) the cost of production relates to out-of-date prices

Method	Advantages	Disadvantages
2 LIFO	(a) production is charged with costs that are close to current economic values (b) the stores ledger account is self-balancing: there are no balancing adjustments to be written off to the profit and loss account	(a) it is arithmetically cumbersome (b) the closing stock is valued at much older prices that may bear little relationship to current economic prices (c) this method is not acceptable for tax purposes
3 Periodic weighted average	(a) it is simple to calculate (b) the issue price relates both to quantities purchased and to changing prices (c) it is easy to adopt because the price is not calculated until the period has ended (d) it achieves a compromise between the lowest and highest prices (e) it is not distorted by the quantities purchased	(a) the price cannot be calculated until the period has ended (b) prices in previous periods are ignored (c) it lags behind current economic prices (d) it may not relate to any price actually paid (e) it may be necessary to write off balancing adjustments to the profit and loss account
4 Continuous weighted average	(a) previous period prices are taken into account (b) it is easy to calculate (c) it relates the prices of goods purchased to quantities purchased (d) it produces a price that is not distorted either by low or high prices paid, or by small or large quantities purchased (e) a new price is calculated on new receipts of goods, so the price is constantly being updated	(a) it lags behind current economic prices (b) it may not relate to prices actually paid (c) it may be necessary to write off balancing adjustments to the profit and loss account

Precise rules cannot be laid down for the choice of a pricing method. LIFO is largely unsuitable for use in the UK because of its tax disadvantages. The periodic weighted average method is somewhat impracticable since it can only be used *after* the period has ended. FIFO attempts to match the physical issue of the goods by using the oldest prices first. In the case of some purchases (such as liquids and grains), this may largely be a theoretical advantage, because there can be no certainty that the goods being issued necessarily relate to the order in which they were purchased. On balance, the continuous weighted average method would appear to be the one that is most suitable: it is easy to calculate, and it does not result in the use of an extreme range of prices. None of these methods would be adopted if the company operates a standard costing system, but even standard costs can lead to some considerable problems. We will be looking at these in Chapter 18.

As we have seen, the charging of material costs to production is not a straightforward exercise. It is usually clear what *quantity* of material has been transferred to production (if not, then it would be treated as an indirect cost), but it may be much more difficult to price it. This problem arises because it is often not possible to distinguish between different purchases of goods, and hence to isolate each individual price.

In future, as modern production techniques become more sophisticated, direct material pricing may become less of a problem. Many companies are now installing what are called 'just-in-time' (JIT) production methods, and these methods may also be applied to purchasing. We will come back to JIT in Chapter 20.

The need to use an estimated price (irrespective of the method adopted), means that the total cost of the unit must also be an estimate. In turn, this also means that the value of any closing stock must also be any estimate, and that will then affect the the entity's financial accounts. However, as we shall see in the next chapter, the problems become more acute, because we also have to estimate how much *indirect* cost we are going to charge each unit. It follows that it is normally impossible to talk about the true cost of anything, since costs can only be true in an arithmetical sense. This point will be developed in greater detail in the next chapter.

We can now move on to have a look at the other main type of direct cost: labour.

DIRECT LABOUR

Labour costs include the cost of employees' salaries, wages, bonuses, and the employer's national insurance and pension fund contributions. Wherever it is economically viable to do so, we will want to charge labour costs to each specific unit, otherwise they will have to be treated as part of indirect costs.

The identification and pricing of direct labour is much easier than is the case with direct material. Basically, the procedure is as follows:

1 Employees working on specific units will be required to keep a record of how many hours they spend on each unit.
2 The total hours worked on each unit will then be multiplied by their hourly rate.

3 A percentage amount will added to the total to allow for the employer's labour costs (e.g. national insurance, pension fund contributions and holiday pay).

4 The total amount is then charged directly to that unit.

The procedure is illustrated in Exhibit 14.7.

Exhibit 14.7 The charging of direct labour cost to production

Alex and Will are working on Unit X. Alex is paid £10 an hour, and Will £5. Both men are required to keep an accurate record of how much time they have spent on Unit X. Alex spends 10 hours and Will 20. The employer has estimated that it costs him an extra 20% on top of what he pays them to meet his contributions towards national insurance, pension contributions and holiday pay.

Required:
Calculate the direct labour cost of producing Unit X.

Answer to Exhibit 14.7

Calculation of the direct labour cost:

	Hours	Rate per hour	Total
		£	£
Alex	10	10	100
Will	20	5	100
			200
Employer's costs (20%)			40
Total direct labour cost			£240

It should be made clear that, in practice, it is by no means easy to obtain an accurate estimate of the direct labour cost of one unit. We start from an assumption that, if it is very difficult to do so, then probably it will be costly and therefore not worthwhile. But even in those cases where there is no doubt that employees are working on one unit (as in Exhibit 14.7), we are dependent upon them keeping an accurate record. If you have ever had to do this in your own job, you will know that this is not easy, especially if you are frequently being switched from one job to another. It is also difficult to account for all those five minutes spent chatting in the corridor!

Notwithstanding the difficulties, however, it is important that management should emphasize to the employees just how important it is that they do keep an accurate record of their time. Labour costs may form a high proportion of total cost (especially in service industries), so tight control is important. This is particularly so, of course, if tender prices are based on total unit cost. A high cost could mean that the company fails to get a contract, whereas too low a cost diminishes profit.

OTHER DIRECT COSTS

Apart from material and labour costs, there may be other types of costs that can be economically identified with specific units. These are, however, relatively rare, because unlike material and labour, it is usually difficult to trace a physical link to specific units. It only occurs, therefore, in some very special cases. For example, the company may hire specialist plant for work on a specific unit. It is then easy to identify the physical link between the unit and the plant, and to identify the hire charge with the unit.

Notwithstanding the difficulties of identifying other expenses with production, it is important to do so wherever possible. Otherwise, the indirect charge becomes bigger and bigger, and that causes even more problems in building up the cost of a specific unit.

CONCLUSION

This chapter has dealt specifically with *direct* costs, i.e. those costs that can be economically identified with specific cost units. We have emphasized that, even where such an exercise is viable, there are still considerable problems. In identifying direct material cost, for example, it is usually necessary to estimate its cost. This may be done by adopting a well-established pricing method, such as FIFO, LIFO, periodic weighted average, continuous weighted average, or a standard cost, but this still does not disguise the fact that, whichever method is used, they all lead to an *estimated* charge. This means, of course, that the value of any closing stock must also be an estimate. Thus, it is not possible to argue that there is any one true cost. Indeed, a cost may only be accurate in the arithmetical sense, because it is usually based on a whole series of assumptions.

It is not usually too difficult to estimate direct labour costs, provided that accurate time records are kept by employees working on specific units. However, where employees switch from one job to another in quick succession (as with supervisory time) it may be difficult to keep an accurate record. Thus, supervisory time, for example, may have to be treated as an indirect cost.

There are occasionally some other costs that can be charged directly to production. These are comparatively rare, and are usually so obvious that no great difficulty arises in treating them as direct costs.

Key points	
	1 **Unit costing serves three main purposes: (a) in valuing closing stock; (b) in estimating selling prices; and (c) in planning and controlling overall costs.**

> **2** The procedure involves identifying those costs that are economically identifiable with a specific unit. It may be impossible to identify some costs with a specific unit, but with other costs, while it may be possible, it either becomes very expensive or may not be worthwhile.
>
> **3** Some materials can be readily identified with specific units, but their purchase price is not always known. If these are to be charged to specific units, an estimated price has to be determined. The most common methods are FIFO, LIFO, periodic weighted average, continuous weighted average, and standard cost.
>
> **4** Wherever possible, labour costs should also be charged directly to specific units. This is not usually as difficult as it is with materials.
>
> **5** Some other services may also be identifiable with a specific unit, and if their costs can be economically determined, they should be charged directly to production.

CHECK YOUR LEARNING

1 Fill in the missing blanks in each of the following statements:
  (a) Expenditure which can be economically identified with a specific saleable unit is known as a _____ _____.
  (b) Overhead comprises _____ material cost _____ labour cost, and _____ expenses.
  (c) Goods purchased for incorporation into products for sale are known as _____ _____.
  (d) Labour costs include employees' _____ and _____, bonuses, employer's national insurance and pension fund contributions.

2 List three methods of charging the cost of direct materials to production.

3 What is the term used to describe a planned or an estimated cost?

4 Is the following statement true or false?
  When prices are rising, using current economic prices to charge materials to production results in a lower level of profit.   True/False

Answers 1 (a) direct cost (b) indirect; indirect; indirect (c) raw materials (d) salaries; wages
2 FIFO; LIFO; weighted average (periodic or continuous)
3 standard costing
4 True

QUESTIONS

14.1

The following stocks were taken into stores as follows:

1.1.X1 1000 units @ £20 per unit.
15.1.X1 500 units @ £25 per unit.

There were no opening stocks.
On 31.1.X1 1250 units were issued to production.

Required:
Calculate the amount which would be charged to production on 31 January 19X1 for the issue of material on that date using each of the following methods of material pricing:

1 FIFO (first-in, first-out);
2 LIFO (last-in, first-out); and
3 periodic weighted average.

14.2

The following information relates to material ST 2:

		Units	Unit price £	Value £
1.2.X2	Opening stock	500	1.00	500
10.2.X2	Receipts	200	1.10	220
12.2.X2	Receipts	100	1.12	112
17.2.X2	Issues	400	–	–
25.2.X2	Receipts	300	1.15	345
27.2.X2	Issues	250	–	–

Required:
Calculate the value of closing stock at 28 February 19X2 assuming that the continuous weighted average method of pricing materials to production has been adopted.

14.3

You are presented with the following information for Trusty Limited:

19X3	Purchases (units)	Unit cost £	Issues to production (units)
1 January	2 000	10	
31 January			1 600
1 February	2 400	11	
28 February			2 600
1 March	1 600	12	
31 March			1 000

Note: There was no opening stock.

Required:
Calculate the value of closing stock at 31 March 19X3 using each of the following methods of pricing the issue of materials to production:

1 FIFO (first-in, first-out);
2 LIFO (last-in, first-out); and
3 continuous weighted average.

14.4

The following information relates to a certain raw material taken into stock:

	Receipts		Issues to production
	Units	Value	Units
		£	
1.4.X4	50	350	
3.4.X4	30	213	
5.4.X4			60
9.4.X4	20	139	
11.4.X4			25
14.4.X4			10
18.4.X4	35	252	
23.4.X4	60	423	
26.4.X4			100
30.4.X4	45	315	

The opening stock was 20 units at a value of £120.

Required:
Using the periodic weighted average method of pricing the issue of materials to production, calculate the value of the closing stock as at 30 April 19X4.

14.5

The following information relates to Steed Limited for the year to 31 May 19X5:

	£
Sales	500 000
Purchases	440 000
Opening stock	40 000
Closing stock value using the following pricing methods:	
1 FIFO (first-in, first-out)	90 000
2 LIFO (last-in, first-out)	65 000
3 Periodic weighted average	67 500
4 Continuous weighted average	79 950

Required:
Prepare Steed Limited's gross profit for the year to 31 May 19X5 using each of the above closing stock values.

14.6

Iron Limited is a small manufacturing company. During the year to 31 December 19X2 it has taken into stock and issued to production the following items of raw material, known as XY1:

Date 19X2	Receipts into stock			Issues to production
	Quantity (litres)	Price per unit £	Total value £	Quantity (litres)
January	200	2.00	400	
February				100
April	500	3.00	1 500	
May				300
June	800	4.00	3 200	
July				400
October	900	5.00	4 500	
December				1 400

Notes:
1 There were no opening stocks of raw materials XY1.
2 The other costs involved in converting raw material XY1 into the finished product (marketed as *Carcleen*) amounted to £7000.
3 Sales of *Carcleen* for the year to 31 December 19X2 amounted to £20 000.
4 For the purpose of this question, an accounting period is defined as the calendar year.

Required:
(a) Illustrate the following methods of pricing the issue of materials to production:
  1 first-in, first-out (FIFO);
  2 last-in, first-out (LIFO);
  3 periodic weighted average;
  4 continuous weighted average.
(b) Calculate the gross profit for the year using each of the above methods of pricing the issue of materials to production.

ADDITIONAL QUESTIONS (WITHOUT ANSWERS)

14.7

The folowing information relates to one of Osprey's stores ledger accounts:

Date 19X8	Receipts		Issues
	Quantity (kilos)	Price per kilo £	Quantity (kilos)
January	145	10	100
February	180	9	170
March	240	11	150
April	110	11	250
May	220	12	200
June	150	15	165

Stock at 1 January 19X8: 20 kilos at £11.50 per kilo.

Required:
Calculate the cost of the closing stock of the above materialas at 30 June 19X8 using each of the following stock valuation methods:

(a) FIFO (first-in, first-out);
(b) LIFO (last -in, first-out); and
(c) continuous weighted average.

14.8
Waters has recorded the following information in one of its stores ledger accounts:

19X9	Receipts		
	Quantity (units)	Cost per unit £	Sales (units)
January	290	6	200
February	580	9	700
March	410	12	300
April	730	15	600
May	290	5	200
June	410	7	600
July	720	11	700
August	600	9	500
September	580	11	600
October	590	7	700
November	840	11	750
December	280	4	300

At 1 January 19X9 there were 60 units in stock at a total estimated value of £300. The selling price was £10 per unit.

Required:
(a) Compare and contrast the gross profit for the year to 31 December 19X9 using each of the following stock valuation methods:
   (i) FIFO (first-in, first-out);
   (ii) LIFO (last-in, first-out); and
   (iii) continuous weighted average.
(b) Prepare a report for the Board of Directors outlining which stock valuation method you would recommend.

DISCUSSION QUESTIONS

14.9
Examine the argument that arbitrary apportionments of material costs to production are of no assistance to managers when they come to take decisions about product costs.

14.10
'It is rarely possible to calculate precisely the cost of anything, so there is no point in trying.' How far do you go along with this assertion in respect of the cost of materials?

14.11
'Direct material costing is 100 years out of date.' Discuss.

CHAPTER 15

Absorption costing

Emap board split over plan to change structure of board

By Raymond Snoddy

The board of Emap, the publishing, commercial radio and exhibitions group, has been split over proposals to make it easier to remove directors and which could reduce the number of non-executives.

The company plans to change its articles of association at its annual general meeting on July 18 so that a director can be removed given a majority of 75 per cent of directors. It is also seeking to remove a requirement that the board must have a minimum of five non-executives.

Emap currently has 13 directors, six of whom are non-executive, including the chairman. Two long-serving Emap non-executives, Professor Kenneth Simmonds, Professor of marketing and international business at the London Business School, and Mr Joe Cooke, a former managing director of the Daily Telegraph Group, are publicly opposing the changes and have written to the company expressing disapproval. Both intend to vote against the proposed changes at the meeting.

The row raises serious issues of corporate governance over what degree of unanimity is required for the removal of directors and over the importance of maintaining a strong block of non-executives.

Sir Frank Rogers, chairman of Emap for 17 years and the man responsible for introducing the five non-executives rule, last night said he would vote against the changes. He is a significant individual shareholder.

Mr Cooke and Prof Simmonds believe it is inappropriate to give 75 per cent of the board power to remove a director without reference to the shareholders. Such a provision would remove shareholder protection from any minority of directors who believe a majority board decision is not in the interests of shareholders.

The new article to be voted on later this month specifies simply that there should be a minimum of three directors.

Mr Robin Miller, chief executive of Emap, said last night the board had always accepted the rules produced by the Cadbury committee into corporate governance, and would continue to honour them. Cadbury specifies there should be an appropriate number of non-executive directors and that this is usually seen as a minimum of three.

The Financial Times, 3 July 1996

Exhibit 15.0 In the meantime, someone has to do the accounts

In the last chapter, we dealt with the treatment of direct costs. Direct costs were defined as that expenditure which can be economically identified and specifically measured against relevant cost objects. In this chapter, we will examine the treatment of indirect costs, i.e. those costs that cannot be economically identified with a specific unit. The total of such costs is known as *overhead*. Overhead includes material costs, labour costs, and other types of cost.

If the recommendations outlined in Chapter 13 are accepted, and all costs are first allocated (i.e. charged to) a specific cost centre, then as far as specific units are concerned, indirect costs will arise from two main sources:

1 from production cost centres: those costs that cannot be economically identified with specific cost objects (even though it may have been possible to identify them initially with a specific production cost centre);

2 from service cost centres: those costs that are not directly identifiable with production cost centres, and so they must all be indirect costs as far as specific units are concerned.

There is no obvious way of identifying indirect costs with specific units (otherwise, there would not be indirect costs), so if we want to calculate the total cost of producing a particular unit, the indirect costs have to be shared out.

We explain how this is done in subsequent sections. The procedure is also outlined in diagrammatic form in Exhibit 15.1.

Learning objectives	**By the end of this chapter, you will be able to:**
	● **describe the nature of indirect production costs;**
	● **apportion service costs to production cost centres;**
	● **absorb indirect costs into cost units;**
	● **identify non-production costs;**
	● **assess the usefulness of absorption costing.**

PRODUCTION OVERHEAD

It was suggested in Chapter 13 that if cost accounting is going to be used as part of a control system, it is necessary for all costs within an entity to become the direct responsibility of a designated cost centre manager. In this section, we will examine how the total production overhead eventually gets charged to specific units. It is quite a complicated procedure, so we will take you through it in stages.

Exhibit 15.1 Flow of costs in an absorption costing system

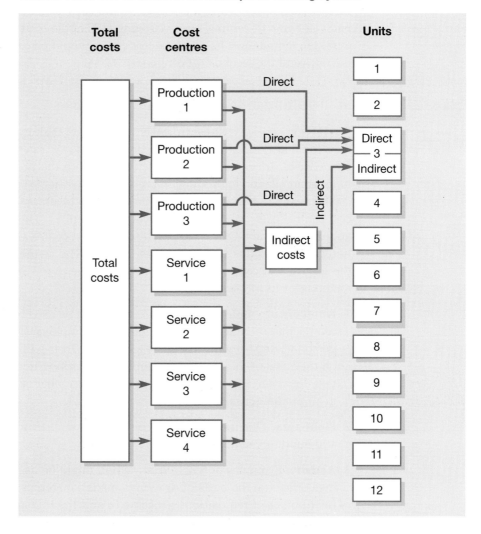

Stage 1: Allocate all costs to specific cost centres

We cannot emphasize too strongly the importance of allocating all costs to specific cost centres. Allocation is the process of charging whole items of cost either to cost centres (or to cost units), i.e. they can be easily identified with the cost centre (or cost unit) so there is no need to apportion the cost. It is not always easy to allocate every type of cost to an easily identifiable cost centre, and sometimes it is necessary to select a particular cost centre even though its manager may only be remotely responsible for the expenditure.

For control purposes, however, it will still be necessary to charge such costs to a particular cost centre, and then, at some later stage, to *apportion* (i.e. share) them among those cost centres that have benefited from the service provided. For example, most cost centres could be expected to be charged with their

313

share of factory rates, and so they would probably be apportioned on the basis of floor space. Thus, if the rates for the factory amounted to £5000, and it had just two cost centres, one occupying 60% of the total floor space, and the other the remaining 40%, the first cost centre would be charged with £3000 of the rates and the second cost centre with £2000.

Stage 2: Share out the production service cost-centre costs

Production service cost-centre costs will contain mainly allocated costs, but they could also include some apportioned costs (e.g. rates). By definition, service cost-centre costs are not directly related to the production of specific units, so in relation to production units, they must all be indirect costs.

The next stage in unit costing, therefore, is to share out the total service cost-centre costs among the production cost centres. This is usually done by apportioning the total cost for each service cost centre among those production cost centres that benefit from the service. The method used to apportion the service cost-centre costs may be very simple. A few of the more common methods are as follows:

1 **Numbers of employees**. This method would be used for those service cost centres that provide a service to individual employees, e.g. the canteen, the personnel department, and the wages office. Costs will then be apportioned on the basis of the number of employees working in a particular production department as a proportion of the total number of employees working in all production cost centres.

2 **Floor area**. This method would be used for such cost centres as cleaning and building maintenance.

3 **Activity**. Examples of where this method might be used include the drawings office (on the basis of drawings made), materials handling (based on the number of requisitions processed), and the transport department (on the basis of vehicle operating hours).

A problem arises in dealing with the apportionment of service cost-centre costs when service cost centres provide a service for each other. For example, the wages office will probably provide a service for the canteen staff, and in turn, the canteen staff may provide a service for the wages staff. Before the service cost-centre costs can be apportioned among the production cost centres, therefore, it is necessary to make sure that service cost-centre costs are charged out to each other.

The problem becomes a circular one, however, because it is not possible to charge (say) some of the canteen costs to the wages office until the canteen has been charged with some of the costs of the wages office. Similarly, it is not possible to charge out the wages office costs until part of the canteen costs have been charged to the wages office. The treatment of *reciprocal* service costs (as they are called) can become an involved and time-consuming process unless a clear policy decision is taken about their treatment. There are three main ways of dealing with this problem:

1 **Ignore interdepartmental service costs**. If this method is adopted, the respective service cost-centre costs are only apportioned among the production cost centres. Any servicing that the service cost centres provide for each other is ignored.

2 **Specified order of closure**. This method requires the service cost centre costs to be closed off in some specified order and apportioned among the production cost centres and the remaining service cost centres. As the service cost centres are gradually closed off, there will eventually be only one service cost centre left. Its costs will then be apportioned among the production cost centres. Some order of closure has to be specified, and this may be quite arbitrary. It may be based, for example, on those centres which provide a service for the largest number of other service cost centres, or it could be based on the cost centres with the highest or the lowest cost in them prior to any interdepartmental servicing. It could also be based on an estimate of the benefit received by other centres.

3 **Mathematical apportionment**. Each service cost centre's total cost is apportioned among production cost centres and other service cost centres on the basis of the estimated benefit provided. The effect is that additional amounts keep being charged back to a particular service cost centre as further apportionment takes place. It can take a very long time before there is no more cost to charge out to any of the service cost centres, but when it is reached, all the service cost centre costs will then have been charged to the production cost centres. This method involves a great deal of exhaustive arithmetical apportionment, and it is also very time consuming, especially where there are a great many service cost centres. Although it is possible to carry out the calculations manually, it is more easily done by computer program.

In choosing one of the above methods, it should be remembered that they all depend upon an *estimate* of how much benefit one department receives from another. Such an estimate amounts to no more than an informed guess. It seems unnecessary, therefore, to build an involved arithmetical exercise on the basis of some highly questionable assumptions. We would suggest that in most circumstances interdepartmental servicing charging may be ignored.

We have covered some fairly complicated procedures in dealing with Stage 1 and 2, so before moving on to Stage 3 we use Exhibit 15.2 to illustrate the procedure.

Exhibit 15.2 Charging overhead to cost centres

You are provided with the following indirect cost information relating to the New Manufacturing Company Limited for the year to 31 March 19X5:

	£
Cost centre	
Production 1: indirect expenses (to units)	24 000
Production 2: indirect expenses (to units)	15 000
Service cost centre A: allocated expenses	20 000
Service cost centre B: allocated expenses	8 000
Service cost centre C: allocated expenses	3 000

Additional information:
The estimated benefit provided by the three service cost centres to other cost centres is as follows:

Service cost centre A: Production 1 50%; Production 2 30%; Service cost centre B 10%; Service cost centre C 10%.

Service cost centre B: Production 1 70%; Production 2 20%; Service cost centre C 10%.

Service cost centre C: Production 1 50%; Production 2 50%.

Required:
Calculate the total amount of overhead to be charged to cost centre units for both Production cost centre 1 and Production cost centre 2 for the year to 31 March 19X5.

Answer to Exhibit 15.2

NEW MANUFACTURING COMPANY LIMITED
Overhead distribution schedule for the year to 31 March 19X5

Cost centre	Production		Service		
	1	2	A	B	C
	£	£	£	£	£
Allocated indirect expenses	24 000	15 000	20 000	8 000	3 000
Apportion service cost-centre costs:					
A (50 : 30 : 10 : 10)	10 000	6 000	(20 000)	2 000	2 000
B (70 : 20 : 0 : 10)	7 000	2 000	–	(10 000)	1 000
C (50 : 50 : 0 : 0)	3 000	3 000	–	–	(6 000)
Total overhead to be absorbed by specific units	£44 000	£26 000	–	–	–

Tutorial notes

1 Units passing through Production cost centre 1 will have to share total overhead expenditure amounting to £44 000. Units passing through Production cost centre 2 will have to share total overhead expenditure amounting to £26 000. Units passing through both departments may be identical: for example, they might be assembled in cost centre 1 and packed in cost centre 2.

2 The total amount of overhead to be shared amongst the units is £70 000 (44 000 + 26 000 or 24 000 + 15 000 + 20 000 + 8000 + 3000). The total amount of overhead originally collected in each of the five cost centres does not change.

3 This exhibit does involve some interdepartmental re-apportionment of service cost-centre costs. However, no problem arises because of the basis upon which the question requires the respective service cost-centre costs to be apportioned.

4 The objective of apportioning service cost-centre costs is to charge them out to the production cost centres so that they can be charged to specific units.

Stage 3: Absorption of production overhead

Once all the indirect costs have been collected in the production cost centres, the next step is to charge the total amount to specific units. This procedure is known as *absorption*.

The method of absorbing overhead into units is normally a simple one. Accountants recommend a single factor, preferably one that is related as closely as possible to the movement of overhead. In other words, an attempt is made to choose a factor which directly correlates with the amount of overhead expenditure incurred. Needless to say, like so much else in accounting, there is no obvious factor to choose! Indeed, if there was an obvious close relationship, it is doubtful whether it would be necessary to distinguish between direct and indirect costs.

There are six main methods that can be used for absorbing production overhead. All six methods adopt the same basic equation:

$$\text{Cost centre overhead absorption rate} = \frac{\text{Total cost centre overhead}}{\text{Total cost centre activity}}$$

A different absorption rate will be calculated for each production cost centre, so by the time that a unit has passed through various production cost centres, it may have been charged with a share of overhead from a number of production cost centres.

The six main absorption methods are as follows.

This method is the simplest to operate. It is calculated as follows:

Specific units

$$\text{Absorption rate} = \frac{\text{Total cost centre overhead}}{\text{Number of units processed in the cost centre}}$$

The same rate would be applied to each unit, thus it is only a suitable method if the units are identical.

Direct material cost

$$\text{Absorption rate} = \frac{\text{Total cost centre overhead}}{\text{Cost centre total direct material cost}} \times 100$$

The direct material cost of each unit is then multiplied by the absorption rate.

It is unlikely that there will normally be a strong relationship between the direct material cost and the level of overheads. There might be some special cases, but they are probably quite unusual, e.g. where a company uses a high level of precious metals and its overheads strongly reflect the cost of protecting those materials.

Direct labour costs

$$\text{Absorption rate} = \frac{\text{Total cost centre overhead}}{\text{Cost centre total direct labour cost}} \times 100$$

The direct labour cost of each unit is then multiplied by the absorption rate.

Overheads tend to relate to the amount of time that a unit spends in production, so this method may be particularly suitable since the direct labour cost is a combination of hours worked and rates paid. It may not be appropriate, however, where the total direct labour cost consists of a relatively low level of hours worked and of a high labour rate per hour, because the cost will not then relate very closely to time spent in production.

Prime cost

$$\text{Absorption rate} = \frac{\text{Total cost centre overhead}}{\text{Prime cost}} \times 100$$

The prime cost of each unit is then multiplied by the absorption rate. This method assumes that there is a close relationship between prime cost and overheads. In most cases, this is unlikely to be true.

As there is probably no close relationship between either direct materials or direct labour and overheads, then it is unlikely that there will be much of a correlation between prime cost and overheads. Hence, the prime cost method tends to combine the disadvantages of both the direct materials and the direct labour cost methods without having any real advantages of its own.

Direct labour costs

$$\text{Absorption rate} = \frac{\text{Total cost centre overhead}}{\text{Cost centre total direct labour hours}}$$

The direct labour hours of each unit are then multiplied by the absorption rate.

This method is highly acceptable, especially in those cost centres that are labour intensive, because time spent in production is related to the cost of overhead incurred.

Machine hours

$$\text{Absorption rate} = \frac{\text{Total cost centre overhead}}{\text{Cost centre total machine hours}}$$

The total machine hours used by each unit is then multiplied by the absorption rate.

This is a most appropriate method to use in those departments that are machine intensive. There is probably quite a strong correlation between the amount of machine time that a unit takes to produce and the amount of overhead incurred.

These absorption methods are illustrated in Exhibit 15.3.

Exhibit 15.3 Calculation of overhead absorption rates

Old Limited is a manufacturing company. The following information relates to the assembling department for the year to 30 June 19X8:

	Assembling department Total £000
Direct material cost incurred	400
Direct labour incurred	200
Total factory overhead incurred	100
Number of units produced	10 000
Direct labour hours worked	50 000
Machine hours used	80 000

Required:

Calculate the overhead absorption rates for the assembling department using each of the following methods:

(a) specific units;
(b) direct material cost;
(c) direct labour cost;
(d) prime cost;
(e) direct labour hours; and
(f) machine hours.

Answer to Exhibit 15.3

(a) Specific units:

$$\text{OAR} = \frac{\text{TCCO}}{\text{Number of units}} = \frac{100\,000}{10\,000} = \underline{\underline{£10.00 \text{ per unit}}}$$

(b) Direct material cost:

$$\text{OAR} = \frac{\text{TCCO}}{\text{Direct material cost}} \times 100 = \frac{100\,000}{400\,000} \times 100 = \underline{\underline{25\%}}$$

(c) Direct labour cost:

$$\text{OAR} = \frac{\text{TCCO}}{\text{Direct labour cost}} \times 100 = \frac{100\,000}{200\,000} \times 100 = \underline{\underline{50\%}}$$

(d) Prime cost:

$$\text{OAR} = \frac{\text{TCCO}}{\text{Prime cost}} \times 100 = \frac{100\,000}{400\,000 + 200\,000} \times 100 = \underline{\underline{16.67\%}}$$

(e) Direct labour hours:

$$\text{OAR} = \frac{\text{TCCO}}{\text{Direct labour hours}} = \frac{100\,000}{50\,000} = \underline{\underline{£2.00 \text{ per direct labour hour}}}$$

(f) Machine hours:

$$\text{OAR} = \frac{\text{TCCO}}{\text{Machine hours}} = \frac{100\,000}{80\,000} = \underline{\underline{£1.25 \text{ per machine hour}}}$$

Exhibit 15.3 illustrates the six absorption methods outlined in the text. You will appreciate, of course, that in practice, only one absorption method would be chosen for each production cost centre, although different production cost centres may adopt different methods, e.g. one may choose a direct labour hour rate, and another may adopt a machine hour rate.

The most appropriate absorption rate method will depend upon individual circumstances. A careful study would have to be made of the correlation between (a) direct materials, direct labour, other direct expenses, direct labour hours, and machine hours; and (b) total overhead expenditure. However, it is generally accepted that overhead tends to move with time, so the longer a unit spends in production, the more overhead that particular unit will generate. Thus, each individual unit ought to be charged with its share of overhead based on the *time* that it spends in production.

This argument suggests that labour intensive cost centres should use the direct labour hour method, while machine intensive departments should use the machine hour method.

A COMPREHENSIVE EXAMPLE

At this stage it would be useful to illustrate overhead absorption in the form of a comprehensive example, although it would clearly be impracticable to use one that involved hundreds of cost centres. In any case, we are trying to demonstrate the principles of absorption costing, and too much data would obscure those principles. Thus, the example contains only the most basic information.

Exhibit 15.4 Overhead absorption

Oldham Limited is a small manufacturing company producing a variety of pumps for the oil industry. It operates from one factory that is geographically separated from its head office. The components for the pumps are assembled in the assembling department; they are then passed through to the finishing department where they are painted and packed. There are three service cost centres: administration, stores and work study.

The following costs were collected for the year to 30 June 19X6:

Allocated cost centre overhead costs:	£000
Administration	70
Assembling	25
Finishing	9
Stores	8
Work study	18

Additional information:

1 The allocated cost centre overhead costs are all considered to be indirect costs as far as specific units are concerned.

2 During the year to 30 June 19X6, 35 000 machine hours were worked in the assembling department, and 60 000 direct labour hours in the finishing department.

3 The number of employees working in each department was as follows:

Administration	15
Assembling	25
Finishing	40
Stores	2
Work study	3
	85

4 During the year to 30 June 19X6, the stores received 15 000 requisitions from the assembling department, and 10 000 requisitions from the finishing department. The stores department did not provide a service for any other department.

5 The work study department carried out 2000 chargeable hours for the assembling department, and 1000 chargeable hours for the finishing department.

6 One special pump (code named MEA 6) was produced during the year to 30 June 19X6. It took 10 machine hours of assembling time, and 15 direct labour hours were worked on it in the finishing department. Its total direct costs (material and labour) amounted to £100.

Required:
(a) Calculate an appropriate absorption rate for:
  (i) the assembling department; and
  (ii) the finishing department.
(b) Calculate the total factory cost of the special pump.

Answer to Exhibit 15.4

(a)   **OLDHAM LIMITED**
         Overhead distribution schedule for the year to 30 June 19X6

	Production		Service		
Cost centre	Assembling	Finishing	Adminis-tration	Stores	Work study
	£000	£000	£000	£000	£000
Allocated overhead costs (1)	25	9	70	8	18
Apportion administration (2):					
25 : 40 : 2 : 3	25	40	(70)	2	3
Apportion stores (3):					
3 : 2	6	4	–	(10)	–
Apportion work study:					
2 : 1	14	7	–	–	(21)
Total overhead to be absorbed	£70	£60	–	–	–

Tutorial notes
1 The allocated overhead costs were given in the question.
2 Administration costs have been apportioned on the basis of employees. Details were given in the question. There were 85 employees in the factory, but 15 of them were employed in the administration department. Administration costs have, therefore, been apportioned on a total of 70 employees, or £1000 per employee. The administration department is the only service department to provide a service for the other service departments, so no problem of inter-departmental servicing arises.
3 The stores costs have been apportioned on the number of requisitions made by the two production cost centres, that is 15 000 + 10 000 = 25 000, or 3 to 2.
4 The work study costs have been apportioned on the basis of chargeable hours i.e. 2000 + 1000 = 3000, or 2 to 1.

Calculation of chargeable rates:
1   Assembling department:

$$\frac{\text{TCCO}}{\text{Total machine hours}} = \frac{70\,000}{35\,000} = \text{£2.00 per machine hour}$$

2   Finishing department:

$$\frac{\text{TCCO}}{\text{Total direct labour hours}} = \frac{60\,000}{60\,000} = \text{£1.00 per direct labour hour}$$

It would seem appropriate to absorb the assembling department's overhead on the basis of machine hours because it appears to be a machine intensive department. The finishing department appears more labour intensive, so its overhead will be absorbed on that basis.

(b) MEA 6: Calculation of total factory cost

	£	£
Direct costs (as given)		100
Add: factory overhead:		
Assembling department (10 machine hours × £2.00 per MH)	20	
Finishing department (15 direct labour hours × £1.00 per DLH)	15	35
Total factory cost		£135

You are now recommended to work throught Exhibit 15.4 without reference to the answer.

NON-PRODUCTION OVERHEAD

In this chapter, we have concentrated on the apportionment and absorption of *production* overheads. Most companies will, however, incur expenditure on activities that are not directly connected with production activities. For example, there could be selling and distribution costs, research and development costs, and head office administrative expenses. How should all of these costs be absorbed into unit cost?

Before this question can be answered, it is necessary to find out why we should want to apportion them. There are three main reasons:

1 **Control**. The more that an entity's costs are broken down, the easier it is to monitor them. It follows that just as there is an argument for having a detailed system of responsibility accounting at cost centre level, so there is an argument for having a similar system at unit cost level. However, in the case of non-production expenses, this argument is not a very strong one. We have seen that in order to calculate the production cost of a unit it is necessary to apportion a whole range of costs, and then to select a number of appropriate absorption methods. The practice of absorbing fixed production overhead into specific units is a highly questionable procedure, but for control purposes, the absorption of non-production fixed overheads is even more questionable.

The relationship between units produced and non-production overhead is usually so remote, that no meaningful estimate of the benefit received can be made. Consequently, the apportionment of non-production overhead is merely an arithmetical exercise, and no manager could be expected to take responsibility for such costs that have been charged to his cost centre, still less for any that have then been built into unit cost. From a control point of view, therefore, the exercise is not very helpful.

2 **Selling price**. In some cases, it might be necessary to add to the production cost of a specific unit, a proportion of non-production overhead in order to determine a selling price that covers all costs and allows a margin for profit. This system of fixing selling prices may apply in some industries, e.g. in tendering for long-term contracts, or in estimating decorating costs. In most cases, however, selling prices are determined by the market, and companies are not usually in a position to fix their selling prices based on cost with a percentage added on for profit (this is known as cost-plus pricing).

Even when selling prices cannot be based on total cost, however, it may be useful to have an idea of the company's total unit costs in relation to its selling prices, but it must be clearly recognized that the calculation of such total units costs can only provide a general guide.

3 **Stock valuation**. You might think that a total unit cost will be required for stock valuation purposes, since it will be necessary to include the cost of closing stocks in the annual financial accounts. However, there is an accounting standard that deals with the valuation of stocks (SSAP 9), and it does not permit the inclusion of non-production overhead in stock valuation. Thus, a company is unlikely to apportion non-production overhead for internal stock valuation purposes if a different method has to be adopted for financial reporting purposes.

It is obvious from the above summary that there are few benefits to be gained by charging a proportion of non-production overhead to specific cost units. In theory, the exercise is attractive, because it would be both interesting and useful to know the *actual* (or true) cost of each unit produced. In practice, however, it is impossible to arrive at any such cost, so it seems pointless to become engaged in spurious arithmetical exercises just for the sake of neatness.

The only real case for apportioning non-production overhead applies where selling prices can be based on cost. What can be done in those situations? There is still no magic formula, and an arbitrary estimate has still to be made. Sometimes a percentage is applied to the total production cost. This is bound to be somewhat questionable, since there can be no close relationship between production and non-production activities. It follows that the company's tendering or selling price policy should not be too rigid if it is based on this type of cost-plus pricing.

It is with some reservation, therefore, that, just in case you do come across the apportionment of non-production overhead in your own company, we introduce you to several ways in which non-production overhead could be apportioned to specific units. Remember though that this is largely an arithmetical exercise, and it does not achieve any further degree of control. If your company does adopt this procedure, you should put your accountants through a fairly severe cross-examination before you accept it. There are three main methods of apportioning non-production overhead to specific units and they are as follows:

1 **Administrative overhead**
   Administrative overheads could be absorbed by relating the total cost of the overhead to the total cost of production. The formula is:

$$\text{Absorption rate} = \frac{\text{Total administrative overhead}}{\text{Total production cost}} \times 100$$

The absorption rate is then applied to the total production cost of each unit.
It is also possible that in some circumstances the following formula could be adopted:

$$\text{Absorption rate} = \frac{\text{Total administrative overhead}}{\text{Total sales revenue}} \times 100$$

The formula is then applied to the selling price of each particular unit.

2 **Research and development overhead**
   As with administrative overhead, a research and development overhead absorption rate may be calculated on the basis of total production cost, i.e:

$$\text{Absorption rate} = \frac{\text{Total research and development overhead}}{\text{Total production cost}} \times 100$$

The rate is then applied to the total production cost of each unit.

3 **Selling and distribution overhead**
   The absorption rate for selling and distribution overhead can again be calculated by reference to the total cost of production, i.e.:

$$\text{Absorption rate} = \frac{\text{Total selling and distribution overhead}}{\text{Total cost of production}} \times 100$$

The rate is then applied to the total production cost of each unit. Alternatively, it might be related to the sales revenue. The formula would then be:

$$\text{Absorption rate} = \frac{\text{Total selling and distribution overhead}}{\text{Total sales revenue}} \times 100$$

The absorption rate would then be applied to the selling price of each unit.

It must be emphasized once again that the absorption of non-production overhead among specific units does not help in *controlling* costs. It is largely an arithmetical exercise, and it may only be of some use when selling prices are fixed on a cost-plus basis.

Before leaving this chapter, there is one further problem in absorbing fixed production overhead that we need to deal with. This is done in the next section.

PREDETERMINED RATES

An absorption rate can, of course, be calculated on an historical basis (i.e. after the event), or it can be predetermined (i.e. calculated in advance).

As we have tried to emphasize all the way through this chapter, there is no close correlation between fixed overhead and any particular measure of activity: it can only be apportioned on what seems to be a reasonable basis. However, if we know the total actual overhead incurred, we can make sure that it is all charged to specific units, even if we are not sure of the relationship it has with any particular unit.

To do so, of course, we cannot calculate an absorption rate until we know (a) the *actual* cost of overheads, and (b) the *actual* activity level (whether this is measured in machine hours, direct labour hours, or on some other basis). In other words, we can only make the calculation when we know what has happened.

The adoption of historical absorption rates is not usually very practicable. We have to wait until the actual period is over before an absorption rate, can be calculated, the products costed and the customers invoiced. We would, therefore, normally wish to calculate an absorption rate in advance. This is known as a *predetermined* rate.

In order to calculate a predetermined absorption rate, we have to estimate both the overhead which we think the company will incur, and the direct labour hours or machine hours that we expect to work (if we are using hours as the method of absorbing overhead). If one or other of these estimates turns out to be inaccurate, then we would have either under-charged our customers (if the rate was too low), or over-charged them (if the rate was too high).

This situation could be very serious for the company. Low selling prices caused by using a low absorption rate could have made the company's products very competitive, but there is not much point in selling a lot of units if they are being sold at a loss. Similarly, a high absorption rate may result in a high selling price. Thus, each unit may make a large profit, but not enough units may be sold to enable the company to make an overall profit.

The use of predetermined absorption rates may, therefore, result in an under- or an over-recovery of overhead. Overhead may be under- or over-absorbed if the company has under- or over-estimated the actual cost of the overhead or the actual level of activity (irrespective of how it is measured). The difference between the actual overhead incurred and the total overhead charged to production (calculated on a predetermined basis) gives rise to what is known as a *variance*. If the actual overhead incurred is in excess of the amount charged out, the variance will be *adverse*, i.e. the profit will be less

Exhibit 15.5 The under- and over-recovery of overhead by using predetermined rates

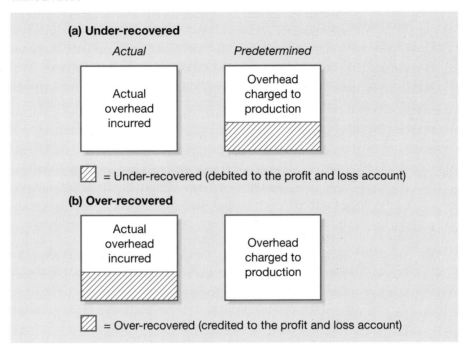

than expected. However, if the total overhead charged to production was less than was estimated, then the variance will be *favourable*. (The effect of this procedure is shown in diagrammatic form in Exhibit 15.5.) Other things being equal, a favourable variance gives rise to a higher profit, and an adverse variance results in a lower profit.

It is a cardinal rule in costing that variances should be written off to the profit and loss account at the end of the costing period in which they were incurred. It is not considered fair to burden the next period's accounts with the previous period's mistakes. In other words, it is as well to start off a new accounting period unburdened by the past.

Throughout this chapter we have clearly expressed many reservations about the way in which accountants have traditionally dealt with overheads. In recent years, dissatisfaction about overhead absorption has become widespread, and now a different technique called *activity-based costing* (ABC) is being advocated. ABC is examined in Chapter 20.

CONCLUSION

Absorption costing aims to help management plan and control a company's operations more effectively and efficiently; it may be necessary for stock valuation purposes, and in some industries it may be used in determining selling prices.

The technique is a highly questionable one. It depends initially on being able to determine those costs that can be economically identified with and specifically measured against specific relevant cost objects (direct costs), and those that cannot (indirect costs). This distinction is not always easy to make in practice, and there is a danger that more and more costs will be then identified as indirect.

The technique is carried out in a number of stages. The first stage is to allocate all costs to appropriate cost centres. The second stage is to apportion those costs that provide a benefit to other cost centres. The third stage is to apportion service cost-centre costs among relevant production cost centres. The fourth stage is to absorb the total overhead collected in each production cost centre into specific units.

The apportionment and the absorption stages both depend upon a relationship being established between the overhead cost and an appropriate measure of activity, even though such relationships are likely to be somewhat distant. Non-production overhead is also sometimes absorbed into unit costs, but the relationship between this type of expenditure and production activity is even more remote than it is for production overhead. For control purposes, therefore, it is not recommended, although it is sometimes done if selling prices are fixed on a cost-plus pricing basis.

Overhead absorption rates have usually to be predetermined, because it is impracticable to wait until the period has ended before production is charged with a share of overheads. If this were the case, then it would take some time before goods were eventually invoiced to customers. The use of predetermined rates means that some overhead may be over- or under-absorbed at the period end, and, as a result, a favourable or an adverse variance will arise. The variance will be favourable or adverse depending upon whether the cost and/or the level of activity has been over- or under-estimated. Variances should be written off to the profit and loss account for the period in which they were incurred. They should not be carried forward and hence become a charge in the next period's accounts.

Any variances that do arise may have a very serious long-term effect, as it could mean that the company could be either under- or over-pricing its products. Under-pricing may lead to an under-recovery of total cost, whilst over-pricing could result in a reduction in sales volume. Ultimately, this could lead to a lower level of profit.

Absorption costing is a technique which must be used with caution. It is necessary for stock valuation purposes, but as long as managers are aware of its limitations, it can also be useful in helping to control the company's production costs.

Key points

> 1 **Indirect costs are those that are not economically identifiable with and specifically measurable against specific relevant cost objects. Indirect costs are collectively referred to as overhead.**

2   In order to charge unit costs with a share of fixed production overhead, all costs should first be allocated to specific cost centres.

3   The cost of those services that provide a benefit for other cost centres should then be apportioned to those cost centres that have benefited from the service.

4   Costs collected in those service cost centres that provide a direct service to production cost centres should be apportioned to those production cost centres.

5   An absorption rate for each production cost centre should then be calculated by using either the direct labour hour or machine hour method.

6   The absorption rate calculated for each production cost centre is used to charge each production unit passing though it with a share of the overhead.

7   The total production cost of each unit can be calculated as follows: direct material + direct labour + direct expenses + apportioned production overhead.

8   The absorption of non-production overhead is not recommended, except where it is necessary for pricing purposes.

9   Absorption rates will normally be predetermined.

10 Under- or over-absorbed overhead should not be carried forward to the next period's accounts.

CHECK YOUR LEARNING

1   State whether each of the following assertions is either true or false:
   (a)   Some costs can be both a direct departmental cost and an indirect unit cost.   True/False
   (b)   All service costs are indirect as far as units are concerned.   True/False
   (c)   Prime cost is the best method to use in absorbing overhead in a machine department.   True/False
   (d)   Some service costs are included in unit costs.   True/False
   (e)   The absorption of non-production overhead into production units helps control the cost.   True/False

2   List three methods of absorbing production overheads into specific units.

3   In general, how could non-production overheads be absorbed into product costs?

1 (a) true   (b) true   (c) false   (d) true   (e) false
2   direct material cost; direct labour hour; machine hour
3   as a proportion of total production cost

QUESTIONS

15.1

Scar Limited has two production departments and one service department. The following information relates to January 19X1:

		£
Allocated expenses		
Production department: A		65 000
B		35 000
Service department		50 000

The allocated expenses shown above are all indirect expenses as far as individual units are concerned.

The benefit provided by the service department is shared amongst the production departments A and B in the proportion 60 : 40.

Required:
Calculate the amount of overhead to be charged to specific units for both production department A and production department B.

15.2

Bank Limited has several production departments. In the assembly department it has been estimated that £250 000 of overhead should be charged to that particular department. It now wants to charge a customer for a specific order. The data relevant are:

	Assembly department	*Specific unit*
Number of units	50 000	–
Direct material cost (£)	500 000	8.00
Direct labour cost (£)	1 000 000	30.00
Prime cost (£)	1 530 000	40.00
Direct labour hours	100 000	3.5
Machine hours	25 000	0.75

The accountant is not sure which overhead absorption rate to adopt.

Required:
Calculate the overhead to be absorbed by a specific unit passing through the assembly department using each of the following overhead absorption rate methods:

1   specific units;
2   percentage of direct material cost;
3   percentage of direct labour cost;
4   percentage of prime cost;
5   direct labour hours; and
6   machine hours.

15.3

The following information relates to the activities of the production department of Clough Limited for the month of March 19X3:

	Production department	Order number 123
Direct materials consumed (£)	120 000	20
Direct wages (£)	180 000	25
Overhead chargeable (£)	150 000	
Direct labour hours worked	30 000	5
Machine hours operated	10 000	2

The company adds a margin of 50% to the total production cost of specific units in order to cover administration expenses and to provide a profit.

Required:

(a) Calculate the total selling price of order number 123 if overhead is absorbed using the following methods of overhead absorption:

1 direct labour hours;

2 machine hours.

(b) State which of the two methods you would recommend for the production department.

15.4

Burns Limited has three production departments (processing, assembly and finishing) and two service departments (administration and work study). The following information relates to April 19X4:

	£
Direct material:	
Processing	100 000
Assembling	30 000
Finishing	20 000
Direct labour:	
Processing (£4 × 100 000 hours)	400 000
Assembling (£5 × 30 000 hours)	150 000
Finishing (£7 × 10 000 hours) + (£5 × 10 000 hours)	120 000
Administration	65 000
Work study	33 000
Other allocated costs:	
Processing	15 000
Assembling	20 000
Finishing	10 000
Administration	35 000
Work study	12 000

Apportionment of costs:

	Process %	Assembling %	Finishing %	Work study %
Administration	50	30	15	5
Work study	70	20	10	–

Total machine hours: Processing 25 000

All units produced in the factory pass through the three production departments before they are put into stock. Overhead is absorbed in the processing department on the basis of machine hours, on the basis of direct labour hours in the assembling department, and on the basis of the direct labour cost in the finishing department.

The following details relate to unit XP6:

	£	£
Direct materials:		
Processing	15	
Assembling	6	
Finishing	1	22
Direct labour:		
Processing (2 hours)	8	
Assembling (1 hour)	5	
Finishing (1 hour × £7 + 1 hour × £5)	12	25
Prime cost		£47

XP6: Number of machine hours in the processing department = 6

Required:
Calculate the total cost of producing unit XP6.

15.5
Outlane Limited's overhead budget for a certain period is as follows:

	£000
Administration	100
Depreciation of machinery	80
Employer's national insurance	10
Heating and lighting	15
Holiday pay	20
Indirect labour cost	10
Insurance: machinery	40
property	11
Machine maintenance	42
Power	230
Rent and rates	55
Supervision	50
	£663

The company has four production departments: L, M, N and O. The following information relates to each department.

Department	L	M	N	O
Total number of employees	400	300	200	100
Number of indirect workers	20	15	10	5
Floor space (square metres)	2 000	1 500	1 000	1 000
Kilowatt hours	30 000	50 000	90 000	60 000
Machine maintenance hours	500	400	300	200
Machine running hours	92 000	38 000	165 000	27 000
Capital cost of machines (£)	110 000	40 000	50 000	200 000
Depreciation rate of machines (on cost)	20%	20%	20%	20%
Cubic capacity	60 000	30 000	10 000	50 000

Previously the company has absorbed overhead on the basis of 100% of the direct labour cost. It has now decided to change to a separate machine hour rate for each department.

The company has been involved in two main contracts during the period, the details of which are as follows:

Department	Contract 1: Direct labour hours and machine hours	Contract 2: Direct labour hours and machine hours
L	60	20
M	30	10
N	10	10
O	–	60
	100	100

Direct labour cost per hour in both departments was £3.00.

Required:
(a) Calculate the overhead to be absorbed by both contract 1 and contract 2 using the direct labour cost method.
(b) Calculate the overhead to be absorbed using a machine hour rate for each department.

15.6
Sarah Limited has two production cost centres (D and P) and three service cost centres (1, 2, and 3). The following information relates to June 19X6:

Allocated costs	£000
Production cost centres:	
D	45
P	35
Service cost centres:	
1	160
2	71
3	34

All of the above costs are indirect as far as individual production units are concerned.

The service cost centres provide a service both for the production cost centres and for each other. The estimated benefit provided by each service cost to the other cost centre is as follows:

	Production		Service		
	D	P	1	2	3
	%	%	%	%	%
Service: 1	55	20	–	15	10
2	45	40	5	–	10
3	50	10	20	20	–

Required:
Calculate the total amount of overhead to be absorbed by production cost centre D and production cost centre P.

ADDITIONAL QUESTIONS (WITHOUT ANSWERS)

15.7
Doyle Limited makes a special type of floor covering. The process involves three production cost centres, L, M, and N, and two service cost centres, I and O.

The budgeted overhead expenditure for the year to 31 December 19X7 is as follows:

	Total
	£000
Canteen expenses	200
Depreciation	300
Heating and lighting	90
Indirect labour production costs	500
Rent, rates, and insurance	100
Repairs and maintenance	60
	£1250

Other information:

	Cost centre				
	L	M	N	I	O
Budgeted direct labour hours (000s)	50	50	25	–	–
Budgeted machine hours (000s)	100	50	20	–	
Capital value of plant and machinery (£000)	1 500	1 000	250	200	50
Cubic capacity (metres)	30 000	30 000	20 000	5 000	5 000
Direct allocation: repairs and maintenance (£000)	20	20	10	5	5
Floor areas (sq. metres)	4 000	3 000	1 000	1 000	1 000
Number employed	40	30	15	10	5

Required:
(a) Prepare a statement showing the total overhead cost budgeted for each cost centre:

(b) Calculate an appropriate budgeted overhead absorption rate for each of the three production cost centres.

15.8
Greaves Limited has prepared the following budget for the year to 31 March 19X8:

	Production cost centres	
	F	G
Costs:	£000	£000
Direct materials	100	30
Direct labour	300	250
Other direct expenses	40	10
Allocated overheads	30	20
Apportioned overheads	50	30
Other information:		
Total budgeted direct labour hours	30 000	25 000
Total budgeted machine hours	40 000	5 000

All units manufactured by Greaves flow through cost centre F and cost centre G.

During the year to 31 March 19X8, the company manufactured a special new unit called 'tacko'. Tacko's actual direct costs per unit were as follows:

	£
Direct materials	90
Direct labour	200
Direct expenses	10

One unit of tacko required 10 direct labour hours and 15 machine hours in cost centre F, and 30 direct labour hours and 5 machine hours in cost centre G.

Required:
(a) Calculate for *each* cost centre five different methods of absorbing production overheads:
(b) By adopting the most appropriate absorption rates, calculate the total cost of producing one unit of tacko.

DISCUSSION QUESTIONS

15.9
'Precision for precision's sake.' Is this statement true of the attempt to absorb non-produnction overhead into product costs?

15.10
Some non-accountants believe that the technique of overhead absorption was devised simply to provide jobs for accountants. How far do you agree?

15.11
How should reciprocal service costs be dealt with when calculating product costs?

CHAPTER 16

Marginal costing

Magnum shares tumble on worse-than-expected £3.1m loss

Management shake-up: Wide-ranging boardroom re-shuffle announced in bid to reverse power supply manufacturer's ailing fortunes

By Paul Stokes

Magnum Power saw its share price slump over 30 per cent yesterday after it unveiled worse-than-expected losses and warned it would not now break even this year as originally forecast.

At the same time the Livingston-based power supply manufacturer announced that its co-founder, Vincent Lavin, was stepping down from his role as managing director, to be replaced on a part-time basis by Alex Wilson, a senior executive with American electronics firm, SCI.

Auditors Arthur Andersen also expressed their concerns, saying there was a strong likelihood Magnum would need additional finance within the next year, adding: 'There can be no guarantee such funding will become available when required'.

Magnum shares fell 29p at one point. After a late rally they closed off 23p at 54p, compared to a float price of 35p and an institutional placing only two months ago which raised £1.5 million at 140p a share. Fellow Scottish hi-tech stock Memory Corporation slumped in sympathy, losing 15p to 75p.

The slide in Magnum's share price, which cut the company's market capitalisation to £23.76 million, makes it clearly vulnerable to a takeover from rival power supply manufacturers who could buy it just to acquire its technology.

Earlier Magnum revealed it had plunged £3.1 million into the red in the year to the end of May, about £1 million adrift of target and a 35 per cent increase on the previous year's loss of £2.3 million. Sales were £627,448 against £111,000.

Mr Wilson, who will retain his full-time role with SCI, supervising its European plants in Irvine, Grenoble and Barcelona, said he would devote three days a week to turning Magnum around.

He said: 'It is going to be tough, we will go through hell over the next nine months. But this is a good company with a good product, and we are going to be successful.'

Mr Lavin's move follows the departure of finance director and fellow founder, Ian Irvin, and means both the key figures who started Magnum have now quit their executive positions.

John Johnston, fund manager at Scottish Amicable, which holds a 13 per cent stake in Magnum, said: 'An entrepreneurial management team brought the stock to market very successfully but we have discovered very painfully over the last 18 months that they did not have the skills to run a plc.'

Robert Hynd, Magnum's company secretary, blamed the widening losses on Magnum's failure to convert its prototypes into products, and orders into sales.

He said the management and board changes, including the appointment of a group director of operations in Douglas McKenzie, would address this problem.

Magnum is now negotiating with manufacturers to produce its systems, which provide constant power to computers when the electricity supply fails.

At the same time it is quitting its own manufacturing operation at Girvan, employing 15, which will be sold to its management or shut at a cost of £225,000 to Magnum.

This will reduce monthly overheads, which have already been cut to £200,000, by a further £50,000 a month, Mr Hynd said.

The Scotsman, 28 June 1996

Exhibit 16.0 Even breaking even is hard to do for some

As was suggested in Chapter 13, once a company has decided to install a cost accounting system and it has chosen an appropriate product costing system, it has to decide how it should deal with fixed production overhead. It has two choices: it can either absorb fixed overheads into product costs, or it can ignore them. The first approach is known as absorption costing, and the second approach is known as *marginal* costing. We examined *absorption* costing in the last chapter, while in this one we are going to look at marginal costing.

You will recall that absorption costing may provide some misleading information, especially if it is used for short-term decision making. The main problem arises because it requires all costs to be shared out among specific units, irrespective of whether those costs change as a result of greater or lesser activity. This procedure lends weight to the argument that those costs that do not change with activity (i.e. fixed costs) should not be charged to specific units.

This argument is a very attractive one, especially when it is related to short-term problems. As the chapter develops, we hope to convince you about the usefulness of marginal costing, but first we must have another look at what we mean by fixed costs.

By the end of this chapter, you will be able to:

- **describe the difference between a fixed cost and a variable cost;**

- **use marginal costing in managerial decision making;**

- **analyse its importance when taking decisions.**

FIXED COSTS

In absorption costing, we do not recognize the distinction between fixed costs and variable costs. Those costs were referred to in Chapter 13 and the formal CIMA definitions are as follows:

> Fixed cost: a cost which is incurred for an accounting period, and which, within certain output and turnover limits, tends to be unaffected by fluctuations in the levels of activity (output or turnover).
> Variable cost: a cost which varies with a measure of activity.

In absorption costing we disregard the fact that fixed costs will not be affected by changes in levels of activity, and yet some fixed costs are charged to specific units even though they may not have been affected by a change in the level of activity. This questionable procedure can best be illustrated by an example.

Suppose that we are costing a particular car journey by someone who already owns a car, and that the car is fully taxed and insured. The main cost of the journey will be that spent on petrol (although the car may depreciate more quickly, and it might require more servicing). The tax and insurance costs will not be affected by one particular journey: they are fixed costs, no matter how many extra journeys are undertaken. Thus as far as a specific journey is concerned, we are only interested in the *extra* cost, i.e. the cost of the petrol. The decision to estimate only the extra cost of the journey (or for that matter, the extra cost of producing one more unit) gives rise to the system known as marginal costing.

The formal CIMA definition is:

> Marginal costing: the accounting system in which variable costs are charged to cost units and fixed costs of the period are written off in full against the aggregate contribution.

In the above example, if we used absorption costing in estimating the cost of the journey, we would add up all the costs of running the car over (say) a year and divide the total cost by its annual mileage. The average (or absorbed cost) per mile would then be applied to the mileage expected to be incurred on that particular journey. It would clearly be absurd to cost it in this way: the total cost of running the car will not be affected by the journey. What we need to calculate is the marginal (or the extra) cost of the journey. This would then be contrasted with the cost of other forms of transport, such as rail or air. Even then, the cost may not be the sole criterion in deciding whether to use the car, the train, or the 'plane, because we would also need to take into account non-quantifiable factors, such as comfort and convenience. This latter point illustrates that, in managerial decision making, *non-financial* factors have also to be taken into account.

In costing the extra cost of a car journey, we are effectively ignoring the *fixed* costs of owning a car. They do form part of the overall cost of car owner-ship, of course, and they do have to be taken into account when deciding how much it costs to run a car. Once the car has been purchased, however, the fixed costs can be ignored as far as a specific journey is concerned.

Managers in industry face similar decisions. These decisions can also best be solved by using marginal costing. An absorbed cost is not very helpful in deciding upon the outcome of a specific event, e.g. in reducing selling prices or in contracting for new work. In taking such specific decisions, the com-pany's fixed costs may not be immediately affected. In the long run, of course, even the fixed costs may change, e.g. if the company expands (or contracts) on any scale.

Nonetheless, marginal costing is extremely useful in decision making gen-erally, although it is especially useful in dealing with short-term decisions. We explain how it works in the next section.

METHOD

Cost accounting records are usually kept on the basis of absorption costing, even if marginal costing is used in many decision-making situations. One of the main reasons for adopting absorption costing in record keeping is that, for financial accounting purposes, SSAP 9 states that production overheads should be included in the value of the closing stocks.

It would be possible to keep the cost books on a marginal costing basis, but this would mean that extra work would be involved in converting them into a format suitable for financial reporting requirements. In practice, it is much easier to keep the books on an absorption basis, and then adapt them for deci-sion making. Nonetheless, the management should be made fully aware of the danger of ignoring fixed costs in any kind of decision-making situation. In the long run, the company must recover all of its costs if it is to survive, even if it may be perfectly legitimate to ignore fixed costs in the short term.

In theory, marginal costing is a very simple system to adopt, although in practice, there are some considerable problems to overcome. These problems arise largely because of the assumptions that have been built into the system. These assumptions may be summarized as follows:

1 it is possible to analyse total costs into fixed costs and variable costs;
2 fixed costs remain constant in the short term irrespective of the level of activity;
3 fixed costs do not bear any relationship to specific units produced;
4 variable costs tend to vary in *direct* proportion to activity;
5 some costs are semi-variable, i.e. they contain an element of both fixed and variable costs (electricity costs and telephone charges, for example, both contain a fixed rental element with a variable charge depending upon the use made of the service).

While these assumptions are somewhat simplistic, they are useful in helping to arrive at decisions where it is safe to ignore fixed costs.

The marginal costing procedure is basically very simple. All that is required is to classify total cost into its fixed and variable elements, instead of into its direct and indirect elements, as in absorption costing.

An example of a marginal cost statement is shown in Exhibit 16.1.

Exhibit 16.1 A typical marginal cost statement

| | Product | | | |
| | A | B | C | Total |
	£000	£000	£000	£000
Sales revenue (1)	100	70	20	190
Less: Variable cost of sales (2)	30	40	10	80
Contribution (3)	70	30	10	110
Less: Fixed costs (4)				60
Profit/(Loss) (5)				£50

Tutorial notes
1 The total sales revenue would be analysed into different product groupings (in this example for products A, B, and C).
2 The variable costs include direct materials, direct labour costs, other direct expenses and variable overhead. In most cases, direct costs are the same as variable costs, but there can be some instances of where they are not the same, for example, a machine operator's salary that is fixed under a guaranteed annual wage agreement.
3 The term *contribution* is used to describe the difference between the sales revenue and the variable cost of those sales. A positive contribution helps to pay for the fixed costs.

4 The fixed costs include all the other costs that do not vary in direct proportion to the sales revenue. Fixed costs are assumed to remain constant over a period of time. They do not bear any relationship to the units produced or the sales achieved, and therefore it is not possible to apportion them amongst the individual products. The total of the fixed costs can *only* be deducted from the total contribution.

5 Total contribution less the fixed costs gives the profit (if the balance is positive) or a loss (if the balance is negative).

It can be seen from Exhibit 16.1 that it is possible to express the information in equation form, i.e.:

$$
\begin{aligned}
\text{Let} \quad S &= \text{sales revenue} \\
V &= \text{variable costs} \\
C &= \text{contribution} \\
F &= \text{fixed costs} \\
P &= \text{profit} \\
\text{Therefore:} \quad S - V &= C \\
C - F &= P \\
\text{or} \quad C &= F + P \\
\therefore \quad S - V &= F + P
\end{aligned}
$$

The equation $S - V = F + P$ is known as the *marginal cost equation*, and it captures the essence of marginal costing. We will explain how it is applied in the next section.

APPLICATION

By using the marginal cost equation, we can speedily cost any specific decision that the management is thinking of taking. Indeed, even if a decision might require a change in the basic marginal costing assumptions, e.g. if a decision might affect the level of fixed costs, the data can be amended relatively easily. This applies for two main reasons:

1 we can normally assume that fixed costs will remain constant, and they will not normally be affected by a particular decision;

2 we can calculate the contribution at any level of sales activity (since the variable costs are assumed to vary in direct proportion to the sales revenue), and then deduct the fixed costs in total (adjusted if necessary).

These points are illustrated in Exhibit 16.2.

Exhibit 16.2 Examples of changes in variable cost and contribution

	Product			
	One unit	*100 units*	*1000 units*	*%*
	£	£	£	
Selling price	10	1 000	10 000	100
Less: Variable costs	6	600	6 000	60
Contribution	£4	£400	£4 000	40%

Tutorial notes

1 The variable cost per unit is 60%, and the contribution 40% of the sales revenue.
2 The relationship is assumed to hold good no matter how many units are sold.
3 For every unit sold, the company makes a contribution of £4.
4 The fixed costs are ignored, because they are assumed not to change with the level of activity.

Once all the fixed costs have been covered by the total contribution, each extra unit sold results in an additional amount of profit equal to the contribution earned by that unit. Note, however, that profit is not necessarily the same as contribution. This will only be the case once the total contribution has covered the fixed costs. The point is illustrated in Exhibit 16.3.

Exhibit 16.3 Effect on profit at varying levels of activity

Activity in units	*1000*	*2000*	*3000*	*4000*	*5000*
	£	£	£	£	£
Sales	10 000	20 000	30 000	40 000	50 000
Less: Variable costs	5 000	10 000	15 000	20 000	25 000
Contribution	5 000	10 000	15 000	20 000	25 000
Less: Fixed costs	10 000	10 000	10 000	10 000	10 000
Profit/(loss)	£(5 000)	–	£5 000	£10 000	£15 000

Tutorial notes

1 The exhibit illustrates five levels of activity: from 1000 units to 5000 units.
2 At each level of activity, the fixed costs remain constant.
3 At each level of activity, the variable costs remain in direct proportion to the sales revenue, i.e. 50%. This means that the relationship of contribution to sales is also 50%.

It can be seen from Exhibit 16.3 that only when the fixed costs have been covered by the contribution (at an activity level of 2000 units) does any further increase in contribution equal an increase in profit. At an activity level of 2000 units, the company's sales revenue is just sufficient to cover its total costs: at this level it makes neither a profit nor a loss. This is referred to as its *break-even point*: CIMA defines this as 'the level of activity at which there is neither profit nor loss'.

The relationship of contribution to sales is known (rather confusingly) as the *profit/volume* (or P/V) *ratio*. Note that it does not mean profit in relationship to sales, but the contribution in relation to sales.

The P/V ratio is extremely useful. Once it has been calculated, we can apply it to any level of sales, deduct the fixed costs, and hence arrive at the new profit on the amended level of sales. Sometimes, of course, the fixed costs will be affected by a change in activity, but if they do change, only a minor adjustment needs to be made to the marginal equation in order to allow for the movement in the level of fixed costs.

The relationships that we have described above are sometimes presented in the form of a chart known as a *break-even chart*. The formal CIMA definition of such a chart is 'a chart which indicates approximate profit or loss at different levels of sales volume within a limited range'.

Accountants believe that it is sometimes much easier to make the point about the relationship between sales, variable costs and fixed costs if it is presented diagrammatically. A break-even chart is illustrated in Exhibit 16.4. The Exhibit is based on the same data as used in Exhibit 16.3.

Exhibit 16.4 shows quite clearly the relationships that are assumed to exist when marginal costing is adopted. Thus the sales revenue, the variable costs and the fixed costs are all assumed to be linear, i.e. they are all represented by straight lines from a point where there is no activity right through to infinity. In practice, these relationships are not likely to remain linear over such a wide range of activity, and the basic marginal costing assumptions may only be valid over a narrow range.

While this point may appear to create some difficulty in using marginal costing, it should be appreciated that wide fluctuations in activity are not normally experienced, and so it is usually possible to assume that the relationship will be linear.

You must remember that the information presented in the format described above is only a *guide* to management. It must not be taken too literally, and in any case, there are many other factors that must also be taken into account.

Another major problem associated with a break-even chart is that it does not show clearly the actual *amount* of profit/loss (a ruler has to be applied to the chart). In order to avoid this problem, the data can be displayed in the form of a *profit/volume chart*. This is a chart (it is sometimes referred to as a *graph*) that shows the effect of changes in sales volume or value on the contribution and on the overall profit. The construction of such a chart is illustrated in Exhibit 16.5 using the same data as in Exhibit 16.3.

Exhibit 16.4 A break-even chart

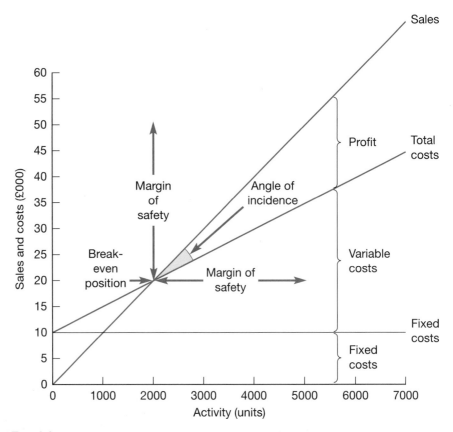

Tutorial notes
1 The total cost line is a combination of the fixed costs and the variable costs. It thus ranges from a total cost of £10 000 (fixed costs only) at a nil level of activity, to £35 000 when the activity level is 5000 units (fixed costs of £10 000 + variable costs of £25 000).
2 The angle of incidence is the angle formed between the sales line and the total cost line. The wider the angle, the greater the amount of profit. A wide angle of incidence plus a wide margin of safety (see 3 below) indicates a highly profitable position.
3 The margin of safety is the distance between the sales achieved and the sales level needed to break even. It can be measured either in units (along the x axis) or in sales revenue terms (along the y axis).
4 Activity (measured along the x axis) may be measured either in units, or as a percentage of the theoretical maximum level of activity, or in terms of sales revenue.

We must not give the impression that marginal costing has no problems, so it would be useful if we summarize in the next section some of the major criticisms that can be levelled at the technique.

Exhibit 16.5 A profit/volume chart

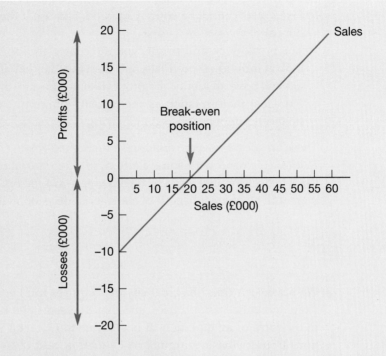

Tutorial notes

1 The x axis can be represented either in terms of units, as a percentage of the theoretical maximum level of activity, or in terms of sales revenue.
2 The y axis represents profits (positive amounts) or losses (negative amounts).
3 With sales at a level of £50 000, the profit is £15 000. The sales line cuts the x axis at the break-even position, and if there are no sales, the loss equals the fixed costs of £10 000.

CRITICISMS

The assumptions adopted in preparing marginal cost statements lead to a number of important reservations about the technique. These are as follows:

1 Costs cannot be easily divided into fixed and variable categories.
2 Variable costs do not vary in direct proportion to activity at all levels of activity, e.g. the cost of direct materials may change as a result of shortages of supply, or through bulk buying, while direct labour costs may be fixed in the short run, since the company may need to give a minimum period of notice to employees before they can be dismissed.
3 The fixed costs will change to some extent as activity increases or decreases.
4 It is difficult to decide over what period of time costs do remain fixed: in the long run all costs become variable in the sense that the company can avoid them altogether, e.g. by going into liquidation!

5 A specific decision affecting one product may in turn affect other products, especially if they are complementary, e.g. a garage sells both oil and petrol.

6 Fixed costs cannot be entirely ignored, because if the company is to survive it must recover all of its costs.

7 The break-even and profit/volume charts are too simplistic: they do not look at individual products, and they assume that any change in one product will have an identically proportionate effect on all the other products.

8 Non-cost factors (such as the security of supplies or the availability of finance) cannot be ignored in arriving at a specific decision.

These are all very severe criticisms of marginal costing. Nonetheless, provided that (a) it is used with some caution, (b) the information is only treated as a *guide* to decision making, and (c) other non-cost factors are taken into account, it can still be of great benefit in managerial decision making.

FORMULAE

We have seen that marginal costing requires total cost to be classified into fixed and variable categories, and that the respective relationships can be put in the form of an equation. It is possible to extract a number of other equations from the basic marginal cost equation, and these can be quite useful in examining specific problems.

For convenience, the main ones are summarized below:

1 Sales – variable cost of sales = contribution $\qquad S - V = C$

2 Contribution – fixed costs = profit/(loss) $\qquad C - F = P/(L)$

3 Break-even (B/E) point = contribution – fixed costs $\qquad C - F$

4 B/E in sales value terms = $\dfrac{\text{fixed costs} \times \text{sales}}{\text{contribution}}$ $\qquad \dfrac{F \times S}{C}$

5 B/E in units = $\dfrac{\text{fixed costs}}{\text{contribution per unit}}$ $\qquad \dfrac{F}{C \text{ per unit}}$

6 Margin of safety (M/S) in sales value terms = $\dfrac{\text{profit} \times \text{sales}}{\text{contribution}}$ $\qquad \dfrac{P \times S}{C}$

7 M/S in units = $\dfrac{\text{profit}}{\text{contribution per unit}}$ $\qquad \dfrac{P}{C \text{ per unit}}$

The application of some of these formulae is examined in Exhibit 16.6.

Exhibit 16.6 Example showing the use of the marginal cost formulae

The following information relates to Happy Limited for the year to 30 June 19X8:

Number of units sold: 10 000

	Per unit	Total
	£	£000
Sales	30	300
Less: Variable costs	18	180
Contribution	12	120
Less: Fixed costs		24
Profit		£96

Required:
In value and unit terms calculate the following:
(a) the break-even position; and
(b) the margin of safety.

Answer to Exhibit 16.6

(a) Break-even position in value terms:

$$\frac{F \times S}{C} = \frac{24\,000 \times 300\,000}{120\,000} = \underline{\underline{£60\,000}}$$

Break-even in units:

$$\frac{F}{C \text{ per unit}} = \frac{24\,000}{12} = \underline{\underline{2000 \text{ units}}}$$

(b) Margin of safety in value terms:

$$\frac{P \times S}{C} = \frac{96\,000 \times 300\,000}{120\,000} = \underline{\underline{£240\,000}}$$

Margin of safety in units:

$$\frac{P}{C \text{ per unit}} = \frac{96\,000}{12} = \underline{\underline{8000 \text{ units}}}$$

Check that you understand the significance of the answer to Exhibit 16.6. You might also use the data to prepare both a break-even chart and a profit/volume chart.

AN ILLUSTRATIVE EXAMPLE

It would now be helpful to incorporate the principles behind marginal costing into a simple example. Exhibit 16.7 outlines a typical problem which a board of directors might well face.

Exhibit 16.7 Marginal costing example

Looking ahead to the financial year ending 31 March 19X5, the directors of Problems Limited are faced with a budgeted loss of £10 000. This is based on the following data:

Budgeted number of units   10 000

	£000
Sales revenue	100
Less: Variable costs	80
Contribution	20
Less: Fixed costs	30
Budgeted loss	£(10)

The directors would like to aim for a profit of £20 000 for the year to 31 March 19X5. Various proposals have been put forward, none of which require a change in the budgeted level of fixed costs. These proposals are as follows:
1 Reduce the selling price of each unit by 10%.
2 Increase the selling price of each unit by 10%.
3 Stimulate sales by improving the quality of the product; this would increase the variable cost of the unit by £1.50 per unit.

Required:
(a) For each proposal calculate:
   (i)   the break-even position in units in value terms;
   (ii) the number of units required to be sold in order to meet the profit target.
(b) State which proposal you think should be adopted.

Answer to Exhibit 16.7

Problems Limited
(a) (i) and (ii)

Workings:	£
Profit target	20 000
Fixed costs	30 000
Total contribution required	£50 000

The budgeted selling price per unit is £10 (100 000/10 000).

The budgeted outlook compared with each proposal may be summarized as follows:

Per unit:	Budgeted position	Proposal 1	Proposal 2	Proposal 3
	£	£	£	£
Selling price	10	9	11	10.00
Less: Variable costs	8	8	8	9.50
(a) Unit contribution	£2	£1	£3	£0.50
(b) Total contribution required to break even (= fixed costs) (£)	30 000	30 000	30 000	30 000
(c) Total contribution required to meet the profit target (£)	50 000	50 000	50 000	50 000
∴ no. of units to break even [(b)/(a)]	15 000	30 000	10 000	60 000
∴ no. of units to meet the profit target [(c)/(a)]	25 000	50 000	16 667	100 000

(b)
Comments:
1 By continuing with the present budget proposals, the company would need to sell 15 000 units to break even, or 25 000 units to meet the profit target. Thus in order to break even the company needs to increase its sales by 50%, or by 250% to meet the profit target.
2 A reduction in selling price of 10% per unit would require sales to increase by 300% in order to break even, or by 500% to meet the profit target.
3 By increasing the selling price of each unit by 10%, the company would only have to sell at the budgeted level to break even, but its unit sales would have to increase by two-thirds to meet the profit target.
4 By improving the product at an increased variable cost of £1.50 per unit, the company would require a sixfold increase to break even, or tenfold to meet the profit target.

Conclusion:
It would appear that increasing the selling price by 10% would be a more practical solution for the company to adopt. In the short run at least, it will break even, and there is the possibility that sales could be sufficient to make a small profit. In the long run this proposal has a much better chance of meeting the profit target than do the others. Some extra stimulus would be needed, however, to lift sales to this level over such a relatively short period of time. In any case, it is not clear why an increase in price should increase sales, unless the product is one which only sells at a comparatively high price, such as cosmetics and patent medicines. It must also be questioned whether the cost relationships will remain as indicated in the exhibit over such a large increase in activity. In particular, it is unlikely that the fixed costs will remain entirely fixed if there is such a large increase in sales.

LIMITING FACTORS

We saw in Exhibit 16.7 that when optional decisions are considered, the aim will always be to maximize contribution, because the greater the contribution, the more chance there is of covering the fixed costs and hence of making a profit. When managers are faced with a choice, therefore, between (say) producing product A at a contribution of £10 per unit, or of producing product B at a contribution of £20 per unit, they would normally choose product B. Sometimes, however, it may not be possible to produce unlimited quantities of product B because there could be a limit on how many units could either be sold or produced.

Such limits are known as limiting factors (or key factors). CIMA defines these as 'anything which limits the activity of an entity'.

Limiting factors may arise for a number of reasons, e.g. it may not be possible to sell more than a certain number of units; there may be production restraints (such as shortages of raw materials, skilled labour, or factory space); or the company may not be able to finance the anticipated rate of expansion.

If there is a product that cannot be produced and sold in unlimited quantities, then it is necessary to follow a simple rule in order to decide which product to concentrate on producing. The rule can be summarized as follows:

> **Choose that work which provides the maximum contribution per unit of limiting factor employed.**

This sounds very complicated, but it is, in fact, quite simple to use. The procedure is illustrated below:

1 Assumption: direct labour is in short supply.
2 Calculate the contribution made by each product.
3 Divide the contribution each product makes by the number of direct labour hours used in making each product.
4 The solution = the contribution per direct labour hour employed (i.e. the limiting factor).

Thus if we had to choose between two jobs (say), A and B, we would convert A's contribution and B's contribution into the amount of contribution earned for every direct labour hour worked on A and on B, respectively. We would then opt for that job which earned the most contribution per direct labour hour. The application of key factors is illustrated in Exhibit 16.8.

Exhibit 16.8 Application of key factors

Quays Limited manufactures a product for which there is a shortage of raw materials known as PX. During the year to 31 March 19X7, only 1000 kilograms of PX will be available. PX is used in manufacturing both product 8 and product 9. The following information is relevant:

Per unit	Product 8	Product 9
	£	£
Selling price	300	150
Less: Variable costs	200	100
Contribution	£100	£50
P/V ratio	$33\frac{1}{3}$	$33\frac{1}{3}$
Kilograms of PX required	5	2

Required:
State which product Quays Limited should concentrate on producing.

Answer to Exhibit 16.8

	Product 8	Product 9
	£	£
Contribution per unit	100	50
Limiting factor per unit	5	2
∴ contribution per kilogram	£20	£25

Choice:
Product 9 because it gives the highest contribution per unit of limiting factor.

Check:
Maximum contribution of product 8:

> 200 units (1000/5) × contribution per unit = 200 × 100 = £20 000

Maximum contribution of product 9:

> 500 units (1000/2) × contribution per unit = 500 × 50 = £25 000

In Exhibit 16.8 it was assumed that this was only one limiting factor, but there could be many more. This situation is illustrated in Exhibit 16.9

Exhibit 16.9 Example of marginal costing using two key factors

Information:
1 Assume that it is not possible for Company XL to sell more than 400 units of product 9.
2 The company aims to sell all of the 400 units. If it did, the total contribution would be £20 000 (400 × 50).
3 The 400 units would consume 800 units of raw materials (400 × 2 kilograms), leaving 200 kilograms for use in producing product 8.
4 Product 8 requires 5 kilograms per unit of raw materials, so 40 units could be completed at a total contribution of £4000 (40 × 100).

Summary of the position:

	Product 8	Product 9	Total
Units sold	40	400	
Raw materials (kilograms used)	200	800	1 000
Contribution per unit (£)	100	50	
Total contribution (£)	4 000	20 000	24 000

Note: The £24 000 total contribution compares with the contribution of £25 000 which the company could have made if there were no limiting factors affecting the sales of product 9.

CONCLUSION

Marginal costing is particularly useful in short-term decision making, but it is of less value when decisions have to be viewed over the long term. The system revolves around two main assumptions:

1 some costs remain fixed, irrespective of the level of activity;
2 other costs vary in direct proportion to sales.

These assumptions are not valid over the long term, but, provided that they are used with caution, they can be usefully adopted in the short term.

It should also be remembered that marginal costing is only a *guide* to decision making, and that other non-cost factors have to be taken into account.

Key points	

1 **In marginal costing, total cost is analysed into fixed costs and variable costs.**

2 **As fixed costs are assumed to be unrelated to activity, they are ignored in making short-term managerial decisions. Fixed costs are also ignored in stock valuations.**

3 **A company will aim to maximize the *contribution* that each unit makes to profit.**

4 **The marginal cost relationship can be expressed in the form of an equation: $S - V = F + P$, where S = sales, V = variable costs, F = fixed costs, and P = profit.**

5 **It may not always be possible to maximize unit contribution, because materials, labour, or finance may be in short supply.**

6 **In the long run, fixed costs cannot be ignored.**

CHECK YOUR LEARNING

1 Fill in the missing blanks in each of the following sentences:
  (a) A ____ ____ is a cost which is incurred for a period, and which, within certain outputs and turnover limits, tends to be unaffected by fluctuations in the levels of activity.
  (b) Costs which tend to vary with the level of activity are known as ____ ____

2 Complete the following equations:
  (a) sales revenue – ____ = contribution
  (b) contribution – fixed costs = ____
  (c) break-even point = ____ – ____
  (d) break-even point in units = $\dfrac{\text{fixed costs}}{}$
  (e) $\dfrac{\text{profit} \times \text{sales}}{\text{contribution}}$ = _____

3 What term is used to describe anything that restricts the level of activity of an entity?

Answers
1 (a) fixed cost (b) variable costs
2 (a) variable cost of sales (b) profit/(loss) (c) contribution – fixed costs
  (d) contribution per unit (e) margin of safety (in sales value terms)
3 limiting (or key) factor

QUESTIONS

16.1
The following information relates to Pole Limited for the year to 31 January 19X2:

	£000
Administration expenses:	
Fixed	30
Variable	7
Semi-variable (fixed 80%, variable 20%)	20
Materials:	
Direct	60
Indirect	5
Production overhead (all fixed)	40
Research and development expenditure:	
Fixed	60
Variable	15
Semi-variable (fixed 50%, variable 50%)	10
Sales	450

Selling and distribution expenditure:

Fixed	80
Variable	4
Semi-variable (fixed 70%, variable 30%)	30

Wages:

Direct	26
Indirect	13

Required:
Using the above information, compile a marginal cost statement for Pole Limited for the year to 31 January 19X2.

16.2
You are presented with the following information for Giles Limited for the year to 28 February 19X2:

	£000
Fixed costs	150
Variable costs	300
Sales (50 000 units)	500

Required:
(a) Calculate the following:
    (i) the break-even point in value terms and in units; and
    (ii) the margin of safety in value terms and in units.
(b) Prepare a break-even chart.

16.3
The following information applies to Ayre Limited for the two years to 31 March 19X2 and 19X3, respectively:

Year	Sales	Profits
	£000	£000
31.3.19X2	750	100
31.3.19X3	1000	250

Required:
Assuming that the cost relationships had remained as given in the question, calculate the company's profit if the sales for the year to 31 March 19X3 had reached the budgeted level of £1 200 000.

16.4
The following information relates to Carter Limited for the year to 30 April l9X3:

Units sold	50 000
Selling price per unit	£40
Net profit per unit	£9
Profit/volume ratio	40%

During 19X4 the company would like to increase its sales substantially, but to do so it would have to reduce the selling price per unit by 20%. The variable cost per unit will not change, but because of the increased activity, the company will have to invest in new machinery which will increase the fixed costs by £30 000 per annum.

Required:
Given the new conditions, calculate how many units the company will need to sell in 19X4 in order to make the same amount of profit as it did in l9X3.

16.5

Puzzled Limited would like to increase its sales during the year to 3l May 19X5. To do so, it has several mutually exclusive options open to it:

1 reduce the selling price per unit by 15%;
2 improve the product resulting in an increase in the variable cost per unit of £1.30;
3 spend £15 000 on an advertising campaign;
4 improve factory efficiency by purchasing more machinery at a fixed extra annual cost of £22 500.

During the year to 31 May l9X4, the company sold 20 000 units. The cost details were as follows:

	£000
Sales	200
Variable costs	150
Contribution	50
Fixed costs	40
Profit	£10

These cost relationships are expected to hold in l9X5.

Required:
State which option you would recommend and why.

16.6

Micro Limited has some surplus capacity. It is now considering whether it should accept a special contract to use some of its spare capacity. However, this contract will use some specialist direct labour which is in short supply.
The following details relate to the proposed contract:

	£
Contract price	50 000
Variable costs:	
Direct materials	10 000
Direct labour	30 000

4000 direct labour hours would be required in order to complete the contract.
The company's budget for the year during which the contract would be undertaken is as follows:

	£000
Sales	750
Less: Variable costs	500
Contribution	250
Less: Fixed costs	230
Profit	£20

Direct labour hours: 50 000 maximum available during the year.

Required:
State, giving your reasons, whether the special contract should be accepted.

ADDITIONAL QUESTIONS (WITHOUT ANSWERS)

16.7
The following information relates to Mere's budget for the year to 31 December 19X7:

Product	K	L	M	Total
	£000	£000	£000	£000
Sales	700	400	250	1350
Direct materials	210	60	30	300
Direct labour	100	200	200	500
Variable overhead	90	60	50	200
Fixed overhead	20	40	40	100
	420	360	320	1100
Profit/(loss)	280	40	(70)	250
Budgeted sales (units)	140	20	25	

Note:
Fixed overheads are apportioned on the basis of direct labour hours.

The directors are worried about the loss that product M is budgeted to make, and various suggestions have been made to counteract the loss, viz.:
1 stop selling product M;
2 increase its selling price by 20%;
3 reduce its selling price by 10%;
4 reduce its costs by purchasing a new machine costing £350 000, thereby decreasing the direct labour cost by £100 000 (the machine would have a life of five years; its residual value would be nil).

Required:
Evaluate each of these proposals.

16.8

Temple Limited has been offered two new contracts, the details of which are as follows:

Contract	1	2
	£000	£000
Contract price	1 000	1 500
Direct materials	300	300
Direct labour	300	600
Variable overhead	100	100
Fixed overhead	100	200
	800	1 200
Profit	200	300
Direct materials required (kilos)	50 000	100 000
Direct labour hours required	10 000	25 000

Note:
The fixed overhead has been apportioned on the basis of direct labour cost.

Temple is a one-product firm. Its budgeted cost per unit for the year to 31 December 19X8 is summarized below:

	£
Sales	6000
Direct materials (100 kilos)	700
Direct labour (200 hours)	3000
Variable overhead	300
Fixed overhead	1000
	5000
Profit	1000

The company would only have the capacity to accept one of the new contracts. Unfortunately, materials suitable for use in all of its work are in short supply, and the company has estimated that only 200 000 kilos would be available during the year to 31 December 19X8.

Even more worrying is the shortage of skilled labour, and only 100 000 direct labour hours are expected to be available during the year.

The good news is that there may be an upturn in the market for its normal contract work.

Required:
Advise management which contract to accept.

DISCUSSION QUESTIONS

16.9

'It has been suggested that while marginal costing is fine in theory, fixed costs cannot be ignored in practice.' Discuss this statement.

16.10

'The marginal costing technique described in text books is too simplistic, and it is of little relevance to management.' How far do you agree with this statement?

16.11

Do break-even charts and profit graphs help management to take more meaning-ful decisions?

CASE STUDY

A special order

Learning objectives

After preparing this case study, you will be able to:

● describe the circumstances in which total absorption costing may be used as a means of pricing;

● outline the technique of marginal costing;

● prepare a report suitable for presentation to management containing data based on the marginal costing technique.

Background

LOCATION   Fast Clean Products Limited: the Managing Director's office

PERSONNEL   Stanley Newton: Managing Director
Omar Khan: Mini-supermarket owner
Ralph Timmins: Production Manager
Su Yamamoto: Distribution Manager
Gerald White: Chief Accountant

Synopsis

Fast Clean Products Limited manufactures household cleaning products, operating from a small factory on the outskirts of Leeds. The company has always been reasonably profitable, although for the last two years it has been producing well under capacity, largely as a result of a general reduction in consumer spending.

Stanley Newton, the Managing Director of the company, has been assiduously reading the financial press, and he has come to the conclusion that there is not likely to be an upturn in the market for at least the next 12 months. He assumes, therefore, that Fast Clean Products is also unlikely to see a revival in its fortunes for at least that time.

Stanley spends a lot of time playing golf. Some months ago he had got talking to a new member of the golf club, Omar Khan, who told him that he owned a chain of mini-supermarkets. The other day, Stanley was going through his morning mail and, rather to his surprise, he found a letter from Omar asking him to quote for a special order.

'Who said that golf was a waste of time?' Stanley asked himself.

He immediately called in his team of senior managers to tell them about the request. 'Can we do it?' he asked each one of them in turn.

Ralph Timmins, the Production Manager, was the first to speak. 'Well, Stanley, we have the capacity at the moment, although we might have to take on more staff. But what happens if trade revives? We certainly could not do this order and satisfy our ordinary trade outlets.'

'As far as I can gather, Ralph, this is a one-off request,' replied Stanley. 'Omar has been let down by his ordinary supplier, and he cannot promise us anything beyond this order.'

He then turned to his Distribution Manager, 'I take it that you will not have any problems in dealing with this order if we take it on?' he queried.

'None whatsoever, Stanley,' replied Su. 'As you know, we have not laid-off any of the distribution staff. And, to be quite honest, most of them have forgotten what it's like to work hard.'

Stanley made a mental note that, order or no order, he must take up this point with Su. 'What on earth are we doing with under-employed staff?' he asked himself.

Su continued, 'And it's also highly unlikely that we would need any more vehicles, although some of the present ones are getting very old.'

'Yes, yes,' intervened Stanley hastily. 'We won't go into that this morning.'

For some time Su had been campaigning for a greater allocation of the capital expenditure budget for the replacement of distribution vehicles.

'So, it seems that we don't anticipate any great problems if we take on this order,' stated Stanley.

'Excuse me, Stanley,' interjected a quiet voice. 'You haven't asked about the costings.' The voice belonged to Gerald White, the company's Chief Accountant.

Gerald was a highly self-effacing member of the management team. He was precise and pedantic, but he was usually right.

'Oh! I don't think that there is any problem there, Gerald,' he replied. 'We shall just cost the job as we normally do, and then charge accordingly.'

Some time ago, Gerald had persuaded Stanley to introduce a cost and management accounting system into the company. Stanley was largely a marketing man, and he was not really interested in accounting. However, like most converts, he was all for an idea once he had accepted it.

'I shall expect you to cost the product on the normal absorption costing lines. I will have a word with you about the precise profit percentage to be added once you have got the details,' said Stanley firmly.

'That may not be wise, Stanley,' responded Gerald.

The others laughed, but Gerald did not see the joke. He carried on regardless.

'These chains of supermarkets are very competitive. You can, I beg your pardon, *one* can guarantee that Mr Khan will have asked other companies to tender and, unless Fast Clean Products is competitive, the order will go elsewhere.'

The room went quiet. Some of the excitement and elation felt by all members of the management team began to evaporate.

'That's just like all you accountants,' interposed Su, who besides looking after distribution also had an interest in sales. 'Gloom, gloom and yet more gloom. You're always looking on the black side. Here we are: for the first time for months we've got the chance of a large new order, and you want to put the brake on it.'

'I am afraid that you have misunderstood me, *Susan*,' Gerald replied quietly. 'Far from wanting to reject the order, I want to ensure that the company is successful. All I meant was that the company's normal accounting procedures may not be appropriate in the case of a 'one-off' order, as some people call it. A total absorbed cost may not, in fact, be the most suitable one to adopt in the case of a special order.'

'But you've always been going on at me,' interjected Su, rather angrily, 'that it's no use making sales if we don't make a profit on them.'

'That is quite correct, *Susan*, but only in the long run. Over a period of time, the company must, of course, cover all of its costs. For a special order, however, it may be profitable to accept that order, provided that the extra costs incurred by undertaking it are less than the amount received from the customer.'

By now, everyone at the meeting had gone unusually quiet. 'I'm not quite sure that I understand you,' said Stanley. 'You seem to be suggesting that we undercut our normal prices, and I don't like the idea of that. But in any case, how do you work out, the "extra" costs of an order?'

'Ah, Stanley, that is an accounting problem of some complexity,' responded Gerald with some satisfaction. 'But I shall be glad to discuss it with you when the accounting team has derived some appropriate costings.'

'Please do,' said Stanley with heavy irony. 'I would like the costings in the morning, *if* you please.'

'Certainly, Stanley. I shall arrange for that. You will have them on your desk at eight o'clock tomorrow morning.'

Stanley realized that he should have known better. Nothing seemed to ruffle the calm of his Chief Accountant. 'Suppose I had asked for them at eight o'clock this evening,' he thought, 'would he have replied, "Certainly, Stanley. I shall arrange for that"?' He answered his own question. 'Probably,' he muttered rather gloomily. 'One of these days I shall put that to the test.'

Required:

1 Prepare a critical appraisal of the marginal cost technique, and then be prepared to defend your arguments in your tutorial group. Be careful to explain why the total absorbed cost of a product may not be an appropriate method of determining the selling price of a special order.

2 Assume that you are Gerald White. Using the information listed in the Appendix, prepare a report suitable for presentation to Stanley Newton.

Appendix   MISCELLANEOUS DATA FOR THE YEAR TO 30 JUNE 19X5

1 Abridged profit and loss account

	£000	£000	£000
Sales			3260
Less: Cost of goods sold			
Direct materials	560		
Direct labour	1660	2220	
Factory overhead		400	
Factory cost of production		2620	
Administration overhead		250	
Selling and distribution overhead		300	
Total operating cost			3170
Operating profit			£90

2 The company uses a total absorption costing system. The selling price of its goods is determined on a cost-plus price basis. A 20% loading for non-manufacturing overhead is added to the total factory cost, to which is added a further 10% for profit. Factory overheads are absorbed into product costs on the basis of machine hours. The machine hour absorption rate for the year to 30 June 19X5 was £2 per hour.

3 Gerald White's team had available to them the following breakdown of overheads for the year to 30 June 19X5:

	Factory	Administration	Selling and Distribution
	%	%	%
Fixed	80	90	60
Variable	20	10	40
Total	100	100	100

4 From the preliminary investigation made, it is expected that Omar Khan's special order would require £75 000 of direct materials. The direct labour cost would be £200 000, and the variable overhead cost, £25 000. The order would involve 40 000 machine hours.

5 Although it is anticipated that prices will rise during the year to 30 June 19X6, Gerald White decided to base his initial costings on the financial results for the year to 30 June 19X5.

PART 6

Planning and control

CHAPTER 17

Budgetary planning systems

Auditors offer to blow whistle on fraud

By Jim Kelly
Accountancy Correspondent

Auditors yesterday offered to give a wider range of assurances about companies, including whether material fraud might be present if the government will agree to limit auditors' legal liability.

The powerful Institute of Chartered Accountants in England and Wales said yesterday the idea was 'an offer on the table' and would be put to the Department of Trade and Industry.

In return for the assurances to shareholders, auditors want the DTI to reform the law of joint and several liability for a wide range of professions and replace it with a form of proportional liability.

Accountants, and many other professionals, complain that under the existing law they can pay all the damages in a case when others, often uninsured, are more to blame.

Mr Graham Ward, head of the institute's working party on the issue, said: 'The present law is fundamentally flawed. It fails to take account of the degree of blame.' While the profession should not have to offer anything back to the government to reform an unfair law, he recognised 'the practicalities' of winning reform. 'It's the way of the world,' he said.

After several years of pressure from the professions, the DTI asked for a special report by the Law Commission last year which eventually rejected radical reform of the law as it

stands. However, the DTI published the findings and asked professionals and others to answer questions about possible reform, including whether auditors would be prepared to give more assurance to shareholders.

Mr Ward said that at the moment auditors limited such assurance because of the threat of litigation under joint and several liability. Specifically the institute has indicated auditors could in future report on how effective a company's internal controls are – a controversial assurance most auditors currently avoid.

Auditors could also give wider assurances on whether a company was a going concern and whether material fraud might be present. A number of other duties, recently outlined by the Auditing Practices Board, could also be taken up.

The institute believes that reform could be achieved in the second parliamentary session of the next government. Mr Ward said that in the long term reform of the law could reduce audit costs by about 5 per cent by reducing insurance premiums.

The institute also wants reform of Section 310 of the Companies Act which forbids auditors to limit their liability by contract but it concedes that there should be greater redress in cases of fraud or personal injury.

The Financial Times, 2 May 1996

Exhibit 17.0 But where does budgeting come into this?

In Part 5 of this book we dealt with the basic principles of cost accounting. Through the analysis, there was an underlying assumption that much of the information had been prepared *after* the event, i.e. on an historical basis. However, the managers of an entity are probably more concerned with looking to what might happen, rather than what did happen. If we are to get the best out of a cost accounting system, we ought to provide management with information about the future as well as the past. It is a relatively easy task to do so by incorporating a control method known as *budgetary control*. Budgetary control is the subject of this chapter.

The CIMA definition of budgetary control is:

> **Budgetary control:** the establishment of budgets relating the responsibilities of executives to the requirements of a policy, and the continuous comparison of actual with budgeted results, either to secure by individual action the objectives of that policy or to provide a basis for its revision.

Budgetary control takes up a lot of time and managerial effort. The system is usually administered by a team of accountants specially employed for the purpose, although it is necessary for the team to be assisted by other personnel. Indeed, if budgetary control is to work effectively, most employees will need to be heavily involved in the entire exercise.

We could go into considerable detail about the system of budgetary control, but in this book we are only concerned with those aspects of it that are of particular relevance to the non-accountant. We shall, therefore, avoid too much detail. In the next section, we outline some of the background to budgeting and budgetary control. This is followed by an explanation of the budget procedure. A further section examines the preparation of functional budgets, while the final section deals with flexible budgets. We start by examining what is meant by the terms 'budget' and 'budgeting'.

By the end of this chapter, you will be able to:

- describe the nature and purpose of budgeting and budgetary control;

- list the steps involved in operating a budgetary control system;

- describe the difference between fixed and flexible budgets.

BUDGETING AND BUDGETARY CONTROL

Budget

The term 'budget' is usually well understood by the layman. Many people, for example, often prepare a quite sophisticated budget for their own household expenses. In fact, albeit in a very informal sense, everyone does some budgeting at some time or other, e.g. by making a rough comparison between the next month's salary and the next month's expenditure. Such a budget may not be very precise, and it may not be formally written down; nonetheless, it contains all the ingredients of what accountants mean by a budget.

The CIMA definition of a budget is:

> **Budget:** a quantitative statement, for a defined period of time, which may include planned revenues, expenses, assets, liabilities and cash flows.

The definition goes on to state that 'a budget provides a focus for the organisation, aids the co-ordination of activities, and facilitates control.'

Essential features It can be seen from the above definition of a budget that a number of essential features can be distinguished. These are as follows:

1. a budget lays down policies that are expected to be pursued in order to meet the overall objectives of an entity;
2. it contains both quantitative and financial data;
3. the data are usually formally documented;
4. it covers a defined future period of time.

In practice, a considerable number of budgets would be prepared, e.g. for sales, production, and administration. These budgets would then be combined into an overall budget known as a *master budget*, comprising (a) a budgeted profit and loss account; (b) a budgeted balance sheet; and (c) a budgeted cash flow statement.

Once a master budget had been prepared, it would be closely examined to see whether the overall plan could be accommodated. It might be the case, for example, that the sales budget indicated a large increase in sales. This may have required the production budgets to be prepared on the basis of this extra sales demand. However, the cash budget might have suggested that the entity could not meet the extra sales and production activity that would be required. In these circumstances, additional financing arrangements may have had to be made, because obviously no organization would normally turn down the opportunity of increasing its sales.

In practice, the preparation of individual budgets can be a useful exercise even if nothing further is then done about them, since the exercise forces management to look ahead. It is a natural human tendency to be always looking back, but past experience is not always a guide for the future. If managers are asked to produce a budget, at least it does encourage them to examine what they have done in relation to what they could do. Nonetheless, the full benefits of a budgeting system are only realized when it is also used for control purposes, i.e. by the constant comparison of actual results with the budgeted results, and then taking any necessary corrective action. This leads us on to consider in a little more detail what we mean by 'budgetary control'.

Budgetary control

Budgetary control has several important features. These are as follows:

1 managerial responsibilities have to be clearly defined;
2 individual budgets lay down a detailed plan of action for a particular sphere of responsibility;
3 managers have a responsibility to adhere to their budgets once the budgets have been approved;
4 the actual performance is constantly monitored and compared with the budgeted results;
5 corrective action is taken if the actual results differ from the budget;
6 departures from budget are only permitted if they have been approved by senior management;
7 variances (i.e. differences) that are unaccounted for will be subject to individual investigation.

Any variance that does occur should be carefully investigated. If it is considered necessary, then the current actual performance will be immediately brought back into line with the budget. Sometimes the budget itself will be changed, e.g. if there is an unexpected increase in sales. Such changes may, of course, have an effect on the other budgets, so it cannot be done in isolation.

Now that we have outlined the nature and purpose of budgeting and budgetary control, we are in a position to investigate how the system works.

PROCEDURE

The budget procedure starts with an examination of the entity's objectives. These may be very simple. They may include, for example, an overall wish to maximize profits, to foster better relations with its customers, or to improve the working conditions of its employees. Once the entity has decided upon its overall objectives, it is in a position to formulate some detailed plans.

These will probably start with a forecast. Note that there is a technical difference between a forecast and a budget. A forecast is a prediction of what is *likely* to happen. The CIMA definition is:

> **Forecast:** a prediction of future events and their quantification for planning purposes.

By comparison, a budget is a formal written statement of what *should* happen.

In order to make it easier for us to guide you through the budgeting process, we will examine each stage individually. This is done in the following sub-sections.

The budget period

The main budget period is usually based on a calendar year. It could be shorter or longer depending upon the nature of the product cycle, e.g. the fashion industry may adopt a short budget period of less than a year, while the construction industry may choose (say) a five-year period. Irrespective of the industry however, a calendar year is usually a convenient period to choose as the base period, because it fits in with the financial accounting period.

Besides determining the main budget period, it is also necessary to prepare sub-period budgets. Sub-period budgets are required for budgetary control purposes, since the actual results have to be frequently compared with the budgeted results. The sub-budget periods for some activities may need to be very short if tight control is to be exercised over them. The cash budget, for example, may need to be compiled on a weekly basis, whereas the administration budget may only need to be prepared quarterly.

Administration

The budget procedure may be administered by a special budget committee, or it may supervised by the accounting function. It will be necessary for the budget committee to lay down general guidelines in accordance with the entity's objectives, and to ensure that individual departments do not operate completely independently. The production department, for example, will need to know what the entity is budgeting to sell, so that it can prepare its own budget on the basis of those sales. However, the detailed production budget must still remain the entire responsibility of the production manager.

This procedure is in line with the concept of responsibility accounting which we outlined in Chapter 13. If the control procedure is to work properly, managers must be given responsibilty for a clearly defined area of activity, such as a cost centre. Thereafter, they are fully answerable for all that goes on there. Unless managers are given complete authority to act within clearly defined guidelines, they cannot be expected to be answerable for something that is outside their control. This means that, as far as budgets are concerned, managers must help prepare, amend and approve their own responsibility centre's budget, otherwise the budgetary control system will not work.

The budgeting process

The budgeting process is illustrated in Exhibit 17.1. Study the Exhibit very carefully, noting how the various budgets fit together.

Later on in the chapter we shall be using a quantitative example to illustrate how the budgeting process works. For the moment, however, it will be *sufficient* to give a brief description.

In commercial organizations, the first budget to be prepared is usually the sales budget. Once the sales for the budget period (and for each sub-budget period) have been determined, the next stage is to calculate the effect on production. This will then enable an agreed level of activity to be determined. The *level of activity* may be expressed in so many units, or as a percentage of the theoretical productive capacity of the entity. Once it has been established, departmental managers can be instructed to prepare their budgets on the basis of the required level of activity.

Let us assume, for example, that 1000 units can be sold for a particular budget period. The production department manager will need this information in order to prepare his budget. This does not necessarily mean that he will budget for a production level of 1000 units, because he will have to allow for the budgeted level of opening and closing stocks.

Exhibit 17.1 The inter-relationship of budgets in a budgeting system

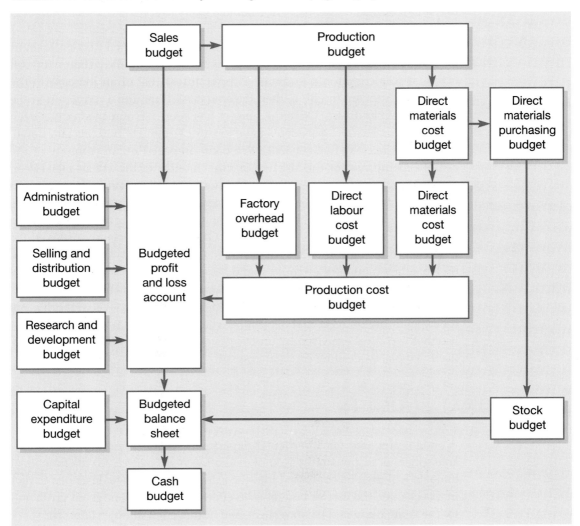

The budgeted production level will then be translated into how much material and labour will be required to meet that particular level. Similarly, it will be necessary to prepare overhead budgets. Much of the general overhead expenditure of the entity (such as factory administrative costs, head office costs, and research and development expenditure) will tend to be fixed, and such overheads will not be directly affected by production levels. However, in some instances, a marked change in activity may lead to a change in fixed costs.

The sales and distribution overhead budget may be the one overhead budget that will not be entirely fixed in nature. An increase in the number of units sold, for example, may involve more van delivery costs.

Not all entities start the budget process with sales. A local authority usually prepares a budget on the basis of what it is likely to spend. The total budgeted expenditure is then compared with the total amount of council tax (after allowing for other income) needed to cover it. The council tax is a form of local authority taxation which replaced the former community charge (or poll tax, as it was commonly known). If the political cost of an increase in the council tax appears too high, then the council will require a reduction in the budgeted expenditure. Once the budget has been set, and the tax has been levied on that basis, departments have to work within the budgets laid down. However, since the budget will have been prepared on an estimate of the actual expenditure for the last two or three months of the old financial year, account has to be taken of any a surplus or short-fall expected in the current year. If the estimate eventually proves excessive, the local authority will have over-taxed. This means that it has got some additional funds available to cushion the current year's expenditure. Of course, if it has under-taxed for any balance brought forward, departments might have to start cutting back on what they thought they could spend.

This process is quite different from the private sector in which the budgeted sales effectively determine all the other budgets. In a local authority, it is the expenditure budgets that determine what the council tax should be, and it is only the control exercised by central government and by the local authority itself that places a ceiling on what is spent.

FUNCTIONAL BUDGETS

A budget prepared for a particular department, cost centre, or other identifiable sphere of responsibility is known as a *functional budget*. All the functional budgets will then be combined into the *master budget*. As we described earlier in this chapter, the master budget is, in effect, a combined budgeted profit and loss account, budgeted balance sheet, and budgeted cash flow statement.

An initial draft of the master budget may well not be acceptable to the senior management of the entity. This may be because the entity cannot cope with that particular budgeted level of activity, e.g. as a result of production or cash constraints. Indeed, one of the most important budgets is the *cash budget*. The cash budget translates all the other functional budgets (including that for capital expenditure) into cash terms. It will show in detail the pattern of cash inputs and outputs for the main budget period, as well as for each sub-budget period. If it shows that the entity will have difficulty in financing a particular budgeted level of activity (or if there is going to be a period when cash is exceptionally tight), the management will have an opportunity to seek out alternative sources of finance.

This latter point illustrates the importance of being aware of future commitments, so that something can be done in advance if there are likely to be constraints (irrespective of their nature). The master budget usually takes so long to prepare, however, that by the time that it has been completed, it will be almost impossible to make major alterations. It is then tempting for senior management to make changes to the functional budgets without referencing them back to individual cost centre managers. It is most unwise to make changes in this way, because it is then difficult to use such budgets for control purposes. If managers have not agreed to the changes, they will argue that they can hardly take responsibility for budgets which have been imposed on them.

A descriptive analysis makes it difficult to see clearly how all the functional budgets fit together, so the procedure is illustrated in the next section by using a quantitative example.

AN ILLUSTRATIVE EXAMPLE

It would obviously be very difficult to observe the basic procedures involved in the preparation of the functional budgets if we used an extremely detailed example, so Exhibit 17.2 cuts out all the incidental information. As a result, it only illustrates the main procedures, but this will enable you to see how all the budgets fit together.

Exhibit 17.2 Preparation of functional budgets

Sefton Limited manufactures one product known as EC2. The following information relates to the preparation of the budget for the year to 31 March 19X9:
1 Sales budget details for product EC2:
    Expected selling price per unit: £100.
    Expected sales in units: 10 000.
    All sales are on credit terms.
2 EC2 requires 5 units of raw material E and 10 units of raw material C. E is expected to cost £3 per unit, and C £4 per unit. All goods are purchased on credit terms.
3 Two departments are involved in producing EC2: machining and assembly. The following information is relevant:

	Direct labour per unit of product (hours)	Direct labour rate per hour £
Machining	1.00	6
Assembling	0.50	8

4 The finished production overhead costs are expected to amount to £100 000.
5 At 1 April 19X8, 800 units of EC2 are expected to be in stock at a value of £52 000, 4500 units of raw material E at a value of £13 500, and 12 000 units of raw materials are planned to be 10% above the expected opening stock levels as at 1 April 19X8.
6 Administration, selling and distribution overhead is expected to amount to £150 000.

7   Other relevant information:
  (a) Opening trade debtors are expected to be £80 000. Closing trade debtors are expected to amount to 15% of the total sales for the year.
  (b) Opening trade creditors are expected to be £28 000. Closing trade creditors are expected to amount to 10% of the purchases for the year.
  (c) All other expenses will be paid in cash during the year.
  (d) Other balances at 1 April 19X8 are expected to be as follows:

		£	£
(i)	Share capital; ordinary shares		225 000
(ii)	Retained profits		17 500
(iii)	Proposed dividend		75 000
(iv)	Fixed assets at cost	250 000	
	Less: Accumulated depreciation	100 000	
			150 000
(v)	Cash at bank and in hand		2 000

8 Capital expenditure will amount to £50 000 payable in cash on 1 April 19X8.
9 Fixed assets are depreciated on a straight-line basis at a rate of 20% per annum on cost.

Required:
As far as the information permits, prepare all the relevant budgets for Sefton Limited for the year to 31 March 19X9.

Answer to Exhibit 17.2

Even with a much simplified budgeting exercise, there is clearly a great deal of work involved in preparing the budgets. To make it easier for you to understand what is happening, the procedure will be outlined step by step.

●   Step 1: Prepare the sales budget

Units of EC2	Selling price per unit £	Total sales value £
10 000	100	1 000 000

●   Step 2: Prepare the production budget

	Units
Sales of EC2	10 000
Less: Opening stock	800
	9 200
Add: Desired closing stock (opening stock +10%)	880
Production required	10 080

- Step 3: Prepare the direct materials usage budget

Direct material:

E: 5 units × 10 080	50 400 units
C: 10 units × 10 080	100 800 units

- Step 4: Prepare the direct materials purchases budget

Direct material	E (units)	C (units)
Usage (as per Step 3)	50 400	100 800
Less: Opening stock	4 500	12 000
	45 900	88 800
Add: Desired closing stock (opening stock+10%)	4 950	13 200
	50 850	102 000
	× £3	× £4
∴ Total value of purchase	£152 550	£408 000

- Step 5: Prepare the direct labour budget

	Machining	Assembling
Production units (as per Step 2)	10 080	10 080
× direct labour hours required	× 1 DLH	× 0.50 DLH
	10 080 DLH	5 040 DLH
× direct labour rate per hour	× £6	× £8
	£60 480	£40 320

- Step 6: Prepare the fixed production overhead budget

Given   £100 000

- Step 7: Calculate the value of the closing raw material stock

Raw material	Closing stock* (units)	Cost per unit £	Total value £
E	4 950	3	14 850
C	13 200	4	52 800
			£67 650

*Step 4

375

- Step 8: Calculate the value of the closing finished stock

	£	£
Unit cost:		
Direct materials:E – 5 units × £3 per unit	15	
C – 10 units × £4 per unit	40	55
Direct labour: Machining – 1 hour × £6 per DLH	6	
Assembling – 0.50 hours × £8 per DLH	4	10
Total direct cost		£65
× units in stock		× 880
		£57 200

- Step 9: Prepare the administration, selling and distribution budget
  Given   £150 000

- Step 10: Prepare the capital expenditure budget
  Given   £50 000

- Step 11: Calculate the cost of goods sold

	£
Opening stock (given)	52 000
Manufacturing cost:	
Production units (Step 2) × total direct cost (Step 3)	
= 10 080 × £65	655 200
	707 200
Less: Closing stock (Step 8: 880 units × £65)	57 200
Cost of goods sold (10 000 units)	£650 000
(or 10 000 units × total direct costs of £65 per unit)	

- Step 12: Prepare the cash budget

	£	£
Receipts		
Cash from debtors		
Opening debtors	80 000	
Sales	1000 000	
	1 080 000	
Less: Closing debtors (15% × £1 000 000)	150 000	930 000

	£	
Payments		
Cash payments to creditors		
Opening creditors	28 000	
Purchases [Step 4: (152 550 + 408 000)]	560 550	
	588 550	
Less: Closing creditors (560 550 × 10%)	56 055	532 495
Wages (Step 5: 60 480 + 40 320)		100 800
Fixed production overhead		100 000
Administration, selling and distribution overhead		150 000
Capital expenditure		50 000
Proposed dividend (19X8)		75 000
		1 008 295

	£
Net receipts	(78 295)
Add: Opening cash	2 000
Budgeted closing cash balance (overdrawn)	£(76 295)

- Step 13: Prepare the budgeted profit and loss account

	£	£
Sales (Step 1)		1 000 000
Less: Variable cost of sales (Step 8: 10 000 × 65)		650 000
Gross margin		350 000
Less: Fixed production overhead (Step 6)	100 000	
Depreciation [(250 000 + 50 000) × 20%]	60 000	160 000
Production margin		190 000
Less: Administration, selling and distribution overhead (Step 9)		150 000
Budgeted net profit		£40 000

- Step 14: Prepare the budgeted balance sheet

	£	£	£
Fixed assets (at cost)			300 000
Less: Accumulated depreciation			160 000
			140 000
Current assets			
Raw materials (Step 7)		67 650	
Finished stock (Step 8)		57 200	
Trade debtors (15% × 1 000 000)		150 000	
		274 850	
Less: *Current liabilities*			
Trade creditors [Step 4: 10% × (152 550 + 408 000)]	56 055		
Bank overdraft (Step 12)	76 295	132 350	142 500
			£282 500
Financed by:			
Share capital			
Ordinary shares			225 000
Retained profits (17 500 + 40 000)			57 500
			£282 500

Exhibit 17.2 is a fairly complicated example, although unnecessary detail has been avoided, e.g. it has been assumed that the company produces only one product, and that the value of the opening stocks at 1 April 19X8 will be the same as the budgeted costs of manufacture in the year to 31 March 19X9. It

might be worthwhile, therefore, to go through the exhibit once again, and make sure that you understand how all the various budgets fit together. You can use as your guide the budgeting process shown in diagrammatic form in Exhibit 17.1. It would then be advisable to have yet another go at Exhibit 17.2, but this time without referring to the solution.

FIXED AND FLEXIBLE BUDGETS

Once the master budget has been agreed, it becomes the detailed plan for future action which everyone is expected to work towards. However, some entities only use the budgeting process as a *planning* exercise. Once the master budget has been agreed, there may be no attempt to use it as a control technique. Thus the budget may be virtually ignored, and it may not be compared with the actual results. If this is the case, then the entity is not getting the best out of the budgeting system.

As was suggested earlier, budgets are particularly useful if they are also used as a means of control. The control is achieved if the actual performance is used to compare it with the budget. Significant variances should then be investigated and any necessary corrective action taken.

The constant comparison of the actual results with the budgeted results may be done either on a *fixed* budget basis or a *flexible* budget basis. A fixed budget basis means that the actual results for a particular period are compared with the original budgets. This is as you would expect, because the budget is a measure. You would get some very misleading results, for example, if you used an elastic ruler to measure distances. Similarly, an elastic-type budget might also give some highly unreliable results. In some cases, however, a variable measure *is* used in budgeting in order to allow for certain circumstances which might have taken place since the budgets were prepared. Accountants call this *flexing* the budget. The CIMA definition of a flexible budget is:

> **Flexible budget:** a budget which, by recognizing different cost behaviour patterns, is designed to change as volume of activity changes.

It may seem a little contradictory to argue that the budget should be changed once it has been agreed, but a fixed budget (i.e. one that does not change) can also be misleading. It was explained earlier that in order to prepare their budgets, managers (especially those directly involved in production) will need to be given the budgeted level of activity. Consequently, their budgets will be based on that level of activity, but if the *actual* level of activity is greater (or less) than the budgeted level, managers will have to allow for more (or less) expenditure on materials, labour, and other expenses.

Suppose, for example, that a manager has prepared his budget on the basis of an anticipated level of activity of 70% of the maximum number of units that the plant is capable of producing. The company turns out to be much busier than it expected, and it achieves an actual level of activity of 80%. The production manager is likely to have spent far more on materials, labour, and other expenses than he had originally budgeted. If the actual performance is then compared with the budget (i.e. on a fixed budget basis), it will appear as though he had greatly exceeded what he thought he would spend. No doubt he would then argue that the differences had arisen as a result of a greatly increased level of activity (which may be outside his control). While this may be true, there is no certainty that all of the differences were caused by the increased activity.

Hence, the need to flex the budget, i.e. it needs to be revised on the basis of what it would have been if the manager had budgeted for an activity of 80% instead of 70%. The other assumptions and calculations made at the time the budget was prepared (such as material prices and wage rates) will not be amended.

If the entity operates a flexible budget system, the original budgets may be prepared on the basis of a wide range of possible activity levels. This method, however, is very time consuming, and managers will be very lucky if they prepare one that is identical to the actual level of activity. The best method is to wait until the actual level of activity is known, and then flex the budget on that basis.

This procedure might appear fairly complicated, so it is best if it is illustrated with an example. This is done in Exhibit 17.3.

Exhibit 17.3 Flexible budget procedure

The following information had been prepared for Carp Limited for the year to 30 June 19X6:

	Budget	Actual
Level of activity	50%	60%
	£	£
Costs:		
Direct materials	50 000	61 000
Direct labour	100 000	118 000
Variable overhead	10 000	14 000
Total variable cost	160 000	193 000
Fixed overhead	40 000	42 000
Total costs	£200 000	£235 000

Required:
Prepare a flexed budget operating statement for Carp Limited for the year to 30 June 19X6.

Answer to Exhibit 17.3

CARP LIMITED
Flexed budget operating statement for the year 30 June 19X6

	Flexed budget	Actual costs	Variance: favourable/ (adverse)
	£	£	£
Direct materials (1)	60 000	61 000	(1 000)
Direct labour (1)	120 000	118 000	2 000
Variable overhead (1)	12 000	14 000	(2 000)
Total variable costs	192 000	193 000	(1 000)
Fixed overhead (2)	40 000	42 000	(2 000)
Total costs (3)	£232 000	£235 000	£(3 000)

Tutorial notes

1 All the budgeted variable costs have been flexed by 20% because the actual activity was 60% compared with a budgeted level of 50% (i.e. a 20% increase).
2 The budgeted fixed costs are not flexed because by definition they ought not to change with activity.
3 Instead of using the total fixed budget cost of £200 000 (as per the question), the total flexed budget costs of £232 000 can be compared more fairly with the total actual cost of £235 000.
4 Note that the terms 'favourable' and 'adverse' (as applied to variances) mean favourable or adverse to profit. In other words, profit will be either greater or less than the budgeted profit.
5 The reasons for the variances between the actual costs and the flexed budget will need to be investigated. The flexed budget shows that even allowing for the increased activity, the actual costs were in excess of the budget allowance.
6 Similarly, it will be necessary to investigate why the actual activity was higher than the budgeted activity. It could have been caused by inefficient budgeting, or by quite an unexpected increase in sales activity. While this would normally be welcome, it might place a strain on the productive and financial resources of the entity. If the increase is likely to be permanent, management will need to make immediate arrangements to accommodate the new level of activity.

It should be emphasized that the primary purpose of a budgetary control system is to control as closely as possible the activities of the entity. There will invariably be differences between the actual and the budgeted results, no matter how carefully the budgets are prepared. This does not matter unduly, as long as it is possible to find out why there were differences, and to take action before it is too late to do something about them.

CONCLUSION

It has been suggested in this chapter that the full benefits of a cost accounting system can best be gained if it is combined with a budgetary control system. The preparation of budgets is a valuable exercise in itself, for it forces management to look ahead to what might happen, rather than to look back to what did happen. However, it is even more valuable if it is also used as a form of control.

Budgetary control enables actual results to be measured frequently against an agreed budget (or plan). Departures from that budget can then be quickly spotted, and steps taken to correct any unwelcome trends. However, the comparison of actual results with a fixed budget may not be particularly helpful if the actual level of activity is different from that budgeted. It is advisable, therefore, to compare actual results with a flexed budget.

As so many of the functional budgets are based upon the budgeted level of activity, it is vital that it is calculated as accurately as possible, since an error in estimating the level of activity could affect all of the company's financial and operational activities. Thus it is important that any difference between the actual and the budgeted level of activity is carefully investigated.

Key points	
	1 **A budget is a plan.**
	2 **Budgetary control is a cost control method that enables actual results to be compared with the budget, thereby enabling any necessary corrective action to be taken.**
	3 **The preparation of budgets will be undertaken by a budget team.**
	4 **Managers must be responsible for producing their own functional budgets.**
	5 **Functional budgets are combined to form a master budget.**
	6 **A fixed budget system compares actual results with the original budgets.**
	7 **A flexible budget system compares actual results with the original budget, flexed (or amended) to allow for any difference between the actual level of activity and the budgeted level.**

CHECK YOUR LEARNING

1 Fill in the missing words in each of the following sentences:
   (a) A budget is a _____ expressed in money.

(b) The continuous comparison of actual with budgeted results is known as
_____ _____.

(c) A _____ budget is one which recognizes different cost behaviour patterns.

2 Over what period of time might a budget normally be prepared?
(a) three months (b) a year (c) two years (d) five years (e) none of these

3 What is the term normally given to the overall budgeted profit and loss account, budgeted balance sheet, and budgeted cash flow statement?

4 (a) In a manufacturing entity, which budget will normally be prepared first?
(b) What is the main determinant of a local authority's budget?

Answers
1 (a) plan (b) budgetary control (c) flexible
2 (b) a year
3 master budget
4 (a) sales budget (b) estimate of total expenditure

QUESTIONS

17.1
You are presented with the following information for Moray Limited:

Budgeted sales units for the six months to 30 June 19X1

January	200
February	250
March	370
April	400
May	500
June	550

Additional information:
1 Opening stock at 1 January 19X1 was expected to be 320 units.
2 Desired closing stock level at 30 June 19X1 was 450 units.

Required:
Calculate the minimum number of units to be produced each month if an even production flow is to be established.

17.2
You have been presented with the following budgeted information relating to Jordan Limited for the six months to 31 December 19X2:

	July	August	September	October	November	December
Sales (units)	70	140	350	190	150	120
Closing stock (units)	230	370	200	190	180	100

Additional information:
Opening stock at 1 July 19X2 is expected to be 100 units.

Required:
Calculate the monthly production levels required to meet the above budgeted data.

17.3
The directors of Dalton Limited have been presented with the following budgeted information for the six months to 30 June 19X3:

	January	February	March	April	May	June
Sales (units)	90	150	450	150	130	120

Additional information:
1 The opening stock at 1 January 19X3 is expected to be 100 units.
2 Units are only available for sale in the period following the month in which they were manufactured.

Required:
Calculate the minimum number of units to be produced each month in order to meet the budgeted monthly sales figures, assuming that the directors wish to adopt the minimum possible production flow.

17.4
The following information has been prepared for Tom Limited for the six months to 30 September 19X4:

Budgeted production levels Product X

	Units
April	140
May	280
June	700
July	380
August	300
September	240

Product X uses two units of component A6 and three units of component B9. At 1 April 19X4 there were expected to be 100 units of A6 in stock, and 200 units of B9. The desired closing stock levels of each component were as follows:

Month end 19X4	A6 (units)	B9 (units)
30 April	110	250
31 May	220	630
30 June	560	340
31 July	300	300
31 August	240	200
30 September	200	180

During the six months to 30 September 19X4, component A6 was expected to be purchased at a cost of £5 per unit, and component B9 at a cost of £10 per unit.

Required:
Prepare the following budgets for each of the six months to 30 September 19X4:
1 direct materials usage budget; and
2 direct materials purchase budget.

17.5

Don Limited has one major product which requires two types of direct labour to produce it. The following data refer to certain budget proposals for the three months to 31 August 19X5:

Month	Production units
30.6.X5	600
31.7.X5	700
31.8.X5	650

Direct labour hours required per unit:

	Hours	Budgeted rate per hour £
Production	3	4
Finishing	2	8

Required:
Prepare the direct labour cost budget for each of the three months to 31 August 19X5.

17.6

Gorse Limited manufactures one product. The budgeted sales for period 6 are for 10 000 units at a selling price of £100 per unit. Other details are as follows:

1 Two components are used in the manufacture of each unit:

Component	Number	Unit cost of each component £
XY	5	1
WZ	3	0.50

2 Stocks at the beginning of the period are expected to be as follows:
   (a) 4000 units of finished goods at a unit cost of £52.50.
   (b) Component XY: 16 000 units at a unit cost of £1.
       Component WZ: 9600 units at a unit cost of £0.50.

3 Two grades of employees are used in the manufacture of each unit:

Employee	Hours per unit	Labour rate per hour £
Production	4	5
Finishing	2	7

4 Factory overhead is absorbed into unit costs on the basis of direct labour hours. The budgeted factory overhead for the period is estimated to be £96 000.

5 The administration, selling and distribution overhead for the period has been budgeted at £275 000.

6 The company plans a reduction of 50% in the quantity of finished stock at the end of period 6, and an increase of 25% in the quantity of each component.

Required:
Prepare the following budgets for period 6:
1 sales;
2 production quantity;
3 materials usage;
4 materials purchase;
5 direct labour;
6 the budgeted profit and loss account.

17.7

The following budget information relates to Flossy Limited for the three months to 31 March 19X7:
1 Budgeted profit and loss accounts:

Month	31.1.X7	28.2.X7	31.3.X7
	£000	£000	£000
Sales (all on credit)	2000	3000	2500
Cost of sales	1200	1800	1500
Gross profit	800	1200	1000
Depreciation	(100)	(100)	(100)
Other expenses	(450)	(500)	(600)
	(550)	(600)	(700)
Net profit	£250	£600	£300

2 Budgeted balance sheets:

Budgeted balances	31.12.X6	31.1.X7	28.2.X7	31.3.X7
	£000	£000	£000	£000
Current assets:				
Stocks	100	120	150	150
Debtors	200	300	350	400
Short-term investments	60	–	40	30
Current liabilities:				
Trade creditors	110	180	160	150
Other creditors	50	50	50	50
Taxation	150	–	–	–
Dividends	200	–	–	–

3 Capital expenditure to be incurred on 20 February 19X7 was expected to amount to £470 000.
4 Sales of plant and equipment on 15 March 19X7 are expected to raise £30 000 in cash.
5 The cash at bank and in hand on 1 January 19X7 was expected to be £15 000.

Required:
Prepare Flossy Limited's cash budget for each of the three months during the quarter ending 31 March 19X7.

17.8

Chimes limited has prepared a flexible budget for one of its factories for the year to 30 June 19X8. The details are as follows:

% of Production capacity	30%	40%	50%	60%
	£000	£000	£000	£000
Direct materials	42	56	70	84
Direct labour	18	24	30	36
Factory overhead	22	26	30	34
Administration overhead	17	20	23	26
Selling and distribution overhead	12	14	16	18
	£111	£140	£169	£198

Additional information:

1 The company is only operating at 45% of its capacity, and an increase in capacity during the year to 30 June 19X8 is unlikely. At that capacity, the sales revenue has been budgeted at a level of £135 500.

2 It would be possible to close the factory down for 12 months, and then re-open it again on 1 July 19X8 when trading conditions were expected to improve. The costs of doing so are estimated to be as follows:

	£000
Redundancy and other closure costs	30
Property and plant maintenance during the year to 30 June 19X8	10
Re-opening costs	20

However, £30 000 would be saved as a result of a reduction in general company and factory fixed overheads.

Required:
Determine whether the factory should be closed during the year to 30 June 19X8.

ADDITIONAL QUESTIONS (WITHOUT ANSWERS)

17.9

Avsar Limited has extracted the following budgeting details for the year to 30 September 19X9:

1 Sales: 4000 units of V at £500 per unit
           7000 units of R at £300 per unit

2 Materials usage (units):

| | Raw material | | |
	O1	I2	L3
V	11	9	12
R	15	1	10

3 Raw material costs (per unit):

	£
O1	8
I2	6
L3	3

4 Raw material stocks:

| | Units | | |
	O1	I2	L3
At 1 October 19X8	1300	1400	400
At 30 September 19X9	1400	1000	200

5 Finished stocks:

| | Units | |
	V	R
At 1 October 19X8	110	90
At 30 September 19X9	120	150

6 Direct labour:

| | Product | |
	V	R
Budgeted hours per unit	10	8
Budgeted hourly rate (£)	12	6

7 Variable overhead:

| | Product | |
	V	R
Budgeted hourly rate (£)	10	5

8 Fixed overhead: £193 160 (to be absorbed on the basis of direct labour hours).

Required:
(a) Prepare the following budgets:
   (i)   sales;
   (ii)   production units;
   (iii) materials usage;
   (iv) materials purchase; and
   (v)   production cost.
(b) Calculate the total budgeted profit for the year to 30 September 19X9.

17.10
The following budgeted trading, and profit and loss accounts, and balance sheets, relating to the three months to 31 March 19X4, have been prepared for Ramsay Limited:

Trading, profit and loss accounts	January	February	March
	£000	£000	£000
Sales	200	300	400
Opening stock	15	20	30
Purchases	145	220	330
	160	240	360
Less: Closing stock	20	30	80
	140	210	280
Gross profit	60	90	120
Less: Expenses	20	30	40
Profit	40	60	80

Balance sheets	1.1.X4	31.1.X4	28.2.X4	31.3.X4
	£000	£000	£000	£000
Fixed assets at cost	390	400	410	420
Less: Accumulated depreciation	155	160	166	180
	235	240	244	240
Investments	18	50	35	60
Current assets:				
Stocks	15	20	30	80
Trade debtors	20	25	45	100
Prepayments	2	2	3	10
Cash and bank	4	3	2	–
	41	50	80	190
Current liabilities:				
Bank overdraft	–	–	–	(8)
Trade creditors	(35)	(40)	(50)	(90)
Accruals	(3)	(4)	(3)	(2)
Taxation	(30)	(30)	–	–
Dividends	(20)	(20)	–	–
	(88)	(94)	(53)	(100)
Debenture loans	–	–	–	(4)
	£206	£246	£306	£386
Capital and reserves:				
Share capital	200	200	200	240
Profit and loss account	6	46	106	146
	£206	£246	£306	£386

Note:
It is not expected that there will be any disposal of fixed assets during the three months to 31 March 19X4.

Required:
Prepare Ramsay's cash budget for *each* of the three months to 31 March 19X4, respectively.

DISCUSSION QUESTIONS

17.11
The Head of Department of Business and Management at Birch College has been told by the Vice Principal (Resources) that his department budget for the next academic year is £150 000. What comment would you make about the system of budgeting used at Birch College?

17.12
Suppose that when all the individual budgets at Sparks plc are put together there is a shortfall of resources needed to support them. The Board suggests, therefore, that all departmental budgets should be reduced by 15%. As the company's Chief Accountant, how would you respond to the Board's suggestion?

17.13
Does a fixed budget serve any useful purpose?

17.14
'It is impossible to introduce a budgetary control system into a hospital because, if someone's life needs saving, it has to be saved irrespective of the cost.' How far do you agree with this statement?

It can't be done

Learning objectives

After preparing this case study, you will be able to:

- describe the nature and purpose of budgetary control;

- outline the accounting treatment of research and development expenditure in financial accounts;

- assess the behavioural implications of implementing and operating a budgetary control system.

Background

LOCATION   Glass Products Plc: the Managing Director's office.

PERSONNEL   Ken Whalley: Managing Director
               Philippa Morgan: Public Relations Manager
               Dr Ross Hunt: Director of Research and Development

Synopsis

Ken Whalley, the Managing Director of Glass Products Public Limited Company, had called a meeting of the senior management. Rumours had been rife in the company for some months that a big new initiative was afoot, but nobody had any real idea what was going on. Now all had been revealed.

Ken had reminded his audience that the company once had a near monopoly in its supply of glass products to the home market. In more recent years, however, international trade barriers had broken down, and the company was now finding it increasingly difficult to maintain the scale of operations that was needed to support its high level of fixed costs. Indeed, all employees had become aware last year that the situation was extremely serious when no annual bonus was paid.

'We are going to have to look at all our operations,' Ken explained to the senior managers. 'We might have to cut out unprofitable products, reduce costs, and, wherever possible, go for a big increase in our sales. That's going to mean a big change for everyone.'

'Do you exclude redundancies?' Philippa Morgan, the Public Relations Manager asked immediately.

'No,' Ken replied, 'but what we aim to do is to expand. Any surplus labour we have we would hope to absorb into other activities. If we can't, then of course some staff would have to be laid off.'

There was an immediate murmur from his audience.

Ken hastily spoke again. 'I repeat, we shall only make someone redundant if all the other things we are going to do don't work. I have asked you here today to talk about those other things.'

Ken then went into some detail about what the Board had in mind, including the introduction of a sophisticated budgetary control system. 'At the moment,' he explained, 'our management reporting procedures are little better than a back of an envelope exercise. That's got to change. It's going to mean creating responsibility centres. It's going to mean managers doing some serious budgeting. And it's going to mean those same managers answering for what goes wrong.'

'Would this system be introduced into the research and development department?' asked Dr Ross Hunt, the Director of Research and Development activities.

'Yes,' replied Ken. 'No department will be excluded, and in the case of R and D, you will become a function. Within that function you will have a number of cost centres, or if you like, smaller departments.'

'Each one working towards a separate budget?' queried Ross.

'That is so,' responded Ken, who was now answering Ross's questions somewhat warily.

'That's impossible,' retorted Ross. 'You can't budget for R and D. You don't know where an experiment is going to take you, and so you don't know what it's going to cost.'

'Dr Hunt …'

Ross broke in again. 'Look at our opaque products!' he explained triumphantly.

Ross was, in fact, referring to one of the company's most successful product ranges. For years, millions of pounds had been spent on researching into opaque products. It was just about to be abandoned, when the technical problems were overcome. The products had been sold widely, and the company had made a fortune.

'Dr Hunt,' Ken began again, 'if you don't mind, I don't want to go into too much detail at this stage. Perhaps we could have a chat sometime?'

Ross nodded his head, but he decided to say nothing further.

Ken got through his agenda without further interruption, and the meeting was eventually concluded at 4.55 pm, just in time for everyone to go home no later than the usual time of 5 o'clock.

The next day, Ken sent for Ross Hunt. He tried to explain to him the benefits of a budgetary control system. It was hard going. Eventually, Ken realized that Ross's main objection was that he thought that he would never be allowed to spend more than a fixed amount of cash, and he was particularly worried because he knew that he would have to agree to this months ahead of when he planned to spend it.

Ken explained that Ross had misunderstood the purpose of budgeting control. In response, Ross came back on an earlier point: it would be difficult for him to work out in advance what he was going to spend. He tried to explain to Ken, 'You just don't know where an experiment is going to take you. It would be madness to stop just when a breakthrough might be round the corner.'

Ken was getting a little weary. 'Yes, but Ross. That would mean that once you start on a project you never stop it, just because eventually it *might* pay off. The company can't go on supporting all your projects because one day they may be successful.'

Ross counterattacked by remarking that this was not his problem: he just looked after R and D.

Ken's retort was crushing. 'Ah, but that's just where you are wrong: it is your responsibility. You might not have thought so up to now, but it's certainly going to be so in the future.'

The meeting ended at that point, because Ken had to rush off to Brussels. But he did so a very worried man. Research and Development expenditure was an important element in total cost, and Dr Ross Hunt could cause a lot of trouble. In any case, Ken knew that a budgetary control system would not work unless it had the support of everyone in the company.

Required:

1 Consult a number of management accounting textbooks in your library, and then write a brief description of each of the following terms:

(a) responsibility accounting;	(g) pure (or basic) research;
(b) division;	(h) applied research;
(c) function;	(i) development;
(d) profit centre;	(j) budget;
(e) investment centre;	(k) budgetary control.
(f) cost centre;	

2 Explain how you think (a) research expenditure, and (b) development expenditure should be dealt with in preparing a company's financial accounts.

3 Obtain a number of company annual reports and accounts covering a particular sector of the economy, for example, chemicals, electronics, pharmaceuticals. Assess the treatment of research and development expenditure and its importance in relation to the company's other costs.

4 Assume that the directors of Glass Products Plc intend to introduce a budgetary control system throughout the company. Outline the arguments that you would use in convincing the Director of Research and Development that it would be possible to introduce such a system into his area of responsibility, and that it would be of benefit to him and everyone in the company.

CHAPTER 18

Standard costing systems

Jersey to shield accountants' assets

By Phillip Jeune in Jersey and Jim Kelly

The partners of Britain's leading accountancy firms will now be able to protect their personal assets from law suits by registering their partnership in Jersey.

The island's parliament yesterday voted by 25–19 to allow limited liability partnerships to be established on the island.

Under the new law, the details of which still have to be approved, firms are still liable to be sued, as are negligent partners, but the assets of the rest of the partners are safe.

Two leading UK firms, Ernst & Young and Price Waterhouse, helped the Jersey authorities draft the law and both are enthusiastic about taking up registration, which partners will vote on later this year.

There is strong pressure on the government to allow limited partnerships in the UK. The possibility that the firms might register off-shore has also prompted fears that the move might damage the reputation of the City.

The Department of Trade and Industry is looking at a wide range of options on professional liability. It is expected to make an announcement on the reform of partnership laws soon.

There was strong opposition to the proposals in Jersey from politicians who feared that it would put the reputation of the island's finance centre at risk. But Senator Pierre Horsfall, the president of the finance committee, insisted that it would enhance the island's status.

Mr Austin Mitchell, the UK Labour MP with an interest in accountancy, has criticised the Jersey proposals as being bad for the consumer.

The Financial Times, 3 July 1996

Exhibit 18.0 Never mind the real work, let's look after ourselves!

Standard costing is similar to budgetary control, except that in standard costing a budget is prepared for each unit (or each process), instead of just for each particular department. The budgeted unit (or process) cost is referred to as the *standard* cost.

The technique is also similar to budgetary control in that the standard cost of each unit is compared with the actual unit cost. Immediate action is then taken to correct any adverse trends.

The chapter is divided into two main sections. In the first section we examine the background to standard costing and its administration, including the types of standards, their preparation and performance measurement. The second section deals with variance analysis, including both cost and sales variances.

We start with the background to standard costing.

<table>
<tr><td>

Learning objectives

</td><td>

By the end of this chapter, you will be able to:

- **describe the nature and purpose of standard costing;**

- **identify the main steps involved in implementing and operating a standard costing system;**

- **calculate three performance measures and four variances;**

- **describe the importance of standard costing and variance analysis.**

</td></tr>
</table>

BACKGROUND

It will be helpful if we first give you two key definitions put forward by CIMA:

Standard cost: the planned unit cost of the products, components or services produced in a period.
Standard: a benchmark measurement, of resource usage, set in defined conditions.

It was suggested in the opening paragraphs that there were close similarities between budgetary control and standard costing, the main difference being that standard costing is more detailed. For example, besides calculating a total variance between the actual cost of a particular unit and the standard cost, the variance is also analysed into the elements of cost. The degree of analysis depends partly upon management requirements, and partly upon the type of product being produced. This type of detailed analysis is known as *variance analysis*, which is defined by CIMA as:

> **Variance analysis:** the evaluation of performance by means of variances, whose timely reporting should maximise the opportunity for managerial action.
>
> **Variance:** the difference between a planned, budgeted or standard cost and the actual cost incurred.

The calculation of variances is largely a routine arithmetical exercise, and as a non-accountant you are unlikely to become involved. Instead, you are much more likely to be responsible for investigating *why* variances have arisen. It is much easier to investigate the possible causes, however, if you have some idea of where to look for them. If you know, for example, that a variance has been caused mainly because of over-spending on direct materials, then you can begin to investigate whether there was an increase in material prices or whether more materials were used.

It is unlikely that all entities need (or will want) a standard costing system. Standard costing is particularly suited to manufacturing industries producing identifiable products, although there is no reason why it cannot be adopted in non-manufacturing entities. Furthermore, it should be noted that in order to prepare standard costs, it is necessary to compile a budget for each cost centre. Consequently, while it is quite possible to have a budgetary control system without having a standard costing system, it is impossible to have standard costing without budgetary control.

In the following sub-sections some of the requirements of a standard costing system are outlined.

ADMINISTRATION

The responsibility for administering a standard costing system is normally delegated either to a special budget committee or the accounting function.

The standard costing period

The overall period for which the standards are prepared will usually conform with the main and sub-budget periods. It may also be necessary (as it sometimes is with budgeting) to adopt fairly short standard periods, e.g. where market and production conditions are subject to frequent changes, or where it is difficult to plan very far ahead. As the selling price charged to customers will usually be based on the standard cost of a particular unit, it would be unwise to fix the selling price on out-of-date information, so in some circumstances it may be subject to fairly frequent changes.

Types of standard

The preparation of standard costs requires great care and attention. As each element of cost is subject to detailed arithmetical analysis, it is important that the initial information is accurate. Indeed, the information produced by a standard costing system will be virtually worthless if subsequent analyses reveal that variances were caused by inefficient budgeting and standard setting.

In preparing standard costs, management will need to be informed of the level of activity to be used in preparing the standard costs (i.e. whether the entity will need to operate at say 80% or 90% of its theoretical capacity). An activity level should be chosen that is capable of being achieved. It would be possible to choose a standard that was *ideal*, i.e one that represented a performance that could be achieved only under the most favourable of conditions. Such a standard would, however, be unrealistic, because it is rare for ideal conditions to prevail. An ideal standard is a standard which is attainable under the most favourable conditions and where no allowance is made for normal losses, waste and machine downtime.

A much more realistic standard is called an *attainable* standard. An attainable standard is one that the entity can expect to achieve in reasonably efficient working conditions. In other words, it accepts that some delays and inefficiencies (such as normal losses, waste and machine downtime) will occur, but it assumes that management will attempt to minimize them.

You may also come across the term *basic cost standards*. These are standards that are left unchanged over long periods of time. This enables some consistency to be achieved in comparing actual results with the same standards over a substantial period of time, but the standards may become so out of date that meaningful comparisons are not possible.

Preparation and information required

Standard costing is a sophisticated means of planning and controlling a company's operations. Standard costs are time consuming to prepare, and costly to produce, and the entire system is expensive to operate. The technique requires so much detailed information that most employees need to be convinced of its value if it is to work properly, so it does call for considerable team work.

There is no point in having a standard costing system if those who are supposed to benefit do not want it. If standard costing is to operate effectively its purpose must be understood by the employees, because they will have to provide the basic information. If this is done ineffectively or inefficiently, then any decision based upon it will be questionable.

The types of information required to produce standard costs can be summarized as follows:

1 **Direct materials:** types, quantities and price.
2 **Direct labour:** grades, numbers and rates of pay.
3 **Variable overhead:** the total variable overhead cost analysed into various categories, such as employee and general support costs.

4 **Fixed overhead:** the total fixed overhead analysed into various categories such as employee costs, building costs and general administration expenses.

From the above information, it can be seen that the standard cost of a particular unit comprises four main elements: (a) direct materials; (b) direct labour; (c) variable overhead; and (d) fixed overhead. In turn, each element comprises two factors, viz. quantity and price. The total standard cost of a specific unit may be built up as shown in Exhibit 18.1. The exhibit is based on some fictitious data.

Exhibit 18.1 Calculation of the total standard cost of a specific unit using absorption costing

	£
1 Direct materials	
Quantity × price (2 units × 5)	10
2 Direct labour	
Hours × hourly rate (5 hours × 10)	50
3 Variable overhead	
Hours × variable overhead absorption rate per hour	
(5 hours × 6)	30
4 Fixed overhead	
Hours × fixed overhead absorption rate per hour	
(5 hours × 3)	15
TOTAL STANDARD COST PER UNIT	£105

Note: The exhibit assumes that the unit cost is calculated on the basis of standard *absorption* costing. This is the most common method of standard costing, although it is possible to adopt a system of standard *marginal* costing.

Standard hours and the absorption of overhead

Assuming that the standard costs are prepared on the basis of absorption costing, overhead will be absorbed on the basis of *standard* hours (you will recall that in a non-standard costing system, overhead is absorbed on the basis of actual hours). A standard hour represents the amount of work that should be performed in an hour, given that it is produced in standard conditions, i.e. in *planned* conditions. CIMA puts it as follows:

> **Standard hour or minute:** the amount of work achievable, at standard efficiency levels, in an hour or minute.

Each unit is given a standard time of so many hours in which to produce the work, and it is against that standard that the actual hours will be compared.

In order to calculate the standard overhead cost of a unit, remember that the standard overhead absorption rate for the period is multiplied by the number of standard (not actual) hours that the unit should have taken to produce. The absorption of overhead by multiplying the standard absorption rate by the standard hours is a significant departure from that approach adopted in a non-standard costing system. This is a most important point, and it will be returned to a little later on in the chapter.

Sales variances

Some companies also prepare standard costings for sales, although they are not as common as cost variances. If sales variances are required, the difference between the actual sales revenue and the standard revenue is analysed into a number of appropriate sales variances, such as price and quantity. A detailed analysis of the budgeted sales will be needed in order to obtain the following information:

1 the range and number of each product to be sold;
2 the selling price of each product;
3 the respective periods in which sales are to take place;
4 the geographical areas in which they are to be sold.

Performance measures

Management may find it useful if some performance measures are extracted from the standard costing data. There are three particularly important ones. They assist in informing managers about the level of efficiency of the entity, help them to spot unfavourable trends, and enable them to take immediate corrective action.

Before these performance measures are examined, we must emphasize once again that in standard costing, actual costs are compared with the standard cost of the *actual* level of activity. It is tempting to compare the actual cost with the budgeted cost, but it is not customary to do so in standard costing. By comparing the actual cost with the standard cost of the actual production, the budget is, in effect, being flexed. This means that any variances that do then arise can be more realistically assessed, as the same level of activity is being used to measure the actual costs against the budgeted costs. The relationship between actual, budgeted and standard is shown in diagrammatic form in Exhibit 18.2.

Exhibit 18.2 The constituent elements in three important capacity ratios

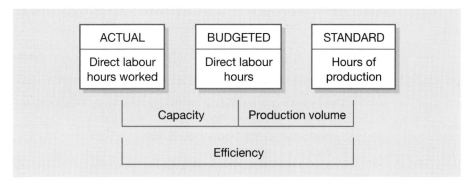

Bearing this point in mind, the performance measures can now be introduced. They are all expressed as ratios, and they are as follows:

The efficiency ratio This ratio compares the total standard (or allowed) hours of units produced with the total actual hours taken to produce those units. It is calculated as follows:

$$\frac{\text{Standard hours produced}}{\text{Actual direct labour hours worked}} \times 100$$

The efficiency ratio enables management to check whether the company has produced the units in more or less time than had been allowed.

The capacity ratio The capacity ratio compares the total actual hours worked with the total budgeted hours. It is calculated as follows:

$$\frac{\text{Actual direct labour hours worked}}{\text{Budgeted direct labour hours}} \times 100$$

This ratio enables management to ascertain whether all of the budgeted hours were used to produce actual units.

The production volume ratio This ratio compares the total allowed hours for the work actually produced with the total budgeted hours. It is calculated as follows:

$$\frac{\text{Standard hours produced}}{\text{Budgeted direct labour hours}} \times 100$$

The production volume ratio enables management to compare the work produced (measured in terms of standard hours) with the budgeted hours of work. This ratio gives management some information about how effective the company has been in using the budgeted hours.

Note that in the case of all three ratios, machine hours may be substituted for direct labour hours.

The efficiency, capacity, and production volume ratios are illustrated in Exhibit 18.3.

Exhibit 18.3 Calculation of efficiency, capacity and production volume ratios

The following information relates to the Frost Production Company Limited for the year to 31 March 19X4:
1 Budgeted direct labour hours: 1000.
2 Budgeted units: 100.
3 Actual direct labour hours worked: 800.
4 Actual units produced: 90.

Required:
Calculate the following performance ratios:
(a) the efficiency ratio;
(b) the capacity ratio; and
(c) the production volume ratio.

Answer to Exhibit 18.3

(a) The efficiency ratio:

$$\frac{\text{Standard hours produced}}{\text{Actual direct labour hours worked}} \times 100 = \frac{900^*}{800} \times 100 = \underline{\underline{112.5\%}}$$

* Each unit is allowed 10 standard hours (1000 hours/100 units), and since 90 units were produced, the total standard hours of production = 900.

It would appear that the company has been more efficient in producing the goods than was expected. It was allowed 900 hours to do so, but it produced them in only 800 hours.

(b) The capacity ratio:

$$\frac{\text{Actual direct labour hours worked}}{\text{Budgeted hours}} \times 100 = \frac{800}{1000} \times 100 = \underline{\underline{80\%}}$$

In this case, all of the time planned to be available (the capacity) was not utilized, either because it was not possible to work 1000 direct labour hours, or because the company did not undertake as much work as it could have done.

(c) The production volume ratio:

$$\frac{\text{Standard hours produced}}{\text{Budgeted hours}} \times 100 = \frac{900^*}{1000} \times 100 = \underline{\underline{90\%}}$$

* As calculated for the efficiency ratio.

It appears that if 90 units had been produced in standard conditions, another 100 hours would have been available (10 units x 10 hours). In fact, since the 90 units only took 800 hours to produce, at least another 20 units could have been produced in standard conditions.

$$\frac{1000 - 800}{10} = \underline{\underline{20 \text{ units}}}$$

Comments on the results

The budget allowed for 100 units to be produced and each unit was expected to take 10 direct labour hours to complete, a total budgeted activity of 1000 direct labour hours. However, only 90 units were actually produced. If these units had been produced in standard time, they should have taken 900 hours (90 units $\times$ 10 direct labour hours). These are the standard hours produced. In fact, the 90 units were completed in 800 actual hours. It appears, therefore, that the units were produced more efficiently than had been expected. The management will still need, of course, to investigate why only 90 units were produced and not the 100 budgeted units.

The background to standard costing and its administration has now been covered, so it is possible to examine what is meant by variance analysis.

VARIANCE ANALYSIS

As was seen above, the difference between actual costs and standard costs consists of two main variances: price and quantity. These variances may either be favourable (F) to profit, or adverse (A). This means that the actual prices paid or costs incurred can be more than was anticipated (adverse to profit), or less than anticipated (favourable to profit). Similarly, the quantities used in production can result in more being used (adverse to profit) or less than expected (favourable to profit).

Each element of cost can be analysed into price and quantity variances (although different terms may be used). Sales and cost variances are shown in diagrammatic form in Exhibit 18.4, while the main cost variances are also summarized below. Sales variances are dealt with later on in the chapter.

1　Direct material: Total = price + usage
2　Direct labour: Total = rate + efficiency
3　Variable production overhead: Total = expenditure + efficiency
4　Fixed production overhead: Total = expenditure + volume *

* The fixed production overhead volume variance is usually sub-analysed as follows:
　Volume = capacity + productivity

Exhibit 18.4 Analysis of the main standard cost variances

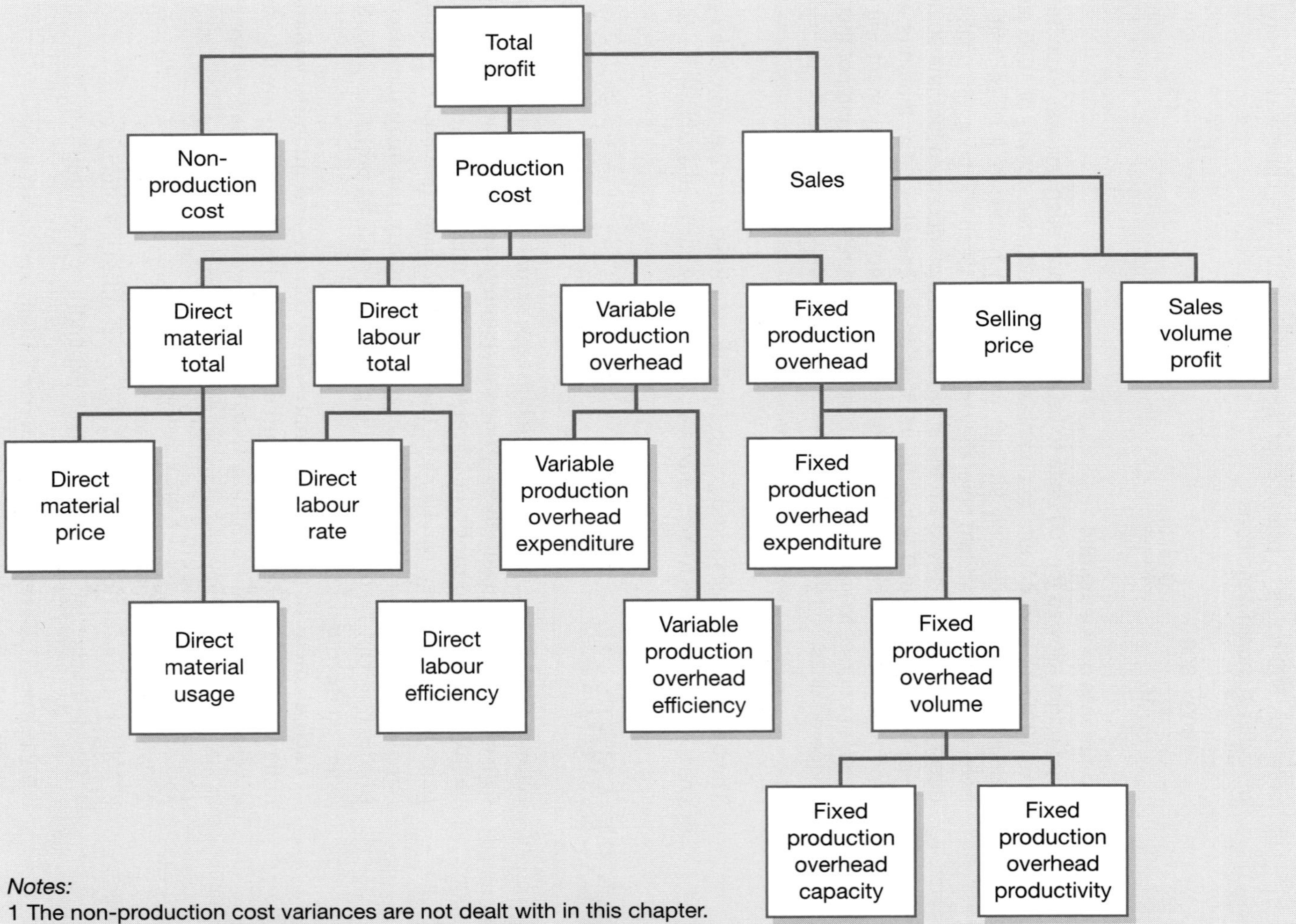

Notes:
1 The non-production cost variances are not dealt with in this chapter.
2 The sales volume profit variance can be analysed into (a) sales mix profit variance; and (b) sales quantity profit variance.
3 The direct material usage variance can be analysed into (a) direct material mix variance and (b) direct material yield variance.

Variance analysis formulae

Before we explain how to calculate cost variances, it would be useful if the basic formulae were first summarized. You will then find it convenient to refer back to this summary when examining later exhibits.

The formulae used in calculating the main standard cost variances are as follows:

Direct materials

1 Total = (actual price per unit × actual quantity used) – (standard price per unit × standard quantity for actual production)
2 Price = (actual price per unit – standard price per unit) × total actual used
3 Usage = (total actual quantity used – standard quantity for actual production) × standard price

These relationships are also shown in Exhibit 18.5.

Exhibit 18.5 Calculation of direct material variances

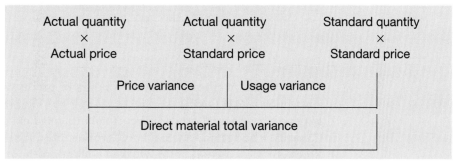

Direct labour

1 Total = (actual hourly rate × actual hours) – (standard hourly rate × standard hours for actual production)
2 Rate = (actual hourly rate – standard hourly rate) × actual hours worked
3 Efficiency = (actual hours worked – standard hours for actual production) × standard hourly rate

These relationships are also shown in Exhibit 18.6.

Exhibit 18.6 Calculation of direct labour variances

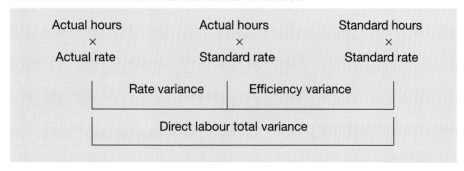

Variable production overhead

1 Total = actual overhead − (standard hours for actual production × variable production overhead absorption rate (V.OAR))
2 Expenditure = actual expenditure − (actual hours worked) × V.OAR
3 Efficiency = (standard hours of production − actual hours worked) × V.OAR

These relationships are also shown in Exhibit 18.7.

Exhibit 18.7 Calculation of variable production overhead variances

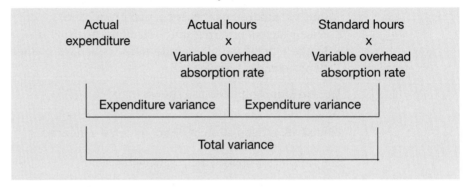

Fixed production overhead

1 Total = actual overhead − (standard hours of production × fixed overhead absorption rate (F.OAR))
2 Expenditure = actual expenditure − total budgeted expenditure
3 Capacity = budgeted − (actual hours worked × F.OAR)
4 Productivity = (actual hours worked − standard hours for actual production) × F.OAR
5 Volume = budgeted expenditure − (standard hours for actual production × F.OAR)

Note: Capacity = productivity + volume

These variances are also shown in Exhibit 18.8.

Exhibit 18.8 Calculation of fixed production overhead variances

Actual expenditure	Budgeted expenditure	Actual hours × Fixed overhead absorption rate	Standard hours × Fixed overhead absorption rate
Expenditure variance	Capacity variance	Productivity variance	
Expenditure variance	Volume variance		
Total variance			

AN ILLUSTRATIVE EXAMPLE

The main cost variances will now be examined by using an illustrative example. The details are contained in Exhibit 18.9.

Exhibit 18.9 Calculation of the main cost variances

The following information has been extracted from the records of the Frost Production Company Limited for the year to 31 March 19X4:

Budgeted costs per unit:	£
Direct materials (15 kilograms × £2 per kilogram)	30
Direct labour (10 hours × £4 per direct labour hour)	40
Variable overhead (10 hours × £1 per direct labour hour)	10
Fixed overhead (10 hours × £2 per direct labour hour)	20
Total budgeted cost per unit	£100

The following budgeted data are also relevant:
1 The budgeted production level was 100 units.
2 The total standard direct labour hours amounted to 1000.
3 The total budgeted variable overhead was estimated to be £1000.
4 The total budgeted fixed overhead was £2000.
5 The company absorbs both fixed and variable overhead on the basis of direct labour hours.

Actual costs:	£
Direct materials	2100
Direct labour	4000
Variable overhead	1000
Fixed overhead	1600
Total actual costs	£8700

Note: 90 units were produced in 800 actual hours, and the total actual quantity of direct materials consumed was 1400 kilograms.

Required:
Calculate the direct materials, direct labour, variable production overhead and fixed production overhead cost variances.

Answers to Exhibit 18.9

To begin the answer to this question, first summarize the total variance for each element of cost:

Actual units produced	Actual costs(1)	Total standard cost for actual production	Variance
	£	£	£
Direct materials	2100	2700 (1)	600 (F)
Direct labour	4000	3600 (2)	400 (A)
Variable production overhead	1000	900 (3)	100 (A)
Fixed production overhead	1600	1800 (4)	200 (F)
Total	£8700	£9000	£300 (F)

Notes:
(a) F = favourable to profit; A = adverse to profit.
(b) The numbers in brackets refer to the tutorial notes below.

Tutorial notes
1 The standard cost of direct material for actual production = the actual units produced × the standard direct material cost per unit, i.e. 90 × £30 = £2700.
2 The standard cost of direct labour for actual production = the actual units produced × standard direct labour cost per unit, i.e. 90 × £40 = £3600.
3 The standard variable cost for actual performance = the actual units produced × variable overhead absorption rate per unit, i.e. 90 × £10 = £900.
4 The fixed overhead cost for the actual performance = the actual units produced × fixed overhead absorption rate, i.e. 90 × £20 = £1800.

As can be seen from Exhibit 18.9, the total actual cost of producing the 90 units was £300 less than the budget allowance. An investigation would need to be held in order to find out why only 90 units were produced when the company had budgeted for 100. Furthermore, although the 90 units have cost £300 less than might have been expected, a number of other variances have contributed to the overall variance. Assuming that these variances are considered significant, they would need to be carefully investigated in order to find out what caused them. Both the direct materials and the fixed production overhead, for example, cost £600 and £200, respectively, less than the budget allowance, while the direct labour cost £400 and the variable production overhead £100 more than might have been expected.

As a result of calculating variances for each element of cost, it would now be much easier for management to investigate why the actual production cost was £300 less than might have been expected. However, by analysing the variances into their major causes, the accountant can provide even greater guidance. In order to explain how this is done, each element of cost and its constituent variances will be examined, and then a brief explanation will be given of their possible causes.

Direct materials

1 Price = (actual price per unit – standard price per unit) × total actual quantity used.

$$\text{The price variance } \therefore = (£1.50 - 2.00) \times 1400 \text{ kg} = £700 \text{ (F)}$$

The actual price per unit was £1.50 (£2100/1400) and the standard price was £2.00 per unit. There was, therefore, a total saving (as far as the price of the materials was concerned) of £700 (£0.50 × 1400). This was favourable (F) to profit.

2 Usage = (total actual quantity used – standard quantity for actual production) x standard price.

$$\text{The usage variance } \therefore = (1400 - 1350) \times £2.00 = £100 \text{ (A)}$$

In producing 90 units, Frost should have used 1350 kilograms (90 × 15 kg), instead of the 1400 kilograms actually used. If this extra usage is valued at the standard price (the difference between the actual price and the standard price has already been allowed for), there is an adverse usage variance of £100 (50 kg × £2.00).

3 Total = price + usage:

$$= £700 \text{ (F)} + £100 \text{ (A)} = £600 \text{ (F)}$$

The £600 favourable total variance was shown earlier in the cost summary in Exhibit 18.9. This variance might have arisen because Frost purchased cheaper materials. If this were the case, then it probably resulted in a greater wastage of materials, perhaps because the materials were of an inferior quality.

Direct labour

1 Rate = (actual labour hourly rate – standard labour hourly rate) × actual hours worked.

$$\text{The rate variance } \therefore = (£5.00 - 4.00) \times 800 \text{ DLH} = £800 \text{ (A)}$$

The actual hourly rate is £5.00 per direct labour hour (DLH) (£4,000/800) compared with the standard rate per hour of £4. Every extra actual hour worked, therefore, resulted in an adverse variance of £1.00, or £800 in total (£1.00 × 800).

2 Efficiency = (total actual hours worked – total standard hours for actual production) × standard hourly rate.

$$\text{The efficiency variance } \therefore = (800 - 900) \times £4.00 = £400 \text{ (F)}$$

The actual hours worked were 800. However, 900 hours would have been allowed for the 90 units actually produced (90 × 10 DLH). If these hours were valued at the standard hourly rate (differences between the actual rate and the standard rate have already been allowed for when calculating the rate variance), a favourable variance of £400 arises. The favourable efficiency variance has arisen because the 90 units took less time to produce than allowed for in the budget.

3 Total = rate + efficiency:

$$£800 \ (A) + £400 \ (F) = £400 \ (A)$$

The £400 adverse variance was shown earlier in the cost summary in Exhibit 18.9. It arises because the company paid more per direct labour hour than had been budgeted, although this was offset to some extent by the units being produced in less time than the budgeted allowance. This variance could have been caused by using a higher grade of labour than had been intended. Unfortunately, the higher labour rate per hour was not completely offset by greater efficiency.

Variable production overhead

Not all accountants consider it necessary to analyse the variable production overhead total variance into sub-variances. The adverse variance of £100 (A) (as shown earlier in the summary of variances in Exhibit 18.9), arises because the variable overhead absorption rate was calculated on the basis of a budgeted cost of £10 per unit. In fact the absorption rate ought to have been £11.11 per unit (£1000/90), because the total actual variable cost was £1000. There would, of course, be no variable production overhead cost for the ten units that were not produced.

If the variable production overhead total variance is analysed into sub-variances, the result would be as follows:

1 Expenditure = actual variable overhead expenditure − (actual hours worked × variable production overhead absorption rate).

$$\therefore \ \text{Expenditure variance} = £1000 - (800 \times £1.00) = £200 \ (A)$$

2 Efficiency = (standard hours of production − actual hours worked) × variable production overhead absorption rate.

$$\therefore \ \text{Efficiency variance} = (900 - 800) \times £1.00 = £100 \ (F)$$

3 Total = expenditure + efficiency:

$$= £200 \text{ (A)} + £100 \text{ (F)} = £100 \text{ (A)}$$

Fixed production overhead

1 Expenditure = actual expenditure – budgeted expenditure.

$$\text{Expenditure variance} = £1600 – £2000 = £400 \text{ (F)}$$

The actual expenditure was £400 less than the budgeted expenditure. This means that the fixed production overhead absorption rate was £400 higher than it needed to have been if there had not been any other fixed overhead variances.

2 Volume = budgeted overhead – (standard hours of production × fixed production overhead absorption rate).

$$\text{Volume variance} \therefore = £2000 – (900 \times £2.00) = £200 \text{ (A)}$$

As a result of producing fewer units than expected, £200 less overhead has been absorbed into production.

3 Capacity = budgeted overhead – (actual hours worked × fixed production overhead absorption rate).

$$\text{Capacity variance} \therefore = £2000 – (800 \times £200) = £400 \text{ (A)}$$

The capacity variance shows that the actual hours worked were less than the budgeted hours. Other things being equal, therefore, not enough overhead would have been absorbed into production. It should be noted that the capacity variance will be favourable when the actual hours are in excess of the budgeted hours. This might seem odd, but it means that the company has been able to use more hours than it had originally budgeted. As a result, it should have been able to produce more units, thereby absorbing more overhead into production. This variance links with the capacity ratio calculated earlier in the chapter. The capacity ratio showed that only 80% of the budgeted capacity had been utilized, so probably not as much overhead was absorbed into production as had been originally expected.

4 Productivity = (total actual hours worked – total standard hours for actual production) × fixed production overhead absorption rate.

$$\text{Productivity variance} \therefore = (800 – 900) \times £2.00 = £200 \text{ (F)}$$

This variance shows the difference between the 900 standard hours that the work is worth (90 × 10 = 900 hours), compared with the amount of time that it took to produce those units (i.e. 800 hours). As was emphasized earlier, in a standard costing system overhead is absorbed on the basis of standard hours. Assuming that the budgeted fixed overhead expenditure had been equal to the actual fixed overhead expenditure, production would have been charged with £200 of extra overhead, because the 90 units were produced in less time than the standard allowance. The factory has been more efficient in producing the goods than might have been expected. This variance complements the efficiency ratio of 112.5% which was illustrated earlier in the chapter in Exhibit 18.3.

Remember that the capacity variance + the productivity variance = the volume variance.

$$\text{Volume variance} \therefore = £400 \text{ (A)} + £200 \text{ (F)} = £200 \text{ (A)}$$
$$\text{(see also 2 above).}$$

5 Fixed production overhead total variance.

This variance was calculated earlier (shown on the summary of variances in Exhibit 18.9). The simplified formula is as follows: Total = expenditure + volume:

$$= £400 \text{ (F)} + £200 \text{ (A)} = £200 \text{ (F)}$$

The actual activity was less than the budgeted activity. Thus, less fixed overhead was absorbed into production. However, the overhead expenditure was budgeted at a level of £2000, but the actual expenditure was only £1600. The over-estimate of expenditure, therefore, compensated for the over-estimate of activity. This means that the 90 units actually produced were charged £200 more of overhead than was necessary. If the selling price were based on the standard cost, it is possible that this over-estimate could make the eventual selling price of the products less competitive. In this example, the variance would appear to be very small.

A considerable number of variances have now been illustrated. Using the formulae listed on pages 403–4, you are now recommended to attempt Exhibit 18.9 without reference to the solution.

SALES VARIANCES

Sales variances are not common in practice, but if they are adopted there is a choice between two different types:

1 variances based on profit (using absorption costing);
2 variances based on contribution (using marginal costing).

Exhibit 18.10 shows sales variances based on absorption costing, while Exhibit 18.11 shows sales variances based on marginal costing.

The formulae used in calculating sales variances are summarized below. The summary is divided in two parts. The first part shows the formulae for sales variances based on profit, and the second part shows the formulae for sales variances based on contribution.

1 **Sales variances based on profit**

   (a) sales variances:

$$[\text{actual quantity} \times (\text{actual selling price per unit} - \text{standard cost per unit})]$$
$$- (\text{budgeted quantity} \times \text{standard profit per unit})$$

   (b) selling price variance:

$$\text{actual quantity} \times (\text{actual selling price per unit} -$$
$$\text{budgeted selling price per unit})$$

Exhibit 18.10 Analysis of sales variance using absorption costing

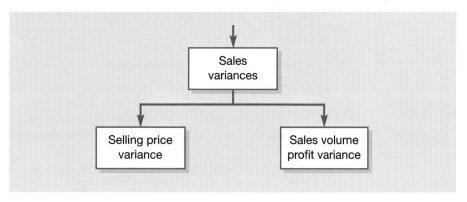

Exhibit 18.11 Analysis of sales variance using marginal costing

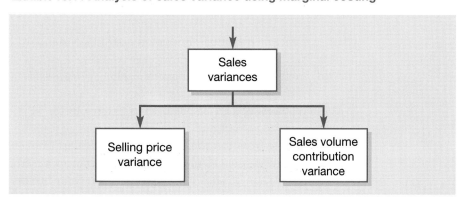

(c)   sales volume profit variance:

(actual quantity – budgeted quantity) × standard profit

(d)   note that the sales variances = selling price + sales volume.

These relationships are also shown in Exhibit 18.12.

Exhibit 18.12 Calculation of sales variances based on profit

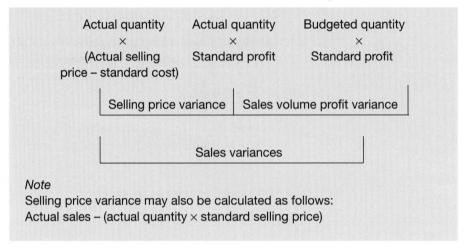

Note
Selling price variance may also be calculated as follows:
Actual sales – (actual quantity × standard selling price)

2 **Sales variance based on contribution**
   (a)   sales variances:

[actual quantity × (actual selling price per unit – standard
variable cost)] – (budgeted quantity × standard contribution)

(b)   selling price variance:

actual quantity × (actual selling price per unit – budgeted
selling price per unit)

(c)   sales volume contribution variance:

(actual quantity – budgeted quantity) × standard contribution

(d)   note that the sales variances = selling price + sales volume contribution.

These relationships are also shown in Exhibit 18.13.

You will note from the above formulae that, apart from substituting 'contribu-tion' for 'profit', the calculation of sales variances based on profit is identical to the calculation of sales variances based on contribution.

Exhibit 18.13 Calculation of sales variances based on contribution

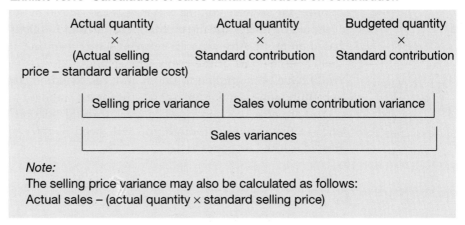

Note:
The selling price variance may also be calculated as follows:
Actual sales – (actual quantity × standard selling price)

The use of these formulae is illustrated in Exhibit 18.14.

Exhibit 18.14 Example using sales variance formulae

The following data relate to Frozen Limited for the year to 31 July 19X9:

	Budget/standard	Actual
Sales (units)	100	90
Selling price per unit	£10	£10.50
Standard absorption cost per unit	£7	–

Required:
Calculate the sales variances (based on profit).

Answer to Exhibit 18.14

(a) selling price variance:
   actual quantity × (actual selling price per unit – budgeted selling price per unit)= 90 × (10.50 – 10) = (90 × 0.5) = £45 (F)

The actual selling price per unit was £0.50 more than the standard selling price, so the variance is favourable. Other things being equal, the profit would be £45 higher.

(b) sales volume profit variance:
   (actual quantity – budgeted quantity) × standard profit
   = (90 – 100) × 3 = £30 (A)

This variance arises because the number of units sold fell below the budgeted level. Other things being equal, this would result in less profit of £30.

(c) sales variances:
   [actual quantity × (actual selling price per unit – standard cost per unit)] –
   (budgeted quantity × standard profit per unit)
   = [90 × (10.50 –7)] – (100 × 3)
   = 90 × 3.50 = 315 – 300 = £15 (F)

In Exhibit 18.14, the favourable selling price of £45 (or £0.50 per unit) helped to offset the adverse volume variance of £30 caused by selling ten fewer units. It should be noted that the standard cost is used in calculating sales variances based on profit. Any variance between actual costs and standard costs will be dealt with as part of the cost variance analysis. Also note that the Exhibit could have been applied to sales variances based on contribution simply be substituting the standard marginal cost for the standard absorption cost.

You are now recommended to work through Exhibit 18.14 without reference to the answer, although you will need to refer to the sales variance formulae listed on pages 411–3.

OPERATING STATEMENTS

As has been seen, the calculation of standard cost variances is a complex arithmetical process. The process can become more complicated if the variances outlined in the preceding sections are analysed into even more sub-variances (e.g. sales mix and sales quantity, and direct material mix and direct material yield). Fortunately, as a non-accountant, it is unlikely that you will ever have to calculate such variances for yourself. However, it is important for you to have some knowledge of how variances are calculated so that you are in a better position to investigate how they may have occurred. Indeed, your main role will probably be to carry out a detailed investigation of the causes of variances, and then to take any necessary corrective action.

It is, however, very difficult to carry out a meaningful variance analysis if you have no idea what you are supposed to be investigating. Hence, you ought to be able to define the main variances, and to have some knowledge of how they have been calculated so that you know where to begin looking for any discrepancies.

Once all the variances have been calculated, they may usefully be summarized in the form of an operating statement. There is no standardized format for such statements, but the one shown in Exhibit 18.15 is reasonably representative.

Exhibit 18.15 Preparation of a standard cost operating statement

Exhibit 18.9 gave some information relating to the Frost Production Company Limited for the year to 31 March 19X4. The cost data used in that exhibit will now be used in Exhibit in 18.15, but some additional information is required.

Additional information:
1 Assume that the budgeted sales were 100 units at a selling price of £150 per unit.
2 90 units were sold at £160 per unit.
3 Actual non-production overhead expenditure was as follows:

	£
Administration	750
Research and development	150
Selling and distribution	300

Required:
Prepare a standard cost operating statement for the year to 31 March 19X4.

Answer to Exhibit 18.15

Frost Production Company Limited standard cost operating statement for the year to 31 March 19X4:

	£
Budgeted profit [100 × (150 – 100)]	5000
Sales volume profit variance (1)	(500)
Standard margin of actual sales	4500
Selling price variance (2)	900
Actual margin of actual sales	5400

Cost variance: (3)	Adverse £	Favourable £	
Direct materials:			
Price		700	
Usage	100		
Direct labour:			
Rate	800		
Efficiency		400	
Variable production overhead			
Expenditure	200		
Efficiency		100	
Fixed production overhead			
Expenditure		400	
Capacity	400		
Productivity		200	
	1500	1800	300
Operating profit			5700
Less: Actual non-production overhead:			
Administration		750	
Research and development		150	
Selling and distribution		300	1200
Actual profit			£4500

Tutorial notes

1 Sales volume profit variance
    = (Actual quantity – budgeted quantity) × standard profit
    = (90 – 100) × 50 – £500 (A)

2 Selling price variance
= actual quantity × (actual selling price per unit – budgeted selling price per unit)
= 90 × (£160 – 150) = £900 (F)

3 Details of cost variances were shown in the answer to Exhibit 18.9 on page 406.

The format used in Exhibit 18.15 is particularly helpful because it shows the link between the budgeted profit and the actual profit. Thus, management can trace the main causes of sales and cost variances. In practice, the statement would also show the details for each product.

The operating profit statement will help management decide where to begin an investigation into the causes of the respective variances. It is unlikely that they will all need to be investigated. It may be company policy, for example, to investigate only those variances that are particularly significant, irrespective of whether they are favourable or adverse. In other words, only *exceptional* variances would be investigated, and a policy decision would have to be taken on what was meant by exceptional.

CONCLUSION

We have now come to the end of a long and complex chapter. You may have found that it has been extremely difficult to understand just how standard cost variances are calculated. Fortunately, it is unlikely that as a non-accountant you will ever have to calculate variances for yourself. It is sufficient for your purposes to understand their meaning, and to have some idea of the arithmetical foundation on which they are based.

Your job will largely be to investigate the causes of the variances, and to take necessary action. A standard costing system is supposed to help management plan and control the entity much more tightly than can be achieved in the absence of such a system. However, it can only be of real benefit if it is welcomed by those managers whom it is supposed to help. It can hardly be of help if it just produces a great deal of incomprehensible data. After reading this chapter, it is hoped that the data will now mean something to you.

In the next chapter we move on to deal with capital investment appraisal, but before doing so, you would be well advised to work your way through this chapter once again.

Key points

1 A standard cost is the planned cost of a particular unit or process.

2 Standard costs are usually based on what is reasonably attainable.

3 Actual costs are compared with standard costs.

4 Corrective action is taken if there are any unplanned trends.

5 Three performance measures used in standard costing are: the efficiency ratio, the capacity ratio, and the production volume ratio.

6 Variance analysis is an arithmetical exercise that enables differences between actual and standard costs to be broken down into the elements of cost.

7 The degree of analysis will vary, but usually a total cost variance will be analysed into direct material, direct labour, variable overhead and fixed overhead variances. In turn, these will be analysed into quantity and expenditure variances, although an even more detailed analysis is possible.

8 Sales variances may also be calculated, but they are not very common. There are two main types: sales variances based on profit, and sales variances based on contribution. Like cost variances, sales variances may also be analysed in greater detail, e.g. selling price and sales volume.

9 The variances help in tracing the main causes of differences between actual and budgeted results, but they do not explain what has actually happened.

CHECK YOUR LEARNING

1 What is a standard?

2 List four main steps in setting up a standard costing system.

3 Name three performance measures used in standard costing.

4 Complete the following equations:
   (a) _____ = direct material price + direct labour usage
   (b) Direct labour total = _____ + direct labour efficiency
   (c) Variable production overhead total = variable production expenditure + _____
   (d) Fixed production overhead total = fixed production expenditure + _____ + fixed productivity volume
   (e) Sales variances = _____ + sales volume profit

Answers
1 A predetermined measurable quantity set in defined conditions.
2 (a) set up a unit responsible for implementing it;
   (b) select an appropriate standard costing period;
   (c) determine the type of standard to be adopted;
   (d) obtain the information necessary to calculate the standards.
3 efficiency; capacity; production volume
4 (a) direct material total   (b) direct labour rate   (c) variable production overhead efficiency   (d) fixed production overhead capacity   (e) selling price

QUESTIONS

18.1
You are presented with the following information for X Limited:
Standard price per unit: £10.
Standard quantity for actual production: 5 units.
Actual price per unit: £12.
Actual quantity: 6 units.

Required:
Calculate the following variances:
1 direct materials cost variance;
2 direct materials price variance; and
3 direct materials usage variance.

18.2
The following information relates to Malcolm Limited:
Budgeted production: 100 units.
Unit specification (direct materials): 50 kilograms × £5 per kilogram = £250.
Actual production: 120 units.
Direct materials used: 5400 kilograms at a total cost of £32 400.

Required:
Calculate the following variances:
1 direct materials cost;
2 direct materials price; and
3 direct materials usage.

18.3
The following information relates to Bruce Limited:
Actual hours: 1000.
Actual wage rate per hour: £6.50.
Standard hours for actual production: 900.
Standard wage rate per hour: £6.00.

Required:
Calculate the following variances:
1 direct labour cost;
2 direct labour rate; and
3 direct labour efficiency.

18.4

You are presented with the following information for Duncan Limited:

Budgeted production: 1000 units.

Actual production: 1200 units.

Standard specification for one unit: 10 hours at £8 per direct labour hour.

Actual direct labour cost: £97 200 in 10 800 actual hours.

Required:

Calculate the following variances:

1 direct labour cost;
2 direct labour rate; and
3 direct labour efficiency.

18.5

The following overhead budget has been prepared for Anthea Limited:

Actual fixed overhead: £150 000.

Budgeted fixed overhead: £135 000.

Fixed overhead absorption rate per hour: £15.

Actual hours worked: 10 000.

Standard hours of production: 8000.

Required:

Calculate the following fixed overhead variances:

1 fixed production overhead variance;
2 expenditure variance;
3 volume variance;
4 capacity variance; and
5 productivity variance.

18.6

Using the data contained in the previous question, calculate the following performance measures:

1 efficiency ratio;
2 capacity ratio; and
3 production volume ratio.

18.7

The following information relates to Osprey Limited:

Budgeted production: 500 units.

Standard hours per unit: 10.

Actual production: 600 units.

Budgeted fixed overhead: £125 000.

Actual fixed overhead: £120 000.

Actual hours worked: 4900.

Required:

Calculate the following fixed overhead variances:

1 fixed production overhead;
2 expenditure;
3 volume;
4 capacity; and
5 productivity.

18.8
Using the data from the previous question, calculate the following performance measures:
1   efficiency ratio;
2   capacity ratio; and
3   production volume ratio.

18.9
Milton Limited has produced the following information:
Total actual sales: £99 000.
Actual quantity sold: 9000 units.
Budgeted selling price per unit: £10.
Standard variable cost per unit: £7.
Total budgeted units: 10 000 units.

Required:
Calculate the sales variances.

18.10
You are presented with the following information for Doe Limited:

Budget sales	100 units
Per unit:	
Budget selling price	£30
Less: Budget variable cost	20
Contribution	10
Actual sales	120 units
Actual selling price per unit	£28

Required:
Calculate the sales variances.

18.11
The following data relate to Judith Limited:

	Budget specification	
Production at sales budget		2 000 units
Per unit	£	£
Selling price		150
Less: Variable costs:		
Direct materials (7 kilos × £10 per kilo)	70	
Direct wages (5 DLH × £5 per DLH)	25	
Fixed overhead (5 DLH × £6 F.OAR)	30	125
Budgeted profit per unit		£25
Actual production and sales		2 200 units
Actual selling price per unit		£145
Actual cost:		
Direct material (8 kilos × £9 per kilo)		£72 per unit
Direct wages (4 DLH × £6 per DLH)		£24 per unit
Total actual fixed overhead		£65 000

Required:
(a) Calculate the following performance measures:
    1 efficiency ratio;
    2 capacity ratio; and
    3 production volume ratio.
(b) Calculate the following variances:
    1 selling price;
    2 sales volume contribution;
    3 sales variances (in total);
    4 direct materials cost;
    5 direct materials price;
    6 direct materials usage;
    7 direct labour cost;
    8 direct labour rate variance;
    9 direct labour efficiency;
    10 fixed production overhead;
    11 fixed production overhead expenditure;
    12 fixed production overhead volume;
    13 fixed production overhead capacity; and
    14 fixed production overhead productivity.
(c) Prepare the standard cost operating statement for the period.

ADDITIONAL QUESTIONS (WITHOUT ANSWERS)

18.12

The budgeted selling price and standard cost of a unit manufactured by Smillie Limited is as follows:

	£
Selling price	30
Direct materials (2.5 kilos)	5
Direct labour (2 hours)	12
Fixed production overhead	8
	25
Budgeted profit	5

Total budgeted sales: 400 units

During the period to 31 December 19X2, the actual sales and production details were as follows:

	£
Sales (400 units)	13 440
Direct materials (1260 kilos)	2 268
Direct labour (800 hours)	5 200
Fixed production overhead	3 300
	10 768
Profit	2 672

Required:
Prepare a standard cost operating statement for the period to 31 December 19X2.

18.13

Mean Limited manufactures a single product, and the following information relates to the actual selling price and actual cost of the product for the four weeks to 31 March 19X3:

	£000
Sales (50 000 units)	2250
Direct materials (240 000 hours)	528
Direct labour (250 000 hours)	1375
Variable production overhead	245
Fixed production overhead	650
	2798
Loss	(548)

The budgeted selling price and standard cost of each unit was as follows:

	£
Selling price	55
Direct materials (5 litres)	10
Direct labour (4 hours)	20
Variable production overhead	5
Fixed production overhead	15
	50
Budgeted profit	5

Total budgeted production: 40 000 units.

Required:
Prepare a standard cost operating statement for the four weeks to 31 March 19X3, utilizing as many variances as the data permit.

DISCUSSION QUESTIONS

18.14

Is it likely that a standard costing system is of any relevance in a service industry?

18.15

'Standard costing is all about number crunching, and for someone on the shop floor, it has absolutely no relevance.' Do you agree with this statement?

18.16

'Sales variance calculations are just another example of accountants playing around with numbers.' Discuss.

CHAPTER 19

Capital expenditure and investment

Allen asks for extra £16m

ALLEN, the plant hire-to-housebuilding group, has celebrated its 50th birthday this year with record profits, and is asking shareholders for £16 million to fund future growth.

Profits in the year to the end of March rose 26.8 per cent to £7.9 million, fuelled by a 44 per cent jump in operating profits in its hire services division to £4.4 million. The final dividend is 4.15p, up from 3.5p, lifting the total to 6.65p from 5.5p.

Hire services, which runs 114 depots under the Speedy name, has expanded rapidly through acquisitions and organic growth.

The cost of acquisitions, together with spending on land for housebuilding and capital equipment, has lifted Allen's gearing level, the ratio of borrowings to shareholders' funds, to 74 per cent, above the 60 per cent normal internal limits of the group.

Allen has launched a rights issue offering one new share at 250p for every five held, against yesterday's unchanged closing price of 283p, to raise £16 million, which will cut gearing to 17 per cent and enable the company to continue its expansion.

The Scotsman, 28 June 1996

Exhibit 19.0 A rights issue is one way of financing capital expenditure

As was seen in Chapter 17, the budgetary process usually starts with the preparation of the sales forecast. The forecast then enables the production manager to assess whether he is likely to have the productive capacity to meet it. If the capacity is not available, then the sales budgets will have to be prepared on what can be produced. In the long run, of course, the entity will want to maximize its sales. If the forecasts suggest a sustained growth in sales, therefore, additional capital expenditure may be required, such as for new factories, plant, and equipment. Expenditure on such proposals is known as *capital investment* (CI), and accountants refer to the process of investigating them as *capital investment appraisal*. CIMA defines capital investment appraisal as follows:

> **Capital investment appraisal:** an evaluation of the costs and benefits of a proposed investment in operating assests.

Thus capital investment may be considered to be part of the capital budgeting process. It involves both the selection of long-term investments and the financing of them, and these are the matters that are going to be considered in this chapter. We are only going to deal with them briefly, however, as the detailed considerations are well outside the scope of this book. The main purpose is to give you an overall appreciation of what is involved in capital investment appraisal, as it is unlikely that as a non-accountant you will have to deal with the involved arithmetical calculations. We intend to use only simple examples, but these should enable you to grasp the main principles behind the technique.

The chapter is divided into three main sections. In the first section, we outline the background to CI appraisal. The following section examines the main accounting techniques used in selecting individual projects, and the final section summarizes the main sources of finance available for capital investment.

Learning objectives	**By the end of this chapter, you will be able to:**

- **describe what is meant by capital investment appraisal;**
- **identify five capital investment appraisal techniques;**
- **recognize the significance of such techniques;**
- **list three main sources of financing capital investment projects.**

BACKGROUND

We explained in an earlier chapter that accountants distinguish between capital expenditure and revenue expenditure (the same distinction also applies to income). The actual delineation between capital and revenue is somewhat imprecise. Generally, any expenditure that is likely to be of benefit in more than one accounting period is to be classed as capital expenditure. The more formal definition, of capital expenditure offered by CIMA is:

> **Capital expenditure:** the cost of acquiring, producing or enhancing fixed assets.

The CIMA definition of a fixed asset is as follows:

> **Fixed asset:** any asset, tangible or intangible, acquired for retention by an entity for the purpose of providing a service to the business, and not held for resale in the normal course of trading.

By contrast, revenue expenditure is expenditure that is of benefit in only one time period. The CIMA definition is:

> **Revenue expenditure:** expenditure on the manufacture of goods, the provision of services or on the general conduct of the entity, which is charged to the profit and loss account in the accounting period of sale.

In this chapter, we are primarily concerned with capital expenditure, and we can see from the above definition that it is likely to have a number of important characteristics. These can be summarized as follows:

1 it will probably involve substantial expenditure;
2 the benefits may be spread over very many years;
3 it is difficult to predict what the benefits will be;
4 it will help the company to achieve its organizational objectives;
5 it will have some impact on the company's employees.

Indeed, if the company is to survive, and especially if it wants to grow, it will need to invest continuously in capital projects. Existing fixed assets will begin to wear out, and more efficient ones will become available. Furthermore, capital expenditure may be required not just in the administration, production, and stores departments, but also on social and recreational facilities. Similarly in the public sector, universities and colleges may be faced with capital expenditure decisions that go beyond providing lecture halls and tutorial rooms, e.g. student accommodation and union facilities.

Irrespective of where the demand for capital expenditure arises, however, all entities face two common problems: (a) the priority to be given to individual projects; and (b) how they can be financed. Hence, competing projects will need to be ranked according to either their importance, or their potential profitability.

The techniques involved in the selection of projects are examined in the next section.

SELECTING PROJECTS

There is little point in investing in a project unless it is likely to make a profit. The exceptions are those projects that are necessary on health, social, and welfare grounds, and these are particularly difficult to assess. In other cases, there are five main techniques that accountants can use in CI appraisal. They are shown in diagrammatic form in Exhibit 19.1. They are examined in each of the following sub-sections.

Payback

The payback method is an attempt to estimate how long it would take before a project begins to pay for itself. For example, if a company was going to spend £300 000 on purchasing some new plant, the accountant would calculate how many years it would take before £300 000 had been received back in cash. The recovery of an investment in a project is usually measured in terms of *net cash flow*. Net cash flow is the difference between cash received and cash paid during a defined period of time. In order to adopt this method, therefore, the following information is required:

1 the total cost of the investment;
2 the amount of cash instalments to be paid back on the investment;
3 the accounting periods in which the instalments will be paid;
4 the cash receipts and and any other cash payments connected with the project;
5 the accounting periods in which they fall.

As this method measures the rate of recovery of the original investment in terms of net cash flow, it follows that non-cash items (such as depreciation, and profits and losses on sales of fixed assets) are not taken into account.

Exhibit 19.1 Methods of capital investment appraisal

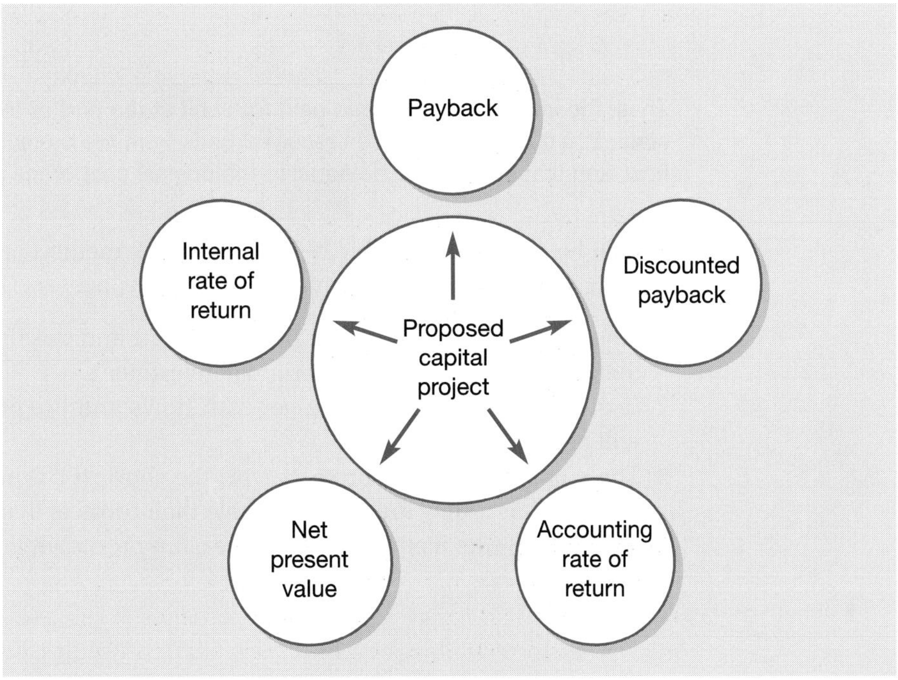

The payback method is illustrated in Exhibit 19.2.

Exhibit 19.2 The payback method

Miln Limited is considering investing in some new machinery. The following information has been prepared to support the project:

	£000	£000
Cost of machinery		20
Expected net cash flow:		
Year 1	1	
2	4	
3	5	
4	10	
5	10	30
Net profitability		£10

Required:
Calculate the prospective investment's payback period.

Answer to Exhibit 19.2

The payback period is as follows:

	£000
Cumulative net cash flow:	
Year 1	1
2	5
3	10
4	20
5	30

Thus, the investment will have paid for itself at the end of the fourth year. At that stage £20 000 will have been received back from the project in terms of net cash flow, and that sum would be equal to the original cost of the project.

As can be seen from Exhibit 19.2, the payback method is a fairly straightforward technique, but it does have several disadvantages. These are as follows:

1 An estimate has to be made of the amount and the timing of cash instalments due to be paid on the original investment.
2 It is difficult to calculate the net cash flows and the period in which they will be received.
3 There is a danger that projects with the shortest payback periods may be chosen even if they are less profitable than projects that have a longer payback period (the method does not measure profitability, only cash flow).

4 The total amount of the overall investment is ignored, and comparisons made between different projects may result in a misleading conclusion. Thus a project with an initial investment of £10 000 may have a shorter payback period than one with an initial investment of £100 000, although in the long run the larger investment may prove more profitable.

5 The technique ignores any net cash flows received after the payback period.

6 The timing of the cash flows is not taken into account: £1 received now is preferable to £1 received in five years' time. Thus, a project with a short payback period may recover most of its investment towards the end of its payback period while another project with a longer payback period may recover most of the original investment in the first few years. There is clearly less risk in accepting a project which recovers most of its cost very quickly than there is in accepting one where the benefits are much more long term.

Notwithstanding these disadvantages, the payback method has something to be said for it. While it may appear to be rather simplistic, it does help managers to compare projects, and to think in terms of how long it takes before a project has recovered its original cost. The timing problem can also be overcome by adopting what is called the *discounted payback method*.

Discounted payback

As was explained above, the simple payback method ignores the timing of net cash receipts. This problem can be overcome by *discounting* the net cash receipts. You will probably be familiar with discounting in your everyday life. You know, for example, that if you put £91 into the building society, and the rate of interest is 10% per annum, your original investment will be worth about £100 [£91 + 9 (10% × 91)] at the end of the year. We could look at this example from another point of view. Assuming a rate of interest of 10% per annum, what amount of money do you have to invest in the building society in order to have £100 at the end of the year? The answer is, of course, £91 (ignoring the old 10p). In other words, £91 received now is about the same as £100 received in a year's time. This is what is meant by *discounting*. The procedure is as follows:

1 future net cash flows are calculated;
2 an appropriate rate of interest is estimated;
3 the net cash flows are then reduced to their *present value* by multiplying them by a discount factor.

In the case of the building society example above, the discount factor is actually 0.9091 (i.e. £100 × 0.9091 = £90.91). To check: take the £90.91 and add the year's interest, i.e. (90.91 × 10% = 9.091 + 90.91 = 100.00). You will not have to calculate discount factors: these are available in readily available tables, and one is included in Appendix 2 on page 459.

To check that you understand the point about discounting, turn to Appendix 2. Look along the top line for the appropriate rate of interest: in this case it is 10%. Work down the 10% column until you come to the line opposite the year (shown in the left-hand column) in which the cash would be received. In this example, the cash is going to be received in one year's time, so it is not necessary to go further than the first line. The present value of £1 receivable in a year's time is, therefore, £0.9091, or £90.91 if £100 is to be received in a year's time.

In order to confirm that you follow the principle behind discounting, try the following example. Assuming a rate of interest of 15% per annum, what is the present value of £200 receivable in three years' time? Consult Appendix 2. The answer is £151.22 (£200 × 0.7561).

You can check this as follows:

	£
At the beginning of the year:	151.22
At the end of year 1, add 15% (151.22 × 15%):	22.69*
	173.91
At the end of year 2, add 15% (173.90 × 15%):	26.09
Total	200.00

* This should really be 22.68. The discount table used in Appendix 2 only goes to four places of decimals, and so some rounding up is usually necessary.

Do you feel reasonably confident that you now know what is meant by the net present value of future net cash flows, and what is involved in discounting? If so, we can move on to examine how discounting can be applied to the payback method (see Exhibit 19.3).

Exhibit 19.3 The discounted payback method

Newland District Council has investigated the possibility of investing in a new project, and the following information has been obtained:

	£000	£000
Total cost of project		500
Expected net cash flows:		
Year 1	20	
2	50	
3	100	
4	200	
5	300	
6	30	700
Net return		£200

Required:
Assuming a rate of interest of 8%, calculate the project's overall return using the following methods:
(a) payback; and
(b) discounted payback.

Answer to Exhibit 19.3

Year	Net cash flow	Cumulative net cash flow	Discount factors	Present value at 8%	Cumulative present value
	£000	£000		£000	£000
0	(500)	(500)	1.0000	(500)	(500)
1	20	(480)	0.9259	19	(481)
2	50	(430)	0.8573	43	(438)
3	100	(330)	0.7938	79	(359)
4	200	(130)	0.7350	147	(212)
5	300	170	0.6860	206	(6)
6	30	200	0.6302	19	13

Using the payback method, the project will have paid for itself after 4 years. However, by discounting the net cash flows, the project will not have paid for itself until after the fifth year. Note also that by using this method, this particular project only just recovers the initial investment.

The discounted payback method has the following advantages:

1 It is relatively easy to understand.
2 It is not too difficult to compute.
3 It focuses on the cash recovery of an investment.
4 It does allow for the fact that cash received now may be worth more than cash receivable in the future.
5 It takes into account more of the net cash flows, since the discounted payback period is always longer than under the simple payback method.
6 It enables a clear-cut decision to be taken, since a project is acceptable if the discounted net cash flow throughout its life exceeds the cost of the original investment.

However, like the simple payback method, it has some disadvantages. These are as follows:

1 It is sometimes difficult to estimate the amount and timing of instalments due to be paid on the original investment.
2 It is difficult to estimate the amount and timing of future net cash receipts and other payments.
3 It is not easy to determine an appropriate rate of interest.
4 In arriving at a decision, net cash flows received after the payback period are ignored.

Irrespective of these disadvantages, the discounted payback method can be usefully and readily adopted by those entities that do not employ staff specially trained in capital investment appraisal techniques.

Accounting rate of return

The accounting rate of return (*ARR*) method attempts to compare the *profit* of a project with the capital invested in it. It is usually expressed as a percentage, i.e.:

$$\text{ARR} = \frac{\text{Profit}}{\text{Capital employed}} \times 100$$

Two important problems arise from this definiton. These may be summarized as follows:

1 The definition of profit. Normally, the average annual net profit earned by the project would be used. However, as was explained in earlier chapters, accounting profit can be subject to a number of different assumptions and distortions (e.g. depreciation, taxation, and inflation), and so it is relatively easy to arrive at different profit levels depending upon the accounting policies adopted. The most common definition is to take profit before interest and taxation. The profit included in the equation would then be a simple average of the profit the project earns over its entire life.
2 The definition of capital employed. The capital employed could be either the initial capital employed in the project, or the average capital employed over its life.

Thus, depending upon the definitions adopted, the ARR may be calculated in one of two ways, as follows:

1 Using the original capital employed:

$$\text{ARR} = \frac{\text{average annual net profit before interest and taxation}}{\text{initial capital employed on the project}} \times 100$$

2 Using the average capital employed:

$$\text{ARR} = \frac{\text{average annual net profit before interest and taxation}}{\text{average annual capital employed on the project *}} \times 100$$

$$* = \frac{\text{initial capital employed} + \text{residual value}}{2}$$

The two methods are illustrated in Exhibit 16.4.

Exhibit 19.4 The accounting rate of return method

Bridge Limited is considering investing in a new project, the details of which are as follows:

Project life		5 years
	£000	£000
Project cost		50
Estimated net profit:		
Year 1	12	
2	18	
3	30	
4	25	
5	5	
Total net profit	£90	

The estimated residual value of the project at the end of year 5 is £10 000.

Required:
Calculate the accounting rate of return of the proposed new project.

Answer to Exhibit 19.4

The accounting rate of return would be calculated as follows:
(a)   Using the initial capital employed:

$$\frac{\text{Average annual net profits}}{\text{Cost of the investment}} \times 100$$

Average annual net profits = 18 000 (90 000/5)

$$\therefore \text{Accounting rate of return} = \frac{18\ 000}{50\ 000} \times 100 = \underline{\underline{36\%}}$$

(b)   Using the average capital employed:

$$\frac{\text{Average annual net profits}}{\text{Average capital employed}} \times 100$$

$$= \frac{18\ 000}{\frac{1}{2}\ (50\ 000 + 10\ 000)} \times 100 = \underline{\underline{60\%}}$$

Like the payback and discounted payback methods, the accounting rate of return method has several advantages and disadvantages. These are as follows:

Advantages
1 The method is compatible with a similar accounting ratio used in financial accounting.
2 It is relatively easy to understand.
3 It is not difficult to compute.
4 It draws attention to the notion of overall profit.

Disadvantages
1 Net profit can be subject to different definitions, e.g. it can mean net profit before or after allowing for depreciation on the project.
2 It is not always clear whether the original cost of the investment should be used, or whether it is more appropriate to substitute an average for the amount of capital invested in the project.
3 The use of a residual value in calculating the average amount of capital employed means that the higher the residual value, the lower the ARR, e.g. with no residual value, the ARR on a project costing £100 000 and an average net profit of £50 000 would be 100%, i.e.:

$$\frac{50\,000}{\frac{1}{2} \times (100\,000 + 0)} \times 100 = 100\%$$

whereas with a residual value of (say) £10 000, the ARR would be 90.9%, i.e.:

$$\frac{50\,000}{\frac{1}{2} \times (100\,000 + 10\,000)} \times 100 = 90.9\%$$

Estimating residual values is very difficult, and so the assumption adopted can make all the difference between one project and another.
4 The method gives no guidance on what is an acceptable rate of return.
5 The benefit of earning a high proportion of the total profit in the early years of the project is not allowed for.
6 It does not take into account the time value of money.

With all of these disadvantages, you might wonder whether the ARR method can ever be used. However, it may be suitable where very similar short-term projects are being considered.

Net present value

One of the main disadvantages of both the payback and ARR methods of CI appraisal is that they ignore the time value of money. This concept has already been explained when the discounted payback method was examined.

There are two other methods that also follow this concept: the net present value method, and the internal rate of return method. In this sub-section, the net present value (NPV) method is examined.

The NPV method recognizes that cash received today is preferable to cash receivable sometime in the future. There is more risk in having to wait for future cash receipts and, while a smaller sum, may be obtained now, at least it is available for other purpose For example, it can be invested, and the subsequent rate of return may then compensate for the smaller amount received now (or at least be equal to it).

As was seen earlier in the chapter, £91 received now (assuming a rate of interest of 10%) is just as beneficial as receiving £100 in a year's time. This is also the principle behind the NPV method of CI appraisal. Basically, it involves taking the following steps:

1 the annual net cash flows expected to arise from the project are calculated;
2 an appropriate rate of interest, or required rate of return is selected;
3 the discount factors appropriate to the chosen rate of interest or return is obtained;
4 the annual net cash flow is multiplied by the appropriate discount factors;
5 the present values for each of the net cash flows are added together;
6 the total net present value is compared with the initial outlay;
7 the project may be accepted if the total NPV is positive (a negative factor might suggest that the project should be rejected, but other factors would have to be taken into account).

This procedure is outlined in Exhibit 19.5.

Exhibit 19.5 The net present value method

Rage Limited is considering two capital investment projects. The details are outlined as follows:

Project	1	2
Estimated life	3 years	5 years
Commencement date	1.1.X1	1.1.X1
	£000	£000
Project cost at 1.01.X1	100	100
Estimated net cash flows:		
Year to: 31.12.X1	20	10
31.12.X2	80	40
31.12.X3	40	40
31.12.X4	–	40
31.12.X5	–	20

The company expects a rate of return of 10% per annum on its capital employed.

Required:
Using the net present value method of project appraisal, assess which project would be more profitable.

Answer to Exhibit 19.5

RAGE LIMITED

Project appraisal:

Year	*Net cash flow*	*Project 1 Discount factor*	*Present value*	*Net cash flow*	*Project 2 Discount factor*	*Present value*
	£	10%	£	£	10%	£
31.12.X1	20 000	0.9091	18 182	10 000	0.9091	9 091
31.12.X2	80 000	0.8264	66 112	40 000	0.8264	33 056
31.12.X3	40 000	0.7513	30 052	40 000	0.7513	30 052
31.12.X4	–	–	–	40 000	0.6830	27 320
31.12.X5	–	–	–	20 000	0.6209	12 418
Total present value			114 346			111 937
Less: Initial cost			100 000			100 000
Net present value			£14 346			£11 937

Tutorial notes
The discount factors have been obtained from the discount table shown in Appendix 2.

Although both projects have a positive NPV, project 1 should be chosen in preference to project 2, because its NPV is higher.

The advantages and disadvantages of the NPV method are as follows:

Advantages
1 Using net cash flows emphasizes the importance of liquidity.
2 Different accounting policies are not of relevance, as they do not affect the calculation of the net cash flows.
3 The time value of money is taken into account.
4 It is easy to compare the NPV of different projects, and to reject projects that do not have an acceptable NPV.

Disadvantages
1 Some difficulties may be incurred in estimating the initial cost of the project and the time periods in which instalments must be paid back (this is a common problem in CI appraisal).

2 It is difficult to estimate accurately the net cash flow for each year of the project's life (a difficulty which is again common to most other methods of project appraisal).

3 It is not easy to select an appropriate rate of interest: this is sometimes referred to as the *cost of capital*, i.e. the cost of financing an investment. One rate that could be chosen is that rate which the company could earn if it decided to invest the funds outside the business (the external rate of interest). Alternatively, an internal rate of interest could be chosen. This rate would be based on an estimate of what return the company expects to earn on its existing investments. In the long run, if its internal rate of return is lower than the external rate, then it would appear more profitable to liquidate the company and invest the funds elsewhere. A local authority, however, may not have the same difficulty, because it would probably use a rate of interest which is set by central government.

NPV is considered to be a highly acceptable method of CI appraisal. It does take into account the timing of the net cash flows, the project's profitability, and the return of the original investment. However, an entity would not necessarily accept a project just because it had an acceptable NPV, as there are many non-financial factors that must be allowed for. Furthermore, other less profitable projects may go ahead, perhaps because they are concerned with employee safety or welfare.

Internal rate of return method

An alternative method of investment appraisal based on discounted net cash flow is known as the *internal rate of return* (IRR). This method is very similar to the NPV method. However, instead of discounting the expected net cash flows by a predetermined rate of return, the IRR method seeks to answer the following question:

> What rate of return would be required in order to ensure that the total NPV equals the total initial cost?

In theory, a rate of return that was lower than the entity's required rate of return would be rejected. In practice, however, the IRR would only be one factor to be taken into account in deciding whether to go ahead with the project. The method is illustrated in Exhibit 19.6.

Exhibit 19.6 The internal rate of return method

Bruce Limited is considering whether to invest £50 000 in a new project. The project's expected net cash flows would be as follows:

Year	£000
1	7
2	25
3	30
4	5

Required:
Calculate the internal rate of return for the proposed new project.

Answer to Exhibit 19.6

BRUCE LIMITED
Calculation of the internal rate of return:

Step 1: Select two discount rates
The first step is to select two discount rates, and then calculate the net present value of the project. The two rates usually have to be chosen quite arbitrarily, although they should preferably cover a narrow range. One of the rates should produce a positive rate of return, and the other rate a negative rate of return. As far as this question is concerned, rates of 10% and 15% will be chosen to illustrate the method.

Year	Net cash flow	Discount factors		Present value	
				10%	15%
	£	10%	15%	£	£
1	7 000	0.9091	0.8696	6 364	6 087
2	25 000	0.8264	0.7561	20 660	18 903
3	30 000	0.7513	0.6575	22 539	19 725
4	5 000	0.6830	0.5718	3 415	2 859
Total present values				52 978	47 574
Initial cost				50 000	50 000
Net present value				£2 978	£(2 426)

The project is expected to cost £50 000. If the company expects a rate of return of 10%, the project will be accepted, because the NPV is positive. However, if the required rate of return is 15% it will not be accepted, because its NPV is negative. The maximum rate of return that will ensure a positive rate of return must, therefore, lie somewhere between 10% and 15%, so the next step is to calculate the rate of return at which the project would just pay for itself.

Step 2: Calculate the rate of return
To do so, it is necessary to interpolate between the rates used in Step 1. This can be done by using the following formula:

$$IRR = \text{Positive rate} + \left\{ \frac{\text{Positive NPV}}{\text{Positive NPV} + \text{Negative NPV*}} \times \text{Range of rates} \right\}$$

*The negative sign is ignored.

Thus: IRR $= 10\% + \left\{\dfrac{2978}{(2\,978 + 2426)} \times (15\% - 10\%)\right\}$

$= 10\% + (0.5511 \times 5\%)$

$= 10\% + 2.76\%$

$= \underline{12.76\%}$

The project will be profitable provided that the company does not require a rate of return in excess of about 13%. Note that the method of calculation used above does not give the precise rate of return (because the formula is only an approximation), but it is adequate enough for decision-making purposes.

Exhibit 19.6 demonstrates that the IRR method is similar to the NPV method: (a) the initial cost of the project has to be estimated, as well as the future net cash flows arising from the project; and (b) the net cash flows are then discounted to their net present value using discount tables.

The main difference between the two methods is that the IRR method requires a rate of return to be estimated in order to give an NPV equal to the initial cost of the investment. The main difficulty arises in deciding which two rates of return to use, one which will give a positive NPV or one which will give a negative NPV. The range between the two rates should be as narrow as possible. You will find that if you use a trial and error method, you may have to try many times before you arrive at two suitable rates!

The advantages and disadvantages of the IRR method may be summarized as follows:

Advantages
1 Care has to be taken in estimating the initial cost of a project.
2 Emphasis is placed on liquidity.
3 Attention is given to the timing of net cash flows.
4 An appropriate rate of return does not have to be calculated.
5 It gives a clear percentage return on an investment.

Disadvantages
1 It is not easy to understand.
2 It is difficult to determine which of two suitable rates to adopt unless a computer is used.
3 It gives only an approximate rate of return.
4 In complex CI situations, it can give some misleading results, e.g. where there are negative net cash flows in subsequent years, and where there are mutually exclusive projects.

As a non-accountant, you do not need to be too worried about the details of such rather technical considerations. All you need to know is that, in practice, the IRR method has to be used with some caution. This takes us on to the choice of method.

Choice of method and other points

The description of CI appraisal techniques has been kept deliberately simple. Non-accountants will not normally be expected to involve themselves in the detailed calculations behind the various methods. You will, however, want to know which method your accountant is using, and the major disadvantages of each. For example, you should question him most carefully if he uses the ARR method. Why? Could he not at least try the discounted payback method? Why has the NPV method not been used?

It is suggested that unless there are very good reasons why your entity is unable to adopt it, you should adopt the NPV method. Otherwise, go for the discounted payback method. The ARR method is not recommended, and it is not necessary for most entities to become involved in complex IRR calculations.

There are two other matters that ought to be mentioned before this section is left: the effect of inflation and taxation on CI appraisal.

1 The effect of inflation (i.e. when prices go up, £1 now is worth less than £1 receivable in the future) can be taken into account in either of two ways:
   (a) by including an allowance for inflation in the calculation of net cash flows, e.g. it might be assumed that £1 now will be the same as £1.20 in a year's time;
   (b) by amending the expected rate of return to allow for inflation, i.e. the return will have to be higher; so that instead of (say) 8% per annum, it might have to be 10%.
2 The effect of taxation. Often there is a time-lag between when the profit is earned on a project, when cash is received for it, and when tax will be payable on the profits. Also, some tax allowances may be given on certain types of capital investment. Thus the timing of taxation payments will have an important effect on the calculation of net cash flows.

Inflation and taxation are just two of the problems inherent in determining future net cash flows. No doubt you will have begun to see why in practice such an exercise is difficult and complex. Happily, as a manager, you can leave the details to your accountant, but at least you should now be in a position to ask him some searching questions to make sure that you know what he is doing – and why.

Once the entity has decided which projects to accept, it has then to find the funds to finance them.

SOURCES OF FINANCE

As far as a company is concerned, there are basically five main sources of funds available for financing capital investments. They are as follows:

1 **From retained profits.** For most companies, this is probably the main source of funds.

2 **By issuing more shares for cash.** This can be an expensive administrative operation. If preference shares are issued, the company is committing itself to paying preference dividends. If it issues ordinary shares, the total amount of ordinary dividends paid out is likely to increase, even if the same rate of dividend is maintained. Thus, if its profits do not match its expectations, the company may have difficulty in meeting a higher amount of dividend.

3 **By long-term borrowing.** The company could issue debentures to pay for its capital investment programme. The debenture interest would be allowable against corporation tax, but the company could become very high geared if it issued more long-term debt. This might cause a problem if profits began to decline and it was committed to paying out a high proportion of its earnings in the form of debenture interest.

4 **By short-term borrowing.** This may be achieved by delaying payments to trade creditors, or by obtaining overdraft facilities at the bank. Capital investments financed by short-term borrowings are clearly very risky: loans may be called in at short notice, and they may not be renewable.

5 **By leasing and hire purchase contracts.** In the last 20 years or so, leasing has become a popular way of obtaining the use of fixed assets, probably because of the substantial tax advantages which the method used to attract. These tax advantages have now been reduced, and leasing as a form of financing is not quite as popular as it used to be. Hire purchase is also a quite common form of financing, but it is an expensive method as a result of the high rate of interest which is usually charged on such arrangements.

Not-for-profit entities, such as local authorities and large charities, also have formidable problems in CI appraisal. A local authority, for example, will be severely constrained by central government in the amount that it is allowed to borrow for capital investment. It cannot issue shares in the same way that a company can, although it can borrow money from the general public on a long-term basis. In fact, a local authority may raise finance for capital expenditure from a number of sources: (a) by obtaining loans and grants from central government and other bodies (such as the EU); (b) by borrowing on the open market; (c) by providing for it out of revenue (i.e. through the council tax); and (d) by making leasing and hire purchase arrangements. A charity can similarly borrow, lease and hire, but it may also be able to depend on a substantial level of donations and legacies.

You will recall that in an earlier part of this chapter, it was argued that CI appraisal forms part of the budgeting process. The budget will have identified what projects need to be undertaken. Usually there are so many competing ones that the entity has to rank them in some order of priority. Some priority has also to be given to those projects that do not necessarily contribute directly to profit, such as those that are perhaps necessary on health, social or welfare grounds. In the case of a local authority, there will be competing claims for the replacement of schools or the building of new social service centres. Such claims cannot really be based on 'profitability', and the calculation of 'net cash flow' is largely irrelevant, so it is difficult to use the techniques that have been outlined in this chapter.

In such instances, capital expenditure may have to be based on an estimate of 'need', i.e. a concept that is difficult to define. Hence, a decision to build a school in a certain area may be determined by the projected growth in the child population in that area, or it may be related to the fact that the local primary school is over 100 years old. When it comes to a decision by the full council (instead of the education committee), such considerations may be overturned because of a perceived need to satisfy electors in an entirely different part of the district. Indeed, if there are several high-ranking claims, the decision will inevitably be taken on political grounds.

In a commercial context, however, capital expenditure programmes will be determined partly by financial and partly by non-financial considerations, and the results of a CI appraisal method (such as the ones outlined earlier in this chapter) will form only part of the overall decision. The projects that are approved will need to be so scheduled that the implementation of them matches the availability of the finance (irrespective of its source). In most circumstances, companies finance their capital expenditure programmes out of retained earnings, but with large projects they may have to issue more shares or engage in long-term borrowing. If this is the case, there may well be a considerable time-lag before a project can proceed.

CONCLUSION

CI appraisal is a complex and time-consuming exercise. It is not possible to be totally accurate in determining the viability of individual projects, but a reasoned comparison can be made between them.

Managers tend to be very enthusiastic about their own sphere of responsibility. Thus, the marketing manager may be sure that additional sales will be possible, the production director certain that a new machine will pay for itself, and the data processing manager convinced that a new computer is essential.

In choosing between such competing projects, the accountant's role is to try to assess their costs, and to compare them with the possible benefits. Once a choice has been made, he then has to ensure that the necessary finance will be available for them. CI appraisal should not be used as a means of blocking new projects. It is no different from all the other accounting techniques. It is meant to provide additional guidance to management, and, ultimately, it is the responsibility of management to ensure that other factors are taken into account.

Key points

1 **Capital investment appraisal forms part of the budgeting process.**

2 **There are five main methods of determining the viability of a project:**

> (a) payback;
> (b) discounted payback;
> (c) accounting rate of return;
> (d) net present value;
> (e) internal rate of return.
>
> 3 All these methods have their advantages and disadvantages, but the recommended methods are discounted payback and net present value.
>
> 4 Capital expenditure may be financed out of a variety of sources: by short-term and long-term borrowing, and by leasing and hire purchase. A company may also finance projects out of retained profits and by issuing shares, while a not-for-profit entity may use revenue income, grants, special loans, and legacies.

CHECK YOUR LEARNING

1 Insert the missing word or words in each of the following statements:
   (a) The evaluation of costs and benefits of proposed investments in specific fixed assets is known as _____ _____ _____.
   (b) The _____ of _____ is the cost of financing an investment, expressed as a percentage rate.
   (c) _____ _____ _____ refers to the discounting of the net cash flows of a capital project to ascertain present value.

2 List five methods used in capital investment appraisal.

3 Identify (a) three main sources of finance available to a limited liability company in financing a capital investment, and (b) two main sources for a local authority.

Answers
1 (a) capital investment appraisal (b) cost (of) capital (c) discounted cash flow
2 payback; discounted payback; accounting rate of return; net present value; (e) internal rate of return
3 (a) retained profits; issue of shares; leasing (b) long-term borrowing; through the council tax.

QUESTIONS

19.1
Prospect limited is considering investing in some new plant. The plant would cost £1 000 000 to implement, it would last 5 years, and it would then be sold for

£50 000. The relevant profit and loss accounts for each year during the life of the project are as follows:

Year to 31 March	19X1	19X2	19X3	19X4	19X5
	£000	£000	£000	£000	£000
Sales	2000	2400	2800	2900	2000
Less: Cost of goods sold					
Opening stock	–	200	300	450	350
Purchases	1600	1790	2220	1960	1110
	1600	1990	2520	2410	1460
Less: Closing stock	200	300	550	350	50
	1400	1690	1970	2060	1410
Gross profit	600	710	830	840	590
Less: Expenses	210	220	240	250	300
Depreciation	190	190	190	190	190
	400	410	430	440	490
Net profit	200	300	400	400	100
Taxation	40	70	100	100	10
Retained profits	£160	£230	£300	£300	£90

Additional information:

1 All sales are made and all purchases are obtained on credit terms.
2 Outstanding trade debtors and trade creditors at the end of each year are expected to be as follows:

Year	Trade debtors	Trade creditors
	£000	£000
19X1	200	250
19X2	240	270
19X3	300	330
19X4	320	300
19X5	400	150

3 Expenses would all be paid in cash during each year in question.
4 Taxation would be paid on 1 January following each year end.
5 Half the plant would be paid for in cash on 1 April 19X0, and the remaining half (also in cash) on 1 January 19X1. The resale value of £50 000 will be received in cash on 31 March 19X6.

Required:
Calculate the annual net cash flow arising from the purchase of this new plant.

19.2
Buchan Enterprises is considering investing in a new machine. The machine will be purchased on 1 January 19X1 at a cost of £50 000. It is estimated that it would

last for 5 years, and it will then be sold at the end of the year for £2000 in cash. The respective net cash flows estimated to be received by the company as a result of purchasing the machine during each year of its life are as follows:

Year	£	
1	8 000	(excluding the initial cost)
2	16 000	
3	40 000	
4	45 000	
5	35 000	(exclusive of the project's sale proceeds)

The company's cost of capital is 12%.

Required:
Calculate (a) the payback period for the project; and (b) its discounted payback period.

19.3

Lender Limited is considering investing in a new project. It is estimated that it will cost £100 000 to implement, and that the expected net profit after tax will be as follows:

Year	£
1	18 000
2	47 000
3	65 000
4	65 000
5	30 000

Required:
Calculate the accounting rate of return of the proposed project.

19.4

The following net cash flows relate to Lockhart Limited in connection with a certain project which has an initial cost of £2 500 000:

Year	Net cash flow £000	
1	800	(excluding the initial cost)
2	850	
3	830	
4	1200	
5	700	

The company's required rate of return is 15%.

Required:
Calculate the net present value of the project.

19.5

Moffat District Council has calculated the following net cash flows for a proposed project costing £1 450 000:

Year	Net cash flow	
	£000	
1	230	(excluding the initial cost)
2	370	
3	600	
4	420	
5	110	

Required:
Calculate the internal rate of return generated by the project.

19.6

Marsh Limited has investigated the possibility of investing in a new machine. The following data have been extracted from the report relating to the project:

Cost of machine on 1 January 19X6: £500 000.
Life: 4 years to 31 December 19X9.
Estimated scrap value: Nil.
Depreciation method: Straight-line.

Year	Accounting profit after tax	Net cash flows	
	£000	£000	
1	100	50	(excluding the initial cost)
2	250	200	
3	250	225	
4	200	225	
5	–	100	

The company's required rate of return is 15%.

Required:
Calculate the return the machine would make using the following investment appraisal methods:
1 payback;
2 accounting rate of return;
3 net present value; and
4 internal rate of return.

ADDITIONAL QUESTIONS (WITHOUT ANSWERS)

19.7

Nicol Limited is considering investing in a new machine. The machine would cost £500 000. It would have a life of five years and a nil residual value. The company uses the straight-line method of depreciation.

It is expected that the machine will earn the following extra profits for the company during its expected life:

Year	Profits
	£000
1	200
2	120
3	120
4	100
5	60

The above profits also represent the extra net cash flows expected to be generated by the machine (i.e. they exclude the machine's initial cost and the annual depreciation charge).

The company's cost of capital is 18%.

Required:
(a) Calculate:
    (i) the machine's payback period; and
    (ii) its net present value.
(b) Advise management as to whether the new machine should be purchased.

19.8

Hewie Limited has some capital available for investment, and is considering two projects, only one of which can be financed. The details are as follows:

	Project	
	1	2
Expected life (years)	4	3
	£000	£000
Initial cost	600	500
Expected net cash flows (excluding the initial cost)		
Year		
1	10	250
2	200	250
3	400	50
4	50	–
Residual value	Nil	Nil

Required:
Advise management on which project to accept.

DISCUSSION QUESTIONS

19.9

In capital expenditure appraisal, management cannot cope with any technique that is more advanced than payback. How far do you think that this assertion is likely to be true?

19.10

'All capital expenditure techniques are irrelevant because (a) they cannot estimate accurately future cash flows; and (b) it is difficult to select an appropriate discount rate.' Discuss.

19.11

Do any of the traditional capital investment appraisal techniques help in determining social and welfare capital expenditure proposals?

19.12

'We can all dream up new capital expenditure proposals', asserted the Managing Director, 'but where is the money coming from?' Has he a point: how might they be financed?

CHAPTER 20

Contemporary issues in management accounting

Appraisal schemes fail

By Peter Marsh

Companies' attempts to institute formal ways of appraising employees' performance, sometimes linking this to pay, often fail because managers do not have time to do the job properly, according to a survey of 30 companies conducted by Industrial Relations Services, a consultancy specialising in employment trends, to be published this weekend.

The Financial Times, 3 July 1996

Exhibit 20.0 Time – the main problem in dealing with new developments

In Parts 5 and 6, we concentrated on examining some fairly basic conventional management accounting techniques. In this chapter, we outline some of the more recent developments that are taking place in management accounting. However, unless you work for a very forward-looking management, it is unlikely that many of them will have yet been introduced into your entity. Indeed, some of the newer techniques may turn out to be not particularly useful, and they may be abandoned before most managers have heard of them.

Learning objectives

By the end of this chapter, you will be able to:

● **outline the nature and purpose of activity-based costing;**

● **describe what is meant by just-in-time production and total quality management;**

● **identify three other recent developments in management accounting.**

BACKGROUND

Most of the traditional cost accounting techniques referred to in Chapter 13 are used to some extent in both the public and private sectors. These techniques were developed many years ago at a time when the economy was very different from what it is now. Manufacturing industry used to be much more significant, and direct labour costs formed a much greater part of total cost than is the case in the late 1990s.

The public sector has also changed. In local government, for example, the Local Authority Treasurer's Department used to be primarily responsible for providing information for rating purposes. Thereafter, it was largely a matter of keeping the books of account. Now, the accent is very much on obtaining value for money, i.e. in ensuring that, for every £1 spent, the community gets the maximum possible benefit. In addition, many local services are put out to tender, and the local authority is no longer directly responsible for many of the services that it administers on behalf of the public.

In these changed circumstances, the practice of management accounting is also beginning to change. Progress has been slow because, unlike financial accounting, it is not subject to either statutory or mandatory professional accounting requirements. The need to adapt arises from two main sources: (a) the overall change in the national economic and financial climate; and (b) the need for British industry to begin to compete with the Japanese (and other emerging countries) in world markets.

There is now some discussion in management accounting circles of the need to adopt new techniques to meet the changing operational circumstances of British industry, and many of the larger UK companies have now adopted some of these newer techniques. A few of the more important developments are briefly examined in the following sections.

ACTIVITY-BASED COSTING

Activity-based costing (ABC) was virtually unknown in the UK prior to 1988. Much interest has been expressed in the technique, and it is now sometimes referred to as *activity-based management* (ABM), as it is believed that its basic ideas go well beyond cost accounting. The CIMA definition of ABC is:

> Activity-based costing: an approach to the costing and monitoring of activities which involves tracing resource consumption and costing final outputs.

The technique came about as a result of the great unease arising from the traditional way of absorbing overheads, i.e. on the basis of cost centre activity measured usually in terms of direct labour hours or machine hours. In Chapter 15, we were fairly critical of this method, and it now seems to have been generally recognized that a new method is required.

As you might imagine, ABC is not an easy technique to understand. Basically, it revolves around a recognition that specific activities cause costs to arise. Thus, if it is possible to isolate the activities that cause the costs, it will be possible to absorb overheads much more fairly on the basis of those activities (instead of using the simple direct labour hour or machine hour method).

This argument has given rise to the use of the term 'cost drivers' to describe a measure of the activities performed. CIMA simply defines a cost driver as 'any factor which causes a change in the cost of an activity'. For example, in order to manufacture certain products, a number of orders may have to be placed, the material may have to be handled several times, and the machines may need re-setting. All of these activities will have an effect on overheads, so it seems only fair to charge some products less for overheads than others, e.g. if less orders are placed, materials are only handled once, and the machines do not have to be re-set. All of these activities can be described as cost drivers, i.e. the number of orders, the number of times handled, and the number of set-ups.

Do you get the basic idea? In effect, instead of charging overheads to production by using just one factor, ABC adopts a considerable number, depending upon how many activities can be isolated within a particular entity.

It is obviously a much more involved and costly system of achieving some control over overheads than the ones that were described in Chapter 15. The proponents of ABC claim that it avoids over-costing high volume products and under-costing low volume ones. This benefit arises because the cost drivers reflect the activity generated by particular products. In traditional overhead absorption, units are charged with a share of the total cost centre overheads based on the total direct labour hours (or the total machine hours) worked in that cost centre. In an ABC system, if both products A and B require one set-up, but A consists of one unit and B 1000, they will both be charged the same amount of overhead.

ABC is still at an early stage of development in the UK, and so for the time being it is not necessary to go into any further detail. As a non-accountant, it is sufficient for you to have heard of the technique, to know what is meant by a cost driver, and to be aware that cost drivers (rather than direct labour hours or machine hours) are used to apportion overheads.

JUST-IN-TIME MANUFACTURING

Chapter 14 dealt with the problem of charging direct materials to production. A relatively new technique, known as just-in-time (JIT), may help this problem to be avoided.

CIMA defines JIT as follows: 'A system whose objective is to produce or to procure products or components as they are required by a customer or for use, rather than for stock.' When applied to production, it is defined as:

A production system which is driven by demand for finished products whereby each component on a production line is produced only when needed for the next stage.'

To illustrate this technique, let us assume that you are having some construction work done at home. The contract supervisor has to schedule the work so that once the foundation and walls have been built, the joiner and glaziers are ready to fit the windows. They are then followed in turn by the plumber, the electrician, and the plasterer. All of these tradesmen will, of course, require materials to be delivered as and when they are require. If there is a delay in one tradesman arriving, or in some materials not being to hand, the whole job could be stopped. In other words, it is vital that all of the various tasks are closely synchronized and timed.

In essence, this forms the basis of JIT. The technique is now becoming widespread in British industry (although it has been common in Japan for many years). It can also be applied to the *purchasing* function. Just-in-time purchasing is defined by CIMA as: 'A purchasing system in which material purchases are contracted so that the receipt and usage of material, to the maximum extent possible, coincide.'

JIT purchasing has some very important implications for cost accounting, especially in respect of material pricing, as it practically solves the problem for us! If materials are ordered for a specific job, and they are then delivered straight onto the production line, there should hardly be any difficulty in identifying their cost. Thus under a JIT system, material pricing is not a major issue.

There are also additional benefits. Ordering straight to production reduces the cost of ordering, handling, storing, issuing, and the risk of stock deterioration or obsolescence. Of course, some problems may arise from following the principle. For example, if the supplier is late in delivering a particular order, or there is some interruption to supplies, the entire production staff might have to be laid off. Nonetheless, JIT has some exciting possibilities, and its future looks well assured.

TOTAL QUALITY MANAGEMENT

Total quality management (TQM) is another management technique that has begun to take off in the UK. It is now sometimes referred to as Quality Management (QM). TQM can be introduced into any entity irrespective of whether it is profit- or non-profit making.

CIMA defines TQM as follows:

> **Total quality management:** the continuous improvement in quality, productivity and effectiveness obtained by establishing management responsibility for processes as well as outputs. In this every process has an identified process owner and every person in an entity operates within a process and contributes to its improvement.

The term 'quality' is elusive. For example, we can refer to a quality car (like a Rolls Royce), but in the context of TQM, we can also mean a small, mass-produced car which is as high quality as it is possible to get in terms of its basic specification.

The concept of TQM can be summed up in the phrase 'getting it right first time'. In other words, it is less expensive to make sure that all tasks and duties are always completed correctly the first time that they are undertaken. Getting it right the first time means that there will be savings on internal failures (e.g. the cost of wastage, re-working, re-inspection, downgrading, and discounting), and also on external costs (e.g. field repairs, handling, legal costs, lost sales, and warranties). However, there could be some additional costs on prevention (planning, training, and operating the system) and on appraisal (administration, audit, and inspection).

TQM is a technique that involves every employee in an entity from the chairman downwards. Accountants are automatically included. In addition, the management accounting function will have some responsibility towards collecting and reporting on appraisal, prevention, and internal and external prevention costs. However, it is rather curious that accountants have not yet become heavily involved in the implementation and operation of TQM systems. In the past, they have tended to get involved in everything!

It is not known to what extent traditional management accounting practices may (or will) have to change in order to accommodate a TQM system. Thus the question that accountants are probably going to have to consider is: 'Does a traditional cost and management accounting system become obsolete if a TQM system is installed?'

OTHER DEVELOPMENTS

A number of other developments are taking place in management accounting. These are summarized below.

Life-cycle costing
In an advanced manufacturing environment, planning and prototype decisions taken in the early stages of a product's development have an important impact throughout its entire life. Management accounting has a role to play in providing information for planning and control at the design stage of a product, and thereafter, in plotting the product's life-time costs and revenues.

This technique is known as 'life-cycle costing', and CIMA defines it as follows: 'The maintenance of physical asset cost records over the entire asset lives, so that the decisions concerning the acquisition, use or disposal of the assets can be made in a way that achieves the optimum asset usage at the lowest possible cost to the entity.' It is also possible to apply the term to the calculation of cost, not just during the product's life, but also during the pre-production stage.

Target costing Target costing is one of a number of techniques imported from Japan. Before a product is designed, the marketing function sets a selling price that will capture a designated share of the market. The product will then have to be designed in such a way that the total unit cost plus an allowance for profit does not exceed the target market price. CIMA defines a target cost as follows: 'A product cost estimate derived by subtracting a desired profit margin from a competitive market price.'

Strategic management accounting Strategic management accounting (SMA) is yet another relatively new development that has arisen out of traditional management accounting practices. There is no agreed satisfactory definition, but we can start by first explaining what is meant by 'strategic'. Strategic (the adjective) relates to strategy (the noun). Strategy is often used in a military context meaning a co-ordinated approach to gaining advantage against an enemy. Used in a business sense, therefore, it can be defined as a co-ordinated approach by a business to gaining a competitive advantage.

Thus strategic management accounting can be considered to be a co-ordinated set of actions aimed at supplying information to management for decision making in order to enable a competitive advantage to be gained in the market place. This means that under an SMA system, the information supplied to management will be far more extensive than is usually the case with traditional management accounting, and it may encompass (a) accounting and non-accounting data; (b) financial and non-financial information; (c) quantitative and qualitative material; and (d) be obtained from both internal and external sources. The amount of data collected will clearly be very extensive, and it may include information, for example, about the entity's competitors, its customers and suppliers, the economy, governmental policy matters, and changes in statutory requirements.

In a book of this nature, it is unnecessary to go into greater detail about SMA, but if you would like to know more, you might like to refer to a book by Malcolm Smith called *New Tools for Management Accounting: Putting Non-financial Indicators to Work*, published by Pitman Publishing (London) in 1995. SMA is covered in Chapter 3 (pages 11 to 90). Although the chapter is quite a long one, it is quite well laid out, and as long as you take it slowly, you should not find it too difficult.

CONCLUSION

It should be stressed that some of the techniques that have been considered in this chapter are not yet widely applied in British manufacturing or service industries, so you may not come across them. It may well be that some of the new techniques prove to be little more than gimmicks, and they could soon be forgotten. Nonetheless, there is no doubt that traditional management accounting is locked into an economic, financial, and political culture that has long ceased to exist. It revolves around, for example, procedures that are more appropriate for an economy based on manufacturing industry than one that is more service orientated, so there is a need to develop a more up-to-date management accounting structure.

Notwithstanding these criticisms, however, this chapter has been able to indicate that management accounting has entered a phase in which new ideas are being worked upon. In particular, two relatively new techniques (activity-based costing and just-in-time purchasing) may help to limit the major disadvantages of traditional absorption costing, i.e. the affinity of overheads to production units, and the material pricing problem. By contrast, the other developments considered in this chapter may take a little longer before they become generally accepted.

Key points	1 Some new developments are taking place in management accounting, such as activity-based costing, just-in-time purchasing, and total quality management.
	2 Other more recent developments include life-cycle costing, target costing, and strategic management accounting.

CHECK YOUR LEARNING

1 What do the following initials mean:
   (a) ABC
   (b) JIT
   (c) TQM?

2 Give an example of a cost driver.

3 State whether each of the following assertions is true or false:
   (a) Strategic management accounting incorporates external
       information into the reporting system.   True/False
   (b) Abnormal gains should be absorbed into process costs.   True/False
   (c) A contract must be completed before any profit can be taken True/False

Answers	1 (a) activity-based costing (b) just-in-time (c) total quality management
	2 number of set-ups
	3 (a) true (b) false (c) false

QUESTIONS

20.1
Describe in one sentence what is meant by 'activity-based costing'.

20.2
How far does 'just-in-time purchasing' help to avoid the material pricing problem?

20.3
List five features of a total quality management system.

DISCUSSION QUESTIONS

20.4
'Activity-based costing is just a fad and a fashion.' Discuss.

20.5
Do you think that management accountants have any role to play in the implementation and operation of a total quality management system?

20.6
'Ugh!' snorted the Chairman when confronting his Chief Accountant. 'Strategic management accounting is another of those techniques dreamed up by you and your mates to keep you all in jobs.' Could the Chairman have a point?

Further reading

This book contains sufficient material for most first-year modules in accounting for non-accounting students. Some modules may require additional information, however, and most students may find it necessary to consult other books when attempting some exercises and case studies.

There are many very good acounting books available for *accounting* students, but they usually go into considerable technical detail. Non-accounting students must use them with caution, otherwise they will be completely lost. In any case, non-accounting students do not need to process vast amounts of highly specialist data. It is sufficient for their purpose if they have an understanding of where accounting information comes from, why it is prepared in that way, what it means, and what reliance can be placed on it.

Bearing these points in mind, the following books are worth considering:

Financial accounting

Elliott, B. and Elliott J.: *Financial Accounting and Reporting*, 2nd e., Prentice Hall, Hemel Hempstead, 1996

This is a well received book which is now into its second edition. It should be a very useful reference book for non-accounting students.

Holmes, G. and Sugden, A.: *Interpreting Company Reports and Accounts*, 5th e., Woodhead-Faulkner, Cambridge, 1994

A well-established text that deals with company financial reporting in some detail.

Wood, F.: *Business Accounting*, Volumes 1 and 2, 7th e., Pitman Publishing, London, 1996 (Volume 2, F. Wood and A. Sangster)

Wood is the master accounting textbook writer. His books can be recommended with absolute confidence.

Management accounting

Arnold, J. and Hope, T.: *Accounting for Management Decisions*, 3rd e., Prentice Hall, Hemel Hempstead, 1996

This book is aimed at first- and second-year undergraduate and professional courses. Non-accounting students should be able to follow it without too much difficulty.

Drury, C.: *Management and Cost Accounting*, 4th e., Chapman and Hall, London, 1996

This book has become the established British text on management accounting. It is a big book in every sense of the word. Non-accounting students should only use it for reference.

Wilson, R.M.S. and Chua, W.F.: *Managerial Accounting – method and meaning*, 2nd e., Chapman and Hall, London, 1993

This book is another first- and second-year undergraduate text. It has much more of a behavioural approach than most other management accounting books. It is a bit heavy going, but it is useful to see how management accounting can be approached from a completely different angle.

Ashton, D., Hopper, T. and Scapen, R.W. (Eds.): *Issues in Management Accounting*, 2nd e., Prentice Hall, Hemel Hempstead, 1996

This book will be useful for those students who are interested in current developments in management accounting. However, be warned! It is written in an academic style, and some of the chapters are very hard-going.

APPENDIX 2

Discount table

Present value of £1 received after n years discounted at i%

n \ i	1	2	3	4	5	6	7	8	9	10
1	0.9901	0.9804	0.9709	0.9615	0.9524	0.9434	0.9346	0.9259	0.9174	0.9091
2	0.9803	0.9612	0.9426	0.9246	0.9070	0.8900	0.8734	0.8573	0.8417	0.8264
3	0.9706	0.9423	0.9151	0.8890	0.8638	0.8396	0.8163	0.7938	0.7722	0.7513
4	0.9610	0.9238	0.8885	0.8548	0.8227	0.7921	0.7629	0.7350	0.7084	0.6830
5	0.9515	0.9057	0.8626	0.8219	0.7835	0.7473	0.7130	0.6806	0.6499	0.6209
6	0.9420	0.8880	0.8375	0.7903	0.7462	0.7050	0.6663	0.6302	0.5963	0.5645

n \ i	11	12	13	14	15	16	17	18	19	20
1	0.9009	0.8929	0.8850	0.8772	0.8696	0.8621	0.8547	0.8475	0.8403	0.8333
2	0.8116	0.7929	0.7831	0.7695	0.7561	0.7432	0.7305	0.7182	0.7062	0.6944
3	0.7312	0.7118	0.6931	0.6750	0.6575	0.6407	0.6244	0.6086	0.5934	0.5787
4	0.6587	0.6355	0.6133	0.5921	0.5718	0.5523	0.5337	0.5158	0.4987	0.4823
5	0.5935	0.5674	0.5428	0.5194	0.4972	0.4761	0.4561	0.4371	0.4190	0.4019
6	0.5346	0.5066	0.4803	0.4556	0.4323	0.4104	0.3910	0.3704	0.3521	0.3349

APPENDIX 3

Answers to end-of-chapter questions

Chapter 1 1.1 (a) To keep a record of the company's day-to-day progress.
     (b) To prepare the company's annual financial accounts.
     (c) To supply information to the management for decision making and control.
     (d) To operate a system of internal auditing.
     (e) To minimize the company's tax liabilities.

1.2 It is required by law. External auditors report to the shareholders on whether the accounts represent a true and fair view (the discovery of fraud is only incidental to this purpose). Note that small limited companies no longer need to have an audit.

1.3 Accountants collect a great deal of information about an entity's activities and then translate it into monetary terms – a language that everyone understands. The information that is collected can help non-accountants do their job more effectively because it provides them with better guidance upon which to take decisions, but the decision is still theirs. Futhermore, all managers must be aware of the statutory accounting obligations to which their organization has to adhere if they are to avoid taking part in unlawful acts.

1.4 None. The preparation of management accounts is for the entity to decide if it believes that they serve a useful purpose.

1.5 Statutory obligations are contained in the Companies Act 1985. In addition, listed companies have to abide by certain Stock Exchange requirements, and qualified accountants are also bound by a great many mandatory professional requirements.

1.6 To collect and store detailed information about an entity's activities, and then to abstract it and summarize it in the most effective way for whatever purpose it is intended to be used.

Chapter 2 2.1 1 Matching.
     2 Historic cost.
     3 Quantitative.
     4 Periodicity.
     5 Prudence.
     6 Going-concern.

2.2 1 Relevance.
   2 Entity.
   3 Consistency.
   4 Materiality.
   5 Historic cost.
   6 Realization.

2.3 1 Entity.
   2 Objectivity.
   3 Periodicity.
   4 Prudence.
   5 Dual aspect.
   6 Realization.

2.4 1 (a) Prudence.
    (b) The long-term services obtained from a professional footballer are highly unpredictable.
   2 (a) Realization.
    (b) Although it may appear somewhat imprudent to do so, in general the risk is usually small in taking profit prior to the receipt of cash.
   3 (a) Entity.
    (b) The company does not have a legal title to the house.
   4 (a) Prudence.
    (b) The profit cannot be known for some time (although in some cases a proportion may be claimed if the final outcome is reasonably certain).
   5 (a) Materiality.
    (b) It would be unduly pedantic to insist on matching the cost of small stocks of stationery purchased in an earlier period with the revenue of a future period.
   6 (a) Prudence.
    (b) The improvement work may never result in a more successful revenue earning drug. (*Note:* In certain specific instances, earlier period costs on development work may be matched with revenues earned after the work has been completed.)

Chapter 3

3.1 Adam's books of account:

Account

	Debit	Credit
1	Cash	Capital
2	Purchases	Cash
3	Van	Cash
4	Rent	Cash
5	Cash	Sales
6	Office machinery	Cash

3.2 Brown's books of account:

Account

	Debit	Credit
1	Bank	Cash
2	Cash	Sales
3	Purchases	Bank

	4	Office expenses	Cash
	5	Bank	Sales
	6	Motor car	Bank

3.3 Corby's books of account:

Account

		Debit	*Credit*
	1	Purchases	Smith
	2	Cash	Capital
	3	Cash	Sales
	4	Purchases	Cash
	5	Bank	Cash
	6	Machinery	Cash

3.4 Davies's books of account:

Account

		Debit	*Credit*
	1	Bank	Capital
	2	Purchases	Swallow
	3	Cash	Sales
	4	Purchases	Cash
	5	Dale	Sales
	6	Motoring expenses	Bank

3.5 Edgar's books of account:

Account

		Debit	*Credit*
	1	Purchases	Gill
	2	Ash	Sales
	3	Cash	Sales
	4	Purchases	Cash
	5	Gill	Bank
	6	Cash	Ash

3.6 Ford's books of account:

Account

		Debit	*Credit*
	1	Cash	Sales
	2	Purchases	Carter
	3	Holly	Sales
	4	Purchases	Cash
	5	Sales returns	Holly
	6	Carter	Purchases returned

3.7 Gordon's books of account:

Account

		Debit	*Credit*
	1	Purchases	Watson
	2	Cash	Sales
	3	Moon	Sales
	4	Watson	Bank

5	Watson	Discounts received
6	Cash	Moon
7	Discounts allowed	Moon
8	Purchases	Cash

3.8   Harry's books of account:

Account

	Debit	Credit
1	Cash	Capital
2	Bank	Cash
3	Rent	Bank
4	Purchases	Paul
5	Van	Bank
6	Cash	Sales
7	Purchases	Nancy
8	Motoring expenses	Cash
9	Nancy	Purchases returned
10	Mavis	Sales
11	Drawings	Cash
12	Purchases	Cash
13	Sales return	Mavis
14	Nancy	Bank
15	Cash	Mavis
16	Nancy	Discount received
17	Discounts allowed	Mavis
18	Petty cash	Bank

3.9   Ivan's ledger accounts:

Cash Account

		£			£
1.9.X9	Capital	10 000	2.9.X9	Bank	8 000
12.9.X9	Cash	3 000	3.9.X9	Purchases	1 000

Capital Account

		£			£
			1.9.X9	Cash	10 000

Bank Account

		£			£
2.9.X9	Cash	8 000	20.9.X9	Roy	6 000
30.9.X9	Norman	2 000			

Purchases Account

		£			£
3.9.X9	Cash	1 000			
10.9.X9	Roy	6 000			

Roy's Account

		£			£
20.9.X9	Bank	6 000	10.9.X9	Purchases	6 000

Sales Account

	£			£
		12.9.X9	Cash	3 000
		15.9.X9	Norman	4 000

Norman

		£			£
15.9.X9	Sales	4 000	30.9.X9	Bank	2 000

3.10 Jones's ledger accounts:

Bank Account

		£			£
1.10.X1	Capital	20 000	10.10.X1	Petty cash	1 000
			25.10.X1	Lang	5 000
			29.10.X1	Green	10 000

Capital Account

	£			£
		1.10.X1	Bank	20 000

Van Account

		£	£
2.10.X1	Lang	5 000	

Lang's Account

		£			£
25.10.X1	Bank	5 000	2.10.X1	Van	5 000

Purchases Account

		£	£
6.10.X1	Green	15 000	
20.10.X1	Cash	3 000	

Green's Account

		£			£
28.10.X1	Discounts received	500	6.10.X1	Purchases	15 000
29.10.X1	Bank	10 000			

Petty Cash Account

		£			£
10.10.X1	Bank	1 000	22.10.X1	Miscellaneous expenses	500

Sales

	£			£
		14.10.X1	Haddock	6 000
		18.10.X1	Cash	5 000

Haddock

	£			£
14.10.X1 Sales	6 000	20.10.X1 Discounts allowed	600
		31.10.X1 Cash	5 400

Cash Account

	£			£
18.10.X1 Sales	5 000	20.10.X1 Purchases	3 000
31.10.X1 Haddock	5 400		

Miscellaneous Expenses

	£		£
22.10.X1 Petty cash	500		

Discounts Received Account

	£			£
		28.10.X1 Green	500

Discounts Allowed Account

	£		£
30.10.X1 Haddock	600		

3.11 Ken's ledger accounts:

Cash Account

	£			£
1.11.X2 Capital	15 000	2.11.X2 Bank	14 000
27.11.X2 Sales	5 000	28.11.X2 Purchases	4 000
		30.11.X2 Bank	1 000

Capital Account

	£			£
		10.11.X2 Cash	15 000

Bank Account

	£			£
2.11.X2 Cash	14 000	3.11.X2 Rent	1 000
30.11.X2 Main	1 000	26.11.X2 Office expenses	2 000
30.11.X2 Pain	2 000	29.11.X2 Ace	4 000
30.11.X2 Vain	3 000	29.11.X2 Mace	5 000
30.11.X2 Cash	1 000	29.11.X2 Pace	6 000

Rent Account

	£		£
3.11.X2 Bank	1 000		

Purchases Account

	£		£
4.11.X2 Ace	5 000		
4.11.X2 Mace	6 000		
4.11.X2 Pace	7 000		
25.11.X2 Ace	3 000		
25.11.X2 Mace	4 000		
25.11.X2 Pace	5 000		
28.11.X2 Cash	4 000		

Ace's Account

	£		£
29.11.X2 Bank	4 000	4.11.X2 Purchases	5 000
30.11.X2 Discounts received	200	25.11.X2 Purchases	3 000

Mace's Account

	£		£
29.11.X2 Bank	5 000	4.11.X2 Purchases	6 000
30.11.X2 Discounts received	250	25.11.X2 Purchases	4 000

Pace's Account

	£		£
15.11.X2 Purchases returned	1 000	4.11.X2 Purchases	7 000
29.11.X2 Bank	6 000	25.11.X2 Purchases	5 000
30.11.X2 Discounts received	300		

Sales Account

	£		£
		10.11.X2 Main	2 000
		10.11.X2 Pain	3 000
		10.11.X2 Vain	4 000
		27.11.X2 Cash	5 000

Main's Account

	£		£
10.11.X2 Sales	2 000	30.11.X2 Bank	1 000
		30.11.X2 Discounts allowed	100

Pain's Account

	£		£
10.11.X2 Sales	3 000	22.11.X2 Sales return	2 000
		30.11.X2 Bank	2 000
		30.11.X2 Discounts allowed	200

Vain's Account

	£		£
10.11.X2 Sales	4 000	30.11.X2 Bank	3 000
		30.11.X2 Discounts allowed	400

Purchases Returned Account

	£		£
		15.11.X2 Pace	1 000

Sales Returns Account

	£		£
22.11.X2 Pain	2 000		

Office Expenses Account

	£		£
26.11.X2 Bank	2 000		

Discounts Received Account

	£		£
		30.11.X2 Ace	200
		30.11.X2 Mace	250
		30.11.X2 Pace	300

Discounts Allowed Account

	£		£
30.11.X2 Main	100		
30.11.X2 Pain	200		
30.11.X2 Vain	400		

3.12 (a), (b) and (c) Pat's ledger accounts:

Cash Account

	£		£
1.12.X3 Capital	10 000	24.12.X3 Office expenses	5 000
29.12.X3 Fog	4 000	31.12.X3 Grass	6 000
29.12.X3 Mist	6 000	31.12.X3 Seed	8 000
		31.12.X3 Balance c/d	1 000
	£20 000		£20 000
1.1.X4 Balance b/d	1 000		

Capital Account

	£		£
		1.12.X3 Cash	10 000

Purchases Account

	£		£
2.12.X3 Grass	6 000		
2.12.X3 Seed	7 000		
15.12.X3 Grass	3 000		
15.12.X3 Seed	4 000	31.12.X3 Balance c/d	20 000
	£20 000		£20 000
1.01.X4 Balance b/d	20 000		

Grass's Account

	£		£
12.12.X3 Purchases returned	1 000	2.12.X3 Purchases	6 000
31.12.X3 Cash	6 000	15.12.X3 Purchases	3 000
31.12.X3 Balance c/d	2 000		
	£9 000		£9 000
		1.1.X4 Balance b/d	2 000

Seed's Account

	£		£
12.12.X3 Purchases returned	2 000	2.12.X3 Purchases	7 000
31.12.X3 Cash	8 000	15.12.X3 Purchases	4 000
31.12.X3 Balance c/d	1 000		
	£11 000		£11 000
		1.1.X4 Balance b/d	1 000

Sales Account

	£		£
		10.12.X3 Fog	3 000
		10.12.X3 Mist	4 000
		20.12.X3 Fog	2 000
31.12.X3 Balance c/d	12 000	20.12.X3 Mist	3 000
	£12 000		£12 000
		1.1.X4 Balance b/d	12 000

Fog's Account

	£		£
10.12.X3 Sales	3 000	29.12.X3 Cash	4 000
20.12.X3 Sales	2 000	31.12.X3 Balance c/d	1 000
	£5 000		£5 000
1.1.X4 Balance b/d	1 000		

Mist's Account

	£		£
10.12.X3 Sales	4 000	29.12.X3 Cash	6 000
20.12.X3 Sales	3 000	31.12.X3 Balance c/d	1 000
	£7 000		£7 000
1.1.X4 Balance b/d	1 000		

Purchases Returned Account

	£		£
		12.12.X3 Grass	1 000
31.12.X3 Balance c/d	3 000	12.12.X3 Seed	2 000
	£3 000		£3 000
		1.1.X4 Balance b/d	3 000

Office Expenses Account

	£		£
24.12.X3 Cash	5 000		

Tutorial note

It is unnecessary to balance off an account and bring down the balance if there is only a single entry in it.

(d)

PAT

Trial Balance at 31 December 19X3

	£ Dr	£ Cr
Cash	1 000	
Capital		10 000
Purchases	20 000	
Grass		2 000
Seed		1 000
Sales		12 000
Fog	1 000	
Mist	1 000	
Purchases returned		3 000
Office expenses	5 000	
	£28 000	£28 000

3.13 (a) Vale's books of account:

Bank Account

	£		£
1.1.X3 Balance b/d	5 000	31.12.X3 Dodd	29 000
31.12.X3 Fish	45 000	31.12.X3 Delivery van	12 000
31.12.X3 Cash	3 000	31.12.X3 Balance c/d	12 000
	£53 000		£53 000
1.1.X4 Balance b/d	12 000		

Capital Account

		£			£
			1.1.X3	Balance b/d	20 000

Cash Account

		£			£
1.1.X3	Balance b/d	1 000	31.12.X3	Purchases	15 000
31.12.X3	Sales	20 000	31.12.X3	Office expenses	9 000
31.12.X3	Fish	7 000	31.12.X3	Bank	3 000
			31.12.X3	Balance c/d	1 000
		£28 000			£28 000
1.1.X4	Balance b/d	1000			

Dodd's Account

		£			£
31.12.X3	Bank	29 000	1.1.X3	Balance b/d	2 000
31.12.X3	Balance c/d	3 000	31.12.X3	Purchases	30 000
		£32 000			£32 000
			1.1.X4	Balance b/d	3 000

Fish's Account

		£			£
1.1.X3	Balance b/d	6 000	31.12.X3	Bank	45 000
31.12.X3	Sales	50 000	31.12.X3	Cash	7 000
			31.12.X3	Balance c/d	4 000
		£56 000			£56 000
1.1.X4	Balance b/d	4000			

Furniture Account

		£			£
1.1.X3	Balance b/d	10 000			

Purchases Account

		£			£
31.12.X3	Dodd	30 000			
31.12.X3	Cash	15 000	31.12.X3	Balance c/d	45 000
		£45 000			£45 000
1.1.X4	Balance b/d	45 000			

Sales Account

		£			£
			31.12.X3	Cash	20 000
31.12.X3	Balance c/d	70 000	31.12.X3	Fish	50 000
		£70 000			£70 000
			1.1.X4	Balance b/d	70 000

Office Expenses Account

	£			£
31.12.X3 Cash	9 000			

Delivery Van Account

	£			£
31.12.X3 Bank	12 000			

(b)

VALE
Trial balance at 31 December 19X3

	Dr	Cr
	£	£
Bank	12 000	
Capital		20 000
Cash	1 000	
Dodd		3 000
Fish	4 000	
Furniture	10 000	
Purchases	45 000	
Sales		70 000
Office expenses	9 000	
Delivery van	12 000	
	£93 000	£93 000

3.14 (a)   Brian's ledger accounts:

Bank Account

		£			£
1.1.X4	Capital	25 000	2.1.X4	Rent	2 000
23.1.X4	Cash	6 000	25.1.X4	Petty cash	500
26.1.X4	Ann	5 500	29.1.X4	Savoy Motors	4 000
31.1.X4	Capital	5 000	30.1.X4	Linda	8 000
			30.1.X4	Sydney	2 000
			31.1.X4	Rent	2 000
			31.1.X4	Balance c/d	23 000
		£41 500			£41 500
1.2.X4	Balance b/d	23 000			

Capital Account

		£			£
			1.1.X4	Bank	25 000
31.1.X4	Balance c/d	30 000	31.1.X4	Bank	5 000
		£30 000			£30 000
			1.2.X4	Balance b/d	30 000

Rent Account

		£			£
2.1.X4	Bank	2 000			
31.1.X4	Bank	2 000	31.1.X4	Balance c/d	4 000
		£4 000			£4 000
1.2.X4	Balance b/d	4 000			

Purchases Account

		£			£
3.1.X4	Linda	5 000			
5.1.X4	Sydney	3 000			
15.1.X4	Linda	10 000	31.1.X4	Balance c/d	18 000
		£18 000			£18 000
1.2.X4	Balance b/d	18 000			

Linda's Account

		£			£
22.1.X4	Purchases returned	2 000	3.1.X4	Purchases	5 000
30.1.X4	Bank	8 000	15.1.X4	Purchases	10 000
30.1.X4	Discounts received	700			
31.1.X4	Balance c/d	4 300			
		£15 000			£15 000
			1.2.X4	Balance b/d	4 300

Motor Car Account

		£			£
4.1.X4	Savoy Motors	4 000			

Savoy Motors Account

		£			£
29.1.X4	Bank	£4 000	4.1.X4	Motor car	£4 000

Sydney's Account

		£			£
30.1.X4	Bank	2 000	5.1.X4	Purchases	3 000
30.1.X4	Discounts received	100			
31.1.X4	Balance c/d	900			
		£3 000			£3 000
			1.2.X4	Balance b/d	900

Cash Account

		£			£
10.1.X4	Sales	£6 000	23.1.X4	Bank	£6 000

Sales Account

		£			£
			10.1.X4	Cash	6 000
31.1.X4	Balance c/d	14 000	20.1.X4	Ann	8 000
		£14 000			£14 000
			1.2.X4	Balance b/d	14 000

Ann's Account

		£			£
20.1.X4	Sales	8 000	24.1.X4	Sales return	1 000
			26.1.X4	Bank	5 500
			26.1.X4	Discounts allowed	500
			31.1.X4	Balance c/d	1 000
		£8 000			£8 000
1.2.X4	Balance b/d	1 000			

Purchases Returned Account

		£			£
			22.1.X4	Linda	2 000

Sales Returns Account

		£			£
24.1.X4	Ann	1 000			

Petty Cash Account

		£			£
25.1.X4	Bank	500	28.1.X4	Office expenses	250
			31.1.X4	Balance c/d	250
		£500			£500
1.1.X4	Balance b/d	250			

Discounts Allowed Account

		£			£
26.1.X4	Ann	500			

Office Expenses Account

		£			£
28.1.X4	Petty cash	250			

Discounts Received Account

		£			£
			30.1.X4	Linda	700
31.1.X4	Balance c/d	800	30.1.X4	Sydney	100
		£800			£800
			1.2.X4	Balance b/d	800

(b)

BRIAN
Trial balance at 31 January 19X4

	Dr £	Cr £
Bank	23 000	
Capital		30 000
Rent	4 000	
Purchases	18 000	
Linda		4 300
Motor car	4 000	
Sydney		900
Sales		14 000
Ann	1 000	
Purchases returned		2 000
Sales returns	1 000	
Petty cash	250	
Discounts allowed	500	
Office expenses	250	
Discounts received		800
	£52 000	£52 000

3.15

FIELD
Trial balance at 28 February 19X5

	Dr £	Cr £
Bank	13 000	
Cash	2 000	
Capital		15 000
Creditors		4 000
Debtors	10 000	
Drawings	5 000	
Electricity	4 000	
Furniture	7 000	
Office expenses	3 000	
Purchases	50 000	
Sales		100 000
Wages	25 000	
	£119 000	£119 000

3.16

TRENT
Corrected trial balance at 31 March 19X4

	Dr £	Cr £
Bank (overdrawn)		2 000
Capital		50 000
Discounts allowed	5 000	
Discounts received		3 000
Dividends received		2 000
Drawings	23 000	
Investments	14 000	
Land and buildings	60 000	
Office expenses	18 000	
Purchases	75 000	
Sales		250 000
Rates	7 000	
Vans	20 000	
Van expenses	5 000	
Wages and salaries	80 000	
	£307 000	£307 000

3.17

SEVERN
Trial balance at 30 April 19X7

	Dr £000	Cr £000
Advertising	14	
Bank (current)	5	
Bank (deposit)	50	
Bank interest received		1
Capital		100
Cash	8	
Creditors		12
Debtors	30	
Discounts allowed	5	
Discounts received		2
Drawings	45	
Fees received		10
Furniture and fittings	18	
Land and buildings	40	
Motor cars	22	
Motor car expenses	4	
Plant and equipment	37	
Purchases	300	
Purchases returned		15
Rents received		5
Sales		500
Sales returns	20	
Telephone	3	
Wages	44	
	£645	£645

Chapter 4 4.1

ETHEL
Trading, profit and loss account for the year to 31 January 19X1

	£
Sales	35 000
Less: Purchases	20 000
Gross profit	15 000
Less: Expenses:	
Office expenses	11 000
Net profit	£4 000

ETHEL
Balance sheet at 31 January 19X1

Fixed assets	£	£
Premises		8 000
Current assets		
Debtors	6000	
Cash	3000	
	9000	
Less: Current liabilities		
Creditors	3000	6 000
		£14 000
Financed by:		
Capital		
Balance at 1 February 19X0		10 000
Net profit for the year		4 000
		£14 000

4.2

MARION
Trading, profit and loss account for the year to 28 February 19X2

	£000	£000
Sales		400
Less: Purchases		200
Gross profit		200
Less: Expenses:		
Heat and light	10	
Miscellaneous expenses	25	
Wages and salaries	98	133
Net profit		£67

MARION
Balance sheet at 28 February 19X2

Fixed assets	£000	£000
Buildings		50
Current assets		
Debtors	30	
Bank	4	
Cash	2	
	36	
Less: Current liabilities		
Creditors	24	12
		£62
Financed by:		
Capital		
Balance at 1 March 19X1		50
Net profit for the year	67	
Less: Drawings	55	12
		£62

4.3

GARSWOOD
Trading, profit and loss account for the year to 31 March 19X3

	£	£
Sales (63 000 – 3 000)		60 000
Less: Purchases (21 400 – 1 400)		20 000
Gross profit		40 000
Add: Other incomes:		
Discounts received	600	
Investment income received	400	1 000
		41 000
Less: Expenses:		
Advertising	2 300	
Discounts allowed	100	
Electricity	1 300	
Stationery	900	
Wages	38 700	43 300
Net loss		£(2 300)

GARSWOOD
Balance sheet at 31 March 19X3

	£	£	£
Fixed assets			
Machinery			20 000
Office equipment			10 000
		c/f	30 000

	£	£	£
b/f			30 000
Investments			4 000
Current assets			
Trade debtors		6 500	
Other debtors		1 500	
Bank		300	
Cash		100	
		8 400	
Less: Current liabilities			
Trade creditors	5 200		
Other creditors	800	6 000	2 400
			£36 400
Financed by:			
Capital			
Balance at 1 April 19X2			55 700
Less: Net loss for the year		(2 300)	
Less: Drawings		(17 000)	(19 300)
			£36 400

Chapter 5

5.1 (a)

LATHOM
Trading account for the year to 30 April 19X4

	£	£
Sales		60 000
Less: Cost of goods sold:		
Opening stock	3 000	
Purchases	45 000	
	48 000	
Less: Closing stock	4 000	44 000
		£16 000

(b) Under current assets normally as the first item.

5.2 (a)

RUFFORD
Trading account for the year to 31 March 19X5

Stock method	1		2		3	
	£	£	£	£	£	£
Sales (82 000 – 4 000)		78 000		78 000		78 000
Less: Cost of goods sold						
Opening stock	4 000		4 000		4 000	
Purchases (48 000 – 3 000)	45 000		45 000		45 000	
	49 000		49 000		49 000	
Less: Closing stock	8 000	41 000	16 000	33 000	4 000	45 000
Gross profit		£37 000		£45 000		£33 000

(b) For the year to 31 March 19X6, other things being equal, using method 1 would result in a *higher* gross profit than using method 2 (whereas the reverse would be true for the year to 31 March 19X5).

5.3

STANDISH
Trading, profit and loss account for the year to 31 May 19X6

	£	£
Sales		79 000
Less: Cost of goods sold:		
Opening stock	7 000	
Purchases	52 000	
	59 000	
Less: Closing stock	12 000	47 000
Gross profit		32 000
Less: Expenses:		
Heating/light	1 500	
Miscellaneous	6 700	
Wages and salaries	17 800	26 000
Net profit		£6 000

STANDISH
Balance sheet at 31 May 19X6

	£	£
Fixed assets		
Furniture and fittings		8 000
Current assets		
Stock	12 000	
Debtors	6 000	
Cash	1 200	
	19 200	
Less: Current liabilities		
Creditors	4 300	14 900
		£22 900
Financed by:		
Capital		
Balance at 1 June 19X5		22 400
Net profit for the year	6 000	
Less: Drawings	5 500	500
		£22 900

5.4

WITTON
Trading, profit and loss account for the year to 30 June 19X7

	£	£
Sales		30 000
Less: Cost of goods sold:		
Purchases	14 000	
Less: Closing stock	2 000	12 000
Gross profit	c/f	18 000

		b/f	18 000
Less: Expenses:			
Office expenses		8 000	
Motor car: depreciation (20% × 5 000)		1 000	9 000
Net profit			£9 000

WITTON
Balance sheet at 30 June 19X7

	£	£
Fixed assets		
Motor car		5 000
Less: Depreciation		1 000
		4 000
Current assets		
Stocks	2 000	
Debtors	3 000	
Cash	500	
	5 500	
Less: Current liabilities		
Creditors	1 500	4 000
		£8 000
Financed by:		
Capital		
At 1 July 19X6		3 000
Net profit for the year	9 000	
Less: Drawings	4 000	5 000
		£8 000

5.5

CROXTETH
Trading, profit and loss account for the year to 31 July 19X8

	£	£	£
Sales			85 000
Less: Cost of goods sold:			
Opening stock		4 000	
Purchases		70 000	
		74 000	
Less: Closing stock		14 000	60 000
Gross profit			25 000
Less: Expenses:			
Depreciation: delivery vans (30% × 40 000)	12 000		
shop equipment (10% × 8 000)	800	12 800	
Shop expenses		7 200	20 000
Net profit			£5 000

CROXTETH
Balance sheet at 31 July 19X8

Fixed assets	Cost	Accumulated depreciation	Net book value
	£	£	£
Delivery vans	40 000	24 000	16 000
Shop equipment	8 000	3 200	4 800
	48 000	27 200	20 800

Current assets		
Stock	14 000	
Bank	2 000	
	16 000	
Less: Current liabilities		
Creditors	4 800	11 200
		32 000
Financed by:		
Capital		
Balance at 1 August 19X7		35 000
Net profit for the year	5 000	
Less: Drawings	8 000	(3 000)
		£32 000

Tutorial note
Accumulated depreciation:
Delivery vans: 12 000 (b/f) + 12 000 = 24 000.
Shop equipment: 2 400 (b/f) + 800 = 3 200.

5.6 (a) Calculation of the depreciation charge for the year to 31 August 19X9:

	£	£	£	£
1 Land				–
2 Buildings: 2% × 150 000			=	3 000
3 Plant at cost	55 000			
Less: Residual value	5 000			
	50 000 × 5%		=	2 500
4 Vehicles at cost		45 000		
Less: Accumulated depreciation at 31 August 19X8		28 800		
		16 200 × 40%	=	6 480
5 Furniture at cost		20 000		
Less: Residual value		2 000		
		18 000 × 10% = 1 800		
Additions at cost		3 000		
Less: Residual value		300		
		2 700 × 10% =	270	2 070
Total amount of depreciation (charged to the profit and loss account for the year to 31 August 19X9)				£14 050

(b)

BARROW
Balance sheet (extract) at 31 August 19X9

Fixed assets	Cost	Accumulated depreciation	Net book value
	£	£	£
Land	200 000	–	200 000
Buildings	150 000	63 000	87 000
Plant	55 000	40 000	15 000
Vehicles	45 000	35 280	9 720
Furniture	23 000	14 670	8 330
	£473 000	£152 950	320 050

5.7

PINE
Trading, profit and loss account for the year to 30 September 19X2

	£	£
Sales		40 000
Less: Cost of goods sold:		
Purchases	21 000	
Less: Closing stock	3 000	18 000
Gross profit		22 000
Less: Expenses:		
Depreciation: furniture (15% × 8 000)	1 200	
General expenses	14 000	
Insurance (2 000 – 200)	1 800	
Telephone (1 500 + 500)	2 000	19 000
		£3 000

PINE
Balance sheet at 30 September 19X2

	£	£	£
Fixed assets			
Furniture			8 000
Less: Depreciation			1 200
			6 800
Current assets			
Stock		3 000	
Debtors		5 000	
Prepayments		200	
Cash		400	
		8 600	
Less: Current liabilities			
Creditors	5 900		
Accrual	500	6 400	2 200
			£9 000

	£	£	£
Financed by:			
Capital			
At 1 October 19X1			6 000
Net profit for the year			3 000
			£9 000

5.8

DALE
Trading, profit and loss account for the year to 31 October 19X3

	£	£	£
Sales			350 000
Less: Cost of goods sold:			
Opening stock		20 000	
Purchases		240 000	
		260 000	
Less: Closing stock		26 000	234 000
Gross profit			116 000
Less: Expenses:			
Depreciation: office equipment	7 000		
vehicles	4 000	11 000	
Heating and lighting (3 000 + 1 500)		4 500	
Office expenses		27 000	
Rates (12 000 – 2 000)		10 000	
Wages and salaries		47 000	99 500
Net profit			£16 500

DALE
Balance sheet at 31 October 19X3

	Cost	Accumulated depreciation	Net book value
	£	£	£
Fixed assets			
Office equipment	35 000	21 000	14 000
Vehicles	16 000	8 000	8 000
	51 000	29 000	22 000
Current assets			
Stocks		26 000	
Trade debtors		61 000	
Prepayments		2 000	
Bank		700	
		89 700	
Less: Current liabilities			
Trade creditors	21 000		
Accruals	1 500	22 500	67 200
			£89 200

483

	£	£	£
Financed by:			
Capital			
At 1 November 19X2			85 000
Net profit for the year		16 500	
Less: Drawings		12 300	4 200
			£89 200

5.9 (a)

ASTLEY
Adjustments for accruals and prepayments for the year to 30 November 19X4

	Electricity	*Gas*	*Insurance*	*Rates*	*Telephone*	*Wages*
	£	£	£	£	£	£
Cash paid during the year	26 400	40 100	25 000	16 000	3 000	66 800
Add: Prepayments at						
1 December 19X3	–	–	12 000	4 000	–	–
	26 400	40 100	37 000	20 000	3 000	66 800
Less: Accruals at						
1 December 19X3	5 200	–	–	–	1 500	1 800
	21 200	40 100	37 000	20 000	1 500	65 000
Add: Accruals at						
30 November 19X4	8 300	–	–	6 000	–	–
	29 500	40 100	37 000	26 000	1 500	65 000
Less: Prepayments at						
30 November 19X4	–	4 900	14 000	–	200	–
Charge to the profit and loss account for the year to 30 November 19X4	£29 500	£35 200	£23 000	£26 000	£1 300	£65 000

(b)

ASTLEY
Balance sheet at 30 November 19X4

	£
Current assets	
Prepayments (4 900 + 14 000 + 200)	19 100
Current liabilities	
Accruals (8 300 + 6 000)	14 300

5.10

DUXBURY
Trading, profit and loss account for the year to 31 December 19X3

	£	£
Sales		95 000
Less: Cost of goods sold:		
Purchases	65 000	
Less: Closing stock	10 000	55 000
Gross profit	c/f	40 000

	£	£
b/f		40 000
Less: Expenses:		
Depreciation: delivery van (20% × 20 000)	4 000	
Office expenses (12 100 + 400 − 500)	12 000	
Provision for doubtful debts (5% × 32 000)	1 600	17 600
Net profit		£22 400

DUXBURY
Balance sheet at 31 December 19X3

	£	£	£
Fixed assets			
Delivery van at cost			20 000
Less: Depreciation			4 000
			16 000
Current assets			
Stocks		10 000	
Trade debtors	32 000		
Less: Provision for bad and doubtful debts	1 600	30 400	
Prepayment		500	
Cash		300	
		41 200	
Current liabilities			
Trade creditors	5 000		
Accrual	400	5 400	35 800
			£51 800
Financed by:			
Capital			
Balance at 1 January 19X3			40 000
Net profit		22 400	
Less: Drawings		10 600	11 800
			£51 800

5.11 (a)

BEECH

Balance sheet (extracts) at	19X4	19X5	19X6	19X7
	£	£	£	£
Current assets				
Trade debtors	60 000	55 000	65 000	70 000
Less: Provision for bad and doubtful debts (10%)	6 000	5 500	6 500	7 000
	54 000	49 500	58 500	63 000

(b)   Profit and loss accounts: increase/decrease in provision for bad and doubtful debts:

	£	£
Year to:		
31 January 19X4		6 000 (New)
31 January 19X5	5 500	
Less: Provision at 31 January 19X4	6 000	500 (Decrease)
31 January 19X6	6 500	
Less: Provision at 31 January 19X5	5 500	1 000 (Increase)
31 January 19X7	7 000	
Less: Provision at 31 January 19X6	6 500	500 (Increase)

5.12

ASH
Trading, profit and loss account for the year to 31 March 19X5

	£	£
Sales		150 000
Less: Cost of goods sold:		
Opening stock	10 000	
Purchases	80 000	
	90 000	
Less: Closing stock	15 000	75 000
Gross profit		75 000
Less: Expenses:		
Bad debt	6 000	
Depreciation: furniture (10% × 9 000)	900	
Electricity (2 000 + 600)	2 600	
Increase in provision for bad and doubtful debts		
[21 000 – 6 000 = (15 000 × 10%) – 1 200]	300	
Insurance (1 500 – 100)	1 400	
Miscellaneous expenses	65 800	77 000
Net loss		£(2 000)

ASH
Balance sheet at 31 March 19X5

	£	£	£
Fixed assets			
Furniture at cost			9 000
Less: Accumulated depreciation			
(3 600 + 900)			4 500
			4 500
Current assets			
Stocks		15 000	
Trade debtors (21 000 – 6 000)	15 000		
Less: Provision for bad and doubtful debts	1 500	13 500	
Prepayment		100	
c/f		28 600	4 500

	£	£	£
b/f		28 600	4 500
Less: Current liabilities			
Trade creditors	20 000		
Accrual	600		
Bank overdraft	4 000	24 600	4 000
			£8 500
Financed by:			
Capital			
Balance at 1 April 19X4			20 500
Less: Net loss for the year		(2 000)	
Less: Drawings		(10 000)	(12 000)
			£8 500

5.13

ELM

Trading, profit and loss account for the year to 30 June 19X6

	£	£	£
Sales (820 000 – 4 000)			816 000
Less: Cost of goods sold:			
Opening stock		47 000	
Purchases (645 000 – 2 000)		643 000	
		690 000	
Less: Closing stock		50 000	640 000
Gross profit			176 000
Add: Other incomes:			
Discounts received		500	
Interest on investments		800	
*Decrease in provision for bad and doubtful debts (42 000 × 5% – 2 300)		200	1 500
			177 500
Less: Expenses:			
Advertising		3 000	
Depreciation: Furniture (15% × 12 000)	1 800		
Vehicles [35 000 – 7 000 × 20%]	5 600	7 400	
Discounts allowed		400	
Electricity (3 200 + 300)		3 500	
General expenses		28 900	
Rates (6 000 – 1 000)		5 000	
Telephone		1 300	
Wages and salaries		77 600	127 100
Net profit			£50 400

*Alternatively, this could be shown as a
  reduction in expenses

ELM
Balance sheet at 30 June 19X6

	Cost £	Accumulated depreciation £	Net book value £
Fixed assets			
Furniture	12 000	3 600	8 400
Vehicles	35 000	12 600	22 400
	47 000	16 200	30 800
Investments at cost			5 000
Current assets			
Stocks		50 000	
Trade debtors	42 000		
Less: Provision for bad and doubtful debts	2 100	39 900	
Prepayment		1 000	
Bank		400	
Cash		100	
		91 400	
Less: Current liabilities			
Trade creditors	13 000		
Accrual	300	13 300	78 100
			£113 900
Financed by:			
Capital			
Balance at 1 July 19X6			73 500
Net profit for the year		50 400	
Less: Drawings		10 000	40 400
			£113 900

5.14

LIME
Trading, profit and loss account for the year to 30 September 19X7

	£	£
Sales		372 000
Less: Cost of goods sold:		
Opening stock	36 000	
Purchases	320 000	
	356 000	
Less: Closing stock	68 000	288 000
Gross profit	c/f	84 000

	£	£
b/f		84 000
Less: Expenses:		
Bad debts	13 000	
Depreciation: office equipment (44 000 – 4 000 × 25%)	10 000	
Insurance (1 800 – 200)	1 600	
Loan interest	7 500	
Loss on disposal of office equipment (4 000 – 3 000 – 500)	500	
Miscellaneous expenses	57 700	
Provision for bad and doubtful debts		
[10% × (93 000 – 13 000) – 2 000]	6 000	
Rates (10 000 + 2000)	12 000	108 300
Net loss		£(24 300)

LIME
Balance sheet at 30 September 19X7

	£	£	£
Fixed assets			
Office equipment at cost (44 000 – 4 000)			40 000
Less: Accumulated depreciation			
(22 000 – 3 000 + 10 000)			29 000
			11 000
Current assets			
Stocks		68 000	
Trade debtors (93 000 – 13 000)	80 000		
Less: Provision for bad and doubtful debts	8 000	72 000	
Prepayment		200	
		140 200	
Less: Current liabilities			
Trade creditors	105 000		
Accrual	2 000		
Bank overdraft	15 200	122 200	18 000
			£29 000
Financed by:			
Capital			
Balance at 10 October 19X6			19 300
Less: Net loss for the year		(24 300)	
Less: Drawings		(16 000)	(40 300)
			(21 000)
Loan (from Cedar)			50 000
			£29 000

5.15

TEAK
Trading, profit and loss account for the year to 31 December 19X8

	£	£
Sales		164 000
Less: Cost of goods sold:		
Opening stock	2 800	
Purchases (83 000 – 6 000)	77 000	
	79 800	
Less: Closing stock	15 800	64 000
Gross profit		100 000
Add: Incomes:		
Building society interest (700 + 800)	1 500	
Dividends (100 + 600)	700	
Interest from Gray	500	2 700
		102 700
Less: Expenses:		
Depreciation: plant and equipment (30 % × 50 000)	15 000	
vehicles [(64 000 – 16 000) × 25%]	12 000	
Office expenses (39 000 + 1 200 – 9 000)	31 200	
Vehicle expenses	12 600	70 800
Net profit		£31 900

TEAK
Balance sheet at 31 December 19X8

	Cost	Accumulated depreciation	Net book value
	£	£	£
Fixed assets			
Plant and equipment	50 000	45 000	5 000
Vehicles	64 000	28 000	36 000
	114 000	73 000	41 000
Investments at cost			5 000
Current assets			
Stocks		15 800	
Short-term loan		10 000	
Trade debtors		13 200	
Debtors (800 + 600)		1 400	
Building society deposit		20 000	
Cash at bank and in hand		400	
		60 800	
Less: *Current liabilities*			
Trade creditors	22 200		
Accrual	1 200	23 400	37 400
			£83 400

	£	£	£
Financed by:			
Capital			
Balance at 1 January 19X8			66 500
Net profit for the year		31 900	
Less: Drawings (6 000 + 9 000)		15 000	16 900
			£83 400

Chapter 6   6.1

MEGG
Manufacturing account for the year to 31 January 19X1

	£000	£000
Direct materials:		
Stock at 1 February 19X0	10	
Purchases	34	
	44	
Less: Stock at 31 January 19X1	12	
Materials consumed		32
Direct wages		65
Prime cost		97
Factory overhead expenses:		
Administration	27	
Heat and light	9	
Indirect wages	13	49
		146
Work-in-progress at 1 February 19X0	17	
Less: Work-in-progress at 31 January 19X1	14	3
Manufacturing cost of goods produced		£149

6.2

MOOR
Manufacturing account for the year to 28 February 19X2

	£	£
Direct materials:		
Stock at 1 March 19X1	13 000	
Purchases	127 500	
	140 500	
Less: Stock at 28 February 19X2	15 500	125 000
Direct wages		50 000
Prime cost		175 000
Factory overheads		27 700
		202 700
Work-in-progress at 1 March 19X1	8 400	
Less: Work-in-progress at 28 February 19X2	6 300	2 100
Manufacturing cost of goods produced		£204 800

6.3

STUART
Manufacturing account for the year to 31 March 19X3

	£000	£000
Direct materials:		
Stock at 1 April 19X2	38	
Purchases	1123	
	1161	
Less: Stock at 31 March 19X3	44	1117
Direct wages		330
Prime cost		1447
Factory overheads		230
		1677
Work-in-progress: at 1 April 19X2	29	
Less: Work-in-progress at 31 March 19X3	42	(13)
Manufacturing cost of goods produced		£1664

Chapter 7   7.1

MARGO LIMITED
Profit and loss account for the year to 31 January 19X1

	£000
Profit for the financial year	10
Tax on profit	3
Profit after tax	7
Proposed dividend (10p × 50)	5
Retained profit for the year	£2

MARGO LIMITED
Balance sheet at 31 January 19X1

	£000	£000	£000
Fixed assets			
Plant and equipment at cost			70
Less: Accumulated depreciation			25
			45
Current assets			
Stocks		17	
Trade debtors		20	
Cash at bank and in hand		5	
		42	
Less: Current liabilities			
Trade creditors	12		
Taxation	3		
Proposed dividend	5	20	22
			£67

Capital and reserves	Authorized	Issued and fully paid
	£000	£000
Share capital (ordinary shares of £1 each)	75	50
Profit and loss account (15 + 2)		17
		£67

7.2

HARRY LIMITED
Profit and loss account for the year to 28 February 19X2

	£000	£000
Gross profit for the year		150
Administration expenses [65 + (10% × 60)]	71	
Distribution costs	15	86
Profit for the year		64
Taxation		24
Profit after tax		40
Dividends: Ordinary proposed	20	
Preference paid	6	26
Retained profit for the year		£14

HARRY LIMITED
Balance sheet at 28 February 19X2

	£000	£000	£000
Fixed assets			
Furniture and equipment at cost			60
Less: Accumulated depreciation			42
			18
Current assets			
Stocks		130	
Trade debtors		135	
Cash at bank and in hand		10	
		275	
Less: Current liabilities			
Trade creditors	25		
Taxation	24		
Proposed dividend	20	69	206
			£224

Capital and reserves	Authorized, issued and fully paid
	£000
Ordinary shares of £1 each	100
Cumulative 15% preference shares of £1 each	40
	140
Share premium account	20
Profit and loss account (50 + 14)	64
	£224

7.3

JIM LIMITED
Trading and profit and loss account for the year to 31 March 19X3

	£000	£000	£000
Sales			270
Less: Cost of goods sold:			
Opening stock		16	
Purchases		124	
		140	
Less: Closing stock		14	126
Gross profit			144
Less: Expenses:			
Advertising		3	
Depreciation: furniture and fittings (15% × 20)	3		
vehicles (25% × 40)	10	13	
Directors' fees		6	
Rent and rates		10	
Telephone and stationery		5	
Travelling		2	
Wages and salaries		24	63
Net profit			81
Corporation tax			25
Net profit after tax			56
Proposed dividend			28
Retained profit for the year			£28

JIM LIMITED
Balance sheet at 31 March 19X3

	Cost	Depreciation	Net book value
	£000	£000	£000
Fixed assets			
Vehicles	40	20	20
Furniture and fittings	20	12	8
	60	32	28
Current assets			
Stocks		14	
Debtors		118	
Bank		11	
		143	
Less: *Current liabilities*			
Creditors	12		
Taxation	25		
Proposed dividend	28	65	78
			£106

	Authorized	Issued and fully paid
	£000	£000
Capital and reserves		
Ordinary shares of £1 each	100	70
Profit and loss account (8 + 28)		36
		£106

7.4

CYRIL LIMITED
Trading, profit and loss account for the year to 30 April 19X4

	£000	£000	£000
Sales			900
Less: Cost of goods sold:			
Opening stock		120	
Purchases		480	
		600	
Less: Closing stock		140	460
Gross profit			440
Add: Income:			
Investment income			5
			445
Less: Expenses:			
Advertising		2	
Auditors' remuneration		6	
Bank interest		4	
Directors' remuneration		30	
Depreciation: buildings	28		
vehicles	9	37	
General expenses		15	
Repairs and renewals (4 – 2)		2	
Wages and salaries		221	317
Net profit			128
Corporation tax			60
Profit after tax			68
Dividends: Proposed ordinary			
(10p per share)		50	
Preference paid		15	65
Retained profit for the year			£3

CYRIL LIMITED
Balance sheet at 30 April 19X4

	Cost £000	Accumulated depreciation £000	Net book value £000
Fixed assets			
Freehold land and buildings	800	130	670
Motor vehicles	36	27	9
	836	157	679
Investments at cost (Market value £35 000)			30
Current assets			
Stocks		140	
Debtors		143	
Prepayment		2	
		285	
Less: Current liabilities			
Bank overdraft	20		
Creditors	80		
Accrual	6		
Taxation	60		
Proposed dividend	50	216	69
			£778

	Authorized, issued and fully paid £000
Capital and reserves	
Ordinary shares of £1 each	500
Cumulative 10% preference shares of £1 each	150
	650
Share premium account	25
Profit and loss account (100 + 3)	103
	£778

7.5

NELSON LIMITED
Trading, profit and loss account for the year to 31 May 19X5

	£000	£000
Sales		800
Less: Cost of goods sold:		
Opening stock	155	
Purchases	400	
	555	
Less: Closing stock	195	360
Gross profit c/f		440

	£000	£000
	b/f	440
Add: Income:		
Investment income		22
		462
Less: Expenses:		
Administrative expenses (257 +13)	270	
Auditors' fees	10	
Debenture interest (12% × 100)	12	
Directors' remuneration	60	
Depreciation: furniture and fittings		
(12.5% × 200)	25	
Wages and salaries (44 − 4)	40	417
Net profit		45
Corporation tax		8
Profit after tax		37
Dividends: Ordinary – interim	20	
– proposed	5	
Preference (paid and payable)	10	35
Retained profit for the year		£2

NELSON LIMITED
Balance sheet at 31 May 19X5

	£000	£000	£000
Fixed assets			
Furniture and fittings at cost			200
Less: Accumulated depreciation			
(48 + 25)			73
			127
Investments at cost (Market value £340 000)			335
Current assets			
Stock		195	
Debtors		225	
Prepayment		4	
Cash at bank and in hand		5	
		429	
Less: Current liabilities			
Creditors	85		
Accruals (13 + 6)	19		
Corporation tax	8		
Proposed dividends: Ordinary	5		
Preference	5	122	307
			£769

Capital and reserves		Authorized	Issued and fully paid
		£000	£000
Ordinary shares of £1 each		500	400
Cumulative 5% preference shares of £1 each		200	200
		700	600
Share premium account			50
Profit and loss account (17 + 2)			19
Shareholders' funds			669
Loans:			
12% Debentures			100
			£769

7.6

KEITH LIMITED
Trading, profit and loss account for the year to 30 June 19X6

	£000	£000
Sales		2100
Less: Cost of goods sold:		
Opening stock	134	
Purchases	1240	
	1374	
Less: Closing stock	155	1219
		881
Add: Income:		
Investment income		4
		885
Less: Expenses:		
Advertising	30	
Auditors' remuneration	12	
Debenture interest (10% × 70)	7	
Directors' remuneration	55	
Electricity	28	
Insurance (17 − 3)	14	
Depreciation: machinery (20% × 420)	84	
vehicles (25% × 80)	20	
Increase in provision for bad and doubtful debts [(5% × 300) − 8]	7	
Office expenses	49	
Rent and rates	75	
Wages and salaries	358	739
Net profit		146
Corporation tax		60
Profit after tax		86
Dividends: Proposed ordinary (400 000 × 10p)	40	
Preference	4	44
Retained profit for the year		£42

KEITH LIMITED
Balance sheet at 30 June 19X6

	Cost £000	Accumulated depreciation £000	Net book value £000
Fixed assets			
Machinery	420	236	184
Vehicles	80	60	20
	500	296	204
Investments (Market value £30 000)			28
Current assets			
Stock		155	
Trade debtors	300		
Less: Provision for bad and doubtful debts (5%)	15	285	
Prepayment		3	
Bank		7	
		450	
Less: Current liabilities			
Creditors	69		
Accruals (7 + 12)	19		
Corporation tax	60		
Proposed dividend	40	188	262
			£494

	Authorized £000	Issued and fully paid £000
Capital and reserves		
Ordinary shares of 50p each	300	200
Cumulative 8% preference shares of £1 each	50	50
	350	250
Profit and loss account (132 + 42)		174
Shareholders' funds		424
Loans:		
10% Debentures		70
		£494

Chapter 8   8.1

DENNIS LIMITED
Cash flow statement for the year ended 31 January 19X2

	£000	£000
Net cash inflow from operating activities		4
Capital expenditure		
Payments to acquire tangible fixed assets		(100)
		(96)
Management of liquid resource and financing		
Issue of ordinary share capital		100
Increase in cash		£4

Reconciliation of operating profit to net cash inflow from operating activities

	£000
Operating profit (60 – 26)	34
Increase in stocks	(20)
Increase in debtors	(50)
Increase in creditors	40
Net cash inflow from operating activities	4

Movement in cash

	At 1.2.X1 £000	Cash flows £000	At 31.1.X2 £000
Cash	6	4	10

8.2

FRANK LIMITED
Cash flow statement for the year ended 28 February 19X2

	£000	£000
Net cash inflow from operating activities		70
Management of liquid resources and financing		
Issue of debenture loan		60
Purchase of investments		(100)
Increase in cash		£30

Reconciliation of operating profit to net cash inflow from operating activities

	£000
Operating profit (40 – 30)	10
Depreciation charges	20
Increase in stocks	(30)
Decrease in debtors	110
Decrease in creditors	(40)
Net cash inflow from operating activities	70

No details of debenture interest were given in the question.

Movement in cash

	At 1.2.X1	Cash flows	At 28.2.X2
	£000	£000	£000
Cash at bank	(20)	30	10

8.3

STARTER

Cash flow statement for the year ended 31 March 19X3

	£	£
Net cash inflow from operating activities		2 500
Capital expenditure		
Payments to acquire tangible fixed assets		(10 000)
		(7 500)
Management of liquid resources and financing		
Capital introduced		20 000
Increase in cash		£12 500

Reconciliation of operating profit to net cash inflow from operating activities

	£
Operating profit	4 000
Depreciation charges	2 000
Increase in stocks	(1 000)
Increase in trade debtors	(5 000)
Increase in trade creditors	2 500
Net cash inflow from operating activities	2 500

Movement in cash

	At 1.4.X2	Cash flows	At 31.3.X3
	£	£	£
Cash at bank	0	12 500	12 500

8.4

GREGORY LIMITED

Cash flow statement for the year ended 30 April 19X4

	£000	£000
Net cash inflow from operating activities		145
Taxation		
Corporation tax paid		(18)
Capital expenditure		
Payments to acquire tangible fixed assets		(150)
		(23)
Equity dividends paid		(35)
		(58)
Management of liquid resources and financing		
Issue of debenture loan		50
Decrease in cash		£(8)

	£000
* Increase in retained profit	10
Proposed dividend	40
Taxation	25
	75

Reconciliation of operating profit to net cash inflow from operating activities

	£000
Operating profit	75*
Depreciation charges	80
Increase in stocks	(40)
Decrease in debtors	20
Increase in creditors	10
Net cash inflow from operating activities	145

Movement in cash

	At 1.5.X3 £000	Cash flows £000	At 30.4.X4 £000
Cash at bank	10	(8)	2

8.5

PILL LIMITED
Cash flow statement for the year ended 31 May 19X5

	£000	£000
Net cash inflow from operating activities		554
Return on investments and servicing of finance		
Interest paid (10% × 40)		(4)
Taxation		
Corporation tax paid (170 + 150 – 220)		(100)
Capital expenditure		
Payments to acquire tangible fixed assets		
[(800 – 600) + 250 – 200]		(250)
		200
Equity dividends paid (150 + 250 – 100)		(300)
		(100)
Management of liquid resources and financing		
Issue of ordinary share capital (550 – 500)		50
Repurchase of debenture loan (190 – 40)		(150)
Decrease in cash		£(200)

Reconciliation of operating profit to net cash inflow from operating activities

	£000
Operating profit [580 + (10% × 40)]	584
Depreciation charges	100
Increase in stocks	(140)
Increase in debtors	(20)
Increase in creditors	30
Net cash inflow from operating activities	554

Movement in cash

	At 1.6.X4 £000	Cash flows £000	At 31.5.X5 £000
Cash	320	(200)	120

8.6

BRIAN LIMITED
Cash flow statement for the year ended 30 June 19X6

	£000	£000
Net cash inflow from operating activities		137
Taxation		
Corporation tax paid		
Tax paid		(52)
Capital expenditure		
Payments to acquire tangible fixed assets	(75)	
Receipts from sales of tangible fixed assets	12	(63)
		22
Equity dividends paid		(20)
Increase in cash		2

Reconciliation of operating profit to net cash inflow from operating activities

	£000
Operating profit	115
Depreciation charges	35
Loss on sale of vehicle	3
Increase in provision for doubtful debts	1
Decrease in stocks	10
Increase in trade debtors	(20)
Decrease in trade creditors	(7)
Net cash inflow from operating activities	137

Movement in cash

	At 1.7.X5 £000	Cash flows £000	At 1.6.X6 £000
Cash	6	2	8

Chapter 9

9.1 **BETTY**

Accounting ratios year to 31 January 19X1:

1 Gross profit ratio:

$$\frac{\text{Gross profit}}{\text{Total sales revenue}} \times 100 = \frac{30}{100} \times 100 = \underline{\underline{30\%}}$$

2 Net profit ratio:

$$\frac{\text{Net profit}}{\text{Sales}} \times 100 = \frac{14}{100} \times 100 = \underline{\underline{14\%}}$$

3 Return on capital employed:

$$\frac{\text{Net profit}}{\text{Average capital}} \times 100 = \frac{14}{\frac{1}{2}(40 + 48)} \times 100 = \underline{\underline{31.8\%}}$$

$$or \ \frac{\text{Net profit}}{\text{Capital}} \times 100 = \frac{14}{48} \times 100 = \underline{\underline{29.2\%}}$$

4 Current ratio:

$$\frac{\text{Current assets}}{\text{Current liabilities}} = \frac{25}{6} = \underline{\underline{4.2 \text{ to } 1}}$$

5 Acid test:

$$\frac{\text{Current assets} - \text{stock}}{\text{Current liabilities}} = \frac{25 - 10}{6} = \underline{\underline{2.5 \text{ to } 1}}$$

6 Stock turnover:

$$\frac{\text{Cost of goods sold}}{\text{Average stock}} = \frac{70}{\frac{1}{2}(15 + 10)} = \underline{\underline{5.6 \text{ times}}}$$

7 Debtor collection period:

$$\frac{\text{Trade debtors}}{\text{Credit sales}} \times 365 = \frac{12}{100} \times 365 = \underline{\underline{44 \text{ days}}} \text{ (rounded up)}$$

9.2 JAMES LIMITED

Accounting ratios year to 28 February 19X2:

1 Return on capital employed:

$$\frac{\text{Net profit before taxation and dividends}}{\text{Average shareholders' funds}} \times 100 = \frac{90}{\frac{1}{2}(600 + 620)} \times 100 = \underline{\underline{14.8\%}}$$

$$or \quad \frac{\text{Net profit before taxation and dividends}}{\text{Shareholders' funds}} \times 100 = \frac{90}{620} \times 100 = \underline{\underline{14.5\%}}$$

2 Gross profit:

$$\frac{\text{Gross profit}}{\text{Sales}} \times 100 = \frac{600}{1200} \times 100 = \underline{\underline{50\%}}$$

3 Mark-up:

$$\frac{\text{Gross profit}}{\text{Cost of goods sold}} \times 100 = \frac{600}{600} \times 100 = \underline{\underline{100\%}}$$

4 Net profit:

$$\frac{\text{Net profit before taxation and dividends}}{\text{Sales}} \times 100 = \frac{90}{1200} \times 100 = \underline{\underline{7.5\%}}$$

5 Acid test:

$$\frac{\text{Current assets} - \text{stock}}{\text{Current liabilities}} = \frac{275 - 75}{240} = \underline{\underline{0.83 \text{ to } 1}}$$

6 Fixed assets turnover:

$$\frac{\text{Sales}}{\text{Fixed assets (NBV)}} = \frac{1200}{685} = \underline{\underline{1.75 \text{ times}}}$$

7 Debtor collection period:

$$\frac{\text{Trade debtors}}{\text{Credit sales}} \times 365 = \frac{200}{1200} \times 365 = \underline{\underline{61 \text{ days}}} \text{ (rounded up)}$$

8 Capital gearing:

$$\frac{\text{Long-term loans}}{\text{Shareholders' funds and long-term loans}} \times 100 = \frac{100}{720} \times 100 = \underline{\underline{13.9\%}}$$

9.3 Accounting ratios year to 31 March 19X3:

	Mark Limited	Luke Limited	John Limited

1 Return on capital employed:
Net profit before taxation and dividends

$$\frac{\text{Net profit before taxation and dividends}}{\text{Shareholders' funds}} \times 100$$

$\frac{64}{250} \times 100$ $\frac{22}{327} \times 100$ $\frac{55}{290} \times 100$

$= 25.6\%$ $= 6.7\%$ $= 19.0\%$

	Mark Limited	Luke Limited	John Limited

2 Capital gearing:
Preference shares + Long-term loans

$$\frac{\text{Preference shares + Long-term loans}}{\text{Shareholders' funds + Long-term loans}} \times 100$$

No preference shares or long-term loans

$\frac{20}{327} \times 100$ $\frac{10 + 100}{390} \times 100$

$= \underline{\underline{6.1\%}}$ $= \underline{\underline{28.2\%}}$

9.4   HELENA LIMITED
Accounting ratios 19X2 to 19X6:

	19X2	19X3	19X4	19X5	19X6
1 Gross profit: $\dfrac{\text{Gross profit}}{\text{Sales}} \times 100$	$\dfrac{30}{130} \times 100$ $= 23.1\%$	$\dfrac{40}{150} \times 100$ $= 26.7\%$	$\dfrac{60}{190} \times 100$ $= 31.6\%$	$\dfrac{70}{210} \times 100$ $= 33.3\%$	$\dfrac{75}{320} \times 100$ $= 23.4\%$
2 Mark-up: $\dfrac{\text{Gross profit}}{\text{Cost of goods sold}} \times 100$	$\dfrac{30}{100} \times 100$ $= 30\%$	$\dfrac{40}{110} \times 100$ $= 36.4\%$	$\dfrac{60}{130} \times 100$ $= 46.2\%$	$\dfrac{70}{140} \times 100$ $= 50\%$	$\dfrac{75}{245} \times 100$ $= 30.6\%$
3 Stock turnover: $\dfrac{\text{Cost of goods sold}}{\text{Average stock}}$	$\dfrac{100}{\frac{1}{2}(20+30)}$ $= 4 \text{ times}$	$\dfrac{110}{\frac{1}{2}(30+30)}$ $= 3.7 \text{ times}$	$\dfrac{130}{\frac{1}{2}(30+35)}$ $= 4 \text{ times}$	$\dfrac{140}{\frac{1}{2}(35+40)}$ $= 3.7 \text{ times}$	$\dfrac{245}{\frac{1}{2}(40+100)}$ $= 3.5 \text{ times}$
4 Trade debtor collection period: $\dfrac{\text{Average trade debtors}}{\text{Credit sales}} \times 365$	$\dfrac{\frac{1}{2}(45+40)}{130} \times 365$ $= 120 \text{ days}$	$\dfrac{\frac{1}{2}(40+45)}{150} \times 365$ $= 104 \text{ days}$	$\dfrac{\frac{1}{2}(70+40)}{190} \times 365$ $= 106 \text{ days}$	$\dfrac{\frac{1}{2}(100+70)}{210} \times 365$ $= 148 \text{ days}$	$\dfrac{\frac{1}{2}(150+100)}{320} \times 365$ $= 143 \text{ days}$
5 Trade creditor payment period: $\dfrac{\text{Average trade creditors}}{\text{Credit purchases}} \times 365$	$\dfrac{\frac{1}{2}(20+20)}{110} \times 365$ $= 67 \text{ days}$	$\dfrac{\frac{1}{2}(25+20)}{110} \times 365$ $= 74.5 \text{ days}$	$\dfrac{\frac{1}{2}(25+25)}{135} \times 365$ $= 68 \text{ days}$	$\dfrac{\frac{1}{2}(30+25)}{145} \times 365$ $= 70 \text{ days}$	$\dfrac{\frac{1}{2}(60+30)}{305} \times 365$ $= 54 \text{ days}$

9.5 HEDGE PLC
Accounting ratios:

1 Dividend yield:

$$\frac{\text{Dividend per share}}{\text{Market price per share}} \times 100 = \frac{7}{350} \times 100 = \underline{\underline{2\%}}$$

2 Dividend cover:

$$\frac{\text{Net profit after taxation}}{\text{Ordinary dividends}} = \frac{70\,000}{35\,000} = \underline{\underline{2 \text{ times}}}$$

3 Earnings per share:

$$\frac{\text{Net profit after taxation}}{\text{Number of ordinary shares in issue}} = \frac{70\,000}{500\,000} = \underline{\underline{14\text{p}}}$$

4 Price/earnings ratio:

$$\frac{\text{Market price per share}}{\text{Earnings per share}} = \frac{3.50}{0.14} = \underline{\underline{25}}$$

9.6 (a)
STYLE LIMITED
Accounting ratios:

1 Gross profit:

	19X5	19X6
$\dfrac{\text{Gross profit}}{\text{Sales}} \times 100$	$\dfrac{525}{1500} \times 100 = \underline{\underline{35\%}}$	$\dfrac{600}{1900} \times 100 = \underline{\underline{31.6\%}}$

2 Mark-up:

$\dfrac{\text{Gross profit}}{\text{Cost of goods sold}} \times 100$	$\dfrac{525}{975} \times 100 = \underline{\underline{53.8\%}}$	$\dfrac{600}{1300} \times 100 = \underline{\underline{46.2\%}}$

3 Net profit:

$\dfrac{\text{Net profit}}{\text{Sales}} \times 100$	$\dfrac{275}{1500} \times 100 = \underline{\underline{18.3\%}}$	$\dfrac{250}{1900} \times 100 = \underline{\underline{13.2\%}}$

4 Return on capital employed:

$\dfrac{\text{Net profit}}{\text{Shareholders' funds}} \times 100$	$\dfrac{275 \times 100}{\frac{1}{2}(900 + 1000)}$ $= \underline{\underline{28.9\%}}$	$\dfrac{250 \times 100}{\frac{1}{2}(900 + 1250)}$ $= \underline{\underline{23.3\%}}$

or		
$\dfrac{\text{Net profit}}{\text{Shareholders' funds}} \times 100$	$\dfrac{275 \times 100}{1000} \times 100$ $= \underline{\underline{27.5\%}}$	$\dfrac{250}{1250} \times 100$ $= \underline{\underline{20.0\%}}$

5 Stock turnover:

$\dfrac{\text{Cost of goods sold}}{\text{Average stock}}$	$\dfrac{975}{\frac{1}{2}(£80 + 100)} = \underline{\underline{10.8 \text{ times}}}$	$\dfrac{1300}{\frac{1}{2}(£100 + 200)} = \underline{\underline{8.7 \text{ times}}}$

6 Current ratio:

$$\frac{\text{Current assets}}{\text{Current liabilities}} \qquad \frac{500}{80} = \underline{\underline{6.3 \text{ to } 1}} \qquad \frac{1000}{210} = \underline{\underline{4.8 \text{ to } 1}}$$

7 Acid test:

$$\frac{\text{Current assets} - \text{stock}}{\text{Current liabilities}} \qquad \frac{500 - 100}{80} = \underline{\underline{5 \text{ to } 1}} \qquad \frac{1000 - 200}{210} = \underline{\underline{3.8 \text{ to } 1}}$$

8 Trade debtor collection period:

$$\frac{\text{Trade debtors}}{\text{Credit sales}} \times 365 \qquad \frac{375}{1500} \times 365 = \underline{\underline{92 \text{ days}}} \qquad \frac{800}{1900} \times 365 = \underline{\underline{154 \text{ days}}}$$

9 Trade creditor payment period:

$$\frac{\text{Trade creditors}}{\text{Purchases}} \times 365 \qquad \frac{80}{995} \times 365 = \underline{\underline{30 \text{ days}}} \qquad \frac{200}{1400} \times 365 = \underline{\underline{53 \text{ days}}}$$

(b) *Brief comments*

The company increased its sales in 19X6 by £400 000 (26.7%). It appeared to achieve this by reducing its profit on goods sold, but the increased activity probably resulted in additional expenses. As a result, even in absolute terms, its net profit was down from £275 000 to £250 000. It should also be noted there is no explanation why an amount was not set aside for taxation or dividends either in 19X5 or 19X6.

Its liquidity position is still healthy, even if its debtor collection period (based on year-end figures) has increased substantially (as has the time taken to pay the creditors). This may be a deliberate policy to stimulate sales or it may be that it has been too busy to encourage its customers to settle their debts.

Not surprisingly, the cash position has deteriorated and at the end of 19X6 the company was in overdraft.

Increased trading activity does not always guarantee survival if the company cannot settle its debts as they fall due. Unless it becomes more efficient in this respect, the company's long-term future could be uncertain.

Chapter 13

13.1 *Financial accounting* is mainly concerned with supplying information to the external users of an entity.

Management accounting is concerned with producing information for use within an entity.

13.2 1 Elements
2 Units
3 Direct and indirect
4 Fixed and variable
5 Controllable and non-controllable
6 Relevant and irrelevant
7 Responsibility
8 Normal and abnormal

13.3 1 Board of directors
2 Divisions
3 Factories or works
4 Functions
5 Cost centres

13.4 A cost centre is a clearly-defined area of responsibility that is charged with its own indentified operating costs. A cost centre may take the form of a department, an area, a machine or an individual (such as a salesperson).

13.5 In *absorption* costing, all production costs (including fixed production overheads) are charged out to individual units or processes.

In *marginal costing*, fixed production overheads are not charged out to individual units or processes.

Chapter 14

14.1 1 FIFO:

		£
1000 units	@ £20 =	20 000
250 units	@ £25 =	6 250
Charge to production		£26 250

2 LIFO:

		£
500 units	@ £25 =	12 500
750 units	@ £20 =	15 000
Charge to production		£27 500

3 Periodic weighted average:

Units		Value £
1 000	@ £20	20 000
500	@ £25	12 500
1 500		£32 500

$$\text{Average} = \frac{32\ 500}{1\ 500} = £21.67$$

Charge to production = 1 250 × 21.67 = £27 088

14.2 MATERIAL ST 2

	Stock	Units	Total stock value £	Average unit price £
1.2.X2	Opening	500	500	1.00
10.2.X2	Receipts	200	220	
		700	720	1.03
12.2.X2	Receipts	100	112	
		800	832	1.04
17.2.X2	Issues	(400)	(416)	
	c/f	400	416	

			£	£
	b/f	400	416	
25.2.X2	Receipts	300	345	
		700	761	1.09
27.2.X2	Issues	(250)	(273)	
28.0.X2	*Closing stock*	£450	£488	

14.3 Closing stock calculations:

1 FIFO:

800 units	@ £12 =	£9 600

2 LIFO:

600 units	@ £12 =	7 200
200 units	@ £10 =	2 000
800		£9 200

3 Continuous weighted average:

	Stock	Units	*Total stock* Value £	*Average unit price* £
1.1.X3	Purchases	2 000	20 000	10.00
31.3.X3	Issues	(1 600)	(16 000)	
		400	4 000	
1.2.X3	Purchases	2 400	26 400	
		2 800	30 400	10.86
28.2.X3	Issues	(2 600)	(28 236)	
		200	2 164	
1.3.X3	Purchases	1 600	19 200	
		1 800	21 364	11.87
31.3.X3	Issues	(1 000)	(11 870)	
		800	£9 494	

14.4 Calculation of closing stock:

	Units	Value £
Total receipts:	240	1692

Periodic weighted average price: $\dfrac{1692}{240} = £7.05$

Total issues: 195 units – all issued at £7.05 = £1375

	£	Units	
In stock at 30.4.X4 *Less*: Issues			
1692 – 1375 =	317	45	(240 – 195)
Add: Stock at 1.4.X4	120	20	
Closing stock at 30.4.X4	£437	65	

14.5

STEED LIMITED

Trading account for the year to 31 May 19X5

	FIFO	LIFO	Periodic weighted average	Continuous weighted average
	£	£	£	£
Sales	500 000	500 000	500 000	500 000
Less: Cost of goods sold:				
Opening stock	40 000	40 000	40 000	40 000
Purchases	440 000	440 000	440 000	440 000
	480 000	480 000	480 000	480 000
Less: Closing stock	90 000	65 000	67 500	79 950
	390 000	415 000	412 500	400 050
Gross profit	£110 000	£85 000	£87 500	£99 950

14.6

(a) Pricing the issue of materials to production:

    1 *First-in, first-out* (FIFO):

       Total receipts   = 2 400 litres

       Total issues   = 2 200 litres

    Therefore closing stock = 200 litres @ £5 per litre = £1 000

    2 *Last-in, first-out* (LIFO):

    Closing stock position at 31 December 19X4:

October receipts	All issued in December	
June receipts:	400 litres issued in July	
	400 litres issued in December	
April receipts:	300 litres issued in May leaving	
	100 litres in stock @ £3.00 per litre =	£300
January receipts:	100 litres issued in February leaving	
	100 litres in stock @ £2.00 per litre =	£200
Closing stock value:		£500

  3 Periodic weighted average:

    Total value of receipts = £9 600

    Total receipts = 2 400 litres

    Therefore periodic weighted average price per litre = £4.00

    Value of stock = £4 × 200 litres = £800

4 *Continuous weighted average:*

Month	Stock balance Quantity	Value	Average price per litre in stock	Issued at per litre
	(litres)	£	£	£
January	200	400	2.00	
February	(100)	(200)		2.00
	100	200		
April	500	1 500		
	600	1 700	2.83	
May	(300)	(849)		2.83
	300	851		
June	800	3 200		
	1 100	4 051	3.68	
July	(400)	(1 472)		3.68
	700	2 579		
October	900	4 500		
	1 600	7 079	4.42	
December	(1 400)	(6 188)		4.42
	200	£891		

(b) Calculation of gross profit:

	Method 1 *FIFO*	2 *LIFO*	3 *Periodic weighted average*	4 *Continuous weighted average*
	£	£	£	£
Sales	20 000	20 000	20 000	20 000
Less: Cost of goods sold:				
Purchases	9 600	9 600	9 600	9 600
Less: Closing stock	1 000	500	800	891
	8 600	9 100	8 800	8 709
Conversion costs	7 000	7 000	7 000	7 000
Manufacturing cost	15 600	16 100	15 800	15 709
Gross profit	£4 400	£3 900	£4 200	£4 291

Chapter 15

15.1 SCAR LIMITED

Overhead apportionment January 19X1:

	Production Department		Service Department
	A	B	
	£000	£000	£000
Allocated expenses	65	35	50
Apportionment of service department's expenses in the ratio 60 : 40	30	20	(50)
Overhead to be charged	£95	£55	–

15.2 BANK LIMITED

Assembly department – overhead absorption methods:

1 Specific units:

$$\frac{\text{Total cost centre overhead}}{\text{Number of units}} = \frac{250\ 000}{50\ 000} = \text{£5 per unit}$$

2 Direct materials:

$$\frac{\text{Total cost centre overhead}}{\text{Direct materials}} \times 100 = \frac{250\ 000}{500\ 000} \times 100 = 50\%$$

Therefore 50% of £8 = £4 per unit

3 Direct labour:

$$\frac{\text{Total cost centre overhead}}{\text{Direct labour}} \times 100 = \frac{250\ 000}{1\ 000\ 000} \times 100 = 25\%$$

Therefore 25% of £30 = £7.50 per unit

4 Prime cost:

$$\frac{\text{Total cost centre overhead}}{\text{Prime cost}} \times 100 = \frac{250\ 000}{1\ 530\ 000} \times 100 = 16.34\%$$

Therefore 16.34% of £40 = £6.54 per unit

5 Direct labour hours:

$$\frac{\text{Total cost centre overhead}}{\text{Direct labour hours}} = \frac{250\ 000}{100\ 000} = \text{£2.50 per direct labour hour}$$

Therefore £2.50 of 3.5 DLH = £8.75 per unit

6 Machine hours:

$$\frac{\text{Total cost centre overhead}}{\text{Machine hours}} = \frac{250\ 000}{25\ 000} = \text{£10 per machine hour}$$

Therefore £10 of 0.75 = £7.50 per unit

15.3 CLOUGH LIMITED

(a) Overhead absorption for March 19X3 – production department:

1   Direct labour hours:

$$\frac{\text{Total cost centre overhead}}{\text{Direct labour hours}} = \frac{150\,000}{30\,000} = £5 \text{ per DLH}$$

Therefore for order number 123: £5 × 5 = <u>£25</u>

2   Machine hours:

$$\frac{\text{Total cost centre overhead}}{\text{Machine hours}} = \frac{150\,000}{10\,000} = £15 \text{ per MH}$$

Therefore for order number 123 : £15 × 2 = <u>£30</u>

Selling price of order number 123:

	Direct labour hours	*Machine hours*
	£	£
Direct materials	20	20
Direct wages	25	25
Prime costs	45	45
Overhead	25	30
Total cost	70	75
Administration + profit (50%)	35	37.50
Selling price	£105	£112.50

(b) As the department appears more labour intensive than machine intensive, use the direct labour hour method.

15.4 BURNS LIMITED

Overhead absorption schedule – April 19X4:

	Departments				
	Processing	*Assembling*	*Finishing*	*Administration*	*Work study*
	£	£	£	£	£
Direct labour	–	–	–	65 000	33 000
Allocated costs	15 000	20 000	10 000	35 000	12 000
				100 000	
Apportion: Administration (50 : 30 : 15 : 5)	50 000	30 000	15 000	(100 000)	5 000
					50 000
Work study (70 : 20 : 10)	35 000	10 000	5 000	–	(50 000)
Overhead to be absorbed	£100 000	£60 000	£30 000	–	–

Calculation of absorption rates:

Processing department: $\dfrac{\text{TCCO}}{\text{Machine hours}} = \dfrac{100\,000}{25\,000} = £4 \text{ per MH}$

Assembling department: $\dfrac{\text{TCCO}}{\text{Direct labour hours}} = \dfrac{60\,000}{30\,000} = £2 \text{ per DLH}$

Finishing department: $\dfrac{\text{TCCO}}{\text{Direct labour cost}} \times 100 = \dfrac{30\,000}{120\,000} \times 100 = 25\%$

Total cost of producing unit XP6:

	£	£
Prime cost		47
Overhead:		
Processing (4 × 6 MH)	24	
Assembling (2 × 1)	2	
Finishing (25% × 12)	3	29
Total cost		£76

15.5 OUTLANE LIMITED

(a) *Overhead charge – direct labour cost method:*

	Contract 1	Contract 2
Direct labour cost:		
DLH × rate per hour = 100 × £3.00	£300	£300
Therefore overhead to be absorbed		
(100%) =	£300	£300

(b) *Overhead charge – machine hour rate method:*
Overhead absorption schedule:

	Apportionment method	L £000	M £000	N £000	O £000
Administration	Total number of employees	40	30	20	10
Depreciation of machinery	Depreciation rate	22	8	10	40
Employer's National Insurance	Total number of employees	4	3	2	1
Heating and light	Cubic capacity	6	3	1	5
Holiday pay	Total number of employees	8	6	4	2
Indirect labour cost	Number of indirect employees	4	3	2	1
Insurance: machinery	Capital cost	11	4	5	20
property	Floor space	4	3	2	2
Machine maintenance	Maintenance hours	15	12	9	6
Power	Kilowatt hours	30	50	90	60
Rent and rates	Floor space	20	15	10	10
c/f		164	137	155	157

			£000	£000	£000	£000
		b/f	164	137	155	157
Supervision	Total number of employees		20	15	10	5
Overhead to be absorbed			184	152	165	162
÷ Machine hours			92	38	165	27
= Overhead absorption rate			£2	£4	£1	£6

		Contract 1			Contract 2	
Department	Machine hours	Absorption rate	Total	Machine hours	Absorption rate	Total
		£	£		£	£
L	60	2	120	20	2	40
M	30	4	120	10	4	40
N	10	1	10	10	1	10
O	–	–	–	60	6	360
Total overhead to be absorbed			£250			£450

15.6 SARAH LIMITED

Overhead absorption schedule for June 19X6:

Cost centre	Production		Service		
	D	P	1	2	3
	£000	£000	£000	£000	£000
Method 1: Specified order of closure					
Allocated costs	45	35	160	71	34
Apportion the service cost-centre costs in the following order (different orders are possible):					
1 (55 : 20 : 15 : 10)	88	32	(160)	24	16
				95	
2 (45 : 40 : – : 10)	45	40	–	(95)	10
3 (50 : 10)	50	10	–	–	(60)
Overhead to be absorbed	£228	£117	–	–	–
Method 2: Ignore inter-department servicing					
Allocated costs	45	35	160	71	34
Apportion the service cost-centre costs as follows:					
1 (55 : 20)	117	43	(160)	–	–
2 (45 : 40)	38	33	–	(71)	–
3 (50 : 10)	28	6	–	–	(34)
Overhead to be absorbed	£228	£117	–	–	–

Chapter 16   16.1

POLE LIMITED
Marginal cost statement for the year to 31 January 19X2

	£000	£000
Sales		450
Less: Variable costs:		
Direct materials	60	
Direct wages	26	
Administration expenses: variable (7 + 4)	11	
Research and development expenditure:		
variable (15 + 5)	20	
Selling and distribution expenditure:		
variable (4 + 9)	13	
		130
		320
Contribution		
Less: Fixed costs:		
Administration expenses (30 + 16)	46	
Materials: indirect	5	
Production overhead	40	
Research and development expenditure		
(60 + 5)	65	
Selling and distribution expenditure		
(80 + 21)	101	
Wages: indirect	13	270
Profit		£50

16.2 GILES LIMITED

(a) (i) *Break-even point:*
In value terms:

$$\frac{\text{Fixed costs} \times \text{sales}}{\text{Contribution}} = \frac{150}{(500 - 300)} \times 500 = £375\,000$$

In units:

	£
Selling price per unit (500 ÷ 50)	10
Less: Variable cost per unit (300 ÷ 50)	6
Contribution per unit	£4

$$\frac{\text{Fixed costs}}{\text{Contribution per unit}} = \frac{150\,000}{4} = 37\,500 \text{ units}$$

(ii) *Margin of safety:*
In value terms:

$$\frac{\text{Profit} \times \text{sales}}{\text{Contribution}} = \frac{50 \times 500}{200} = £125\,000$$

In units:

$$\frac{\text{Profit}}{\text{Contribution per unit}} = \frac{50\ 000}{4} = \underline{\underline{12\ 500\ \text{units}}}$$

16.2 (b) *Break-even chart:*

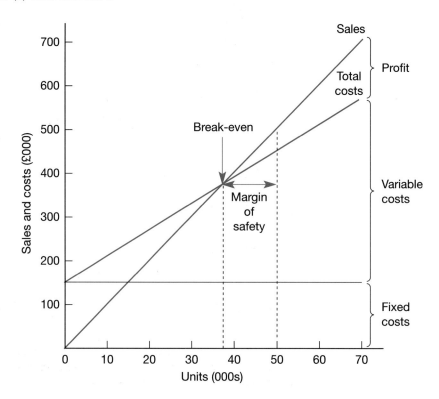

16.3 AYRE LIMITED

Since the company makes a profit of £100 000 on sales of £750 000, all the fixed costs must have been covered. A rise in sales, therefore, of £250 000 (1 000 000 – 750 000) giving an increase in profit of £150 000 (250 000 – 100 000) means that the increased variable cost was £100 000. Therefore the profit/volume ratio is 60% (150/250 × 100) and the variable cost of sales must be 40%.

Year to 31 March 19X3	Budget	Actual
	£000	£000
Budget sales	1200	1000
Less: Variable costs (40%)	480	400
Contribution	720	600
Less: Fixed costs (60% × 1 000 – profit of 250)	350	350
Budget profit	£370	£250

16.4

CARTER LIMITED

Marginal cost statement year to 30 April 19X3

	Per unit	Total
		(50 000 units)
	£	£000
Selling price	40	2000
Variable cost	24	1200
Contribution	16	800
Less: Fixed costs		350
Profit		£450

Budgeted marginal cost statement year to 30 April 19X4

	Per unit	Total
		£000
Selling price (40 – 20%)	32	
Variable costs	24	
Contribution	8	830*
Fixed costs		380
Profit required		£450

*Contribution required = 450 + 350 + 30 (increase in fixed costs) = £830 000

$$\text{Therefore number of units to be sold} = \frac{830\,000}{8} = 103\,750 \text{ units.}$$

103 750 units will have to be sold in 19X4 to make the same amount of profit as in 19X3 if the company reduces its selling price per unit by 20% and increases its fixed costs by £30 000 per annum.

16.5 PUZZLED LIMITED

Option 1 – Reduce the selling price by 15%:

	£
New selling price per unit	8.50
Variable cost per unit	7.50
Contribution per unit	£1.00

$$\text{Therefore break-even} = \frac{\text{Fixed costs}}{\text{Contribution per unit}} = \frac{40\,000}{1.00} = 40\,000 \text{ units}$$

Option 2 – Improve the product:

	£
Selling price per unit	10.00
New variable cost per unit	8.80
Contribution per unit	£1.20

$$\text{Therefore break-even} = \frac{\text{Fixed costs}}{\text{Contribution per unit}} = \frac{40\,000}{1.20} = 33\,333 \text{ units}$$

Option 3 – Advertising campaign:

	£
Selling price per unit	10.00
Variable cost per unit	7.50
Contribution per unit	£2.50

$$\text{Therefore break-even} = \frac{\text{Fixed costs}}{\text{Contribution per unit}} = \frac{£40\,000 + £15\,000}{2.50}$$

$$= 22\,000 \text{ units}$$

Option 4 – Improve factory efficiency:

$$\text{Break-even} = \frac{\text{Fixed costs}}{\text{Contribution per unit}} = \frac{£40\,000 + £22\,500}{2.50}$$

$$= 25\,000 \text{ units}$$

Conclusion:

The advertising campaign would require fewer extra units to be sold in 19X5 compared with 19X4 in order to break even: 22 000 units compared with 16 000 (40 000 ÷ 2.50).

This would require an increase of 10% on the current year's sales just to break even, although it is fewer than the other options. To make the same profit of £10 000 as in 19X4, 26 000 units would have to be sold $\left(\frac{40 + 15 + 10}{2.5}\right)$. Would the campaign also have to be repeated in future years? Has the company got the immediate cash resources in order to carry out the campaign? Can the sales be increased by the required amount simply by advertising?

16.6 MICRO LIMITED

Budgeted contribution per unit of limiting factor for the year:

$$\frac{250\,000}{50\,000} = £5 \text{ per direct labour hour}$$

Contribution per unit of limiting factor for the special contract:

	£	£
Contract price		50 000
Less: Variable costs:		
Direct materials	10 000	
Direct labour	30 000	40 000
Contribution		£10 000

Therefore contribution per unit of limiting factor:

$$\frac{10\,000}{4000} = £2.50 \text{ per direct labour hour}$$

Conclusion:
The special contract earns less contribution per unit of limiting factor than does the *average* of ordinary budgeted work. It may be profitable to accept the contract if either it displaces less profitable work or surplus direct labour hours are available. A careful assessment should be undertaken to ascertain whether much more profitable work would be found than is the case with the contract if it will displace other more profitable contracts that could arise in the near future.

Chapter 17

17.1 MORAY LIMITED

	Units
Total budgeted sales: January to June 19X1	2270
Add: Desired stock at 30 June 19X1	450
	2720
Less: Opening stock at 1 January 19X1	320
∴ Required production units	2400

Monthly average production $= \dfrac{2400}{6} = 400$ units

17.2 JORDAN LIMITED

Budgeted production for the six months to 31 December 19X1:

19X2		Sales (units)	Production* (units)	Balance (units)
1.7	Balance b/f	–	–	100
31.7	Sales	70	–	30
	Production	–	200	230
31.8	Sales	140	–	90
	Production	–	280	370
30.9	Sales	350	–	20
	Production	–	180	200
31.10	Sales	190	–	10
	Production	–	180	190
30.11	Sales	150	–	40
	Production	–	140	180
31.12	Sales	120	–	60
	Production	–	40	100

* Production is the amount needed to reach desired stock levels

17.3 DALTON LIMITED

	Units
Total budgeted sales: January to June 19X3	1090
Less: Expected opening stock at 1 January 19X3	100
	990

Average monthly production required ∴ = 165 (990/6)
Note that: Opening stock – sales = stock remaining + monthly production
= closing stock.

19X3	O/stock	– sales	=	stock remaining	+	monthly production	=	c/stock
January	100	– 90	=	10	+	165	=	175
February	175	– 150	=	25	+	165	=	190
March	190	– 450	=	(260)				

165 units produced in both January and February will not enable the company to meet its monthly budgeted sales figure for March 19X3. In order to do so, it could produce 295 units (165 + 260/2) in both January and February, and produce 150 units per month in March, April, May and June. This would enable the company to meet its budgeted April sales figure and to achieve a reasonably smooth production flow. However, it would mean that by the end of June 19X3, the budgeted closing stock will be 200 units compared with 100 units at 1 January 19X3.

The calculations are as follows:

19X3	O/stock	– sales	=	stock remaining	+	monthly production	=	c/stock
January	100	– 90	=	10	+	295	=	305
February	305	– 150	=	155	+	295	=	450
March	450	– 450	=	0	+	150	=	150
April	150	– 150	=	0	+	150	=	150
May	150	– 130	=	20	+	150	=	170
June	170	– 120	=	50	+	150	=	200

Whether the company would wish to adopt this policy is debatable. It might wish, for example, to keep a minimum number of units in stock (perhaps 100 units) at any one time. This would mean increasing the number of units produced in 19X3, because according to the above figures, the company would be left with only 10 units ready for sale at the end of January 19X3. Another 295 units would, however, be immediately ready for sale in February 19X3. There may also be operational difficulties arising from variable production levels.

17.4 TOM LIMITED

1 *Direct materials usage budget:*

Month	30.4.X4	31.5.X4	30.6.X4	31.7.X4	31.8.X4	30.9.X4	Six months to 30.9.X4
Component:							
A6 (2 units for X)	280	560	1 400	760	600	480	4 080
B9 (3 units for X)	420	840	2 100	1 140	900	720	6 120

2 *Direct materials purchase budget:*

Component A6	30.4.X4	31.5.X4	30.6.X4	31.7.X4	31.8.X4	30.9.X4	Six months to 30.9.X4
Material usage (as above)	280	560	1 400	760	600	480	4 080
Add: Desired closing stock	110	220	560	300	240	200	200
	390	780	1 960	1 060	840	680	4 280
Less: Opening stock	100	110	220	560	300	240	100
Purchases (units)	290	670	1 740	500	540	440	4 180
Price per unit	£5	£5	£5	£5	£5	£5	£5
Total purchases	£1 450	£3 350	£8 700	£2 500	£2 700	£2 200	£20 900

Component B9

Material usage (as above)	420	840	2 100	1 140	900	720	6 120
Add: Desired closing stock	250	630	340	300	200	180	180
	670	1 470	2 440	1 440	1 100	900	6 300
Less: Opening stock	200	250	630	340	300	200	200
Purchases (units)	470	1 220	1 810	1 100	800	700	6 100
Price per unit	£10	£10	£10	£10	£10	£10	£10
Total purchases	£4 700	£12 200	£18 100	£11 000	£8 000	£7 000	£61 000

17.5 DON LIMITED

Direct labour cost budget:

	Quarter			
	30.6.X5	31.7.X5	31.8.X5	*Three months to 31.8.X5*
Grade:				
Production (units)	600	700	650	1 950
Direct labour hours per unit	3	3	3	3
Total direct labour hours	1 800	2 100	1 950	5 850
Budgeted rate per hour (£)	4	4	4	4
Production cost (£)	7 200	8 400	7 800	23 400
Finishing (units)	600	700	650	1 950
Direct labour hours per unit	2	2	2	2
Total direct labour hours	1 200	1 400	1 300	3 900
Budgeted rate per hour (£)	8	8	8	8
Finishing cost (£)	9 600	11 200	10 400	31 200
Total budgeted direct labour cost	£16 800	£19 600	£18 200	£54 600

17.6 GORSE LIMITED

1 *Sales budget:*

Quantity	Selling price £	Sales revenue £
10 000	100	1 000 000

2 *Production quantity budget:*

Sales budget (units)	Closing stock (units)	Opening stock (units)	Production required (units)
10 000	2 000	(4 000)	8 000

3 *Materials usage budget:*

Component	Component usage	Production (units)	Total component usage (units)
XY	5	8 000	40 000
WZ	3	8 000	24 000

523

4 *Materials purchase budget:*

	Component		
	XY	WZ	Total
			£
Budget usage	40 000	24 000	
Stock increase (25%)	4 000	2 400	
Purchase quantities	44 000	26 400	
Cost price per unit	£1	£0.50	
Purchase values	£44 000	£13 200	£57 200

5 *Direct labour budget:*

Grade	Production budget	Budgeted hours per unit	Total budgeted hours	Budget labour rate per hour £	Total direct labour cost £
Production	8 000	4	32 000	5	160 000
Finishing	8 000	2	16 000	7	112 000
			48 000		£272 000

6 *Budgeted profit and loss account:*

Sales units

		10 000
	Per unit	Total
	£	£
Sales revenue	100.00	1 000 000
Less: Costs:		
Production (see workings)	52.50	525 000
Total factory profit	47.50	475 000
Administration, selling and distribution		275 000
Budgeted profit for period 6		£200 000

Workings:	£	£
Unit cost:		
Direct materials:		
Component XY: 5 × £1	5.00	
WZ: 3 × £0.50	1.50	6.50
Direct labour:		
Production: 4 × £5	20.00	
Finishing: 2 × £7	14.00	34.00
		40.50
Production overhead:		
$\dfrac{96\,000}{48\,000}$ = £2 per DLH × 6		12.00
		£52.50

17.7 FLOSSY LIMITED

Cash budget for the three months to 31 March 19X7

	January £000	February £000	March £000
Receipts:			
Debtors (Workings 1)	1 900	2 950	2 450
Sales of plant and equipment	–	–	30
Sales of short-term investments	60	–	10
	£1 960	£2 950	£2 490
Payments:			
Trade creditors (Workings 2)	1 150	1 850	1 510
Other creditors	450	500	600
Capital expenditure	–	470	–
Short-term investments	–	40	–
Tax	150	–	–
Dividends	200	–	–
	£1 950	£2 860	£2 110
Monthly net cash flow	10	90	380
Opening balance	15	25	115
Closing balance	£25	£115	£495

Workings:

1 *Trade debtors*

	January	February	March
Sales	2 000	3 000	2 500
Add: Opening debtors	200	300	350
	2 200	3 300	2 850
Less: Closing debtors	300	350	400
Cash from trade debtors	£1 900	£2 950	£ 2 450

2 *Purchases*

	January	February	March
Cost of goods sold	1 200	1 800	1 500
Add: Closing stock	120	150	150
	1 320	1 950	1 650
Less: Opening stock	100	120	150
Purchases for each quarter	1 220	1 830	1 500
Add: Opening trade creditors	110	180	160
	1 330	2 010	1 660
Less: Closing trade creditors	180	160	150
Cash to trade creditors	£1 150	£1 850	£1 510

17.8 CHIMES LIMITED

Option 1 – Keep the factory open

		45%
Production capacity		
	£000	£000
Sales revenue		135.5
Less: Variable cost of sales:		
Direct materials	63	
Direct labour	27	
Variable overhead:		
Factory (*see* working)	18	
Administration	13.5	
Selling and distribution	9	130.5
Contribution		5
Contribution		
Less: Fixed costs:		
Factory	10	
Administration	8	
Selling and distribution	6	24
Budgeted loss		£(19)

Option 2 – Close the factory

	£000
Costs:	
Redundancy and other closure costs	(30)
Property and plant maintenance	(10)
Re-opening costs	(20)
	(60)
Less: Saving in fixed overheads	30
Net cost of closure	£(30)

Decision:

As the factory will still make a contribution during the year to 30 June 19X8, it should be kept open. However, there may be other non-cost factors to take into account.

Tutorial note:

Factory variable overheads are calculated thus: Factory overhead increases by £4000 for each 10% increase in productive capacity utilization, therefore at 30% level, £12 000 (3 × £4 000) is variable, leaving £10 000 as fixed. The other overheads may be calculated similarly.

Chapter 18

18.1 X LIMITED

		£
1 Direct materials cost variance:		
Actual price per unit × actual quantity = 12 × 6		72
Less: Standard price per unit × standard quantity		
for actual production = 10 × 5		50
		£22 (A)

2 Direct materials price variance:
(Actual price – standard price) × actual quantity
= (12 – 10) × 6 .... £12 (A)

3 Direct materials usage variance:
(Actual quantity – standard quantity) × standard
price = (6 – 5) × 10 .... £10 (A)

18.2 MALCOLM LIMITED

1 Direct materials cost variance: £
Total actual cost 32 400
Less: Standard quantity for actual production ×
standard price = (50 × 120) × £5 .... 30 000

£2 400 (A)

2 Direct materials price variance:
(Actual price – standard price) × actual quantity =
(6* – 5) × 5400 .... £5 400 (A)

*32 400
―――――
5400

3 Direct materials usage variance:
(Actual quantity – standard quantity) × standard
price = (5400 – 6000*) × £5 .... £3 000 (F)

*(120 units × 50 kilograms)

18.3 BRUCE LIMITED

1 Direct labour cost variance: £
Actual hours × actual hourly rate = 1000 × £6.50 ... 6 500
Less: Standard hours for actual production ×
standard hourly rate = 900 × £6.00 .... 5 400

£1 100 (A)

2 Direct labour rate variance:
(Actual hourly – standard hourly rate)
× actual hours = (6.50 – 6.00) × 1000 .... £500 (A)

3 Direct labour efficiency variance:
(Actual hours – standard hours for actual production)
× standard hourly rate = (1000 – 900) × 6.00 .... £600 (A)

18.4 DUNCAN LIMITED

1 Direct labour cost variance: £
Actual direct labour cost 97 200
Less: Standard hours for actual production ×
standard hourly rate = (10 × 1200) × 8 .... 96 000

£1 200 (A)

2 Direct labour rate variance:
(Actual hourly rate − standard hourly rate) × actual
hours = (9* − 8) × 10 800   £10 800   (A)

$$\frac{*97\,200}{10\,800}$$

3 Direct labour efficiency variance:
(Actual hours − standard hours for actual
production) × standard hourly rate
= (10 800 −12 000*) × 8   £9 600   (F)

*1200 x 10 DLH = 12 000

18.5 ANTHEA LIMITED

1 Fixed production overhead variance: £
Actual fixed overhead   150 000
Less: Standard hours of production × fixed
production overhead absorption rate = 8000 × 15   120 000
     £30 000   (A)

2 Fixed overhead expenditure variance:
Actual fixed overhead − budgeted fixed overhead =
150 000 − 135 000   £15 000   (A)

3 Fixed overhead volume variance:
Budgeted fixed overhead − (standard hours of
production × fixed production overhead
absorption rate) = 135 000 − (8000 × 15)   £15 000   (A)

4 Fixed overhead capacity variance:
Budgeted fixed overhead − (actual hours worked
× fixed production overhead absorption rate)
= 135 000 − (10 000 × 15)   £15 000   (F)

5 Fixed overhead productivity variance:
Actual hours worked − standard hours of production
× fixed production overhead absorption rate
= (10 000 − 8000) × 15 000   £30 000   (A)

18.6 ANTHEA LIMITED

Performance measures:

1 Efficiency ratio:
$$\frac{SHP}{Actual\ hours} \times 100 = \frac{800}{10\,000} \times 100 = 80\%$$

2 Capacity ratio:
$$\frac{Actual\ hours}{Budgeted\ hours*} \times 100 = \frac{10\,000}{9000} \times 100 = 111.1\%$$

$$\frac{*135\,000}{15}$$

3 Production volume ratio:

$$\frac{\text{SHP}}{\text{Budgeted hours}} \times 100 = \frac{8000}{9000} \times 100 = \underline{\underline{88.9\%}}$$

18.7 OSPREY LIMITED

1 Fixed production overhead variance:

		£
Actual fixed overhead		120 000

Less: Standard hours of production × fixed
production overhead absorption rate =

$$(600 \times 10) \times \left(\frac{125\,000}{500 \times 10} \right) \qquad \qquad 150\,000$$

$$\underline{\underline{£30\,000}} \quad (\text{F})$$

2 Fixed overhead expenditure variance:
Actual fixed overhead – budgeted fixed overhead =
120 000 – 125 000 $\qquad\qquad\qquad$ $\underline{\underline{£5\,000}}$ (F)

3 Fixed overhead volume variance:
Budgeted fixed overhead – (standard hours of
production × fixed production overhead absorption rate)
= 125 000 – (6000* × 25) $\qquad\qquad$ $\underline{\underline{£25\,000}}$ (F)

4 Fixed overhead capacity variance:
Budgeted fixed overhead – (actual hours worked ×
fixed production overhead absorption rate)
= 125 000 – (4900 × 25) $\qquad\qquad$ $\underline{\underline{£2\,500}}$ (A)

5 Fixed overhead productivity variance:
(Actual hours worked – standard hours of
production) × fixed production overhead absorption rate
= (4900 – 6000*) × 25 $\qquad\qquad$ $\underline{\underline{£27\,500}}$ (F)

*600 units × 10 standard hours

18.8 OSPREY LIMITED

Performance measures:

1 Efficiency ratio:

$$\frac{\text{SHP}}{\text{Actual hours}} \times 100 = \frac{6000}{4900} \times 100 = \underline{\underline{122.4\%}}$$

2 Capacity ratio:

$$\frac{\text{Actual hours}}{\text{Budgeted hours*}} \times 100 = \frac{4900}{5000} \times 100 = \underline{\underline{98\%}}$$

3 Production volume ratio:

$$\frac{\text{SHP}}{\text{Budgeted hours}} \times 100 = \frac{6000}{5000} \times 100 = \underline{\underline{120\%}}$$

(* 10 × 500 = 5000)

529

18.9   MILTON LIMITED

1   Selling price variance:
Actual quantity × (actual selling price per unit – budgeted
selling price per unit) = 9000 × (11* – 10)   £9000   (F)

*$\frac{99\ 000}{9\ 000}$

2   Sales volume contribution variance:
(Actual quantity – budgeted quantity) × standard
   contribution = (9000 – 10 000) × 3   £3000   (A)

3   Sales variances ∴ = 9000 (F) + 3000 (A)   =   £6000   (F)

18.10 DOE LIMITED

1   Selling price variance:
Actual quantity × (actual selling price – budgeted
   selling price) = 120 × (28 – 30)   £240   (A)

2   Sales volume contribution variance:
(Actual quantity – budgeted units) × standard
   contribution = (120 – 100) × 10   £200   (F)

3   Sales variance ∴ = 240 (A) + 200 (F)   =   £40   (A)

18.11 JUDITH LIMITED

(a) 1   Efficiency ratio:
$\frac{\text{SHP}}{\text{Actual hours}} \times 100 = \frac{5 \times 2200}{4 \times 2200} \times 100 = 125\%$

2   Capacity ratio:
$\frac{\text{Actual hours}}{\text{Budgeted hours}} \times 100 = \frac{8800}{5 \times 2000} \times 100 = 88\%$

3   Production volume ratio:
$\frac{\text{SHP}}{\text{Budgeted hours}} \times 100 = \frac{11\ 000}{10\ 000} \times 100 = 110\%$

(b) 1   Selling price variance:
(Actual selling price – budgeted selling price)
   × actual units = (145 – 150) × 2200:   £11 000   (A)

2   Sales volume contribution variance:
(Actual quantity – budgeted units) × standard
   margin = (2200 – 2000) × 25   £5 000   (F)

3   Sales variance = 11 000 (A) + 5000 (F)   £6 000   (A)

4   Direct materials cost variance: £
    Actual quantity × actual price = 2200 × 72   158 400
    Less: Standard quantity for actual production
        × standard price = (7 × 2200) × 10   154 000
                                                                        ─────────
                                                                        £4 400   (A)
                                                                        ═════════

5   Direct materials price variance:
    (Actual price − standard price) × actual
        quantity = (9 − 10) × (2200 × 8)   £17 600   (F)
                                                                        ═════════

6   Direct materials usage variance:
    (Actual quantity − standard quantity)
        × standard price = (8 × 2200) −
        (7 × 2200) × 10   £22 000   (A)
                                                                        ═════════

7   Direct labour cost variance: £
    Actual hours × actual hourly rate =
        (4 × 2200) × 6   52 800
    Less: Standard hours for actual production
        × standard hourly rate = (2200 × 5)
        × 5   55 000
                                                                        ─────────
                                                                        £2 200   (F)
                                                                        ═════════

8   Direct labour rate variance:
    (Actual hourly rate − standard hourly rate)
        × actual hours = (6 − 5) × (4 × 2200)   £8 800   (A)
                                                                        ═════════

9   Direct labour efficiency variance:
    (Actual hours − standard hours for actual
        production) × standard hourly rate =
        (8800 − 11 000) × 5   £11 000   (F)
                                                                        ═════════

10 Fixed production overhead variance: £
    Actual fixed overhead: 65 000
    Less: Standard hours of production × fixed
        production overhead absorption rate =
        (2200 × 5) × 6   66 000
                                                                        ─────────
                                                                        £1 000   (F)
                                                                        ═════════

11 Fixed production overhead expenditure variance:
    Actual fixed overhead − budgeted fixed
        overhead = 65 000 − (30 × 2000)   £5 000   (A)
                                                                        ═════════

12 Fixed production overhead volume variance:
    Budgeted fixed overhead − standard hours of
        production × fixed production overhead
        absorption rate = 60 000 − (11 000 × 6)   £6 000   (F)
                                                                        ═════════

13 Fixed production overhead capacity variance:
   Budgeted fixed overhead – (actual hours worked ×
   fixed production overhead absorption rate) =
   £60 000 – (8800 × 6)   £7 200   (A)

14 Fixed production overhead productivity variance:
   (Actual hours worked – standard hours of
   production) × fixed production overhead
   absorption rate = (8800 – 11 000) × 6   £13 200   (F)

(c) Standard cost operating statement for the period: £
    Budgeted profit (25 × 2000)   50 000
    Sales volume contribution variance (25 × 200)   5 000

    Standard margin of actual sales   55 000
    Selling price variance (5 × 2200)   (11 000)

    Actual margin of actual sales   44 000

	Cost variances:	Adverse £	Favourable £
	Direct materials:		
	Price		17 600
	Usage	22 000	
	Direct labour:		
	Rate	8 800	
	Efficiency		11 000
	Fixed production overhead:		
	Expenditure	5 000	
	Capacity	7 200	
	Productivity		13 200

	Adverse	Favourable	
	£43 000	£41 800	(1 200)
Actual profit			£42 800

Chapter 19

19.1 PROSPECT LIMITED
Calculation of net cash flows:

	Year to 31 March					
	19X1 £000	19X2 £000	19X3 £000	19X4 £000	19X5 £000	19X6 £000
Cash receipts						
Trade debtors (Working 1)	1800	2360	2740	2880	1920	400
Sale of plant	–	–	–	–	–	50
c/f	1800	2360	2740	2880	1920	450

		Year to 31 March					
		19X1	19X2	19X3	19X4	19X5	19X6
		£000	£000	£000	£000	£000	£000
	b/f	1800	2360	2740	2880	1920	450
Cash payments							
Purchase of plant		1000	–	–	–	–	–
Trade creditors							
(Working 2)		1350	1770	2160	1990	1260	150
Expenses		210	220	240	250	300	–
Taxation		–	40	70	100	100	10
		2560	2030	2470	2340	1660	160
Net cash flows		£(760)	£330	£270	£540	£260	£290

	Year to 31 March					
	19X1	19X2	19X3	19X4	19X5	19X6
	£000	£000	£000	£000	£000	£000
Workings:						
1 *Trade debtors*						
Sales	2000	2400	2800	2900	2000	–
Less: Closing trade debtors	200	240	300	320	400	–
	1800	2160	2500	2580	1600	–
Add: Opening trade debtors	–	200	240	300	320	400
Cash received	£1800	£2360	£2740	£2880	£1920	£400

	Year to 31 March					
	19X1	19X2	19X3	19X4	19X5	19X6
	£000	£000	£000	£000	£000	£000
Trade creditors						
Purchases	1600	1790	2220	1960	1110	–
Less: Closing trade creditors	250	270	330	300	150	–
	1350	1520	1890	1660	960	–
Add: Opening trade creditors	–	250	270	330	300	150
Cash purchases	£1350	£1770	£2160	£1990	£1260	£150

19.2 BUCHAN ENTERPRISES

(a) Payback period:

Year	Investment outlay £	Cash inflow £	Net cash flow £	Cumulative cash flow £
1	(50 000)	8 000	(42 000)	(42 000)
2	–	16 000	16 000	(26 000)
3	–	40 00040 000		c/f 14 000

		£	£	£		£
					b/f	14 000
4		–	45 000	45 000		59 000
5		–	37 000	37 000		96 000

Payback period therefore = 2 years, 7.8 months*

*Net cash flow becomes positive in Year 3. Assuming the net cash flow accrues evenly, it becomes positive during August: $(26/40 \times 12) = 7.8$ months (i.e. 2 years and 7.8 months).

(b) Discounted payback period:

Year	Net cash flow	Discount factor @ 12%	Discounted net cash flow	Cumulative net cash flow
	£		£	£
0	(50 000)	1.0000	(50 000)	(50 000)
1	8 000	0.8929	7 143	(42 857)
2	16 000	0.7929	12 686	(30 171)
3	40 000	0.7118	28 472	(1 699)
4	45 000	0.6355	28 598	26 899
5	37 000	0.5674	20 994	47 893

Discounted payback period therefore = 4 years, 1 month*

*Discounted net cash flow becomes positive in Year 4. Assuming the net cash flow accrues evenly throughout the year, it becomes positive in January ($1699/28\,598 \times 12 = 0.7$). This is in contrast with the payback method where the net cash flow becomes positive in August of Year 3.

19.3 **LENDER LIMITED**

$$\text{Accounting rate of return} = \frac{\text{Average annual net profit after tax}}{\text{Cost of the investment}} \times 100$$

$$= \frac{\frac{1}{5}(18\,000 + 47\,000 + 65\,000 + 65\,000 + 30\,000)}{100\,000} \times 100$$

$$= \frac{£45\,000}{100\,000} \times 100$$

$$= \underline{\underline{45\%}}$$

Note: Based on the average investment, the ARR

$$= \frac{45\,000}{\frac{1}{2}(0 + 100\,000)} \times 100$$

$$= \underline{\underline{90\%}}$$

19.4 LOCKHART LIMITED

Net present value:

Year	Net cash flow £000	Discount factor @ 15%	Present value £000
1	800	0.8696	696
2	850	0.7561	643
3	830	0.6575	546
4	1200	0.5718	686
5	700	0.4972	348
Total present value			2919
Initial cost			2500
Net present value			£419

19.5 MOFFAT DISTRICT COUNCIL

Internal rate of return:

Year	Net cash flow £000	Discount factor @ 5%	@ 7%	Present value @ 5% £000	@ 7% £000
1	230	0.9524	0.9346	219	215
2	370	0.9070	0.8734	336	323
3	600	0.8638	0.8163	518	490
4	420	0.8227	0.7629	346	320
5	110	0.7835	0.7130	86	78
Total present value				1505	1426
Initial cost				1450	1450
Net present value				£55	£(24)

Internal rate of return

$$= \text{Positive rate} + \left(\frac{\text{Positive NPV}}{\text{Positive NPV} + \text{Negative NPV}} \times \text{Range} \right)$$

$$= 5\% + \left(\frac{55}{55 + 24} \times 2\% \right)$$

$$= 5\% + 1.4\%$$

$$= \underline{\underline{6.4\%}}$$

Tutorial note:

The selection of discount rates is largely trial and error – remember you are looking for a range of rates within which the present value becomes negative.

19.6 MARSH LIMITED

1 Payback:

Year	Investment outlay £000	Cash inflow £000	Net cash flow £000	Cumulative cash flow £000
1	(500)	50	(450)	(450)
2	–	200	200	(250)
3	–	225	225	(25)
4	–	225	225	200
5	–	100	100	300

$$\text{Therefore payback} = 3 \text{ years} + \frac{(25 \times 12)}{225} = 3 \text{ years, 1.3 months}$$

2 Accounting rate of return:

$$\frac{\text{Average annual net profit after tax}}{\text{Cost of the investment}} \times 100$$

$$= \frac{(100 + 250 + 250 + 200)}{4}$$

$$= \frac{200}{500} \times 100$$

$$= 40\%$$

Note: If the average cost of the investment is used:

$$= \frac{200}{\frac{1}{2}(\pounds 0 + 500)} = \frac{200}{250} \times 100 = 80\%$$

3 Net present value:

Year	Net cash flow £000	Discount factor @ 15%	Present value £000
1	50	0.8696	43
2	200	0.7561	151
3	225	0.6575	148
4	225	0.5718	129
5	100	0.4972	50

Total present value	521
Initial cost	500
Net present value	£21

4 Internal rate of return:

Year	Net cash flow £000	Discount factor @ 15%	Discount factor @ 17%	Present value @ 15% £000	Present value @ 17% £000
1	50	0.8696	0.8547	43	43
2	200	0.7561	0.7305	151	146
3	225	0.6575	0.6244	148	140
4	225	0.5718	0.5337	129	120
5	100	0.4972	0.4561	50	46
Total present value				521	495
Initial cost				500	500
Net present value				£21	£(5)

$$\text{IRR} = \text{Positive rate} + \left(\frac{\text{Positive NPV}}{\text{Positive NPV} + \text{Negative NPV}} \times \text{Range} \right)$$

$$= 15\% + \left(\frac{21}{21 + 5} \times 2\% \right)$$

$$= 15\% + 1.6\%$$

$$= 16.6\%$$

Chapter 20

20.1 *Activity-based costing* is a management accounting technique used to measure the unit cost of products and services based on the benefit received or the demand created by respective units.

20.2 In essence, stock is ordered only when it can be delivered straight to production. Hence there is little difficulty in identifying the actual cost of materials that should be charged to a particular job. This means that there is generally no need to adopt one of the traditional material pricing techniques (such as FIFO, LIFO or average weighted cost) in estimating the cost of direct materials that should be charged to production.

20.3 1 Specific aims and objectives are laid down for the entity.
2 All personnel in the entity are involved in implementing the technique.
3 There is documentation of all activities.
4 Customers' needs and wants are emphasized.
5 The entity's performance is measured from the customers' perspective.

Index